FARM INCOMES, WEALTH AND AGRICULTURAL POLICY

Berkeley Hill is Professor of Policy Analysis in the University of London. He joined the Department of Agricultural Economics of Wye College, University of London, in 1970 after graduating from the Universities of Nottingham (BSc) and Reading (PhD). Research areas have included farm size and efficiency (with D. K. Britton), pluriactivity in agriculture (with Ruth Gasson), and alternative support systems to rural areas (he was a specialist advisor to the House of Lords' Select Committee inquiry into the future of rural society). His major line of investigation has been into incomes of farming, farms and farmers. In this capacity he has acted as advisor, consultant or contractor to the National Audit Office, OECD, the European Commission DG VI and, in particular, Eurostat (the Statistical Office of the European Communities). However, any views expressed here are entirely the responsibility of the author, as is the blame for errors.

Farm Incomes, Wealth and Agricultural Policy
Third Edition

BERKELEY HILL

Ashgate

Aldershot • Burlington USA • Singapore • Sydney

Published by
Ashgate Publishing Ltd
Gower House
Croft Road
Aldershot
Hants GU11 3HR
England

Ashgate Publishing Company
131 Main Street
Burlington
Vermont 05401
USA

Ashgate website: http://www.ashgate.com

British Library Cataloguing in Publication Data
Hill, Berkeley
    Farm incomes, wealth and agricultural policy. - 3rd ed.
    1.Farm income - Europe 2.Agricultural prices - Government
    policy - Europe 3.Agriculture - Europe - Economic aspects
    4.Agriculture and state - Europe
    I.Title
    338.1'3'094

Library of Congress Catalog Card Number: 99-76642

ISBN 0 7546 1132 9

Printed and bound by Athenaeum Press, Ltd.,
Gateshead, Tyne & Wear.

Contents

List of tables

List of figures

Preface

Since the first edition of this book appeared in 1989 there have been substantial changes to the Common Agricultural Policy (CAP) of the European Union (EU), most notably the partial implementation in 1992 of the "MacSharry" proposals of 1991. These imposed price cuts for some major agricultural commodities and compensated farmers by forms of direct payment. Both the cuts and the introduction of direct payments would have been assumed to be politically unacceptable only a few years previously. Reform has been carried further in the direction of reduced market intervention and greater emphasis on direct payments by the *Agenda 2000* package agreed in 1999, which also confirmed rural development as a "second pillar" of the CAP. The reorientation to a more explicit and transparent means of farm support has awakened interest in the distribution of benefit under the CAP and in the overall income situation of those who receive direct payments, with questions being raised about who are the intended target group for agricultural support spending.

Another change has been the growth in information about the incomes of agricultural households in the European Union. Three lines of development have occurred, and the author has been involved in each. First, when this book was initially prepared Eurostat's statistics on the income situation of the agricultural households sector, for which the author has acted as an advisor, were in an early stage of development. Later editions have enabled the progressive consolidation of these Income of the Agricultural Households Sector statistics (until 1998 called the Total Income of Agricultural Households statistics) and the flow of result to be captured, including those for Member States that joined in January 1995. Second, the OECD has undertaken and published a review of farm-level data among its Members, to which the author has made an input. While some Member States are poorly served, others (including the three new Members) have excellent microeconomic data by which relationships between the farm and the overall household can be explored. In particular this has opened up comparisons between what is known about farm family incomes in the EU with the situation in North America. Third, the Directorate-General for Agriculture of the European Commission has reviewed the ways in which it monitors farm incomes at the individual business level and has conducted a more detailed analysis of its data over the 1980s than is routinely possible; again the author was a contractor. Fourth, there has been growth in the number of research publications that, while remaining outside the official statistical system, cast light on the incomes of farmers and their families.

There is much new to be described in this recent information, both in terms of the insight it gives into the structure of the agricultural sector and how this is changing over time, and in terms of the implications it carries for the way that the need for policy is perceived and how it is implemented. This new material largely explained the greater size of the second edition, which also saw substantial revisions and restructuring of the text. This third edition has carried the process further. In particular, the major revision in the way in which the accounts for the agricultural industry in the EU are drawn up, to be implemented in 1999, is covered. The capital balance sheets for agriculture and the way they related to the wealth of the agricultural community has been thoroughly re-examined. Greater attention is given to the information on the US and to how this can provide an enlightening perspective on the European situation. Statistics have been generally updated. However, it is gratifying to observe that the main theme of the book, and the lessons it attempts to draw from the expanding material, has proved remarkably robust.

1 Introduction

Most books have a story line running through them or attempt to make a point. This one is no exception. Rather than allowing the intent of this text to emerge from the material as it is unfolded, with the inherent danger of losing readers in their progress along a path that, inevitably, is strewn with detail, let me start by stating my main thesis.

Agricultural policy in the European Union (EU) is primarily concerned with the incomes of farmers, as are the national policies of most industrialised countries. Of course, there are many other strands within the diffuse fabric of policy. Some have been of greater importance in the past than now - food security, balance of payments, improvements in efficiency of production and marketing. New strands have emerged and risen to prominence in recent decades - conservation of landscape and wildlife, softening the environmental impact of farming practices, animal welfare, employment creation and protection and, particularly in the late 1990s, the development of the rural economy. But the strongest and most enduring strand in the case for public intervention in agriculture, and in particular for the continuation of financial support to it, has been the concern with agricultural incomes. To take a recent example, in the 1990s much attention was given to the need to recast the Common Agricultural Policy (CAP) for budgetary reasons, to enable a more rational use of resources in an interdependent world and for the future development of the Union. These changes were constrained by objections related primarily to incomes. Had agricultural ministers not been so sensitive to the political impact of change on farm incomes, the MacSharry reforms of 1992 and the *Agenda 2000* package of 1999 could have taken a more radical approach to adjusting policy to the contemporary problems faced by the EU.

As will be shown later, the official statements of agricultural policy of both the EU and the UK, especially in the way that they relate to incomes, are expressed in language that is purposely general. From a politician's viewpoint this lack of precision may be useful; no Minister would wish to have around his neck the noose of specific objectives by which his opponents could hang him. There will be a need to retain some flexibility of response in the face of evolving circumstances, and aims that are too detailed and quantified may act as a straightjacket. However a consequence of vague objectives is that there is no certainty of what should be measured in order to evaluate the success or failure of policy actions.

It is entirely proper to monitor the economic performance of agriculture. Within all countries agricultural production contributes to national income, and the calculation of the Net Value Added by agriculture must form an integral part of any system of national accounts. Monitoring also involves surveys of farm businesses to catch the diversity that characterises this industry. But statements of policy intent, as far as they relate to incomes in agriculture, are not to do with production as reflected in this aggregate economic indicator or in business performance measures. Rather, their prime concern is with the personal well-being of individuals and farm households, especially those found on "family farms". Though there is an interest in what is happening to the profitability of agricultural activity and in whether farm operators have enough funds to carry out reinvestment sufficient to at least maintain their output capacity, the stronger message is that it is the *standard of living* of the farm population which is the central policy issue.

But beyond that, quite what is meant as the policy goal for living standards is by no means well articulated in the EU or in most industrialised countries. The prevention of poverty is a major implied objective; the spectre of low income farm families unable to make ends meet is an image with a powerful historical resonance. Another implied objective is equitable living conditions for farm families. The inference is often made that agricultural households are typically in a disadvantaged position *vis-à-vis* other socio-professional groups and that governments must act to narrow the gap between farmers and non-farmers. This raises the question of with which other groups comparisons are to be made. And, lastly, farm households may face particular problems in their living standards because of the inherent variation of farming prosperity from year to year as the result of its dependence on the weather and similar natural phenomena. While the necessity for policy action to dampen fluctuations seems to be commonly accepted, although perhaps more so in some countries than others because of particular climatic conditions and the nature of the crops grown, the stances taken on poverty and comparability issues show marked national differences, particularly when one goes beyond the Member States of the EU.

1.1 Approaches to income

From the above it is apparent that incomes can be looked at from two standpoints, and each at two levels. The first approach is to view income as the reward for a productive activity - farming. This can be done in aggregate, when the agricultural industry is seen as one branch of the economy, or at microeconomic (farm) level. As part of the official industry-level accounts, it is usual to produce an indicator for the amount of value-added remaining to farmers and their families (or, by charging for the unpaid labour of other family members, to farmers and their spouses) as a return for using in agriculture the factors of production that they own (their owned land and capital, and their labour and managerial efforts). These residuals go under a variety of names: in the UK, *Total Income From Farming (TIFF)* and *Farming Income*; in the USA, *Net Farm Income*; in the EU, *Net income from agricultural activity of family labour input,* recently renamed (in association with other changes) as *Entrepreneurial Income,* and by the OECD as *Net Income from Agriculture.* Particularly in the EU, it is common to express these aggregates per unit of labour so that changes over time in the indicators reflect the shrinking resource base among which the rewards from farming are shared. These aggregate indicators and their variants are described in Chapter 3. At the level of the individual farm business, income from production is the reward to the farm entrepreneur for using his/her agricultural resources to generate goods and services. Most of these products are uncontroversially agricultural in nature, although the output is increasingly spread across the industrial classification as farmers explore additional ways of making profits in response to declining opportunities in agriculture, and as businessmen from other sectors buy their way into farming. Again, the surveys of farm accounts that are found in all developed countries tend to use different names for what are, in essence, closely similar concepts of business profit.

The second approach to income is to consider personal incomes, a view that covers the broader flow of resources to farmers that can be spent on consumption goods or saved. In this context it makes sense to talk about farmer households rather than individuals, since the incomes and expenditures of farmer and spouse are usually pooled, and this sharing may also extend to others living in the same house. Farmer households form one part of the households sector of the economy; they have a shared characteristic that separates them from other, non-farmer, groups. (The possible bases of a socio-professional classification will be tackled later). The main interest here concerns the way that agricultural households acquire resources and how they use them to give a standard of living. This involves decisions on the allocation of time and other resources between farming, other income-generating activities, household tasks and leisure. In the personal income approach farmer households can be considered together - the agricultural households sub-sector of the economy - or as individual units.

Succeeding chapters will consider these approaches in turn, assessing the way that income is measured in each, criticising the present methodology and discussing the estimates that are available. There are obvious links between the aggregate and disaggregated levels in each approach. The changes in the income at the individual business level will be reflected in the industry-level figure, and the aggregate indicator, which is usually available earlier, can be used to predict what is likely to be experienced by the single farm business. However, due attention will have to be paid to variations within the overall picture. The range of farming types, sizes, locations and other characteristics mean that the business incomes of individuals may change in ways that are far from the national trend, and group averages for, say, dairy farms may bear no similarity to the performance of other types or to the all-types mean. Even within groups of the same type and size-band there are many factors, including management standards, which will cause a wide dispersion of incomes.

We must not assume that all the income generated by the farming industry accrues to farmers, or that farmers are solely dependent on farming for their livelihoods. Agriculture is no longer exclusively formed of family-operated farms where the whole of the livelihood for the household comes from the farm, and there is doubt whether this has ever been the real situation. A household which occupies a farm is very likely to have one or more members who have income from earnings in other occupations based on the farm (such as tourism) or off the farm (as an employee or self-employed businessman or professional), from investments, pensions or other transfer payments. Many of these people would not normally be considered to be farmers, in that farming is not their main activity.

Later it will be shown that in Europe non-farm sources of income are of great significance, not only to the income situation of farm households but also to what is viewed as an agricultural household. These forms of income reduce the degree to which the household relies on the farm for its livelihood, and for many farming is only a minor source. It is at least questionable whether CAP income support is intended to benefit households that are not primarily dependent on farming, corresponding to over half the total number of holdings in the EU. Non-farm incomes help raise the total incomes of agricultural households to levels that in many countries, on average, compare favourably to national all-households averages, dispelling the myth that farmer households are particularly poor as a group. They also cushion farm families against the inherent instability in their income from farming. In short, to know the farming income of a farm household is no adequate guide to its total income, and to make policy judgements using information on the rewards from agriculture alone is to risk serious misuse of public funds. As a corollary, it is clear that support to agriculture is not reflected in a proportionate way in the total income of farm households; this is particularly true among small farms where other income is found most frequently. Supporting the income from farming is unlikely to have much impact on the total income of these households, yet it will greatly raise the income of the larger producers. Such findings are common among industrialised countries; in the USA, total non-farm income of farm families exceeds their income from farming and has done since the mid-1960s.

So far it has been assumed that it is quite easy to identify what farm families are and hence who comprises the agricultural community. Even if farmers are not entirely, or even largely, dependent on agricultural production for their livelihoods, they are seen essentially as self-employed in their agricultural activities. Many agricultural statistics, not least those on income, adopt the model of the small business in which the farmer is the entrepreneur, where he and his family provide at least some of the capital and labour, and where income is a residual reward to all the factors of production owned by the farm family, including their management and risk-taking. In that farming is undertaken in the EU by units that, in terms of numbers, are predominantly unincorporated businesses (or behave as if they were), there is justification for adopting this convention. This book concentrates on the incomes of such units owned and operated by households. However, it is worth noting, firstly, that this approach excludes the hired workforce in agriculture, who have been shown in countries where they are relatively numerous (including the UK) to be a group where low incomes and poor living standards are often concentrated. Second, non-traditional units are taking an increasing share in agricultural production. For statistical purposes the handful of genuinely corporate farms (in the sense that they were not just family owned businesses arranged as companies for tax purposes) could usually be ignored until the 1990s or treated as if they were not incorporated. However, the enlargement of Germany has brought into the EU many large units with their own legal status and engaging significant numbers of people. They present a challenge to the popular notion of what is a farmer. The people working on these units differ from operators elsewhere in the EU in terms of their employment status, yet do not comfortably fit into the hired worker category. They pose a substantial problem to statisticians over how to treat their labour and hence how their incomes should be measured, something for which a satisfactory solution must be reached before enlargement of the EU brings in many more.

1.2   The income information system

In an ideal world, information would be available to policy-makers and analysts on both the incomes from agricultural production (at industry and farm-firm levels) and the personal incomes of farmers and their households. Of the two approaches it will soon become apparent that the latter is by far the worse served in terms of official statistics. Paradoxically, judged from the stated objectives of agricultural policy, personal incomes would appear to be the more important on which to have comprehensive information since they relate far more directly to standards of living in agriculture. Within the EU the extreme scarcity of detaile d agricultural household income data for all but four or five of the fifteen Member States effectively blocks attempts to reform the CAP in ways which target aid to low income farm households.

This statistical lacuna indicates a substantial breakdown of the information system with regard to agriculture - a failure to service policy adequately. When it comes to analysing the extent of the income problem in the European Union, it is not possible in the present state of statistical knowledge to show the distribution of farmers according to levels of personal income and hence to establish how many low income farm families there are, on which types and sizes of farms they are to be found, the ages of the people involved, and in which regions and countries they are located. Despite advances made in the last few years, comparisons of the income position of farmers with non-farmers are only possible in the broadest of terms. These are matters that might be thought central to the design and operation of an agricultural policy which has income support as a central aim. While policy administrators may not feel the need for data on personal incomes in order to keep the CAP running from year to year in its present form, this opinion is not shared by those whose intent is to reform the CAP into one which is more efficient and manageable at achieving its stated objectives. If ever there were a case for *more* statistics it is in this matter of better coverage of farming households and their incomes.

1.3   A conspiracy of ignorance?

Some detect a conspiracy. Reforms proposed by the Perspectives Green Paper of the European Commission (Commission, 1985b), developed further by the MacSharry proposals of 1991 (Commission, 1991b) and the *Agenda 2000* discussion document of 1997 (Commission of the European Communities, 1997), and advocated by many critics before and since, share a common theme. This is for a changed pattern of aid from one dominated by product price support (which Commissioner MacSharry claimed resulted in 80 per cent of the support going to only 20 per cent of the farmers - by implication those that had large outputs and high incomes) to one of income supplements targeted more to those farmers who could be shown to be in greatest need. However, if this line were followed to a substantial extent, certain countries would find that they received far less from the CAP budget in relation to their contribution than they do now. Other countries, predominantly those with large numbers of small farmers who do not have other part-time jobs, would benefit. The changes that were introduced in the reforms of 1992 and 1999, though they moved prices of some commodities nearer to the world market (especially cereals and oilseeds and protein crops), were accompanied by "compensatory aids" paid on a per hectare basis that, in effect, almost maintained the status quo in terms of the distribution of benefit. In the case of cereals, where in practice the aid payments in the mid-1990s more than compensated for changes in prices actually experienced, the position of the large producer was probably further enhanced. Attempts at "modulation" (changing the impact to the relative advantage of the small farmer) contained in the original MacSharry proposals were defeated. Similarly, between the initial proposals for agricultural reform in *Agenda 2000* (1997) and the agreement of the package in 1999, the notion of "modulation" was watered down by making it optional at the national level, and "capping" payments which any individual could receive was dropped. The conspiracy theory suggests that an information gap is one way to ensure that radical reforms cannot be pursued and hence, at least for a time, the national interest of the potential losers can be protected.

As will be demonstrated, an active conspiracy is not the root cause of the present situation. It stems from the fact that the conceptual framework of the present information systems, and much of the data collecting procedures, were established more than half a century ago. Historical developments have led to the official monitoring systems of incomes in European agriculture being outdated and inadequate, and this applies in the UK as much as elsewhere. Within the EUR 15 only Germany, Denmark, the Netherlands, Finland and Sweden can be described as having adequate information on the total personal incomes of their farmers. The policy problems in the 1930s and 1940s were substantially different from those of the 1990s, yet basically the same sorts of data are still generated. This is a case of *conceptual obsolescence*. Rather than being agents for change, the institutions responsible for official information systems - the conceptual background and data collection - have tended to form part of the problem.

Yet there is still whiff of conspiracy in the resistance to updating the information system in the area of personal incomes of farmers. By and large there is little political or bureaucratic pressure within the EU to make the income position of agricultural households more transparent. Those who might have something to gain - mainly those representing non-farmers - have lacked the impetus necessary to effect change. In the UK there is enough evidence to show that agricultural policy acts as a transfer mechanism of income from the relatively poor (consumers) to the relatively rich (farmers), with a disproportional benefit accruing to the largest farmers whose incomes could not justify further enlargement on grounds of social equity. Though in some other EU Member States farmers may be less privileged as a group, the distributional distortion of benefit from the CAP is widely acknowledged. Pressure groups working for farmers tend to be dominated by the more successful and larger farmers, and the personal interests of these would not be well served by a major change in the income support system. They could hardly be expected to promote actively a more detailed disclosure of the income position of the farming community.

Considerations of narrow national interest may work against obtaining better information. Countries like the UK could find themselves disadvantaged if a more transparent income situation which showed its farmers to be relatively well-off led to a reduction in the sums it could draw from the Community budget while leaving its contributions unaltered.

What may not be immediately apparent is that the provision of fuller information on the income position of farmers may be against the institutional interests of the agricultural bureaucracy, and even perhaps run counter to the personal ambitions of civil servants and ministers. Government agricultural departments and the agriculture Directorate-General of the European Commission are unlikely to accept easily changes which involve a reduction in their powers, budgets and influence. Taking a view of incomes in agriculture that adopts a household approach carries the danger of such changes, so is not welcomed.

Perhaps what is feared most by the agricultural establishment on a European scale, and this must include parts of the agricultural bureaucracy in EU Member States and the European Commission, is the exposure of the lack of uniqueness of poverty in agriculture. While with adequate information it may be possible to demonstrate that there are some farmers whose standards of living are below what the rest of society considers as tolerable and for whom assistance could be justified, there is nothing unique about the poverty of these people. They are households in poverty who happen to occupy farms. However, to recognise this is to expose the weakness of much of the case for continuing the present level of support to agriculture which, as an unwanted by-product, generates surpluses of farm products and a pattern of land use which in some areas is criticised on grounds of the broader social interest. To be seen to be giving special treatment to poverty in agriculture is to open the floodgates of comparison with the way in which many other groups in society have been treated, some of whom could assemble a far more pressing case for assistance from public funds than could farmers.

In the UK, some universities are involved with data collection on farm businesses as contractors to government departments; they have financial and academic reasons for not wishing to disrupt relationships with their sponsoring departments or the farmers who co-operate in providing data. Consequently academics in these universities may prefer not to pursue research that requires data on the household income of farmers.

Where poverty exists among farmers, its causes may have an agricultural base - they may be on farms which are too small or producing a commodity which has undergone a price decline uncompensated by other payments - but the means of relieving this poverty need not be agricultural. There may be many other more cost-effective alternatives to using measures such as product price support, arable area payments and other forms of subsidy that are linked to production now or at some time in the past, mechanisms that benefit the un-needy as well as the needy. In the past such blunt instruments may have been both the most effective way of bringing relief to a wide spectrum of distressed people in agriculture and the only practical means by which this could be brought about. When another goal was agricultural expansion, the additional output that was engendered by the support of farm product prices was welcome. However that is little reason for perpetuating a system linked to agricultural production where preferable alternatives are available. Policy analysts frequently point to the desirability of matching appropriate instruments to particular problems and of the greater efficiency that can result from more precise targeting. In the context of income support this indicates that direct payments should be made to those households found to be in need, and none to those not in need.

To some extent in practice the choice of policy instruments reflects the availability of information by which the measures can be implemented. One defence offered by administrators responsible for the income information system is that agricultural politicians have never expressed much interest in using instruments which would require knowledge on the personal incomes of farmers before they could be implemented. While this may have been true in the past, and even of the UK in the 1980s, this is hard to defend now at EU level with a wider awareness of the inequitable distribution of the benefits brought about by the current instruments, the reduction in influence of the agricultural establishment and a greater willingness to make radical policy change. Clearly, in the absence of information on the total income of farm households little progress could be made towards shifting the mix of policy measures towards a more direct attack on poverty in agriculture. The most obvious way to resolve this chicken-and-egg situation is to collect on a systematic basis the necessary income information. Various methods of doing this are discussed later, including modifications to the system currently used in the EU for monitoring the business incomes of holdings (the Farm Accountancy Data Network – FADN/RICA), drawing on information collected as part of the taxation system, and using the household budget surveys held in all Member States and the associated European Community Household Panel.

1.4   Appropriate indicators

Emphasis has so far been placed on gaps in the information on incomes in agriculture. The term "income" can have a range of meanings, and a concept of income which is appropriate in one context is not suitable for another. In particular, the elements which would be included in an assessment of personal disposable income of households is different from that required when estimating the reward to farmers (and their families) for their contribution to agricultural production. Appropriate concepts will be discussed later. Here it is sufficient to point out that a common feature of policy discussion is the use of the "wrong" income indicator, usually simply because this happens to be available. Macroeconomic indicators relating to the agriculture branch of the economy are often quoted as if they were adequate proxies for the aggregate personal incomes of farmers; similar liberties are taken with microeconomic income parameters generated by the farm business surveys. In many ways, the use of an inappropriate income concept is worse than to admit ignorance, in that the former risks giving a misrepresentation while the latter acknowledges more neutrally a deficiency in the information system. There is an unhappy history of choosing inappropriate indicators not only by interested parties such as farmer organisations but also by ministers, national civil servants and EU officials. While bureaucrats may understand the implications of the methodology they employ and might be cautious in drawing inferences, this reserve does not extend to those with a cause to promote or an interest group to represent.

In North America there is a history of scrutiny of agricultural income data and a substantial body of literature on the appropriate indicators to use for policy purposes (see AAEA, 1972; Martin, 1977 and 1981; Loyns *et al.*, 1983; Brinkman, 1983; Farmer and Strickland, 1986). In the UK, and in the EU generally, agricultural economists have shown only a muted interest in this area despite its centrality to agricultural policy and, indeed, to the activities of the European Union. The reasons for this reticence, already touched on, will be further explored later.

1.5 Wealth

It is axiomatic that farmers have access to land. A variety of arrangements exist by which this can happen, and it is not necessary for a person to own agricultural land to be a farmer. At the turn of the last century four out of five acres in Britain were farmed by operators who rented their land from someone else. However, by far the more common arrangement nowadays in Britain, most countries in the EU and other industrialised countries, is for farmers to own the land they occupy, or at least some of it.

The economic status of any person or family is not simply dependent on their annual income, however this might be defined, but is also a reflection of their wealth. A moment's reflection on the positions of two people of equal (and to illustrate the point most effectively, low) incomes, but the one owning his own house and perhaps a few valuable oil paintings and the other owning nothing, will soon suggest to most observers that one is better off than the other. The wealth-owner has the option to convert his assets (a *stock* concept) into spendable cash (a *flow* concept) by selling or by borrowing against them; the other has no such opportunity.

It happens that most landowning farmers are wealthy people when compared with other groups in society. An agricultural policy aimed at attacking poverty should not ignore the wealth position of the intended beneficiaries. There are good reasons why the manner in which it is taken into account should be carefully considered - the value of farmland can go down as well as up, making substantial differences to the wealth of farmers, and the wealth it represents cannot be fully realised without also losing occupancy for farming purposes - but it should not be ignored. Ways of combining income and wealth in a unified measure of economic status will be considered later. Yet the net worth of agricultural households is firmly set aside by policy-makers when they decide the shape of agricultural policy. A more satisfactory situation would be to explore alternatives to price support for those farmers who are also wealthy as ways of supplementing their incomes; these people might be assisted by a system which enabled them to realise part of their assets.

The agricultural establishment has been very effective at creating in the mind of policy-makers, and even the general public, an insulation between the question of agricultural incomes and agricultural wealth. Most developed countries apply some sorts of capital or wealth taxation, but preferential treatment is usually given to agricultural wealth in the form of land, a situation that typically bids up its price and results in calls for even more favourable tax concessions.

For some policy purposes, setting aside the wealth of the agricultural population can be fully justified; these will be set out later. The point here is that this should be the result of deliberate choice and not, as is largely now the case, an automatic reaction. Where the inclusion of wealth is unambiguously relevant, to ignore it is to distort what would be widely regarded as equity.

1.6 Information and decisions

The absence of adequate information on the incomes of farmers does not stop agricultural policy from being implemented. Rather, it means that decision-makers have a very imperfect picture against which to operate. In practice it seems that, at least in the context of the CAP, the apparent mismatch between the official policy aims and the available information is not considered a substantial handicap. In the annual price-fixing exercise of the CAP, until the early 1990s the most important element of EU policy and still an important event at which many matters of detail of support regimes are decided, income changes seem to be only a background against which other decisions are made. Macroeconomic indicators of income are relied on primarily to show the prosperity of the agricultures of Member States. At EU level microeconomic data have usually not been used for reasons of timing - generally they have been too out-of-date - and this has led to emphasis falling on the industry-wide indicators. Farm-level income data are used primarily by national administrations, for example in the UK for preparing the stance on commodity pricing taken by its ministers and to adjust the special payments given to farming in disadvantaged areas.

Much of the haggling within the CAP boils down to protecting national interests. Decisions on agricultural matters are almost always the preserve of agricultural ministers sitting in a Council (of agricultural ministers) which lacks representatives from other areas of policy who might question the need to support farmers and require evidence for its justification. A national agricultural minister, acting in the "best" tradition of trying to ensure that his farmers get as much as the bargaining conditions allow, and that his country's benefit from the EU budget is protected, will require from civil servants only broad figures on which to make his case. Indeed, too much detail, particularly any which shows that there are better-off farmers as well as those witnessing falls in their incomes, may hamper the argument. Hence broad averages are to be preferred to distributions of incomes, changes of income to absolute figures, and the wealth position of agricultural operators can be conveniently ignored. It is easier to treat farms as businesses rather than to acknowledge that farming households lie at the centre of agricultural policy, households that often have other sources of income.

The way that policy is practised is heavily dependent on the decisions taken and processes used in previous years. In common with all large organisations, there is a strong preference in government agricultural departments and in the European Commission for the continuation of established practices, and this includes the way that incomes are measured and incorporated into policy decisions. Far from implementing the income objective of the CAP as set out in the Treaty of Rome (1957) that established the European Economic Community, with its declared intent of ensuring a fair living standard for the agricultural community, the structure of decision-making results in this issue being kept firmly out of immediate consideration. Only when there is a crisis which threatens the entire CAP is there sufficient fluidity created to allow a more radical review of the way that incomes are taken into account. An example of this was the inchoate interest of the Commission in forms of direct aids to farmers and how they might qualify as "social" cases in the mid-1980s in the face of budgetary pressure. This interest was underlined by the problems of accumulating stocks that led to the MacSharry reform proposals of 1991, implemented in diluted form in 1992 but including direct payments to farmers to "compensate" their incomes for changes made elsewhere. The need to make further changes in policy instruments to accommodate the conditions of GATT and in the face of impending enlargement of the EU further spurred interest in giving support to those farmers who have low incomes, but in ways that does not encourage further production ("decoupling" the income component). The *Agenda 2000* discussion document (1997) again underlined the objective of securing a fair standard of living for the agricultural community, but it is clear that who receives this assurance, the instruments used to give it and the costs incurred have to be given careful consideration in the light of the likely large expansion in number of EU agricultural producers when candidate countries accede early in the next millenium. These crises, coming close together, may have served to change the climate in which the incomes of agricultural households are viewed but, as yet, this has not been matched by significant shifts in the application of policy.

An important statistical step in this period was the decision by Eurostat (in November 1985) to create an indicator at aggregate level of the total disposable income of agricultural households in each Members State. Germany and France had been making such calculations on a national basis for some years prior to 1985. After a long gestation period, results using a harmonised methodology were published by country in 1992 and 1995 (Hill, 1995), since when an annual report has appeared (though the UK is not included because of particular data problems, commented on later). Progress with microeconomic information, which would show, for example, the distribution of incomes among farmer households, is far slower, with nothing yet published officially. Statistical developments are hampered because of resistance primarily from farmers' unions in some countries.

There is a danger that the present level of interest among policy designers in the personal incomes of farmers, already under pressure from some farmer groups and facing apathy from some groups of policy administrators, might evaporate if the CAP reforms introduced in 1992 and 1999 result in a reduction in budgetary pressure or if other events (such as favourable movements in international commodity markets) construe to avoid crises. Against this, it could be argued that, once a new series of income statistics has been created on farmers' household incomes, it is difficult to ignore completely. The information on the total income of agricultural households now being published has substantial implications for policy (see Chapter 5), and as it spreads, interest groups representing non-farmers could be expected to use the results to further their case for the reallocation of EU finance and to maintain the momentum for reform in agricultural policy. In particular, it is clear from existing statistics that many farm families are already diversified in their income sources. This suggests that the development of alternative local employment and entrepreneurial opportunities may be an attractive way of tackling the income problem in agriculture. Already the EU's *Agenda* 2000 package has agreed (in 1999) that rural development is to become the "second pillar" of the CAP, an approach that sees the difficulties of farm families as forming part of a broader set of problems in rural areas. Statistics on the overall income of farm families would play a part in assessing the performance of such a policy.

EU statistics on agricultural households are at present only available for the whole sector. There is a big gap at the microeconomic level. However, all three of the Member States that joined the European Union in January 1995 (Austria, Sweden and Finland) have traditions of measuring the total incomes of their farms and/or of their farmers. They bring their experience in what some other countries believe to be a methodologically difficult area and thereby erode the objections to statistical developments in practice.

Some see a race between, on one hand, the further reform required of the CAP and, on the other, its ultimate collapse under the financial pressure of its present preoccupation with the production of commodities and further enlargement to include countries to the east of the present EU. I am one of these. The fluidity in the thinking about agricultural incomes engendered in the policy process by the prospect of enlargement forms a valuable opportunity to ensure that the CAP, in respect of its income support objective, is directed back to its central and enduring concern with the living standards of the agricultural community. There are plenty of policy instruments usable for this purpose in the bureaucratic cupboard, ranging from modified forms of product price support to means-tested direct income payments. But without the basic information on the personal incomes of farmers and their families, moves in this direction are largely blocked.

1.7 The plan of the rest of the book

The chapters which follow explore in detail various issues that have been raised here. This book originated from an interest in farm incomes and policy in the United Kingdom. However, a national study would be too parochial for the conditions of 2000 since many of the most important policy decisions are made at Union level. Consequently it is vital to be familiar with the picture for the EU as a whole, the income measures used by the European Commission and the patterns found therein, and the way that the information is used. There has also to be an awareness of the income situations in other individual EU Member States, particularly where they have better information on aspects that are poorly covered elsewhere.

And because the problems faced in the EU have parallels in other industrialised countries it is necessary to have mind to the agricultural income information systems of other Western countries, both European, North American and Australasian. Some of these are particularly well provided with information on the incomes of their farmers, and they can be used to illustrate patterns that are evident in the EU, though less fully quantified.

The first step is to investigate evidence for the objectives of agricultural policy, particularly the income aspects (Chapter 2). In light of these, Chapter 3 reviews the concepts of income appropriate to the stated policy objectives and compares these with the indicators currently in use in the EU and elsewhere. The next examines the indicators of the income from agricultural production at industry branch and farm levels and the historical patterns that emerge (Chapter 4). Chapter 5 brings together a comprehensive collection of the macroeconomic and microeconomic data on farm household incomes and presents the empirical evidence by which the income situation of agricultural households can be judged. Wealth is dealt with in Chapter 6. Chapter 7 considers ways in which income information is taken into account in decision making, and outlines the steps by which the statistics might be generated which would allow the CAP to become more closely aligned with its stated objectives on the living standards of the agricultural population.

2 Incomes and Agricultural Policy

Farmers and others closely involved with the practical side of the industry are sometimes perplexed by the changes to which they are required to adjust. They see that farms are tending to get larger and the task of operating them falls increasingly on the shoulders of farm families as hired labour becomes too expensive to employ. Mixed farming has tended to be replaced by specialist forms, and the sizes of enterprises - milking and beef herds, sheep and poultry flocks, crop areas per farm - have almost without exception been on the increase. Part of the drift to larger units might be explained by a natural inclination of successful farmers to grow, but there is also a driving force in the form of economic necessity.

The problem is felt most acutely by the smaller farm. Though the medium and larger businesses may be able to specialise or shed labour, for small farms such responses are not possible. They are non-viable not because they are necessarily inefficient at using land or purchased inputs (indeed, farms occupying small areas are frequently the most intensive users of land), but because they cannot generate enough income for families who wish to operate them on a full-time basis. Over time this threshold is creeping remorselessly upwards. Under such circumstances there is little wonder that farmers and their pressure groups call on governments to protect them from the harsh economic climate which they see as unfair to the farming industry - farmers consider themselves to be victims of forces outside their control and therefore worthy of some form of assistance.

The inevitability of these changes and the underlying causes of the economic pressures on farming which produce the squeeze on incomes will be familiar to readers who have studied basic economics. For others a brief outline of the fundamental principles is first given here. However, the main concern of this chapter is with the reaction that governments have made towards the economic pressures on their farmers, as shown in the declared and implied aims of their agricultural policies. Particular attention is given to the policies of the EU and UK, though it can easily be shown that the support of farm incomes is a feature of virtually all industrialised countries, springing from the similarity of problems they face with respect to their agricultural sectors, though there are differences in the extent to which income issues are given prominence over other considerations, such as trade.

2.1   Fundamental economic forces

Central to the explanation of agriculture's income problems is the tendency for the demand for agricultural products to expand more slowly than does their supply, resulting in a downward pressure on farm prices and on the rewards to be earned from farming (for an extended treatment see Hill and Ray, 1987; Commission, 1994a; Bonnen and Schweikhardt, 1998). Though there is a danger of over-simplification, and some medium-term changes for individual countries do not fit comfortably into the general picture (Gardner, 1992), these fundamentals are at the root of the need for agriculture to adapt and of the income problems it faces.

In developed industrialised countries incomes for society as a whole are of such a level that, as average personal incomes increase, very little of the extra is spent on the products of the agricultural industry - that is, *their income elasticity of demand is low*. Added to this, people will be willing to consume more only if prices fall a great deal, and the price fall (in percentage terms) will greatly exceed the extra demanded (again in percentage terms) - in other words the *price elasticity is also low*. If the population were increasing, the extra mouths would provide an increasing demand for food, but in most western countries the population is either growing very little or is even falling slightly. Consequently the demand for food can be regarded as virtually static.

On the supply side there are two characteristics that are of paramount importance. The first is that most forms of agricultural output are subject to unpredictable year-to-year variations due to external factors, particularly weather. This can result in unstable product prices and large changes in income, though the extent and even the direction of change will depend on factors such as how widespread is the weather impact, whether trade is allowed between areas, intervention by the government to stabilise prices and so on. Some individuals may do well out of such situations; a potato grower with irrigation may reap high profits if all his neighbours lose their crops because of drought and the price of potatoes increases markedly. Some income variation over time will be anticipated by farmers and action will be taken to reduce risks, though there will be a trade-off between the cost of these actions and the risks involved. They will diversify their farms, choosing mixes of enterprises that complement one another in some way. They will maintain reserves of machinery capacity to cope with difficult conditions. They will make forward contracts for prices of inputs and products. Government intervention will be called for to assist in stabilising the situation when the variation is considered excessive, providing assistance in times of unusually severe winter weather or natural disaster (such as widespread flooding) or if it is judged that risk reduction is in the national interest. For example, stable conditions brought about by government intervention were thought essential for encouraging investment and the expansion of production in the in UK in the recovery period after the Second World War.

The second characteristic of agricultural supply, and the more fundamental in terms of agricultural policy in the EU, is its persistent expansion. Since the Second World War technological developments have ensured that farmers have been willing to produce more at given price levels. The capital used by agriculture has risen substantially, and to some extent this has been substituted for labour, which has been much reduced. Many of the technical advances have originated outside the farming industry - new chemicals for disease and pest control, new types of more efficient machines - and in the parts of the agricultural sector not directly involved with commercial farming - plant and animal breeders. In the absence of any substantial annual increase in demand, this rising supply has had a depressing effect on the prices which farmers receive. All the efforts of the CAP to support the prices received by EU farmers have been insufficient to counter the decline in real terms (that is, after inflation has been taken into account). In Chapter 3 it will be shown that in the UK that increases in output have so depressed product prices that over the 1970s and 1980s the value of what farming produced in total (price times quantity) actually fell in real terms.

But the costs that farmers face for the inputs they use - fuel, chemicals, to a large extent labour too - are determined by supply and demand for these inputs in the national economy rather than by farming's requirements alone. The market for these farm inputs is not restricted in the same way as is the market for farm products. Farmers find themselves in a cost-price squeeze; the prices for their products are declining in comparison with the costs they face. As will be shown in Chapter 3, there is a narrowing gap between the value of total farm output and total costs, so that the income of the agricultural industry as a whole arising from production of farm commodities is reduced over time. This does not necessarily mean that the income of individual farmers falls; if enough gave up farming the smaller total income would be shared between a smaller number of individuals and the average might not fall. However, this out-migration is usually slow, and the more common world-wide experience is that there is a depressing effect on individual incomes from farming.

Because of the nature of the structure of agriculture - many small businesses operating independently and each having to accept market prices rather than exercising power over the market - technological advances spread in an inexorable way throughout the farming industry. Many advances need increases in both output and inputs if the potential for higher profits they contain is to be realised; higher yielding cereal varieties obvious need a heavier fertilizer regime that will enable the higher profits they can generate to be reached, and expensive high-capacity tractors are only profitable if the enterprise is big enough for them to be worked near their full potential. If an innovating farmer can spot an output-generating opportunity and exploit it before other farmers catch on, he will be able to increase his revenue while prices are high. By the time the average farmer has adopted the innovation the overall level of output will have risen, putting downward pressure on output prices. The laggards will be forced eventually to either adopt the new technology or quit; falling prices will ensure that their outdated ways of farming do not generate a sufficient return for them to continue.

Declining incomes from farming at both the industry and individual operator levels can thus be seen as an inevitable result of supply expansion, driven by the treadmill of technological advance, exceeding demand expansion. But more than that, it is a part of the economic mechanism by which resources in a growing economy are released from some industries (in our case agriculture) and flow to others. The history of economic development is concerned with the shift of productive resources - notably labour - from those sectors where marginal productivity is low to those where it is higher. Improvements in the productivity of agriculture mean that it is possible to release resources and still maintain the level of food production. Under a market economy the forces of supply and demand will bring this adjustment about by creating a differential between the rewards available in farming and those in other sectors of the economy. In a dynamic economy we should not be at all surprised at low incomes in at least some sectors of agriculture - particularly among those farms which have an inadequate volume of resources (which in effect means too little land). These are signals generated by the market mechanism showing the required direction of change.

A substantial problem arises when the owners of productive resources cannot switch them out of agricultural use and into other lines of production. The reason is that, once locked into the farming industry, they often have little value other than in agriculture. With capital items such as buildings specific to farming uses (such as for dairying) this takes the form of very low scrap values, so it makes economic sense to continue in production as long as variable costs are covered. With farmers it takes the form of low alternatives because of old age, lack of education or experience, or being accustomed to independence or working with a particular type of enterprise. In the 1980s and 1990s the opportunities to work in other industries have been seriously curtailed by the lack of demand for labour there, a symptom of general economic conditions. Due to immobility, farmers with low incomes may be forced to continue in agricultural production in order to gain any livelihood, often in grinding poverty. Their persistence helps to aggravate the cost-price squeeze; they continue to market produce which, with greater factor mobility, would not have been produced.

Even in the absence of technological advance and the adjustments that follow in its wake, the structure of the farming industry implies that there will be a wide range of incomes. Although there is no strong evidence that, beyond the confines of the smallest farms, the average total cost of producing agricultural commodities varies much across the range of farm sizes, the different amounts of resources controlled by the larger farmers will give them bigger absolute business incomes than the smaller ones. Even on farms of the same size and type there is a diversity of management abilities and good fortune which will be reflected in a diversity of income levels.

There is an important (though, as we will see later, inexact) link between the incomes of farm businesses and the personal incomes of the families that operate them. Farming consists of, in the main, businesses that are personally owned and managed by families. Consequently business profits, in addition to being the rewards to farmers as owners of the factors of production, are a major source of their spending power as consumers. On welfare grounds society will wish to see the low incomes of disadvantaged groups of farmers underpinned in some way. The rationale is that these farmers will need assistance because they are poor, not because they are farmers *per se*.

To sum up, there is nothing surprising in the fact that some incomes are low in agriculture. In an industry with an atomistic business structure, diversity in terms of farm sizes, management talent and luck in yields and prices, there will always be the well-off and the poor. The dynamics of economic development adds to this diversity by imposing a cost-price squeeze on the industry; the low incomes which farmers with inadequate resource bases, or the inefficient, or those farming in unsuitable areas, receive are signals from the market that resources should flow out of agriculture and into other uses. But because farm incomes are personal incomes as well as business rewards there are social equity implications to be faced. To alleviate these problems, and to achieve other production-linked objectives, governments have been frequently persuaded to intervene.

2.2   The aims of agricultural policy

The reasons why governments of the Western industrialised countries have become involved with their agricultural sectors differ in detail but share some broad similarities. Many of the reasons for supporting agriculture fall into the "protective" category, in that action is taken to protect the agricultural sector against economic forces which, if unchecked, would result in a diminished prosperity for home farming, lower farm incomes and fewer farmers. The background is formed by the insidious pressure of technological advance that renders outdated the farming structure of earlier periods. Encumbered with immobile resources and spiced by the personal income aspects of farming profits and losses, there will always be a political case to be made for public intervention to ease the lot of farmers, to defend them against the adjustments required by economic forces. The inevitability of these forces does little to dampen the fundamentalist pressure for aid for the small farmer.

   In some cases the trigger for policy action has come from abroad; the protection afforded to the agriculture sectors of France and Germany in the late 19th century (but not in the UK, where a free trade stance was adopted) was engendered by the competition of cheaper food from the New World and Australasia. The legacy of these governments' actions was seen in the structure of small farms that dominated these countries in the 1950s and that are still an issue in the CAP. Another trigger was the historic situation that led to a need to expand the domestic supply of food. This is very much the case in the UK where the framework of intervention was established by the necessity of expanding output rapidly in the face of the near-cessation of food supply from abroad during the Second World War and the desirability of further substituting for imports in the period of post-war recovery. In many of the countries that set up the European Economic Community in 1957 the spectre of starvation was still a vivid memory; the need for greater agricultural output and a more productive farm sector to achieve food security was self-evident. Encouraging more output by supporting the prices of agricultural commodities inevitably enhanced the incomes of producers. Once established, such protective policies are notoriously difficult to dismantle since the adjustment then necessary will involve a degree of catching-up. Effective interest groups and lobbies have built up in most Western countries (Wilson, 1977), so that a gap has been created between the "normative" aspects of agricultural policy - by which is meant the "ought to be" aspects such as the prevention of poverty and correction for externalities - and the "political" aspects - which means the actions which are the most likely to be taken because they benefit those groups with the greatest influence (Cochrane, 1985).

A brief excursion into what is meant by "policy" is necessary here. The policy process can be divided into a number of distinct components (Josling, 1974; Hill, 1990a). In the *background* are the sets of values that the society holds; examples relevant to the present study would be that extreme poverty is bad and that the freedom to transfer to alternative forms of employment is good. From that background springs *myths* about reality, beliefs about the way in which the real world operates; these might include the assumption that supporting home agriculture will give a more secure food supply, or that farmers' incomes are inherently and unfairly low, necessitating public intervention to raise them. In turn, from these "myths" more concrete *objectives* are formed - such as an intention to raise farming incomes. These objectives are determined by the interplay of political influences, and lobbies, such as the UK's National Farmers' Union and COPA (the EU-level association of farmers' unions), will be formed to promote the interests of particular sectors of society. These lobbyists will foster myths that are to the advantage of the groups they represent. Bureaucrats will design and use *policy instruments* (or *mechanisms* or *measures,* the last a particularly confusing term) to achieve the required objectives. In the agricultural contexts these take many forms; product price support is the most costly in terms of CAP spending, brought about by a variety of means, but others include input subsidies, investment grants to assist with farm modernisation or to the reduction of pollution or afforestation, payments to encourage set-aside of land, and more direct forms of income supplementation. The bureaucracy will have its own interests to safeguard, and these may influence the way that policy is translated into action. The final step in the process is the *monitoring* of policy mechanisms to assess their effectiveness; instruments are often improved as a result and more information generated on the way in which the real world works. Often the terms *programme* or *regime* are used to imply a subset of objectives and instruments (such as the CAP's cereal regime).

While the term "agricultural policy" flows glibly, it is frequently used inappropriately and incompletely. Policy is commonly thought of as just the set of instruments applied, mainly by central government, whereas it really means the whole process. Without the other elements, and especially the setting of objectives, these instruments have little meaning. And the agricultural industry is affected not only by measures designed specifically to make an impact on the resources and markets which by common usage are thought of as agricultural but also by a range of general economic and social policies. Some of these, such as the taxation of capital, have had a major influence on the shape of agriculture in the UK and in other countries. Conversely, agricultural policy is believed to have an impact on various non-agricultural aspects of the economy; trade, environment and rural employment are obvious examples. As the extent of interdependence has been increasingly recognised there has been a tendency for the boundaries of the term "agricultural" to grow in both the vertical sense, embracing aspects of the input industries and food processing, and horizontally, to merge with social policy in rural areas, recreation and access to the countryside, pollution control and so on. In consequence, policies which purport to deal primarily with aspects of agriculture must be viewed against a context of general economic policies.

There is no single, well-integrated, coherent agricultural policy designed to serve the requirements of the sector as a whole. This applies to the CAP and, to greater or lesser extents, to national policies. Policy tends to have evolved in response to particular problems as and when they arose, with occasional stocktakings to try to resolve the inevitable inconsistencies that this *ad hoc* type approach produces. There are many examples of conflicts arising between single agricultural policies within countries and between agricultural and non-agricultural ones. For EU Member States, having both CAP and national aspects to their farm policies and implementing a mix of measures related to both, dual-level decision-making represents a further source of inconsistency, with overlapping but not identical sets of objectives.

Concern with incomes is only one of a number of interwoven strands in all Western countries, though it is now evidently the most significant strand. Other common strands have been food security, agriculture's contribution to the balance of payments, improvements to productivity and efficiency, and food prices to consumers. Farming has always been seen as playing a part in the prosperity of rural areas, and since the mid-1970s agriculture has been used as a vehicle for maintaining the size of the population in areas which would otherwise suffer from depopulation; increasingly farming is used for job retention in rural areas generally (OECD, 1983a; Commission, 1988b, 1997). Over time the desirability of higher levels of farm output has waned, to the extent that extra production of most major commodities is embarrassingly expensive in the EU and USA. Improvements in productivity which displace labour are similarly unwelcome when general unemployment is a serious social problem. Since the early 1980s, and notably in the UK, questions of environmental impact have gained importance, with a search for policy instruments which will produce a natural environment more in line with the public perception of what it ought to be and, in some measure, undo the changes for which other parts of agricultural policy can be blamed. Add to the mix the heightened concern with animal welfare, and the balance of strands has demonstrably shifted from those linked to levels of agricultural production - the "productivist" aspect - to those concerned with broader socio-economic issues.

There seems to be general agreement among academics and commentators working in the policy area that income support is now the fundamental objective of agricultural policy in contemporary western Europe and in industrialised capitalist market economies as a group. Incomes hold the key to explaining past policy decisions and, of particular relevance to the 1990s, to the rate at which change is possible. A statistical survey of European agricultural economists showed that the view that "the CAP mainly aims at supporting farm incomes, whereas the other objectives of the Treaty of Rome receive little attention" was clear-cut (Herrmann *et al.*, 1985). And specialist CAP-watchers have little difficulty in identifying the significance of the income strand. To quote Fennell (1985), " Concern with the inadequate level of agricultural incomes has been a dominant feature of farm policy in all developed countries since about the mid-1950s...", a view reinforced later (Fennell, 1997) with the comment that the central importance of income levels in agricultural policy "has been a feature of policy across the developed world, at least since the mid-1950s and in some countries much earlier than that." In a review of OECD countries Winters (1990) confirmed that "The maintanance of farm incomes is probably the major objective of agricultural policy". The "Larsen" report of independent experts to the European Commission on

EU agricultural policy for the 21st century (Commission, 1994a) left no doubt as to their interpretation of the thrust of policy; "Governments in most developed countries have therefore set out to secure a satisfactory and equitable standard of living for farmers and to stabilise agricultural markets and farmers' incomes" and it goes on to show that this was also the stance of the EU. The OECD has observed that "One of the main motivations which has led to the panoply of interventions which characterise the agricultural sectors of OECD countries has been concern about the income of farmers and their families" (OECD, 1995). Similarly, a retired Permanent Secretary of the UK's Ministry of Agriculture, Fisheries and Food when contemplating how the CAP should be revised to fit the future, referred repeatedly to the central importance of the income support to farmers as a determining factor in past policy, and stressed that, where reforms to the CAP bring lower prices and reduced income from farming "This issue will have to be addressed if any programme is to have the slightest chance of being taken seriously" (Ockenden and Franklin, 1995). This list of comments on the central importance of farmer incomes to policy could be greatly extended.

2.3   Official statements of policy for the EU

At this stage it is appropriate to examine official policy statements and descriptions of the aims of agricultural policy, paying particular attention to the references to incomes they contain. The objective of achieving a satisfactory and equitable standard of living for farmers is found in official statements of policy in the EU, Japan, Canada, the USA, and Switzerland (Winters, 1990), though it is not easy to draw a line between those countries that treat this as a primary goal and those others where this aim is implied through the objective of creating the conditions in which an efficient and competitive farming industry can operate. We start first with the EU's Common Agricultural Policy, move to the statements about national policies in the UK and Germany that run alongside the CAP, finally broadening to a representative group of non-EU countries.

The Treaty of Rome's statement of the objectives of the CAP, set out in Article 39, is still used as a reference for the validity of any proposed new policy measures. The Treaty states that "The common agricultural policy shall have as its objectives:

(a)   To increase agricultural productivity by promoting technical progress and by ensuring the rational development of agricultural production and the optimum utilisation of the factors of production, in particular labour;

(b)   *Thus to ensure a fair standard of living for the agricultural community, in particular by the increasing of the individual earnings of persons engaged in agriculture* (emphasis added)

(c)   To stabilise markets.

(d)   To assure the availability of supplies;

(e)   To ensure that supplies reach consumers at reasonable prices."

The Treaty also required the following factors to be taken into consideration when working out and applying the CAP:

(i)   The particular nature of agricultural activity, which results from the social structure of agriculture and from structural and natural disparities between the various agricultural regions;

(ii)   The need to effect any appropriate adjustment by degrees;

(iii)   That in the Member States the agricultural sector is closely linked with the economy as a whole.

The normative nature of "fair" used in connection with the living standards mentioned in (b) should not go unnoticed (emphasis has been added). Such a term does not permit a precise interpretation by which the efficacy of policy in approaching its declared objectives can be judged easily, although there are somewhat stronger possibilities for assessing whether changes resulting from policy bring about a less or more fair situation than was previously the case. However, the fundamental concern in the legislation with the living standards of people engaged in agriculture is abundantly clear.

The three listed factors that should be considered when applying the CAP imply that agriculture should be defended, at least in some areas, against pressures that would reduce incomes and result in farmers going out of business where this can be justified for social and environment reasons. Also farmers must be given time to adjust.

While the Treaty of Rome statement of CAP objectives remains as a foundation, it must be viewed in its historical context. The notion that, under the CAP, earnings should be increased through improvements in productivity is a child of the time of food imports, not one of production surpluses. Policy with regard to income will have developed since these statements were made, and it is reasonable to look for more recent and perhaps more precise objectives. This search will largely be in vain, at least in the forty years until the *Agenda 2000* discussion document of 1997 added a little more flesh. No document from the Council of Ministers has sought to interpret the broad "standard of living" objective of the Treaty of Rome's agricultural policy into more specific, quantified aims. Nor has guidance been given on the priorities of the various directions in which the Treaty states that policy should go, for example in the conflict between living standards of the agricultural population and the food prices paid by consumers (NAO, 1985).

On the other hand, the Commission of the European Communities has produced a flow of documents on the CAP which, while having less authority than the Treaty, are nevertheless a good indication of the way that the fundamental objectives are interpreted in the institution that is responsible for carrying them out. For example, in 1980 the Commission described the CAP as follow: "The Common Agricultural Policy may be characterised as a system of support of farmers' incomes mainly through support of market prices with certain direct aids to incomes" (Commission, 1980b).

In a specialist brochure on incomes in 1984 the Commission stated that

> Although they are not the only factor in an assessment of the economic and social situation in agriculture, agricultural incomes are obviously of key importance. The improvement in the individual incomes of those working in agriculture is indeed, under Article 39 of the Treaty of Rome, one of the fundamental objectives of the Common Agricultural Policy (Commission, 1984b).

The Director General for agriculture put it more bluntly; "If we did not have to take account of the income objective, our task would be much easier. We should propose cuts in many of the common prices" (Commission, 1984a).

The discussion paper *Perspectives on the Common Agricultural Policy* (Commission, 1985b, usually called the Green Paper) marked a major attempt to change the direction of the CAP, by no means the first but possibly the most determined up to that time. Though discussing various options for controlling the expansion of output and escalating costs, and the importance of environmental issues to European agriculture, in many ways it represented a return to fundamentals in the area of income objectives and amply reinforced the basic concern with living standards. The text specifically stated that the original objectives, as laid down in Article 39 of the Treaty,

> .....remain as valid today as when the Treaty was signed in 1957. The task of the Community is not to revise or reinterpret those aims, but to ensure that the means of putting them into effect are adapted to the realities of the present day. The objectives of the CAP are both economic and social in nature. .... The challenge for the Community now is to reconcile the success of the CAP in achieving its economic objectives with the need to continue to fulfil the social objective of assuring a fair standard of living for the agricultural population.

The Green Paper contained the first tentative estimates of the numbers of farmers who would be potential beneficiaries of an attack on poverty through direct income support, and of the costs involved.

Following discussions in 1985 the policy document which emerged *(A Future for Community Agriculture*, Commission (1985c)) contained only a watered-down version of the Green Paper's proposals as far as income support was concerned. However, the intentions of the Commission regarding the future direction of policy were clear. In a memorandum of 18th December 1985 the need to take into account the income problems of small family farms in a more effective and systematic manner when reorienting the CAP more towards the market were stated explicitly. In 1987 proposals for direct income payments were put forward by the Commission though in the form of (a) supplements to tide certain groups of potentially viable but financial precarious farmers over the difficult period of readjustment flowing from the reform of agricultural product prices under the CAP; (b) pre-pensions to elderly farmers to encourage them to leave the land; and (c) a framework for controlling national aids to farm incomes, in recognition of the tendency of governments to introduce such measures in response to local political demands. These proposals were further elaborated in the 1987 *Agricultural Situation in the Community* report (Commission, 1988a) which continued to emphasise the need for a combination of selective income support, not general but concentrated on situations of need, and reform in the system of product price support. The social aspects of the CAP were acknowledged, but so too was the fact that "social considerations have provided an alibi often exploited by those opposing any serious effort to cut back on the indiscriminate support now granted under the CAP" (Commission, 1988a). Also in 1988 the Commission issued a major discussion document (*The Future of Rural Society*) which indicated that agriculture could be instrumental in providing income and employment in rural areas, particularly in the most remote ones where support to farming was critical to the maintenance of a viable population (Commission, 1988b). In the Community's naturally disadvantaged areas (mainly the uplands) the support of farming formed an integral part of the strategy to stimulate regional economic development.

In 1991 the most fundamental reform of the CAP attempted up to that time was instituted, with a reflections paper from the Commission (Commission, 1991a) and proposals for change (Commission, 1991b), known by the name of the Agriculture Commissioner, Ray MacSharry. These described the mechanisms used to support prices and incomes, but observed that the existing system resulted in 80 per cent of the support provided going to 20 per cent of farms, those larger holdings that also accounted for the greater part of the land used by agriculture. "The existing system does not take adequate account of the incomes of the vast majority of small and medium size family farms"(Commission, 1991a). Without any firm evidence the reflections paper went on to assert that "The per capita purchasing power of those engaged in agriculture has improved very little over the period 1975-89. This development is all the more worrying in that over the same period the Community's active agricultural population has fallen by 35 per cent". In the programme for proposed CAP reform the problem of surplus production was to be tackled by a progressive reduction in the support prices of cereals, oilseeds and proteins over three years, cuts starting in 1993/4. Changes in the livestock sector were to be made to allow for the resulting lower costs of feed for beef and sheep. However, these crop price reductions would be accompanied by compensating payments, in the form of aid per hectare on the crops (dependent on compliance with an undertaking to set-aside a proportion of arable land) to counter the resulting anticipated loss in income. There was a studied silence on the key issue of whether these compensatory payments were to be continued indefinitely or reduced over time; consequently uncertainty and ambiguity flourished among commentators and national politicians. As a response to the known pattern of benefit, there were plans to introduce forms of "modulation", in effect achieving a somewhat more equitable distribution of financial support by scaling down the amounts that large farmers would receive. However, these attempts to target aid were largely lost in the political compromise needed to get the proposals through the Council of Ministers in 1992. After the reforms were instigated in 1993/4 a rise in world commodity prices meant that, in practice, for EU cereal farmers in general, market prices failed to fall as much as had been expected when the "compensation" payments were set, so that a degree of overcompensation occurred. For UK producers this was particularly marked as the withdrawal of Sterling from the EU's Exchange Rate Mechanism in 1992 and a fall in its value against the ECU resulted in an increase in support prices and area payments. UK market prices (in £) remained almost level (until 1997), so the "compensation" payments were, in reality a bonus (Cook and Hill, 1999). Again, most of the benefit from this would have gone to the producers with the largest volumes of output.

The central role taken by incomes in EU agricultural policy was further underlined by the *Agenda 2000* discussion document, issued by the Commisison in 1997. This covered three main topics; which of the candidate countries that had applied for membership (mostly in Central and Eastern Europe) should be in the first wave to join (Hungary, Poland, Estonia, the Czech Republic, Slovenia and Cyprus); how the EU should be financed in the future (the new "financial framework", including the fate of the "rebate" that the UK had negotiated first in 1984); third, the further reform of the CAP in ways which took it further along the road of demolishing market support and the greater use of direct payments in compensation, and with the development of alternative sources of income for farmers and their families. The Commission subsequently issued concrete proposals and legal texts (March 1998). The general outline of the proposals for agricultural reform was agreed in principal by agricultural ministers in 1998, and agreement in detail was achieved by the agricultural Council in March 1999 (though not entirely to the Commission's proposals). The matters settled then set the shape of agricultural policy to 2006. This was subject to negotiations on the entire *Agenda 2000* package by the heads of state and government at European Council in Berlin later in March 1999; this watered down some of the details (such as reducing the size of price cuts for cereals from 20% in two equal stages to 15% and delaying changes in the dairy regime from 2003 to 2005). The general framework, however, was not altered.

The *Agenda 2000* reforms were significant to the incomes of farmers and their families in a number of ways. First, the objectives of agricultural policy for the start of the next millennium were articulated with an unusual clarity in a Commission document that, while falling short of the authority of a Treaty, was formally adopted by the Council of agricultural ministers and of the heads of state and government meeting as the European Council. The "new" objectives for the CAP were, as set out in *Agenda 2000*:

- (To) "increase competitiveness internally and externally in order to ensure that Union producers take full advantage of positive world market developments;

- Food safety and food quality, which are both fundamental obligations towards consumers;

- *Ensuring a fair standard of living for the agricultural community and contributing to the stability of farm incomes* (emphasis added);

- The integration of environmental goals into the CAP;

- Promotion of sustainable agriculture;

- *The creation of alternative job and income opportunities for farmers and their families* (emphasis added);

- Simplification of Union legislation".

The assurance given to the fair standard of living of the agricultural community was carried over, word for word, from the 1957 Treaty of Rome, but with no attempt at a greater precision of how these terms should be interpreted. The added mention of stability registers the Commission's concern with one of the fundamental problems facing agriculture.

Second, another important addition among the objectives of agricultural policy was the reference to the creation of alternative job and income opportunities for farmers and their families. This recognised overtly that the support of farming cannot hope to provide an adequate livelihood for everyone currently engaged in farming, and that diversification of income sources was necessary to assist with the aim of ensuring fair living standards. The implication is that measures of total income accruing to farmers will be necessary in order to assess the needs for policies to develop such non-farm opportunities and to monitor the performance of policy.

Third, and closely linked, was the stated aim to pursue in a more active way rural development policy – to form a "second pillar" to the CAP. *Agenda 2000*'s rhetoric declared that the rigid distinction between sectors (agriculture, industry, and services) was out of date, a view long held by many outside the Commission. In practice, it seemed that (at least at the outset) support to farm families comprised the centre of this pillar and accounted for the bulk of spending, with programmes to protect the environment (paying incentives to farmers for less intensive production methods, management of land and natural resources, biodiversity), financial help to farmers for early retirement by elderly farmers and for entry by young ones, incentives to modernisation of potentially viable farms and diversification, for afforestation, and the continuation of payments to farmers in less favoured areas (in particular mountainous regions and areas with specific natural handicaps). All this, however, represented little more than one tenth of sum to be spent on supporting the Common Market Organisations for agricultural commodities. At the same time revisions to the Structural Funds and the Cohesion Fund were to take place (from 2000), with a reduction of the number of objectives from seven to three (two regional objectives and one for human resources). "The new policy explicitly recognises that farming plays a number of roles including the preservation of the rural heritage, while emphasising the creation of alternative source of income as an integral part of rural development policy" (Press notice *Elements of the political agreement of the Agricultural Council 22/02-11/03/1999)*.

2.3.1 The agricultural community and the family farm

These Community-level statements reinforce the notion that the income objective of agricultural policy is fundamentally concerned with the incomes of individuals rather than of the industry *per se*, with special attention being given to those farmers operating under form of disadvantage because of farm size, natural conditions etc.. Beyond that, there is very little that is specific. Perhaps the most remarkable omission is any reference to what constitutes the "agricultural community" which is supposed to benefit from the CAP. At its broadest it might be interpreted as comprising all households containing someone who operates a holding as an independent (self-employed) farmer or who works on one as a hired employee (dependent worker). Or perhaps it might be only those people who spend some working time in agriculture. Though for some statistical purposes the European Commission lumps farmers and hired workers together, in practice the CAP directs its support exclusively at the self employed sector.

The CAP is also ambiguous in its application of support. When the CAP enhances the prices of farm products, all producers benefit to some extent, the larger ones the most (OECD 1996, 1999). Some other forms of aid have excluded those farms where the holder (presumably the head of household in most cases) does not spend most of his time on the farm. Eurostat (the Statistics Office of the European Communities) has recently adopted a definition of an agricultural household, for the purpose of income measurement and comparison, as one where more than half of the income of the head of household (reference person) comes from farming (Hill, 1995). Households of prosperous bankers, other professionals, owners of non-farm businesses and those mainly dependent on property income are not classed as agricultural, however large their farms, if they fail on this income criterion. This approach, while having some logic and being compatible with a systematic breakdown of all households into socio-professional groups, is by no means universally accepted among CAP policy-makers. Meanwhile the CAP price supports, and many other instruments, continue to benefit households which are not considered by Eurostat to be agricultural. This important issue is revisited in Chapter 3.

Some crumb of assistance towards discovering the target group for the CAP is the repeated assertion by policy-makers of the importance given to the support of the family farm. The conference held in Stresa in 1958 to work out the ways in which the Treaty objectives were to be fleshed out and implemented accepted as axiomatic in its final resolution the unanimous wish to safeguard the "familial" structure of agriculture and that every effort should be made to raise their economic and competitive capacity (Fennell, 1987). Confusion seems to have reigned on quite what the term meant, with various generalised descriptions to be found in early CAP documents (Fennell, 1997) that implied that size was the critical characteristic; farms of one, two or (in some documents) three people were cited, which by virtue of the structure of ownership and operation, meant that the family would probably provide all the labour input. It was assumed that agricultural policy instruments would support incomes in such a way that this size of farm could generate and income that, "given rational management, allows a fair family income in relation to comparable groups of workers" (Commission draft proposals, quoted in Fennell, 1997).

Following a lull in interest starting in the mid-1960s and running for two decades, the mid-1980s saw a reawakening in the concept. Reference to the family farm has run though many subsequent Commission documents. In 1988 it was cited as forming an integral part of the Commission's strategy for the future of rural society (Commission, 1988b).

The 1991 Reflections document (Commission, 1991a) considered its reforms to the CAP "taking into account the income problem of small family farms in a more effective and systematic manner". The MacSharry proposals again recognised the need to "maintain economic and social cohesion by safeguarding the position of the vast majority of farmers in the 12 Member States" (Commission, 1991b).

Though oft repeated, quite what is intended by the term "family farm" has never been made clear. Many alternative criteria are possible, of which family ownership, family management, or (probably the intention of the fathers of the CAP) sole operation by the family are front runners (Hill, 1993). The view of what constitutes such a farm is likely to be very different in, for example, the UK (where family ownership of the business is implied, so a family farm can be a large one and employ mainly non-family labour) from that in Greece or Italy (where any hired labour would rule it out). Despite the lack of precise articulation of what is meant by the term, the "family farm" has constituted one of the most powerful "myths" in agricultural policy. However, because of the lack of discrimination that currently characterises the support mechanisms used, much of the support under the current CAP must be going to farms which at least some countries consider not to be family farms.

2.4 National agricultural policies in the EU - the cases of the UK and Germany

Although the agricultural policies of EU Member States are dominated by the CAP, some reference should be made to the official statements of national agricultural policies. In the *United Kingdom* the foundation of national agricultural policy prior to adopting the CAP was the 1947 Agriculture Act. Though largely superseded by the Treaty and subsequent domestic legislation, its influence is still felt in the UK. The income objectives of agricultural policy were only described in the most general of terms. The 1947 Act refers to the aim of

> ... Promoting and maintaining ...a stable and efficient agricultural industry capable of producing such part of the nation's food and other agricultural produce as in the national interest it is desirable to produce in the United Kingdom, and of producing it at minimum prices *consistently with proper remuneration and living conditions for farmers and workers in agriculture and an adequate return on capital* invested in the industry. (emphasis added)

The two major UK White Papers dealing with policy - *Food From Our Own Resources* (HMSO, 1975), and *Farming and the Nation* (HMSO, 1979) either restricted consideration to comments on changes in the aggregate income from production of the agriculture sector (the former) or virtually ignored the topic (the latter). Publications associated with the annual Reviews of Agriculture were also not forthcoming about the income aims of policy in concrete terms.

By far the most detailed official statement of the objectives of agricultural policy operated in the UK, under both CAP and national legislation, was a series of annual published documents (now discontinued) containing the report on Ministerial Information in MAFF (MINIM). This consisted of a record of the objectives and resource use for each of the programmes of work undertaken by the Ministry of Agriculture, Fisheries and Food. First made publicly available in 1984, it was regularly updated and submitted as an aid to management to ministers and senior officials. MINIM was thus not an official statement about the aims of *political* policy but rather was the administrative record of the way that past policy decisions had been implemented. Nevertheless it is surprising that incomes were not mentioned specifically in the list of overall MAFF aims in the 1986 and 1987 MINIMs

Among the stated aims of individual programmes reference was made to incomes only in the context of grant for investment where, for example, the Agricultural and Horticultural Grant Scheme (now terminated) was described as acting "to improve agricultural efficiency and productivity and thereby improving farm incomes and assisting rural areas..." Under the grant schemes operating up to 1985 and part-financed by the EC there was a notion of "comparable income" built in, with a test of eligibility incorporating the demonstration that the income position of the farmer was to be improved by the assisted investment. The expensive series of programmes for commodities (e.g. cereals, beef) were unspecific in their income aims, using terms like "giving due weight to the interests of UK producers" but bracketing them with the interests of consumers, traders and processors. In short, little of precision could be gleaned about the income objectives from the individual measures which had an impact on incomes, except that the relevant sector of the industry seemed to be only those farms which were viable or potentially so, and that it was assumed that improved farm incomes assisted rural areas generally.

The operation of a national agricultural policy, with its own objectives and legal framework, in combination with the CAP is, of course, not confined to the UK. *Germany* forms another example. As in Britain, national legislation (the 'Agriculture Act' of 1955) requires an annual review on the state of German agriculture, the practical manifestation of which is the Green Report (Agrarbericht). This Act institutionalised the generally-held view that farming needed special treatment, an attitude still shared by the main political parties (Hendriks, 1994). The 1987 Report identified four major policy streams, each of which was divided into several specific items. The four long-term objectives were as follows (Agrarbericht 1987 p120, trans. Weltzien):

(a)   The improvement of the standard of living in rural areas combined with an equal participation of agriculture, forestry and fishing in the overall income and welfare development.

(b)   The supply of citizens and the economy with high quality produce from the agricultural sector at reasonable prices, and the protection of consumer nutrition.

(c)   Contributing to the solution of the world's agricultural and food problems and improving external agricultural trade relationships and well as internal German trade connections.

(d)   Contributing to the security and development of natural resources including the landscape and an improvement of animal welfare.

These objectives obviously reflect those of the Treaty of Rome, not surprisingly so as the Treaty was heavily influenced by Germany's earlier national legislation. However, they show an interpretation appropriate to the German standpoint and market developments. For example, there is an absence of any reference to improving productivity. The third objective reflected the contemporary dislocation in international trade of agricultural products. However, the weight given to the standard of living component of agricultural policy is undeniable, and a helpful inflexion is supplied on the breadth of the German view of the intended beneficiaries ("rural areas") and on the way that policy might be interpreted ("equal participation" most probably meaning equal rates of growth).

2.5   Income objectives in non-EU industrialised countries

A brief review of policy aims in some other OECD countries will add perspective to those in the EU, the UK and Germany. Sweden and Finland only adopted the CAP at the start of 1995, so their national agricultural policies up to that date can be used as non-EU examples. *Sweden*'s agricultural policy objectives were laid out in a parliamentary resolution of 1947, which subsequent legislation of 1967 and 1977 consolidated. This included aims covering incomes, production and efficiency. In 1984 the Swedish parliament, while maintaing that the main objective of food policy was security of supplies, both in war and in peace-time, also set as a goal that the economic and social position of farmers operating rationally-managed farms that were capable of providing full-time employment should be equal to that of comparable population groups, taken to be waged workers and salaried employees (Puurunen, 1990). For this purpose, specific calculations of incomes of occupiers of farms of 20-100 hectares of arable land were made during the 1980s up to 1987; survey data were adjusted for known distortion of certain items in order to make better comparisons of living standards (Hill, 1995). These comparisons formed the basis for negotiating agricultural support prices. However, in 1990 the Swedish parliament decided on a new, market-orientated agricultural policy in which farmers were to be treated as all other forms of businessmen, and the explicit comparability aim was abandoned.

In *Finland* the aim of ensuring that farmers' incomes kept pace with those of other groups was incorporated in legislation in 1952 and formed part of the basis for setting agricultural support prices. The various Agricultural Income Acts of the 1980s explicitly stated that the annual income from agriculture on rationally-managed farms requiring the full-time employment of the farm family, and changes in that income, had to be compared with the situation experienced by skilled industrial workers (Puurunen, 1990).

In *Norway* the broad agricultural policy aims relate to food security (such as approximate self-sufficiency in animal products) and to stabilise the population in rural areas, to which agriculture is seen as capable of making a major contribution. The income aim is for the farmer to have an economic and social standard of living equal to that of industrial workers. Legislation of 1965 stipulated that the income generated by a modern and rationally-managed farm that employed one annual worker had to be at least at the same level as the average wage income reached in rationally-managed industry. Agricultural commodity prices were to be adjusted with this in mind; legislation of 1975 set the target of parity by 1982. A resolution of 1976 expanded the basis of comparison to one of living standards, not just income. By the mid-1980s this had become interpreted in agricultural price negotiations as the objective of achieving the same income level for farmers as for industrial workers and, apart from the effects of taxation, the same standard of living. Thus the history of this parity-objective evolved from simple income goals to a more complex approach in which adjustments were made for the cheaper food on farms, the rental value of houses, distance from work, holidays, inconvenient working hours, job security, social insurance and so on. However, in a major revision of policy in 1992 the legislation of 1975 was repealed and replaced with a less committing objective - that farmers have to be provided with the *potential* for income and living standards corresponding with the remainder of the population. This was to be achieved through creating a "robust agriculture", not a very precise term but interpreted as one that had a structure that enabled it to be more internationally competitive and less dependent on raised prices for its products. However, at the same time, the policy revisions recognised that farmers supply non-market goods (environmental, cultural landscape, support of rural society, food security etc.) for which payment should be made. In effect, the lowering of price support combined with increases in direct payments (which have tended to favour the smaller farmer) still left Norwegian agriculture the second most heavily protected among OECD countries (in terms of percent Producer Subsidy Equivalent), exceeded only by Switzerland (Nersten, 1998).

Switzerland has had a general policy aim "To conserve a viable rural population and facilitate the country's food supplies by securing agricultural production", given in its 1951 Agriculture Act. The income objective has been one of striving for comparability in terms of the "fair parity remuneration", defined as the average wage of workers in industry and small own-account operations in rural and semi-urban areas. It is recognised that, while the methods of support used have not permitted full comparability in nominal terms, especially among mountain farmers, this has not prevented farmers making sizeable personal savings, suggesting that the levels of consumption of farmers are lower.

The four countries listed above are examples where there are fairly clearly defined income objectives, with the thread of parity of reward or living standard between the agricultural and non-agricultural population running through them. By way of contrast, agricultural policy in the *USA* is much less concerned with engineering income levels at the level of the individual. It shares with *Canada, Australia* and *New Zealand* an approach of creating a suitable economic environment for farming in which the social aspects of income objectives do not feature within agricultural policy, although there is commonly a general policy on poverty in which farmers are treated on the same basis as other members of society (OECD,

1987; Winters, 1990). In the *USA* the five basic agricultural policy objectives over the last century have been as follows (Vertrees and Morton, 1984):

(i)   To enhance farm income during periods of excess supply

(ii) To achieve reasonable stability in farm prices and incomes

(iii) To provide an adequate and stable supply of food and fibre for consumers at reasonable prices

(iv) To expand farm product exports, and

(v)   To reduce the cost of farm programs to taxpayers.

There is no single official USA policy statement equivalent to Article 39 of the Treaty of Rome which acts as a foundation of later developments. Policy is carried forward primarily using a series of periodic (five year) Farm Acts. If one were determined to seek parallels, it might be noted that in 1948 the US Congress, when providing the Federal Charter for the Commodity Credit Corporation (the agency which operated commodity price support), declared the objectives as "... stabilising, supporting and protecting farm incomes and prices...assisting in the maintenance of balanced and adequate supplies of agricultural commodities,..... facilitating the orderly distribution of agricultural commodities." This list bears an obvious similarity with the broad objectives of the CAP.

In the OECD review of agricultural policies in its members countries, which drew on official national sources for its information, the list of USA policy objectives started as follows: "To provide farmers the opportunity to earn incomes consistent with their management ability and capital investments and commensurate with incomes received in non-agricultural sectors of the economy" (OECD, 1974). Other objectives followed the by now familiar lines of food security, environmental compatibility and rural development. The important point to note is the "enabling" tone of the income objective; that is, conditions are to be created in which comparability can be achieved, rather than the "mechanistic" approach implied in the European countries cited above. Though the 1985 Food Security Act avoided giving specific goals for increasing or maintaining farm income, the administration recognised that many farmers had come to rely on Government payments for an important part of their incomes, and that many farm organisations were unwilling to accept sharp reductions in these receipts (USDA, 1986). This approach was maintained in the Food, Agriculture, Conservation, and Trade Act of 1990 (OECD, 1994). The run-up to the 1995 Farm Bill revealed consensus that product price support "can no longer be justified as necessary to bring the income of poor farmers up to nonfarm levels" but no clear view as to how the system in which most of the benefit goes to the well-off producers and landowners should be changed (Stovall and Hathaway, 1995). Some claim that the 1996 Federal Agricultural Improvement and Reform (FAIR) Act marked a paradigm shift in policy, involving the replacement of the traditional protection of family farming with one emphasising market efficiency (Tweeton and Zulauf, 1997), though history suggests that, in retrospect, this is likely to turn out as more a matter of adjusting balance than one of fundamental change.

It is worth noting, in passing, that in the US context the term "parity" has an additional specific (though now outdated) meaning, in which it referred both to prices and to incomes. The parity price formula was written into the Agricultural Adjustment Act of 1933 and related (originally) to the prices that were in operation in the period 1910-14; for later periods parity prices were those which would have existed if the prices which farmers received for their produce had increased by the same percentage as had the prices which farmers paid. Parity in this context means comparison with what was received by the agricultural sector at some historical period, rather than a comparison between farming and other sectors at the *same* time. In the post-war period much attention was given to parity prices and parity incomes viewed in this uniquely American manner, though the notion of applying these prices as part of policy was gradually abandoned because of the prospects of substantial unmarketable surpluses (Brandow, 1977).

From this brief review is will be seen that, on balance, the agricultural policy of the EU (and UK) falls between the explicitly social approach of some European countries and the environment-creation of North America and Australasia. Among the latter group, while making it clear that there is a deep concern with the living standards of the agricultural community, there is not the detailed articulation of these aims that the European countries share.

2.6 Elucidating the income objectives of agricultural policy

Though important within the policy *milieu*, the income intentions of the CAP and UK national agricultural policy are only imprecisely defined. This is a general characteristic of the CAP and inhibits any systematic or objective evaluation of its effectiveness (NAO, 1985). From an operational standpoint there may be advantages in refraining from a precise articulation of objectives. Income policies form only one part of governmental policies towards agriculture, and general statements can underlie many different practical applications of policy and facilitate the trade-offs between individual applications that inevitably occur (Kirk, 1958). More recently, the UK agriculture departments (MAFF, DAFS now SERAD, WOAD now NAWAD, DANI) voiced the opinion that a more precise definition would not assist the UK in negotiations with other Member States or in its attempts to reform the CAP; they considered that it would be unrealistic to expect agricultural ministers to commit themselves to forward targets which, due to the nature of EC decision-making, they could have no assurance of securing (NAO, 1985).

The absence of closely defined income objectives means that powers of interpretation must be relied on to distil the intentions of policy-makers. Observation of the practice of policy, the speeches of politicians, the reports and discussion papers of civil servants, and the declarations of farmer organisations and pressure groups on their perceptions of the income problems of agriculture indicate that in the EU there are three broad areas of concern (Hill, 1982):

(a)   The general levels of income of those engaged in farming compared with earnings in other sectors (termed the *parity issue*);

(b)   The particularly low incomes in certain regions or sizes of farm (the *poverty issue*);

(c)   The variations of income over time (the *instability issue*).

These are the same trio of central components of "the farm problem" that have been identified in the USA and summarised by Gardner (1992). For example Schultz (1945) identified the farm problem with both "the low earnings of most farm people and the great instability of income from farming". Tweeten (1971) cited the low absolute net incomes and the relatively low rates of return on farm resources and both Brandow (1977) and Tweeten both commented on the variability and instability of incomes. It seems highly likely that these are universal problems faced by the agricultures of industrialised market economies, at least in periods of relative peace in international relations.

Parity and poverty are concerned essentially with the welfare of individual farmers and their dependants, and it is on these two components that most of our attention will be focused in later chapters, where problems of definition and measurement will be faced. Low farm incomes in single years do not throw the recipients immediately into the poverty category; reserves will be drawn on or borrowings made to maintain living standards through times of temporary financial setback. A distinction has to be drawn between those farm households that have to contend with occasional periods of low income and those that suffer hardship from incomes that are persistently low. Instability also has a welfare component. However, when year-to-year fluctuations are anticipated the level of consumption by farmers and their households may have to be curtailed in order to set aside reserves for years of low incomes or to pay for past borrowing in lean years. Farmers may have to be content with generating a safer but lower income, with consequences both for consumption possibilities and the potential for the business to grow.

Both comparability and stability can be interpreted in the business or resource use sense, as well as the personal welfare context. Studies of the relative returns of factors of production in agriculture with uses in other industries have a long history. However, this concern belongs to a period when policy was aimed at expanding total agricultural output by the improved use of resources and with their transfer, especially with the moving of labour trapped in farming to other occupations which offered higher marginal productivities and, consequently, higher incomes. The emergence of agricultural commodity surpluses and a pool of labour unemployment has diminished interest in the comparability of factor rewards. Reasonably stable business conditions are likewise seen as enhancing the efficiency with which resources are employed, including the more rational use of capital. Bearing in mind that some degree of instability is needed if an industry is to respond to changes in supply and demand conditions, including technological advance, there are economic arguments which support the modulation of random short-term variations brought about by external influences like weather and the dampening of price signals which perform no economic function, such as price cycles. However, these issues are distinct from, and now of minor importance compared with, the main thrust of agricultural policy which is directed at the personal incomes of the agricultural population.

When policy makers attempt to interfere with the markets for agricultural products or inputs, they do so primarily with the intent of improving the incomes of farmers. There would be little reason for taking action unless the potential beneficiaries were seen to be disadvantaged in some way - that without assistance they would be unacceptably poor or that there would be an unfair gap between the position of farmers and other members of society. It goes without saying that in the parity issue farmers are typically seen as the relatively disadvantaged group.

Talk of lowering the prices that farmers receive, as a way of reducing production to achieve a better balance in the market, is commonly opposed using arguments which suggest that poverty or unfair comparability would result. It is pointed out that some farm families would be forced to quit because they would be unable to provide themselves with an adequate livelihood. Whether or not this would actually happen on any significant scale, or even if it did, whether this would matter much, is immaterial. As long as it is perceived by people responsible for policy decisions as being the likely result of an action, and the political cost of allowing such an outcome is believed to be high, the short-run poverty or comparability threat will often be sufficient to prevent the change.

Secondary to these three main strands are other issues, some of great importance, which are believed to be related to a significant extent to incomes from farming. Among the most prominent of these are beliefs that incomes from farming have a substantial impact on;

(i)   The level of general economic activity and employment in rural areas, especially in those suffering from unfavourable natural conditions, such as hill and mountain areas, where alternative employment opportunities also tend to be limited. Support for farming in these areas is seen as a way of promoting the viability of the rural economy.

(ii)   The pursuit of practices to conserve the natural environment, with the assumption that adequate farm incomes are a prerequisite for conservation at the farm level.

(iii)   The rate of technological advance. Though not an argument heard so loudly in times of agricultural surpluses, the notion that a prosperous agriculture was necessary to encourage the development of new technology and its uptake through rising levels of investment and capital stocks was built into the thinking of post-war agricultural policy in the UK. A prosperous farming sector produced thriving support industries, with more jobs and income arising from exports of modern machinery and chemicals.

With each of these income-related issues there are alternative ways of bringing about the desired ends other than through changing farm incomes. Indeed, the extent of the dependency on farming is open to question; there may be superior ways of stimulating rural employment or of conservation than by using farming as a vehicle.

2.7   Income information and the general theory of data systems

Given the income objectives of agricultural policy that are stated or implied, the next stage is to consider the sorts of information the policy-makers and administrators need in order to design an efficient, effective and economic set of instruments. Better information leads to a clearer set of ideas of the way that the world works and of the problems that are to be faced, so that the objectives of policy can be put on a firmer base. It also enables the performance of instruments to be viewed against these objectives. Agricultural policies in developed countries are diverse and therefore have complex statistical needs. Nevertheless, the central position held by the income objective necessitates an adequate supply of relevant information. As will become increasingly evident, the statistical system in the EU and UK is far from satisfactory in this respect.

At this stage it is worth bearing in mind the essentials of an "information system".   Such a framework forms a useful basis for examining the role of existing official statistics on incomes (that is, statistics generated or supervised by the government or EU institutions) and how they fall short of what is now required in the policy-making context of the 1990s. An information system can be characterised as having three components (Brinkman, 1983):

(a)   A data system;

(b)   The necessary analysis to transform data into information;

(c)   The decision-maker.

The way that the components fit together is shown in Figure 2.1

The provision of statistics on the incomes of agricultural households is essentially the function of the data system, but the collection, analysis and publication of *data* forms only part of the larger *information* system needed to service policy. An important next step is the interpretation of the analysis, which is the interface between the providers and users of statistics and in which both will be involved. In parallel with the direct servicing of policy there is generally a system of scientific enquiry which is designed to test the basic assumptions of the data system and its interpretation and analysis.

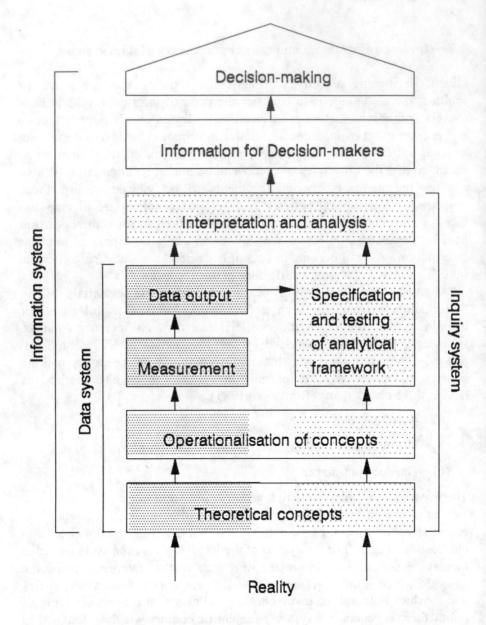

Figure 2.1 An agricultural information system (from Brinkman, 1983)

A property of any data system, and without which its utility is reduced, is its ability to reflect the reality to which policy relates. According to Bonnen (1975, 1977) there are three distinct steps which must be taken before data can be produced which purport to represent reality. In the (inelegant) terms used by Bonnen, these are:

(a) "Conceptualisation",

(b) "Operationalisation" of the concepts (definition of empirical variables), and

(c) Measurement, meaning the actual collection of data.

These steps constitute the data system and are compatible with the overall information framework, shown in Figure 2.1.

Because official statistics are essentially policy-driven, a prerequisite for a successful data system is a search for the fundamental objectives that the data system is required to serve. These will give guidance to the concepts which need to be made operational. Concepts cannot be measured directly, and for the system to be practically possible it is necessary to define empirical variables (measurable entities) which are highly correlated with the object of enquiry. If policy-makers are clear in their objectives, then the task of the statistician in designing the data system is relatively straightforward. If, as is the case with the income objective of agricultural policy, the aims are not clear or have become confused since they were first set out or are in the process of change, the statistician has a more difficult task. A more proactive role has to be adopted, in which decisions have to be made on the sorts of information that policy-makers are likely to want in the future, often at short notice, as they realise that new areas of policy have come on the agenda. Anticipation is important because time is involved in planning new forms of statistics. And resources will be need to be committed to develop statistics before the benefit to policy-makers from having the statistics is apparent, involving a certain amount of courage on the part of managers of data systems in justifying their actions.

The data system can fail for two main reasons. One is inadequacy in the collection mechanism - the size and representative nature of samples, reliability of data entries etc. This is the aspect to which most attention has been paid by statisticians. However, perhaps the more important concerns the relevance of the concepts employed and their associated empirical variables to the problems in hand. Here we are faced with the problems of measurability and the fact that policy is always evolving.

Conceptual obsolescence may occur when the nature of reality changes or the needs of policy shift. The result is that the empirical variables in use no longer represent the aspect of reality that policy-makers wish to know about. Statisticians find themselves using concepts and measurements that belong to previous circumstances. They cannot provide the new forms of information yet continue generating the old for which there is reduced demand and relevance; this represents a waste of skills and other resources.

Pointing out and countering conceptual obsolescence is where the "inquiry system" shown in Figure 2.1 plays a role. This consists of independent observers and researchers who are not involved in the routine work of producing data, often under pressure; they therefore bring a different perspective and may consider issues for which the official statistician has insufficient time. The prime objective of the official statistician may be more concerned with publishing to deadlines rather than with questioning the relevance of the published statistics to the policy questions of today and of tomorrow. Analysis of the behaviour of bureaucracies indicate a preference for the status quo. Changes to established procedures commonly involve resource costs. Frequently changes will be opposed by groups or individuals who see their interests threatened. Countering conceptual obsolescence will have to overcome this type of institutional inertia and devise a new pattern of interest which is conducive to change. Often substantial changes are accepted only when the very existence of the bureaucracy is threatened. In the light of the changing agricultural policy requirements, which display an increasing "people orientation", it is becoming apparent that the utility of official data sources will be much reduced unless they respond to the evolving information requirements.

2.8   In conclusion

The first task of this chapter was to establish the validity of the assertion that support to the living standards of the agricultural population is a central issue in agricultural policy, and the most important brake on the movement towards a CAP which would reduce and eventually eliminate the unwanted production of surpluses. Though living standards are mentioned as basic concerns in the legislation underlying policy in the EU, and appear as important ingredients in the national policies of many countries including the UK, there is a conspicuous lack of official statements of detailed objectives relating to the incomes of farmers. This is despite a growth in the relative importance of incomes within the policy mix, a change brought about by the success of agriculture in achieving, or over-achieving, goals of food security, stable supplies, productivity improvements and so on. Later an explanation of this paradox will be offered. Here it is enough to note its existence.

Having established the importance of living standards to policy, it is necessary to follow through the steps in the data system of conceptualisation and operationalisation. We have to discuss some fundamental issues, such as what is meant by living standards and how they might be measured in a way that would be relevant to practical policy. The nature of the people who form the target group of agricultural policy has also to be considered in some detail, as this will be important to the process of measurement. These fundamental matters are the subject of the next chapter.

3 Conceptual Issues

A central concern of agricultural policy in the EU, the UK and virtually all industrialised countries, is the living standard of farmers and their families. Yet often policy has become dislocated because of the failure of policy-makers to specify more precisely the aspect of the welfare of farmers they are mindful to improve. Often this has resulted in frustrated aims and resources wastefully employed.

The aims of this chapter are, first, to explore what is meant by "standard of living" in the context of agricultural policy. Consideration is given to the problem of measurement and to ways of establishing the minimum standard that a modern society can tolerate for its members. This involves the special problems of establishing poverty lines for households that operate farms, with their uncertain and irregular flow of income and ability to generate part of their food and accommodation requirements from their business resources. Many of these living standard issues involve making comparisons, between farmers on large and small farms, dairy or cropping and in different regions. Particular attention is given to the problems encountered when attempting to compare the standards experienced by farmers and by other members of society.

Second, examination is made of the simplifications which must be accepted when the debate is made in terms of income rather than consumption. It will soon become apparent that "income" is a generic term for a range of concepts, each appropriate for a particular set of circumstances. Much of the confusion which surrounds income policy can be laid at the door of those who use the wrong income concept to analyse a situation, sometimes through ignorance and sometimes with the intent to misinform. The role of capital gains and losses as part of income is discussed.

Third, broadening the assessment of welfare to achieve a more comprehensive assessment of the economic position of farmers and their families means taking on board the value of the assets they own, something of special importance to an industry where low incomes are often found combined with great wealth. The concept of economic status, incorporating both current income and net worth in a single entity, is explored in the context of agricultural policy.

Fourth, consideration is given to the concept of the agricultural community, the target group at which income support is aimed under the CAP. This involves examining alternative criteria that may be used to distinguish agricultural households from those belonging to other socio-professional groups in the policy context. This inevitably involves the recognition that many families who operate farms have income from other sources that not only adds to their total income and affects the way that they manage their business but also has implications for whether or not they can be classed as agricultural households. As part of this attempt to define the target group, some thought is given to the concept of the family farm, as the support of this too is a fundamental tenet of agricultural policy in the EU.

All these points are made in principal as a preparation for the review of the practical measurements of income at the macro-level and micro-levels and their empirical findings which follow in Chapters 4 and 5. Clearing the theoretical decks at this stage will also help to show the extent to which the official routine measurement of the well-being of the agricultural population in the EU falls short of what is necessary to fulfil the objectives of agricultural policy described in Chapter 2.

3.1 Standard of living

Quite what the fathers of agricultural policy had in mind when they laid the framework in statements of intent such as the Treaty of Rome is open to varied interpretation, but the use of the term "standard of living" implies a broad concern with the quality of life of the agricultural population. The way that this quality is reflected in the lives of individuals has many labels - their happiness, utility, satisfaction - but no effective measuring rods.

One approach has been to develop a range of social indicators for various aspects of the quality of life (OECD, 1982: Fox, 1986), and the OECD has identified thirty-three specific indicators grouped under eight major headings: health, education and learning, employment and quality of working life, time and leisure, command over goods and services, physical environment, social environment, and personal safety (see Figure 3.1). Though not arranged in order of priority, clearly the indicators relate to the well-known work on the hierarchy of human needs undertaken by Maslow (1957) and Herzberg (1957).

Social concern	Indicator
Health	
Length of life	Life expectancy
	Perinatal mortality rate
Healthiness of life	Short-term disability
	Long-term disability
Education and learning	
Use of educational facilities	Regular education experience
	Adult education
Learning	Literacy rate
Employment and quality of working life	
Availability of employment	Unemployment rate
	Involuntary part-time work
	Discouraged workers
Quality of working life	Average working hours
	Travel time to work
	Paid annual leave
	Atypical work schedule
	Distribution of earnings
	Fatal occupational injuries
	Work environment nuisances
Time and leisure	
Use of time	Free time
	Free time activities
Command over goods and services	
Income	Distribution of income
	Low income
	Material deprivation
Wealth	Distribution of wealth
Physical environment	
Housing conditions	Indoor dwelling space
	Access to outdoor space
	Basic amenities
Accessibility to services	Proximity of selected services
Environmental nuisances	Exposure to air pollutants
	Exposure to noise
Social environment	
Social attachment	Suicide rate
Personal safety	
Exposure to risk	Fatal injuries / Serious injuries
Perceived threat	Fear for personal safety

Figure 3.1   The OECD list of social indicators (from OECD, 1982)

The quality of life will be related to each of these, though the quantification of many individual indicators (such as fear for personal safety) may be difficult and their aggregation into a single meaningful entity is open to dispute, particularly at the level of society (Scheuch, 1994). Many of the current debates on the state of the nation - such as the controversy over farming technology and the environment, or the condition of the unemployed in city centres, or the public funding of the arts - can be recognised as involving contrary movements in two or more indicators. While general agreement might be reached on whether a change in one indicator was beneficial or harmful, such judgements are far less easy when trade-offs are involved.

The standard of living of the agricultural population no less impinges on a wide range of these social indicators. Farmers are reputed to enjoy a healthy life, high job satisfaction, flexibility of working time, preferential housing conditions, and substantial wealth. On the other hand, they are exposed to considerable risk of personal accident, are usually in poor proximity to public services and education, and find the taking of extended holidays difficult.

All the elements contained in the list of social indicators contribute to the welfare of people in that they relate to basic needs for security, sustenance, self-fulfilment and so on. However, the notion of using such a broad range of components to indicate the level of satisfaction, utility, benefit or whatever name is attached to the satisfying of a need, is beyond the realms of practicality as well as posing severe theoretical problems. The field has to be narrowed down.

Here we are concerned with looking at agricultural policy from an economic standpoint, and to do so involves setting aside those aspects of reality that are beyond the techniques of this discipline to conceptualise or quantify. The first simplification is to abandon the attempt to measure the end product of the process of need satisfaction - the utility or happiness created - in favour of the circumstances which give rise to that satisfaction. This approach pervades economics. Individuals will react with their circumstances to derive their utility, but this is a function of each person's psychology. We are incapable of measuring this utility, so resort to measuring the circumstances which give rise to it. Unfortunately the terms "welfare" or "well-being" are sometimes used as to be synonymous with "utility" and sometimes to describe the circumstances giving rise to it.

The second simplification is to draw a division between the economic and non-economic circumstances of welfare. Little (1957) has neatly described economic welfare, and its relationship to satisfaction, as follows:

> We are .... interested in *economic* welfare. There is no part of well-being called 'economic well-being'. The word 'economic' qualifies not well-being, but the causes or changes in it. If I am interested only in someone's economic welfare, then I interest myself in the economic things that may affect his well-being... ..the economic causes of changes in the happiness of an individual are taken to be those things and services which the individual consumes or enjoys, and which could be exchanged for money, together with the amount and kind of work which the individual does...

However, this description of "economic things" is not entirely satisfactory since, while some items are habitually exchanged for money and other not, others like housework are sometimes traded and sometimes non-traded, dependent on circumstances. In addition, many of the goods and services which are exchangeable for money can be substituted by items which are not exchangeable. Hence an extension of Little's definition is required to include within the economic causes of happiness those "things and services the distribution of which could influence or be influenced by the distribution of money or of those things and services that could be exchanged for money" (Dinwiddy, 1980). This gives an almost open-ended definition, since few contributors to (or detractors from) happiness are entirely beyond the influence of money. Even if a precise delineation of economic causes of welfare could be agreed upon, there would remain the problem of measuring fully those items lying within the boundary and of excluding any indirect influence of those outside.

It follows that economic welfare is not something that is capable of rigorous definition, and any attempt to produce a full definition is unlikely to result in something that is measurable. Nevertheless, the concept is useful in that some items that influence happiness fall closer to Little's (modified) definition than others. Value judgements can be used to select those items that are both relevant to the policy question in hand and are capable of measurement. Thus in the context of the standards of living of farmers, the influence of life expectancy might be excluded on the grounds that this is a non-economic influence on happiness, while the closeness of home and work might be included as exchangeable for money but practically difficult to measure as a determinant of welfare.

A third simplifying assumption, following on from the two above, is that the consumption of a good represents the same amount of welfare to an individual regardless of the personal psychological factors which may result in differences in the pleasure or utility that different individuals derive from it (Grootaert, 1983). Persons with the same consumption patterns are therefore assumed to be at the same level of welfare. This allows meaning to be ascribed to groups of individuals arranged by consumption level. More consumption means higher levels of welfare, with the implication that greater levels of consumption of goods and services are associated with being "better off" and therefore preferable.

3.2 Consumption and living standards

The economic welfare of farmers and their families, as indicated by their standard of living, is determined by their level of consumption of goods and services. Most industrialised countries, and all EU Members States, have household budget surveys from which this sort of information can be gleaned. There is a substantial number of UK studies which examine the theoretical and practical aspects of this approach and which trace the changing British standard of living viewed in this way (for example see Abrams, 1973; Hall, 1976; Toland, 1980; and Halsey, 1987). However, few farmer households are to be found in the basic data sources so little can be said about them as a socio-professional group, although such surveys are more revealing in those countries with larger farming sectors and where therefore they appear in greater numbers in the samples (see Chapter 5). Even if figures for agricultural households were available, statistics on the physical consumption of a heterogeneous collection of goods and services is of limited interest is answering the important questions of agricultural policy; the proportion of farm households with washing-machines is only a partial indicator. Though an impression of the standard of living of the agricultural population could be gained by reviewing a number of these physical series, it is far more desirable from a practical standpoint to have a single overall figure, such as household total consumption expenditure. Eurostat has published data on household expenditure, taken from national household budget surveys, but in the breakdown by socio-professional groups the households headed by self-employed farmers are combined with those of hired workers (see, for example, Eurostat, 1990a; Hagenaars *et.al.,* 1994).

The use of money as a common denominator also needs to take into account that the costs of goods and services are not uniform, so that a given level of consumption expenditure could represent widely differing physical standards of living. This is a particular problem when comparing urban and rural households. It is always necessary to bear in mind too that household spending is only a proxy for consumption, and there are situations where its acceptability breaks down. Not all consumption involves a money outlay; for example, farmers often consume some of the food produced by their farm, at costs lower than paid by non-farmers. Correction will be needed if comparisons are to be made over time, between farmers or (especially) between farmers and non-farmers (Kulshreshtha, 1966, 1967). The value of goods and services consumed over a given period can differ from the actual spending on these items, and it is the latter which is usually measured in household surveys. The gap may arise if, for example, households decide to build up their stocks of food in anticipation of future supply problems - expenditure will exceed consumption. The problem is at its most acute in the case of spending on consumer durables (cars, televisions etc.) where occasional large purchases are involved. The question becomes one of how to apportion the value of the item over their years of service. This could be done if information were available on the expected lives, the purchase price and date of acquisition, but such information (apart from price) is rarely collected in surveys. But if a sufficiently large number of households is taken, the occasional large purchase at the individual level should be smoothed out in the group average.

There is also the problem that households differ in size, and a given level of consumption spending for a large family may represent a much lower living standard per person than for a smaller family. Some equivalence scale must be used to put them on a common base. There are various approaches which can be used to calculate equivalence (reviewed in Van Slooten and Coverdale, 1977; Buhmann *et al.*, 1987; Hagenaars *et al.,* 1994). Observation can be made of the patterns of expenditure of families of differing composition to give a rough idea of the "needs" of each type of family, including the economies of scale in consumption - two can live proportionally cheaper than one. Children could be treated as a cost, and the income of the adults could be compared "net of children" with adults who do not have them. Alternatively, children could be given a weight, say equivalent to one third of an adult on the assumption that their needs were only one third, so that the income of the parents were reduced by the amount attributed to their offsprings. However, it appears that whatever equivalence scales are adopted, arbitrary judgements are inevitable.

The end product is a set of coefficients for the different types of persons found in households (single persons, couples, additional adults, children of various age bands). Summing the coefficients for the entire household gives a total which can be used as a divisor of household expenditure (or income) to give a standardised figure covering households of different compositions. For example, the Irish Household Budget Survey has used a scale in which a couple was treated as unity, a single adult as 0.61, additional adults in a two-adult household as 0.39, the first two children as 0.17 and additional children as 0.14 each. In the UK parallel coefficients (as used in the calculation of Supplementary Benefit Entitlement) were 0.61 for a single adult householder, 1 for a couple, 0.49 for additional adults, 0.18 for children under 4 years rising to 0.38 for 16-18 year olds. The choice of scales and equivalence figures will reflect differences in social conditions, and these are likely to change over time. Though otherwise similar to the British coefficients, in the USA the figure used for late teenagers was substantially higher, which suggests that American families at the time may have been required to support their near-adults more than here.

Consumption levels alone are not adequate guides to living standards; savings too must be taken into account. Savings can be either positive or negative. Low levels of consumption may result from an inadequate disposable income, in which case the low standard of living is the product of necessity. Dis-saving, such as the running down of wealth or the accumulation of debts, can also be a method of sustaining a consumption level beyond the current disposable income, something that might be expected to be a characteristic of agriculture households with their inherent income instability from farming. Even farmers with normally adequate incomes might experience occasional years of enforced dis-saving.

Alternatively, low consumption may reflect a deliberate choice to allocate only a small share of an otherwise adequate disposable income to consumption, and reflect the value judgement of the individual of family, in which case savings will be positive. This leads to one definition of income: "personal economic income" or "personal disposable income" can be regarded as the sum of consumption spending and saving. It follows that how the levels of consumption spending is viewed in a welfare context has to take into account the opportunity to make the choice to consume or not to consume.

In practice, concern about living standards concentrates on those members of society with low levels of consumption because of necessity. Their incomes are low, so their consumption expenditures are also low. Consequently, the choice of whether to investigate low standards of living through information on consumption or through incomes will depend on the data sources that are available. As will become evident, the low income route is the one adopted in most research and statistics on poverty in agriculture.

3.3 The assessment of poverty

Criteria are needed if some members of society, deemed to be worthy of assistance because of their poverty, are to be distinguished from the others. There are a variety of grounds on which society might wish to act because it feels that deprivation exists - social, cultural or educational disadvantage perhaps. What is meant by the term "deprivation" depends on the context (Bradley, Lowe, Wright, 1986) but it is nevertheless a potent concept in justifying social policy. Within the agricultural sector it will commonly be found that various forms of deprivation go together - an inadequate income will tend to be associated with isolation on a small farm, where the family is locked into a restricted set of social contacts and has only a narrow range of access to the facilities provided for society in general. Nevertheless these additional forms of deprivation are separate from (but may be linked with) what we can describe as economic deprivation - poverty or, put another way, situations where people have an insufficient command over the resources needed for living and are excluded from the socio-economic system.

In order to turn this inexact notion of insufficiency into a measure which can be used to guide practical policy some standards have to be set for what is deemed sufficient. One way of doing this is to establish a *poverty line* against which the circumstances of individuals, households or families can be compared. It would be possible to establish a poverty level in terms of a combination of characteristics - for example income plus leisure - so that two people of identical income but one having more leisure than the other might be classified differently. Rather than referring to a poverty line such a situation should use the term boundary. However, it is more usual to simplify the relevant variables to one - that of income.

Poverty lines are by their nature impossible to set without involving value judgements, explicitly or hidden in the assumptions behind what may appear to be objective approaches (Bradley, 1986). A variety of approaches to defining a poverty line have been used or proposed. Two polar positions can be taken - that the poverty line can be set in absolute terms, in which case it would be possible to totally eliminate poverty if every one could be lifted above the poverty line, or that poverty is a relative phenomenon, in which case poverty will never be removed (Hagenaars and van Praag, 1985; Hagenaars *et al.*, 1994). At its most extreme, an absolutist view of poverty would be a situation of deprivation of certain basic goods and services necessary for maintaining physical subsistence. This makes no reference to the well-being of the rest of society. A poverty line under such an approach would correspond to the income required to allow the acquisition of these basic means. This was basically the approach of the seminal work on poverty by Rowntree (1901) and Booth (1902). Rowntree greatly influenced the Beveridge Report and the subsequent levels of income support provided in the UK by the National Assistance Board (later replaced by the Supplementary Benefits Commission) were determined largely in the light of this approach.

A less rigid attitude might set a line somewhat above this subsistence-consumption level to reflect the view of society of what is a minimum acceptable income for its members. Both are absolute figures, though in the latter case the level takes into account more than physical necessities. As Atkinson (1975) points out "It is misleading to suggest that poverty may be seen in terms of an absolute standard which may be applied to all countries and at all times, independent of the social structure and level of development. A poverty line is necessarily defined in relation to social conventions and the contemporary living standards of a particular society". Though a subsistence poverty line may have the appearance of objectivity, the *choice* to define poverty in this way is as subjective as any other based on less clear physical requirements.

The other extreme in poverty line definitions is represented by those which set the line at some percentage of the society's average personal income or at some point in the distribution of incomes- at some percentage of the median income or the lowest decile. Expressed in such a way, poverty will never be eliminated. But this too imposes the judgement of the observer on the measure of poverty. In an attempt to strive for greater objectivity, exercises have been conducted to extract from a representative cross-section of people, using surveys, the assessment of society of where the poverty line lies (Hagenaars and van Praag, 1985). Different representatives perceive poverty according to their circumstances, though suitable weighting can be employed to achieve poverty levels which reflect the mix of views in society. But to adopt a poverty line derived in this way presupposes that society in general is the best assessor of poverty; this is not self-evident.

All poverty lines are arbitrary. The choice of method of their determination depends essentially on the problem in hand and the dominant social values. The absolutist approach is now less in favour because of rising general levels of consumption and changed public perceptions of poverty. Bare physical subsistence criteria have been replaced by ones relating to the ability to participate acceptably in the social system (Van Slooten and Coverdale, 1977). Another set of value judgements is involved when equivalence scales are used to apply poverty lines to families of different sizes and compositions. If the marginal needs of additional household members are given a low rating, then poverty among elderly single-person households is emphasised more strongly and family poverty is emphasised less (Steiner and Wolf, 1996). On the other hand, a high rating will make poverty appear more "rural" and, in the European context, more "southern". Ultimately the setting of a poverty line is not an economic decision but a political one (Madden, 1974).

For practical purposes many countries utilise a poverty line in their welfare policies, though it may not be labelled bluntly as such. Its practical implementation may involve measuring the cost of some single parameter, such as the necessary family expenditure on food, and extrapolating from this to the total income requirement to cover all purposes at the poverty level. The US has a poverty line developed from the USDA's Low Cost Food Plan, the poverty line income being three times this on the grounds that average food expenditure comprised about one third of the typical family's budget (the Orshansky index). This was clearly inappropriate for farm families which produced more of their own food than the typical US family, so the poverty line for farm families was set initially at 60 per cent of the standard line (Bryant, Bawden and Saupe, 1981). Criticism that, while food costs of farmers were lower, this did not necessarily apply to the other components in family budgets, resulted in the gradual narrowing of the farm/non-farm poverty lines to 85 per cent. In Australia the 1973 Henderson Poverty Enquiry (Vincent, 1976) used a farmer poverty line 20 per cent below that for all families. In Canada the similar "low income cut-off" is defined differently for rural and non-rural households (OECD, 1995).

The danger of using a too-narrow income base when assessing the extent of poverty, especially rural poverty, is illustrated by the impact on the numbers of US rural families classed as poor by widening the concept of income from annual money income (used in US official statistics) to include unrealised capital gains and the value of non-market services provided by owner-occupied housing, home-grown food and do-it-yourself activities, all of which are probably more important for farm households than for non-farm ones and especially for poor ones (Gardner, 1975). The "full income" approach attempted to estimate the purchasing power available for consumption and saving in a normal year. In the absence of reliable data by which piecemeal corrections could be made to income data, Gardner used an intricate method based on rates of return on the factors (land, capital and human) used on farms. Because of this, substantial errors were probably involved, but the methodology gives a first approximation of the importance of taking a wider income view. In 1969, on conventional income measurement 20 per cent of rural farm families were below the poverty line; taking a full-income approach reduced this to the range 5 to 14 per cent, dependent on assumptions. A reduction of some 7 to 8 per cent was attributable to a more equal distribution of farm incomes and about 5 per cent to a higher average income.

Poverty lines are easier to use where incomes are stable. The random variation in agricultural incomes from year to year, principally weather-related, means that in some years a farm family could find itself below the line and in others above it. Classification on a single year's income, as is common in income distribution statistics, would be foolish. Evidence from Australia, Denmark and Germany (see Chapter 5) suggests that a distinction should be drawn between the core of farm households that are in a persistent low income situation and those who suffer temporary low incomes. While the former are likely to constitute a welfare problem requiring intervention with public funds, the latter are not. How far low incomes have to fall and for how long before government action is justified is, of course, a matter of political judgement.

Despite methodological difficulties, one might have supposed that the importance of low incomes to agricultural policy would have engendered a substantial body of research and estimation by official statisticians to assess the number of farm families who fall below poverty lines. In the

US, though figures for farmers who are in poverty are published, these do not seem to have been of major importance in shaping agricultural policy. The Australian use of a poverty line for farm families, referred to above, was part of a special investigation that has not been repeated. In the UK no such estimates take place. In most of the EU Member States the information by which such an exercise could be carried out is either not co-ordinated or simply not collected. In the absence of basic data the matter of how best to calculate the poverty line shrinks to irrelevance. One of the exceptions is Ireland where there are special welfare payments for landholders whose incomes fall below specified thresholds (the so-called farmers' dole), and some 20 to 25 per cent of holders seemed to qualify in the 1980s. This represents an imperfect island of knowledge in a sea of ignorance of the extent of poverty among the agricultural population.

3.4 Agricultural incomes and the welfare of farmers

We move now to consider the use of proxies for standards of living in an agricultural context. In practice, it is generally easier to approach standards of living of farmers through the measurement of their incomes. Consumption surveys covering farmers are far less frequent than income surveys and usually only cover farm households, typically in small numbers, as part of a national exercise embracing all household types. As with the consumption approach, incomes should be corrected for differences in living costs, non-traded items, family composition and so on before being used in a welfare context. A few examples exist (in Denmark, Norway and the Netherlands) in which income measurement systems go a step further and allocate it between that part spent on consumption and that part saved, but these are rare.

Income can be defined in a variety of ways, and in agricultural economics the same word is used to carry a variety of conceptually different meanings. These uses fall into two groups - the reward to the activity of farming, and the personal incomes of farmers. In the first group, the term income is used in a *business accounting sense* (Hamilton, 1986) to mean the residual left out of revenue from farm sales after the costs of the business have been paid; these costs comprise purchases from other firms, wages and interest paid, rents paid, depreciation charges and so on. The income residual (net profit) is the reward to the factors of production owned by the farmer and his family and for which no charge has been made (because no one required payment). Many different formulations can be used to estimate this residual, to be considered later. From a functional standpoint, the income remaining to the farmer from his farming business will consist of all four recognised types of factor rewards - interest on the farmer's owned capital, rent on his land (assuming that he owns at least some), wages for his labour and profit for his entrepreneurial input. Essentially the same view is taken in the national accounts when estimating the income from agricultural activity, when the industry is treated as if it were one huge national farm (see Chapter 4). Such an aggregate income concept fits in with the construction of the national accounting system for the estimation of the productive activity of the entire economy. However, all the concepts in this group ignore any income that farmers and their families receive from outside the business to which the accounts relate. In practice these other income sources are significant to the households involved.

The second form of income, *personal income*, is much more appropriate to studies of the economic welfare of the agricultural population. At the risk of stating the obvious, the concern of agricultural policy with living standards relates primarily to the people involved in the industry and their well-being. To be useful to policy-makers, income information will be needed which captures the important link between income and potential consumption. Again, a range of alternative income concepts and ways of measuring them can be found. Frequently policy decisions involve comparisons; between farmers over time and space and between farmers and non-farmers. Under these circumstances two desirable characteristics suggest themselves for the concepts of income adopted; comparability and measurability (Dinwiddy, 1980). *Comparability* is an essential attribute of any definition of income used in a welfare context because there must be confidence that the placing of one income against another has some meaning. This will necessitate a broad definition of income so that important contributions to income are not omitted. To take an example, there would be little confidence in a comparison of two men with identical money incomes if one also received a free house and a firm's car and the other had neither. However, *measurability* is also important, since a heterogeneous collection of information is not of much use unless it can be reduced to a common, money, base. There is an inevitable conflict between the two, since broadening the income concept in the interests of better comparability will inevitably try to bring into the definition items that are inherently difficult to measure, whether in money terms or any other.

There are several general aspects of personal income that must be considered before a precise formulation of an income measure can be presented, and these are reviewed next.

3.5 Aspects of personal income

3.5.1 *General definition of personal income*

A widely accepted definition of personal income is that given by Simons:

> Personal income may be defined as the sum of (1) the market value of rights exercised in consumption and (2) the change in the store of property rights between the beginning and end of the period (Simons, 1938).

Interestingly, the notion underlying this definition is one of consumption. It is important to note that these consumption rights are those which *could* be exercised rather than those which are *actually* used, otherwise a high earner who spent little might be grouped with a low earner who spent everything. Income is not numerically identical to consumption unless changes in the stored rights, in the form of savings, are also taken into account, a point made earlier. We would expect the low-spending high-earner to accumulate savings over the period.

In the absence of any change in the value of the capital owned by the person, positive or negative, personal income obviously corresponds numerically with the value of consumption. This is identical to the notion of income put forward by John Hicks (1946), who defined an individual's income as the maximum value he could consume during a period and still be as well off at the end of the period as he was at the beginning. Note the use of the words "could consume". It follows that increases in "the store of property rights" arising from capital gains form positive contributions to personal income, and losses are negative items, since a person who was enjoying capital gains could spend them on consumption without running down his property rights (maintaining capital "intact"). Capital aspects are considered in detail later. However, it should be pointed out that there is some debate on what is meant by keeping capital intact.

This comprehensive view of income received support in the UK in the Minority Report of the Royal Commission on the Taxation of Profits and

Income (1955) which concluded that "No concept of income can be really equitable which stops short of the comprehensive definition which embraces all receipts which increase an individual's command over the use of scarce resources - in other words his 'net accretion of economic power between two points in time'", a phrase that can be traced back to Haig in 1921. Income therefore includes "the whole of the change in the value of a man's store of property rights ... irrespective of whether the change has been brought about by the current addition to property (or) by accretions to the value of property".

If consumption involves the exercising of rights flowing from individuals, thereby acquiring the goods and services they desire, there must be a balancing set of rights flowing towards individuals and households in the form of income. This is illustrated in Fig. 3.2 (from Cecora, 1986) where the process of income flow into households and its dissipation on goods and services (and saving) is referred to as "subsistence technology".

Notwithstanding the consumption-plus-saving definition of personal income, it is usual to attempt the measurement of income at the stage at which the resources which enable these two activities to take place flow to the person, rather than when they leave. Household budget surveys are concerned primarily with measurement of consumption and saving, but other sources - farm accounts surveys, taxation and social security records - are set up in ways which assess the inward resource flow.

As long as all items on either side are accounted for, it should make no difference to the final estimate. However, where complete information is available there is some suggestions that in practice income measurement tends to understate the level of consumption for typically 80 to 90 per cent of the population (Grootaert, 1983). And in Germany in an agricultural context some of the physical indicators (housing conditions) seem to indicate for farmers higher levels of real consumption than incomes alone might suggest (Cecora, 1986).

3.5.2 The household unit

In an income approach to welfare assessment a full account of all sources of consumption rights must be made, or at least attempted. This implies using the household as the basic unit of income measurement. The logic behind preferring the household rather than the individual as the unit over which measurement is made when assessing personal income is that

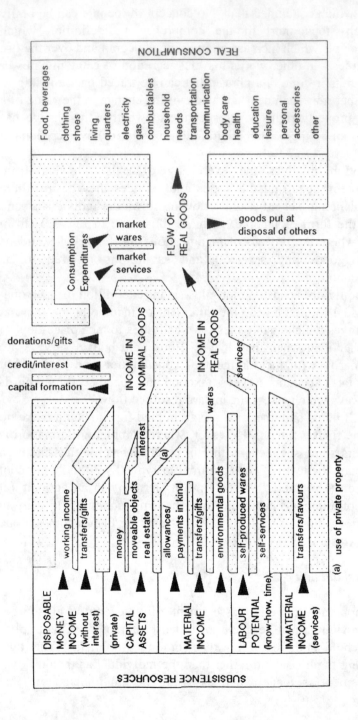

Note: this Figure has been redrawn and modified from Cecora (1986)

Figure 3.2 The "subsistence" of private households

members of households, and especially married couples and their dependent children, usually pool their incomes and spend on behalf of the members jointly.

As will be seen later, the household approach is adopted within the EU by Eurostat for its measurement of the total income of agricultural households (Hill, 1992) and in the USA by the US Department of Agriculture's Farm Costs and Returns Survey (Ahearn *et al.*, 1993) – now relabelled the Agricultural Resource Management Study (ARMS). This is not to deny that, for example, farmer's wives may have some private source of income which they regard as their own, or that the beer money which a farmer spends is the result of a collective decision and is approved of as a necessary line of expenditure. Although there have been some studies of shared decision making within farm households, touching particularly on the roles of spouses and sons (reviewed in Gasson *et al.*,1988) these do not appear to cover spending on consumer items.

Nevertheless, it clearly makes more sense to take the household as the unit for income measurement. Otherwise in a farm family with the business operated as a sole proprietorship all the farming income would be shown against the farmer and his wife and children would be indicated as having zero income, a situation which obviously inaccurately expresses their real position as potential consumers. The problem of aggregating households of different composition can be handled by the use of equivalence scales, as in consumption studies.

Official definitions of households exist for use in national household budget surveys. For the UK it is defined thus:

> A household comprises one person living alone or a group of people living at the same address, sharing their meals and the household, and having sole use of at least one room. All persons in a household must receive from the same person at least one meal a day and spend at least four nights a week (one, if they are married) in the household. The household includes staff, paying guests and tenants, and also anyone living in the household during the period in which expenditure is recorded. Persons who normally live in the household, but who are absent for a period of more than one month, are excluded (Eurostat, 1985).

The condition of living at the same address and sharing catering arrangements is common among the definition of adopted by EU Member States for their household budget surveys (all have one), but there are differences in the way that living-in domestic staff and temporary residents, such as students, are treated. These are peripheral to the main thrust of the definition of the household for the purpose of income studies.

Of far greater import is the role played by adult family members who are in addition to the farmer and spouse and who live in the farm house - usually grown-up children, parents, brothers and sisters. While there would be little dispute over treating a husband and wife with dependent children as a single household unit for the purpose of income assessment, there are problems if other adults also live in the same dwelling. Things are made complex because of the fact that many farms are run by family members working together and many different forms of financial arrangements may exist between them. To take an example, where grown-up children receive a wage from working, though they may make some payment to the farm household for their keep, they probably regard their independently-earned income to be under their own control as far as spending is concerned. The case for *not* including these additional adults in the household unit is particularly strong where they have full-time jobs off the farm and are treated within national tax systems as separate units. To include them in the larger household unit of measurement, when they are clearly financially independent, introduces a degree of artificiality that can undermine the validity of the income statistics. However, even if such grown-up children do not contribute labour to the farm on a regular basis, it seems highly unlikely that they would not help out at seasonal labour peaks; to some extent they still form part of the agricultural labour force.

Much the same problem is faced when retired parents live with their farmer-sons or when other groups of relatives live in the same house. The notion of personal income implies the freedom to dispose at will, and it is far from certain that, for example, the old-age pension of a retired relative living in can be regarded as at the general disposal of the household.

Ideally, a distinction should be drawn between the household as a social unit for domestic budgeting (the housekeeping unit, or *single budget household*, comprising only those people who pool income and expenditure) and the household unit in the domiciliary sense (the *accommodation* or *dwelling household*, consisting of the people living under the same roof). In the absence of a firm information on intra-household financial integration and the diverse forms it takes, a case exists for calculating household incomes using both concepts. Some balance could then be struck between the overstating of income at the disposal of the household incurred by including the income of additional adults and the understatement which would doubtless result from their being excluded. What is appropriate treatment for one country may not apply elsewhere because of differences in degrees of financial integration that will reflect, *inter alia*, social norms and systems of direct taxation. However, the boundaries of the *single budget household* are not simple to define. In reality, family budget surveys differ in their approaches but usually conform to dwelling household (Verma and Gabilondo, 1993). In contrast, taxation statistics when using the *fiscal household* approximate to the *single budget household* (though the move to independent taxation of individuals is eroding this). Unfortunately, within the EU few countries have sufficient data for both approaches to be explored and compared.

3.5.3 Accounting for and valuing non-money income

Income can come two main forms, money and goods, or in the terminology of Figure 3.2, nominal goods and real goods. While accounting system are usually good at capturing money flows, they are less suitable for handling income in the form of goods and services, especially where no exchange between individuals takes place. In attempting to express income as a magnitude of money, it will be necessary to attach values to these goods and services, the relevant question being "How much would the farm family have to pay to consume these items if they did not come in a physical income form?". The problem is one of, firstly, identifying the non-monetary income and, secondly, choosing an appropriate method of valuation. Some examples of income in kind are straightforward. If a farmer's wife is given eggs in exchange for working on a neighbour's holding for a few hours each week, then these eggs clearly form part of her household's income. The method of valuing them may be open to argument, but there would be little doubt that the eggs should be included. The use of petrol paid for by the farm business but used for private outings would also qualify. These are both items that can be substituted by articles bought in the marketplace - shop eggs and petrol bought at the pumps. Goods and services consumed by individuals that are provided in kind by the state and financed from taxation, such as health care and education, also form part of personal income. While for some items (dental treatment, perhaps) the price of similar services from private dentists is an acceptable indicator of the value of those provided by the state healthcare system, for others there may be no parallel market from which values can be taken, or the markets may be so marginal that the prices in them are not satisfactory representatives of the whole (is the price of private education a valid indicator of the value of free state education?). In such cases the average cost of providing these items may have to be substituted as values.

Though there are practical problems of identification and valuation, these forms of income in kind should not be ignored, especially where comparisons of household income are made between countries that have different levels of state activity in the health and education sectors or over time when changes in the level of state provision take place.

But one soon enters deeper waters. What about the value of job satisfaction? If farmers have a fulfilling life, as is often asserted, should something be added to their income in order to reflect this non-monetary benefit? If farmers could be shown to be willing to except an income £x lower than they might earn in other jobs, it might even be possible to put a value on this job-satisfaction. Here we have to remind ourselves that we are concerned primarily with *economic welfare*, that is those economic causes in the form of goods and services. Other causes of satisfaction - so-called "psychic income" - are beyond our consideration. Job satisfaction is not a good or service in the same way that eggs or petrol are and cannot be bought or sold; it cannot be separated from the nature of the job. Nevertheless these forms of psychic income should not be ignored. The importance attached to the intrinsic satisfaction gained from agricultural activities and, particularly among the smaller farmers to the independence afforded has been amply demonstrated (Gasson, 1973). The lack of success of the various UK government and EU funded schemes aimed at encouraging farmers to retire can be explained in part by their failure to recognise the importance of such non-pecuniary rewards from farming. However, the non-tradable nature of these items makes for extreme difficulties in valuation. As an example, paraphrased from Runciman (1974), take a farmer's going to market; is he giving himself a day off under the bogus guise of a commercial purpose, or is he spending all day toiling in the lounge bar of the market tavern trying to sell produce in which he has no interest to people he dislikes in a place from which he is longing to get away? It is because we can only measure the circumstances giving rise to utility and not the utility itself that such items have to be put on one side.

Some forms of income in kind are of particular importance in an agricultural context and require specific mention. These include the fringe benefits associated with farming, some of which are confined to this activity and some widely experienced by self-employed businessmen. The description "fringe" is perhaps unfortunate since it gives the impression that these benefits are unimportant and might be ignored, yet it is precisely these "fringe" elements in the rewards enjoyed by farmers and landowners which those outside the industry frequently find the most attractive. Benefits such as spacious and desirable houses in environments divorced from unwanted encroachments by noisy people and traffic, the ability to pursue space-demanding activities like horse-riding, the availability of field-sports and the opportunity for direct involvement in the protection and conservation of wildlife seem to be precisely the attributes of farming which potential new entrants with adequate fortunes made in other businesses are keenest to secure and which are protected most vigorously when some external change, such as a motorway plan, threatens to take them away.

In an agricultural context two important examples of income in kind where some valuation by imputation is required are the farm household consumption of food materials produced on the home farm (often termed own-consumption) and the domestic accommodation provided by the farmhouse. Food consumed by farm families which they grow themselves, because they have the necessary facilities, involves costs borne by the business (fertilizer, tractor fuel, machinery hire-purchase charges and so on) which are debit items in calculating income from self-employment, so in assessing the total income to the farmer from his business the value of all the goods produced also have to be accounted for, even that part which is not sold but is consumed by the farm household. Another way of looking at home-consumption of farm production is that, in the case of any other household, the food would have to be bought for cash, so the real value of the farm household income is greater than it appears nominally by the extent of the own-consumption. Consequently farm families would be expected to spend less on purchased meat, milk or eggs and so on than other types of households. Choices have to be made on the method of valuation, the options being to use the retail prices, wholesale (or farm-gate) prices, or some estimate of the costs of production. When viewing farm households as consumers, the logical method is to use retail prices, as this represents the cost of the food which farmers are relieved from paying. On the other hand, as assessment of the farm's output, viewed as a business, should use farm-gate prices, as this corresponds with the revenue that is being forgone by the business if the farm household consumes the produce rather than selling it. A retail valuation was adopted by Bellerby (1956, see p.57) in his seminal work on the relative income position of the agriculture and non-agriculture sectors and this is the practice of the Irish Household Budget Survey. However the practice in the European System of Accounts (Eurostat, 1979) in its household sector account has been to use farm-gate prices, with the justification that on farms the foods consumed from own-production do not receive the benefits of packaging, processing and presentation, all of which are reflected in the retail price. Though this particular income adjustment is probably of little importance when comparing the incomes of one group of farmers with other farmers, there could be a substantial impact when ranking farmer incomes against those of other groups in society.

A similar situation exists with respect to other outputs of the farm, such as food for the ponies of the farmer's children or the wood fuel for domestic heating. It makes a great deal of difference whether these are valued at retail or farmgate prices, but in most accounting systems these items would escape totally any income measurement. The loose distinction between resources used for private and for business purposes - the use of the car and telephone and so on, something shared with most forms of self-employment - also raises questions of identification and valuation of non-cash income.

Of importance is the way that property income in kind is treated. Typically the buildings on a farm include a domestic house for the farm family, and sometimes more than one. One benefit which the farm household receives through living in the house is the accommodation it affords; if the house were let it could command a rent, and by occupying the house the family is in effect receiving the benefit in kind. Therefore an imputed rental value must be added to the income of the farm household. It makes no difference whether the farm is owner-occupied or rented; a tenanted farm provides a domestic house benefit as part of the service obtained in exchange for paying the whole-farm agricultural rent. Another way of putting it is to say that, if the farm family did not live in the farm house, it would have to pay a rent for equivalent accommodation, and by living where they do the farmer's household receive a benefit in kind. Similar reasoning would apply, of course, to housing of other socio-professional groups who have accommodation which goes with the job or business, including clergy and prime-ministers. Indeed, all owner-occupiers of domestic houses are receiving a flow of services in kind from their property, and a full assessment of their income should take the value of these services into account. When assessing the incomes of their agricultural households most EU Member States use an imputed value for the income arising from the domestic dwelling (see the IAHS statistics described in Chapter 5), but this is not the treatment in all national household budget surveys (Hagenaars *et al.*, 1994) nor in the

Household Sector of the UK's national accounts, where it is felt that "it would not normally feature in households' perception of their income"(CSO, 1985 p52).

3.5.4 Capital gain and income

A comprehensive definition of income, along the lines suggested by Simons and Hicks, includes not only income in the form of flows of money and real goods but also changes in the store of property rights. The size of this "store" can come either in the form of physical increases, such as the enlargement of a breeding herd by retaining young animals rather than selling them, or through an increase in real value, such as a rise in the market price of land in excess of any general fall in the value of money, so that the owner experiences capital gain.

There is little dispute that an increase in the physical volume of stocks held on farms constitute part of income and should be simply added to the trading surplus in order to estimate income. Finished cattle standing on the farm represent revenue which has not yet been turned into cash, and an increase in the number of them between the beginning and end of an accounting period form part of income (though not of cash-flow).

The real problems arise from capital gains in the form of changes in values. Nevertheless, these gains and losses cannot be ignored. For example, writing of the US, Hathaway (1957) noted that because of them "it is possible for a farm owner who has never enjoyed a high annual income to accumulate substantial assets over his lifetime, and it is also possible for a farmer who has consistently earned good annual income and invested it in his business to reach a point of retirement and have accumulated few or perhaps no assets".

Just as current income could take the form of a flow of goods and services or money, so value gains can come from both physical assets (such as farmland) and financial assets (such as bank loans). Real capital gains (and losses) are possible with livestock and crops; a rise in the market price of potatoes because of a market shortage caused by an interruption of imports is a gain, but this is usually treated as part of current income because of its easily-realised nature by sale. Some forms of capital gain on working capital have been significant, such as the gain on breeding livestock in the 1970s in the UK. However, among the assets used by farming, agricultural land is clearly the most significant source of potential capital gains and losses. As will be seen in Chapter 6, agricultural land in the UK has seen both a substantial rise and a subsequent fall in its price in the post-war period, and despite the latter, capital gain has given a net increase in wealth for many farming households. It is important to stress that it is real capital gain that is part of income, that is, an allowance has to be made for inflation so that the real gain is the potential purchasing power that the wealth represents. Capital losses should also be taken into account of course because these represent a shrinking in the potential spending power of the household; this shrinkage becomes particularly painful if the value of the asset falls to below the size of any loan that was taken out to finance its purchase (situations of so-called "negative equity").

Capital gains and losses can arise from non-tangible items, such as "goodwill" sold with a business. Of greater importance to the incomes of most farmers, however, are the changes in the real values of financial assets - positive money savings and borrowings - which occur when inflation erodes the real value of assets or loans which are designated in nominal (money) terms. Under inflation borrowers enjoy a real increase in their "net accretion of economic power" whereas lenders suffer diminutions. A substantial proportion of the capital gain experienced in North America in the 1970s came in the form of shrinking real value of borrowings. Again, this gain was also experienced in the UK by virtually all house owners with mortgages, so care has to be exercised in ensuring that equivalent treatment is given to farmers and non-farmers when assessing income. The adoption of a definition of personal real income implies that an allowance should be made in the case of all assets for the effect of inflation (Atkinson, 1975).

When capital gains are realised by sale of an asset there is a clear release of purchasing power to the person or household owning the asset. A farmer who sells land at a gain has received an income in excess of the current flow by the extent of the gain. It is not unreasonable to assume that people treat realised gains like any other income. Similarly, though less conspicuously, realised capital losses constitute reductions in purchasing power. Realisation can come in forms other than simple disposal, most notably as borrowing against the increased market value through banks and other credit institutions; realisation in this case does not involve giving up the occupation of the land for farming purposes. In Canada one form of realisation was the lower level of spending by farmers on pension schemes than was common in other occupational groups. Their higher level of consumption was based on the expectation that, with continually rising land prices, the accumulated capital gain would provide an adequate nest egg when the land was sold on retirement. There is a suggestion that farmers have a particularly high propensity to save from capital gains (Bhatia, 1972), a logical extension of the view that gains are a form of forced or involuntary saving (Plaxico and Kletbe, 1979).

When capital gains are not realised, by sale or indirectly, there are problems of measurement and aggregation with current income, but nevertheless it is clear that unrealised gains still constitute part of real personal income as defined by Simons. In a market economy at any time the owner of assets could, at his own option, turn his property value into current spending power. The sum received would be the present value of the discounted rewards to be generated by that asset in the future, including the risk-discounted prospect of capital gain or loss not reflected in the income stream. These rewards need not all be pecuniary ones, though they must be capable of being handled by the market mechanism. For example, people will be prepared to pay a premium for the privacy that a piece of land may bestow, but only if that right to privacy is capable of being protected within the legal framework of property rights. The fact that a farmer chooses not to realise a capital gain in his landholding does not detract from the fact that his potential spending power has risen. In terms of the Simons definition, income is the value of the rights which a person *might have exercised* in consumption without altering the value of his wealth.

Capital gains differ sufficiently from current income (operating gains) in their nature that objections can be made to simply adding the two together. They differ in degrees of *uncertainty*, and *liquidity* (Hill, 1982). An additional element of uncertainty arises because the gain may disappear before it can be realised; the value of capital assets is largely dependent on the expectations of future profitability. Expectations are volatile and can be influenced by a wide range of factors. In the case of agricultural land it is not only the future prosperity of farming that is influential, which will in turn reflect perceptions about the shape of future national and EU agricultural policy, but also the relative attractiveness of alternative forms of investment and ways in which these alternatives are likely to develop, interest rates and their movements, expectations of the desirability of land as a giver of privacy and environment control, and so on. By their very nature of being gains on capital assets, items which are usually distinguished by the fact that they contribute to production over more than one production cycle or more than one accounting year, capital gains will pose a liquidity problem. As was pointed out above, selling land is only one way of turning any gain into cash, but this will often involve a time-consuming and costly process. Quick sales might require giving a substantial discount, eroding the value of the gain. Realisation by sale could be rapid in the case of other capital items such as breeding livestock, stores and machinery, and this is one reason why in farm accounting gains on these items are usually treated as current income and simply added to trading surpluses. If gains are realised by borrowing against the enhanced values of assets, this requires the co-operation of credit institutions. Though any problems encountered by farmers unencumbered by debt and well backed by net worth might be minimal, nevertheless the necessity of having to work through institutions constitutes a liquidity barrier which may pose a real constraint to less well-situated farmers.

When measuring real capital gains over a period, factors that have to be considered include not only the change in nominal values (which may be determined on small and potentially unstable residual markets) but also the marginal rates of tax on income and gains, the rate of inflation and the opportunity cost of capital, expressed as a discount rate (Lee and Rask, 1976). Some of these present practical problems or, in the case of the last, conceptual difficulties (Plaxico and Kletbe, 1979 and 1981). There is also a tendency to undervalue gains by failing to take into account the improved equity position of farmers by whom the asset is being held (Bhatia, 1970, 1971, 1972; Dunford, 1980; Drynan and Hodge, 1981) .

Capital gains have a mixed treatment in actual accounting systems used in agriculture.   In the EU's system of farm account monitoring (FADN/RICA), while gains on breeding livestock are taken as forming part of income, the general practice is to ignore gains on land and financial assets. They do not fit into the concept of the rewards to the fixed factors over a period of a year from farming activity. These gains are also excluded when assessing the aggregate income of agriculture in national accounts because they do not form part of current productive activity. Practical reasons may also impinge on the decisions to treat holding gains and losses on land as falling outside the income accounts. Such is the importance of land in the asset structure of agriculture that if changes in capital values were incorporated into annual accounts, a moderate change in land prices could swamp the income arising from farming operations. Given that land prices are subject to short-term instability reflecting the intentions of a relatively small number of buyers and sellers in a marginal market, the "correct" level of prices is difficult to settle on. Using a moving average of, say, three years' prices is perhaps better, in that not only would the gain be less erratic but the average might well conform more closely to the perception which farmers hold of the land value on which in turn they make their decisions. In Sweden Andersson and Bengtsson (1984) concluded that, when including capital gains and losses in income, it is necessary to look on quite a long period of time but that no general proposal of the method by which they should be incorporated could be made. In practice accounting systems find it more convenient to ignore gains on land when assessing incomes.

Capital gains and losses have been given space here because they have too often been left out when assessing the income position of farmers and their households. While there may be disagreement over how precisely they should be aggregated with current income, there is a general consensus that gains and losses cannot be ignored: "capital gains constitute an important source of returns, impact on the aggregate consumption function and affect investment and production decisions. Wealth accumulation may be superior to income as a simple proxy of the utility surface" (Plaxico and Kletbe, 1979, p.1099). However, it is equally important to ensure that, if comparisons are drawn between farmers and non-farmers, that gains and losses in either group are taken into the exercise.

3.5.5 *The importance of time*

Income is a flow. The notion of a time period over which income is enjoyed, and measured, is integral with the concept and is explicit in the Simons definition, but there is no specific period over which income must be measured. By convention a year is commonly taken as the relevant period; this is not sacrosanct and there may well be other lengths of time which are more appropriate for particular circumstances. However, it is unlikely that a detailed definition of income which is appropriate for one length of time will be equally appropriate for a shorter or longer period.

Looking back over a lifetime and assessing the personal income of a farmer, a full assessment of the personal income could take a very broad view. Not only would the income in cash and kind be covered, but also any capital gains or losses would need to be ascertained. This ex post view of income is related to the notion that consumers, in our case farmer-households, can have a longer-term expectation of their income, which would encompass all income forms, and on which their consumption pattern is determined - the "permanent income hypothesis" put forward by Freidman (1957). There has been very little work done on the relationship of spending and perceived incomes of a longer-term nature in agriculture, although evidence on the personal expenditure of farmers, cited in Chapter 5, suggests that they do not adjust substantially their annual consumption to accommodate shifts in the profits generated by their farms, at least not within the same accounting period.

There are well-established empirical links for the population as a whole between age and income, low incomes being found especially among the young and elderly, and higher levels somewhere in the middle. Farmers as a group tend to be relatively old compared with the rest of society. The 1991 sample survey of manpower in the EU found that 30 per cent of those working in agriculture were aged 55 and over, compared with 10 per cent in other industries and 10 per cent in services (about a quarter of those covered in the figures for agriculture were hired workers, known to be generally younger than self-employed farmers). Figures for the UK were 22 per cent, 12 per cent and 12 per cent respectively. On a yearly basis some of these older farmers would have a low income, but in former times their earnings may well have been substantial.. Their present position might simply reflect changed priorities and the assurance of accumulated savings and other forms of wealth; their ability to consume may be quite adequate. Taking a longer view would reduce the inequality of incomes within the farming community, a general conclusion applicable to many occupations and particularly appropriate in farming where quite large year-to-year variations regarded as normal (Atkinson, 1975).

The longer the period chosen and the more disparate the groups for which comparison is required, the broader the income concept needed for a satisfactory outcome. In the shorter term it may be appropriate to narrow the definition of income to suit the problems in hand. Much of the purpose for income policy and therefore of income measurement hinges on poverty, and in such a situation it may be satisfactory to put on one side those constituents of income that do not in the short run impinge significantly on the amount of cash which a household has to meet its immediate needs. Thus capital gains and imputed rental values might be excluded.

3.6 Disposable income

The income parameter that in practice is usually chosen as the most appropriate indicator of the standard of living of farmers and other socio-professional groups is *net disposable income* (sometimes translated as *available income*), measured over a year (United Nations, 1977; Puurunen, 1990). This acknowledges that spending power should take account not only of the resources flowing into the household in the form of money or goods and services, but also outflows that are beyond the will of the household to influence. A generalised outline of its calculation is shown in Figure 3.3.

Net income from self-employment (independent activity) after deduction of capital consumption
    (a) self-employment in agriculture
    (b) self-employment in other industries
    (c) imputed rental value of owned dwelling
+   Wages and salary, which may be earned in or outside agriculture
(= Primary income)
+   Property income (interest, rent or other property income)
+   Social benefits (pensions and other welfare payments
+   Other current inflows (such as transfers from relatives living and working abroad)
=   Total income
-   Current taxes on income and wealth
-   Social contributions
-   Other current outflows (such as payments of alimony)
=   Net disposable income

Figure 3.3   The definition of net disposable income

On the income side all forms of income are covered, from the farm and elsewhere, net of an allowance for the amount of capital assets used up in production. The value of income received in kind (such as food from the farm) is included, as is also normally an estimate of the rental value of owned dwellings. In addition to this income from gainful activity (self-employment and employment) that coming from property and from welfare and other transfers is included. No account is taken of capital gains and losses are not included. The main outflow will be personal taxation and compulsory social contributions. The balancing item is (net) disposable income.

This concept of net disposable income is used both in microeconomic studies, such as household budget surveys in EU Member States, and in national accounts as agreed in the European System of Accounts (Eurostat 1979, 1995b) in the distribution of income account for the households sector. The general framework will differ in detail whether a macro or micro economic approach is being taken (Anne Harrison, 1999). The main differences lie in the way that insurance payments and claims are treated and what is included among the negative items. Within the national accounts approach all flows between the households sector and other institutional sectors have to be accounted for, so some items appear that would be ignored or treated differently in household budget surveys. For example, insurance claims from accidents to capital assets are positive items in the macroeconomic approach whereas they would not normally be considered as part of income to a household. Interest payments on consumer credit are deducted when reaching disposable income in the national accounts whereas they would normally be considered as items paid out of disposable income in family budget surveys. Such macro-micro disparities present a familiar problem to statisticians (Ruggles and Ruggles, 1986). In the present context the differences should not be overstated; they represented about 15 per cent of the total resources of households in Ireland (Hill, 1995). Nevertheless the conceptual disparity has caused some countries to develop macroeconomic accounts that use balancing income concepts that are closer to those used in microeconomic studies. The Netherlands has a system of Socio-Economic Accounts (Hill, 1994) which differs from the households sector account, but can be reconciled with it. In the UK the construction of an Income and Expenditure of Households Account from 1981 onwards (distinct from the personal sector account) was intended to reflect general perceptions of the nature of disposable income by households (CSO, 1985). The only negative items were taxes on income, National Insurance contributions (excluding employers' contributions) and contributions of employees to occupational pension schemes; on the income side, imputed rent was not included on the grounds that it does not normally feature in households' perception of their income.

In recognition that there are international differences in the extent to which consumption goods are provided by the state out of taxation, there are provisions in the latest set of accounting systems (UN, 1993) to include values of social benefits provided in kind (such as the costs of public health care and state education) in an *adjusted disposable income*. Countries which provide many benefits in this form also tend to tax more heavily, so this adjustment also restores the asymmetry in the account which counts taxes but ignores the benefits to consumption they bring. In practice this concept has not yet been generally implemented, so (unadjusted) disposable income has to be regarded as an incomplete indicator of consumption potential.

Because of the macro-micro problem, the unequal treatment of social benefits in kind, and the disparities between methodologies of countries even when they purport to conform to the same conceptual framework, when confronted with sets of figures on disposable income it is important to know precisely what has gone into their calculation (Hill, 1988). International comparisons of absolute levels are best avoided.

3.7 Multiple-activity households

The days are long gone, if they ever existed, since farmers and their families confined their economic activities solely to farming. Many households that operate farms will receive, in addition to their income from self-employment in agriculture, earnings from other jobs or businesses run by the farmer and his family. They may also have income from property, from pensions or from other transfers. Consequently, their personal incomes will be made up from contributions from several sources; some idea of the magnitudes of these are given in later chapters.

The diverse nature of the incomes accruing to farmers and their households does not appear to be fully appreciated by many policy-makers, judged by their public statements and the types of income statistics they request. Here it is necessary first to challenge the myth that farming households are necessarily primarily dependent on farming for their livelihood. Second, the existence of multiple income sources makes us question what is meant by an agricultural (or farmer) household, since many farm operators will only receive a small proportion of their total income from the farm. In section 3.5.2 above the household was suggested as the appropriate unit for assessing personal income. Particularly on small farms, where there are insufficient opportunities to fully occupy a family, a household approach is likely to show many more farms as having several income sources than if only the farmer is considered.

The EU Farm Structure Surveys find that about one third of the farmers in the EU also have some other gainful activity (OGA); they are part-time, in the sense that not all their working time is spent on their farms. The proportion varies widely, as Table 3.1 shows, though in part this reflects country differences in the thresholds for inclusion in the surveys.

Table 3.1 Proportion of holders and spouses with some other gainful activity (in %), 1983 and 1995

	1983		1995	
	Holders	Spouses	Holders	*Where OGA is the major occupation*
Belgium	33	9	15	*13*
Denmark	34	31	32	*24*
Germany	43	7	45	*39*
Greece	40	9	26	*21*
Spain			28	*23*
France	33	25	25	*14*
Ireland	25	30	34	*20*
Italy	29	17	25	*23*
Luxembourg	19	4	17	*12*
Netherlands	19	1	24	*18*
Austria			40	*34*
Portugal			33	*30*
Finland			50	*23*
Sweden			54	*36*
United Kingdom	25	18	28	*19*
EUR10/EUR 15	33	15	29	*24*

Source: Eurostat Farm Structure Survey

Figures for 1983 refer to holders and spouses separately, not farmer-and-spouse together or households. Including these would revise the figures upwards substantially from the holders-only column. The 1995 figures, for which results for spouses are not available (there are problems of data quality), suggest that a little below a third of holders had an other gainful activity, and for most of them (24 of the 29 per cent) it was the major occupation (a subjective self-assessment based on time allocation), the remaining 5 per cent having an OGA which was a secondary activity. In Germany, Austria, Finland and Sweden four or more holders out of every ten had another activity. Where found the OGA was overwhelmingly the holder's main occupation; only in Finland, with its uniquely high incidence of other activities (which might be explained by forestry) were they predominantly of a secondary nature. Between 1983 and 1995 some changes in the incidence of OGAs among holders are suggested, with reductions for Belgium, Greece and France but rises for Ireland and the Netherlands, though there have been changes in methodology that may prevent direct comparability. It should be borne in mind that these are proportions; between the years shown most countries will have seen falls in absolute numbers.

The bulk of information from Britain and other developed countries suggests that multiple activity is widespread and pervasive among farm households (Gasson, 1988; Hallberg, Findeis and Lass, 1991). Within the mix, degrees of part-time operation of the farm can be found and many ways of combining agriculture with some other income-earning occupation are experienced. Strong indications exist that farm families in OECD countries are generally becoming increasingly dependent on off-farm incomes. Furthermore, though still widely associated with small farms, part-time farming seems to be spreading into larger farm size groups, though in part this may represent a better documentation of what always existed. There is evidence (Harrison, 1975; Gasson, 1986) that part-time farming in the UK exhibits a "U" shaped pattern with respect to size, being relatively common among the smallest farms, falling in the medium-sized group - typically those operated predominantly with family labour where there is little opportunity for the members to engage in off-farm activities - and showing some rise among the largest farms where frequently agriculture is only one of the operator's business interests. A similar picture emerges for the US and Canada (see evidence on incomes by farm size given in Chapter 5).

Apart from noting that agricultural households often have these other gainful activities, it is important in a study of living standards to be aware why these other activities occur. Sometimes the impression is given that part-time farmers are predominantly those being squeezed out of the industry, and for whom the other jobs are necessary but unwelcome. While this may be the case in some countries, it is far from true in the UK; only about one in five seems to fall into this group (Hill, 1987). For the others there is a wide variety of explanations, including taking on a new challenge, providing variety of work and, for those who have come in from other occupations, the domestic environment and the fringe benefits which were discussed earlier (Gasson, 1983, 1986). To take another example, in Denmark pluriactivity is common among young farmers; the tradition of the younger generation buying land from the older using special external loans gives the retiring father a capital sum but the successor and/or spouse will often need to take an off-farm job in order to help pay the interest charges on the loan.

None of this is new. Indeed, according to Fuller (1991) "full-time farming is the aberration in modern farming history and multiple job-holding is the norm." As a universal phenomenon "Multiple job-holding is a flexible mechanism for adjusting to changes in agriculture, family needs, and shocks in the external environment." That these non-farming activities have some impact on the overall household income level is also well-established. A century ago in the UK the Royal Commission appointed to examine the hardship caused to certain large sections of British agriculture in the depression of 1879-96 encountered part-time farming and noted that the attraction of combining farming with another occupation was chiefly for the resulting security, but it was not uncommon for the arrangement to be "extremely profitable". The Report cited the New Forest where smallholders were said to have three sources of livelihood; their farming, common rights to pasture and the collection of fuel and turf, and small businesses such as dealing in small goods and stock. Elsewhere work combined with farming included fishing, retailing, road haulage, wholesale distribution, factory work, mining, and banking. With the addition of management and some more of the professions the list would serve well to describe what has been found in the 1970s and 1980s (Harrison, 1975; Gasson, 1988). Entrants from other occupations were blamed for rising rents. As a Mr. Channing remarked "Further, there have been, and still are, all over England and notably in Scotland, considerable numbers of men, some of whom know nothing of farming, others next to nothing, who have made money in other callings, and deliberately take farms because they prefer a country life, and without much anxiety as to commercial results".

The fact that multiple-activity households exist is enough to establish the importance of assessing not only the income arising from farming and non-farming activities but, as far as is practical, the rewards in the form of flows of goods and services generated by the farm as a place to live. And the existence of a degree of multiple activity throughout the spectrum of farm sizes means that this broad approach to income must be maintained even when considering the larger farming businesses.

3.7.1 Classifying households into agricultural and non-agricultural groups

Multiple-activity households also complicate the classification of households into those who form part of the agricultural population and those who do not. In Chapter 2 it was shown that the Common Agricultural Policy is not precise about who are considered the target group for its activities, yet without some clarification of the nature of the agricultural community it is impossible to know whether the CAP is achieving its central objective of ensuring a fair standard of living for these people. Yet, as will be shown in later chapters, the manner in which the agricultural community is defined has important implications for the numbers of households that qualify and the income results that emerge.

Several criteria can be used to qualify those households that comprise the agricultural community (Hill, 1990b) and the one which is appropriate will depend on the purpose for which these have to be distinguished from other households. *Residence on a farm* is perhaps the most intuitively attractive criterion, but living on an agricultural holding is of little meaning as a basis of classification in many parts of Europe where distances are often small enough for people to commute from farms, often little more than rural houses with particularly large gardens, to their regular place of work in urban areas. Conversely, it is quite possible, though less common in the UK, for farmers to live in towns and for them to commute to their farms. Up to 1983 the USDA produced income statistics for 'farm residents'; a farm was (and still is) defined as an establishment from which a given minimum value ($1,000) of agricultural products was sold or would normally have been sold in a year (USDA, 1988). A set of objections similar to those for Europe led to the discontinuation of the USDA series after almost fifty years, though analysis of farms is still made on this basis (see Banks *et al.*, 1989). Residence does, of course, cover both self-employed and hired workers, and it is evident that, within the context of the CAP, the latter are not given direct assistance to their incomes and standards of living.

Ownership of agricultural land is another possible criterion, perhaps with a minimum size qualification (such as the threshold for inclusion in the EU's Farm Structure Survey) to eliminate large gardens. However, it is inappropriate for the present context, as the CAP is directed at operators of agricultural holdings (holders) and their families, not landowners, though there are good economic arguments for believing that the ultimate beneficiaries of income support are the owners of land, the factor of production in least elastic supply (see Chapter 6). Some but not all of these owners will be farmers.

A more plausible approach in the present context is to define the agricultural community in terms of those people who are dependent on self-employment in farming for part of their livelihood. One way is to look at their pattern of working time; the agricultural community might be taken to be *every household in which at least one member spends some time working in agricultural production*. However, this would include every one who grows some of their own vegetables in their gardens. In order to remove these people some cut-off might be used below which producers would not be considered as "real" farmers, such as a minimum labour input (in days), a minimum area, or a minimum amount of output. Similar cut-offs are encountered in agricultural statistics to set the bottom limits of what constitutes a farm (or agricultural holding). A variant of this would be to treat only those households where the members spend the majority of their time working on their farms as comprising the agricultural community. At the level of the individual it may be relatively easy to collect data on what the respondent declares as his or her "main occupation"; this is often a subjective judgement but is often consistent and relatively stable. However, the use of time allocation at the household level is far more difficult in practice, requiring records of the labour allocation of each household member which will be rarely available. Another drawback of this labour input approach is that the notion of work may be too restricting. It is too simplistic to treat only physical labour as work; on many larger farms this may form only a small part of the operator's activities and it may be difficult or impossible to separate out time spent on managing the farm from that spent managing other activities. The two may even be complementary.

Probably a better basis of classification in the context of the CAP and its income support objective is *income dependency*. At its broadest the agricultural community could be defined as including all households in which anyone makes some income from self-employed farming activity; as noted above, hired (dependent) workers are not usually considered part of the agricultural community for which the CAP aims to provide a "fair standard of living", a view that may well change when the EU's enlargement to the east brings in large numbers of people working on farms arranged as forms of co-operative. This coverage of the households containing self-employed (independent) individuals would include many earning only very small amounts from farming and whose main income came from other sources. Although part of the agricultural community defined in the "broad" way, these households could not be considered as being dependent on farming for their livelihoods. It would appear more sensible to take a more restrictive approach and to include in a "narrow" definition only those households that are mainly dependent on farming for their livelihoods, that is where they derived half or more of their total income from self-employment in agriculture. This basis of classification is compatible with the complete allocation of all households into socio-professional groups, of which agricultural households could form one, and is the system proposed for the disaggregation of the households sector of national accounts in the 1995 ESA (Eurostat, 1995b). By subtraction it should be possible to obtain information on those "marginal" households in which farming generates some income but where it is not the main income source.

The "broad" and "narrow" ways of defining agricultural households, applicable when using either a labour input or an income criterion, are explored further in Figure 3.4. Agricultural activity (time or income) is shown on the horizontal axis and non-agricultural activity on the vertical. On both margins there is a level of activity which can be treated as irrelevant (kitchen garden production, hobby furniture repairing etc.). Only households which are within A or A' are unambiguously agricultural: Those in B are similarly non-agricultural. Those which lie in C or C' use the majority of their labour for agriculture or derive most of their income from it, and could reasonably be labelled as agricultural. The division between A and A' (and C and C') might result from the imposition of some size qualification. If only a small amount of labour was spent in agriculture, even if little or none was used elsewhere, the household might fail to be regarded as agricultural and might be classed as non-

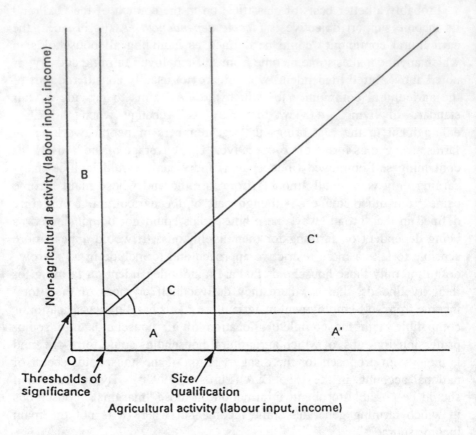

Figure 3.4 Combinations of agricultural and non-agricultural activity

economically active. Qualification tests outside this framework could also be employed; minimum holding areas or output values could be imposed before a household entered the frame.

Though income dependency is attractive as a basis for defining the agricultural community in the "narrow" sense, the target group at which the CAP is aimed is capable of interpretation in terms of both labour and time criteria. These are combined in Figure 3.5 which shows the percentage of income derived from and the percentage of time used for agriculture. On the assumption that a 50 per cent line can be used to divide the agricultural from the non-agricultural, cases falling into quadrant B may be confidently treated as agricultural since they satisfy both criteria.

Similarly those in quadrant D could be classed as non-agricultural, though they operate holdings and are therefore beneficiaries of any price-support regimes for agricultural commodities which might exist. However, D might also include some households which might be regarded as legitimate targets of agricultural policy; households on farms too small to absorb all the available labour (yet too large to be dismissed as not really being farms at all), where there currently are no other opportunities for alternative employment, and where there is major dependence on welfare transfers as a source of income. Policies of farm modernisation or the promotion of rural diversification may offer hope for some of these. Also covered here would be high income households whose farms may be large but whose non-agricultural activities may generate even larger non-farm incomes and where little household labour is spent on the farm, operations being carried out by hired managers and workers.

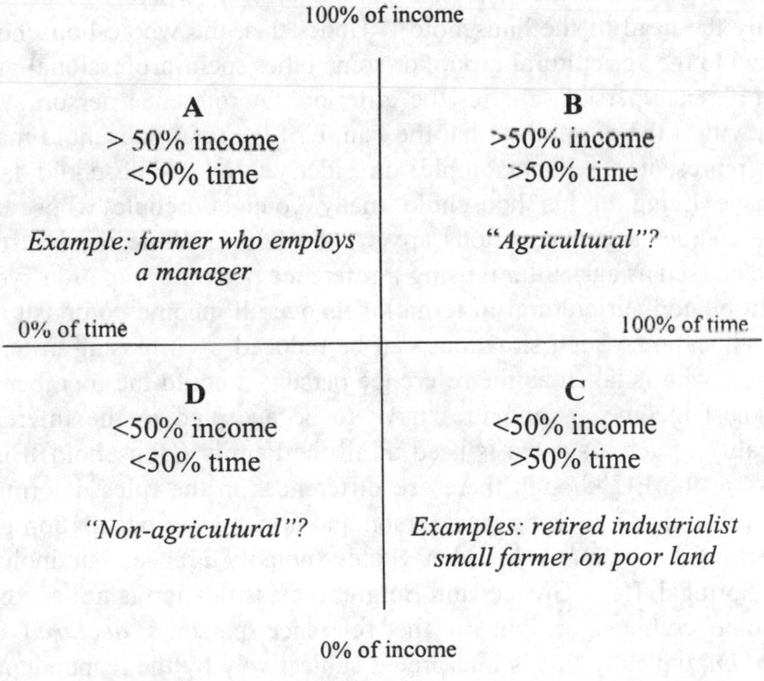

100% of income

A	**B**
> 50% income	>50% income
<50% time	>50% time
Example: farmer who employs	*"Agricultural"?*
a manager	

0% of time   100% of time

D	**C**
<50% income	<50% income
<50% time	>50% time
"Non-agricultural"?	*Examples: retired industrialist*
	small farmer on poor land

0% of income

Figure 3.5 Combining criteria of income composition and labour time allocation

Quadrants A and C contain further complex mixes of farming situations. For example, C would cover, on the one hand, the semi-retired businessmen, filling his time on the farm carrying out unnecessary tasks while receiving a high income from his former business in the form of director's remuneration and dividends on his investments and, on the other, a low-income farm household struggling against severe natural production conditions which absorb most of its available labour but yet which leave it primarily dependent on other sources of income. Quadrant A would include the large-scale farmer who arranges his farm so that he can spend large amounts of time off the holding doing unpaid political work, or in leisure pursuits. A similar approach combining income and occupation (of the operator) has been applied in the USA by Ahearn and Lee (1991).

In practice classification systems based on the characteristics of whole households (income composition or labour input) often prove difficult to implement because of data problems (Hill, 1995). The alternative which has gained ground is the *reference person* system (where this person is typically the head of the household). Under this, the whole household is allocated to the agricultural group, or some other socio-professional group, if the reference person satisfies the criterion. A reference person system carries with it the possibility that the nature of the total household may be poorly represented. For example, an elderly head-of-household farmer may have living in his household many younger people whose main income sources and occupations are off the farm. While the household may be classed as agricultural using a reference person occupation system, it might be non-agricultural in terms of its overall income composition or labour allocation. Such situations can be reduced by imposing criteria to determine who is taken as the reference person; it could the member with the highest income. Anomalies have to be accepted in the interest of practicality. Such a system is used in all the Family (Household) Budget Surveys in the EU, though there are differences in the rules determining who is regarded as the reference person and how his/her occupation group is determined. In many Member States (notably France, but including Spain, Portugal, Italy, Greece, and Belgium) classification is not according to income composition but to the reference person's *declared main occupation*; typically this is interpreted subjectively by the respondent and can be a mixture of income composition and time allocation, or predominantly time.

An important caveat must be borne in mind when applying criteria that involve the selection of households according to their position on a continuum. This is that there must be some degree of *stability in the variable used for classification purposes*. In this respect labour input, or a self-declared subjective judgement of the head of household's "main occupation" are superior to income composition, especially where farming and its inherent income instability is concerned. Not only will the number of agricultural households change where farming is the main income source, but the average income levels of those remaining in the group will alter. Evidence from Germany (Cordts, Deerberg and Hanf, 1984) and Norway (Hegrenes, Hill and Lien, 2000) suggests that taking a three-year period removes most of the unpredictable variation in incomes, an approach supported from French analysis (Brangeon and Jegouzo, 1992). Taking longer periods gives more stability but there is an increasing danger that changing farm structure (changes in the size distribution of the farms concerned) will affect the long-term trend in income variability. There is a tendency for the classification system to respond to changes in the numbers of households in ways which hide the cases in certain categories, and sometimes these are the ones on which greatest interest might be focused. For example, while the number of holdings deriving some income from farming may be declining in a stable and predictable way, if falls in income from farming are concentrated among the small, low-income farms, this may affect the numbers whose main income comes from farming disproportionately. Many of those with the severest income problems will be de-classified from being agricultural households. This is seen in an extreme form when incomes from farming fluctuate and classification (on the basis of income composition) takes place each year. It is quite possible for the residue of households left in the agricultural group to be occupiers of the larger, more successful farms, so that incomes of the smaller number of agricultural households are seen to increase when the general prosperity of agriculture falls (see the example of Denmark quoted in Hill, 1992). Thus it may be necessary to pay attention to both what is happening to numbers and income levels among agricultural households defined in the "narrow" way, but also to what is happening in the "marginal" group where farming is not the main income source.

Even if short-term instability can be eliminated, the households that are labelled as agricultural will not form a constant group over time. In the long term numbers will fall, in line with the historic trend. Agricultural policy reform is likely to accelerate this fall. For example, the households which are most successful in diversification into non-agricultural activities can be expected sooner or later to fall outside the agricultural group defined in the "narrow" sense, and to join some other. Farmers who face a fall in their income from farming without developing other earnings will eventually be excluded from the agricultural category as their welfare transfers grow in relative importance. Thus when commenting on income developments over time, changes in the composition of the group of agricultural households must be borne in mind. If the policy interest were to be to trace the development of income of people who *started* any given period as members of agricultural households, some attempt would have to be made to retain these in the group. This represents a major challenge to the way that official statistics are organised, since longitudinal analysis of a constant sample is at present very rare and data are not organised in ways that makes this easy.

Before leaving household classification it is necessary to refer to the issue of farms on which the operators are not in the technical sense engaged in independent agricultural activity (self-employment). This means, in effect, the operators of farms that are arranged as companies or similar forms. The farmer-directors are not, from a legal perspective, self-employed (as they would be as sole traders or as partners) but rather as salaried employees of their own companies, and any dividends they may receive are similarly not strictly income from self-employment. According to the definition of an agricultural household as one where the head (or the entire household) has self-employment as their main income source, the households headed by hired workers are not included. Applying this rules strictly would mean that the households the operators of company farms would also not be included. In reality, most company farms are family owned and operated businesses that adopt the particular business form primarily for taxation reasons or for other conveniences (such as distributing ownership of a family business among members who do not wish to farm). In their behaviour they act indistinguishably from unincorporated businesses. Indeed, in the EU's Farm Structure Survey some Member States advise their company farms to return themselves as if they were sole-traders or partnerships. A common-sense view would clearly include the households of such farmers as belonging to the agricultural community.

The issue becomes more difficult to handle when considering the large-scale farms in the territory of the former East Germany (GDR). There large farms arranged along co-operative lines and with their own legal entities are still a major force and engage large numbers of people; following enlargement, they are thought to be responsible for some 15% of the agricultural Net Value Added of the entire (enlarged) Germany (Eurostat, personal communication). While there are many households found on them that are dependent on agriculture in a real way, there are (from a legal perspective) no self-employed persons, and consequently no households that belong to the "agricultural community" in the sense with which that term has been used hitherto. A solution to this conceptual problem is being sought, one that is likely to become pressing as the countries of Central and Eastern Europe join the EU.

3.7.2 Decisions of multiple-activity agricultural households

Pluriactivity among farm households implies that some discretion can be exerted in the allocation of resources between competing on-farm and off-farm uses. Adjustment in this allocation can be expected as families experience micro level changes in their needs and as their resources alter with movements through the life cycles of its members. Changes in the external macro-environment, such as a pressure on farm incomes from agriculture's long-term cost-price squeeze, will also result in reallocation of the household's labour, land and capital, with greater shares typically being used for non-farming purposes. But agricultural households are not only economic units concerned with production; they are social units concerned with social goals and the way they behave will reflect a complex mix of motives. No lengthy treatment of explanations for the behaviour of farm households can be given here, but the level and composition of the income of these households must be given a perspective by mentioning some of the most important issues.

Though theoretical work on the economics of peasant households had an early start with Chayanov (1925, not translated into English until 1966 as Thorner *et al.*, 1966), the assumptions of the lack of a labour market and the presence of a flexible supply of land to all households makes this approach of limited utility to studies of the EU in the 1990s. Becker (1976) was responsible for creating renewed interest in the economics of households in general. More recent work in a developed country context sees the farm as comprising a trinity of three entities (Nakajima, 1986);

(a) The farm-firm - concerned with the normal decisions of factor allocation with the conventional objective of profit maximisation. A small extension of this, which does not change its essential nature, is to allow the firm to have both agricultural and non-agricultural enterprises, so that choices have to be made between using resources within the farm businesses and in other uses;

(b) The labourer's household, concerned with providing labour to the farm-firm and/or to the off-farm labour market. The economic problem is how to allocate the household's limited amount of time between spending time on income-earning activities and on leisure, the aim being to maximise utility;

(c) The consumer's household - concerned with the provision of consumption items (housing and food) direct from the farm.

Interest in explaining and modelling the behaviour of farm households in making simultaneous choices in these three dimensions has grown recently in Germany and France (see, for example, Eboli and Turri, 1988; Schmitt, 1989, 1991; Caillevet, Guyomard and Lifran, 1994). Particular attention must be given to whether the decisions of the farm-firm and the labour allocation of the household are separate and independent from each other ("recursive") or not (Kjehdahl, 1995). In the latter case the amount of labour available to the farm and other business activities will depend on decisions of the household on how much to spend on work and how much on leisure.

Much will hinge on whether there are labour markets for the time of the farmer and his family and for agricultural labour which might be hired in and how well they work. If members of farm households can hire in labour where necessary, and if they can sell their own labour at a higher price, it would be quite possible for the farm to respond to, for example, rising prices for the crops brought about by CAP support mechanisms in the way that simple theory of the firm would predict. Examples abound in the UK where the head of farm families or household members work off the farm in lucrative occupations (major businessmen, lawyers, bankers, doctors and dentists etc.) and hire in lower-paid managers and farm workers. But others can be found in which the occupiers of small-scale farms have inflexible full-time jobs as low-paid employees off the holding and where the labour available to the farm would be relatively insensitive to what is happening to the prices of farm commodities. Thus the response of farm households to economic stimuli could be vary varied.

It is also clear that the decisions on how a farm is run cannot be taken in isolation from the other economic activities and income sources that the household may have. As Phimister (1993) has put it "Specifically, in any period the household must decide upon both the level of output and labour input, the level of family labour supply, the level of investment and the level of consumption. Finally, it most also decide ultimately upon the level of the bequest to be passed to the next generation. It is the potential for interactions between these decisions, ... which forms the basis for the case for treating farm households as a distinct type of economic actor". In other words, an approach is needed in which the household is the unit of investigation, covering all its resources and their uses. The need for such an approach is clear from only a few examples. In the short-term, incomes from non-agricultural sources can play a vital part in sustaining the viability of farms; in Denmark many farms operated by relatively young farmers who have bought land from the previous generation are heavily dependent on income from off-farm salaries earned by the farmer and spouse. This will affect the types of enterprises for which the land is used. In the UK farming has been shown to be the beneficiary of investment funds brought in from non-farming businesses or occupations (Harrison, 1975); these can affect the longer-term ability of the farm to generate income. Explaining savings and investment in the Netherlands (Phimister, 1993) and on savings and consumption spending in Norway (Sand, 1999) required information on both incomes from farming and from other sources. And examples are known where the start of a pension being paid to an elderly farmer has led to an increase in the quantity of bought-in foodstuffs used to feed dairy cows.

A good case could be made for measuring the total income of farmer households even if the purpose were solely to explain in a better way their agricultural land use and on-farm investment decisions. However, such an approach would need to take into account the marginal taxation of income to the individuals in agriculture and in their other activities. To a person already facing high marginal tax rates the proportion of profits from the farm taken by this and other unavoidable deductions may be such that there is very little incentive to generate surpluses. Maximum amounts may find themselves being reinvested on the farm as "improvements" that, though not strictly necessary for the farm to operate, are tax-deductible expenses. The farm may be operated primarily for the fringe benefits it offers, perhaps with the hope of some ultimate capital gain and the concessions in property taxes that are commonly offered on agricultural property.

3.8   Family and non-family farms

Chapter 2 pointed out that an enduring theme among the objectives of the CAP has been the desire to support the family farm, although quite what was meant by this term was by no means clear. This feeling is not restricted to the EU (for the USA see, for example, Bartlett, 1993; Hallam, 1993). If policy-makers are really concerned with targeting support to this type of producer, and therefore presumably away from the non-family farm, it is worth giving some consideration to what this concept might mean. Income measurement could then be concentrated on this type of farm.

A widely quoted definition of a farm family business by Gasson *et al.* (1988) it is based on ownership and/or control of business assets. A family farm is one where (a) if there is more than one principal of the business (that is, people who perform entrepreneurial roles), the principals are related by kinship or marriage; (b) business ownership is usually combined with managerial control, and (c) control is passed from one generation to another within the same family. On this basis, nearly all farms in the EU would be classed as family. Later Gasson and Errington (1993) add to their notion of the "ideal" family farm the characteristics that family members (including business principals) do farm work, and that the family lives on the farm.   Commentators viewing the family farm from different perspectives and for different purposes are unlikely to agree on a common definition and, for example, a sociologist may emphasise the internal family relationships and the division of labour by gender. As has been pointed out earlier, the inclusion in the Gasson-Errington description of residence on the farm does not seem particularly helpful in the context of agricultural policy. Furthermore, and important as far as generating statistics on family farms is concerned, this descriptive list is not really sufficiently precise to enable an operational definition to be built. Something more easily applied is needed.

A concept of the "family farm" that considers the *operation* of the farm and the part played by the family's labour for the agricultural processes that take place there is both easy to understand and to apply. Though the founders of the CAP and their successors were not explicit in their indications, the impression is given is that they were primarily implying the concept of family operation (though ownership and control would be associated with this pattern of operation). Academics writing in the policy context have often interpreted the term in this operational way. Pollack

(1985) described the family farm as a unit "typically worked jointly by a married couple and their children or, in many societies, by members of an extended family who live together in a single household". Because of the restricted supply of labour that most families can make available there has been a tendency to assume that family farms are small farms (Gasson *et al.*, 1988; Tranter, 1983). However, it is wrong to assume that "small" and "family" are interchangeable labels.

Hill (1993) reports an analysis of the Farm Accountancy Data Network in which farms are grouped according to a single parameter - the proportion of the total labour input coming from the farm family. "Family" farms were taken (arbitrarily) as those where the family provided more than 95 per cent of total labour over the year; "intermediate" ones were where the family contributed from 50 per cent for 95 per cent; on "non-family" farms the family accounted for less than 50 per cent of the total labour input. In 1989 "family" farms represented 70 per cent of all farms covered by the FADN field of observation (which was itself confined to those deemed to be commercial farms - see Chapter 5) but accounted for just over one-half of total agricultural output. However, there was substantial variation between Member States. Family farms in the UK formed only 41 per cent of numbers in 1989, up from 32 per cent in 1981 as the result of the general displacement of hired workers from the industry. In contrast in Ireland the proportion was 83 per cent in 1989, and in Belgium 81 per cent.

Despite the attention in policy statements given to the support of the family farm, in all EU countries incomes per family member were much lower among "family" farms than among "non-family" farms, very probably resulting from tendency of the former to be smaller. However, in some countries higher incomes per person were associated with ("non-family") farms where the family contributed only very small amounts of labour to agriculture, often less than the equivalent of one unit of full-time labour. This points to better use of family labour, presumably through allocating time to non-farming activities and substituting hired labour on the farm where necessary. Besides securing relatively high incomes from farming, these families would also be enjoying income from outside the farm.

There have been various attempts to "modulate" some CAP support mechanisms so that the largest farmers do not receive payments pro rata to their size. However, no positive discrimination has ever been proposed for the benefit of family farms *per se*. Rather predictably, countries such as the UK (and Portugal) with relatively low shares of family farms judged in the basis of labour input could be expected to resist such moves. In that the attempts to modulate by farm size were defeated, it is almost certain that disagreements between Member States would block any moves in this direction for the family farm. Thus, though it is tempting to speculate on what criteria might be used to operationalise the concept of the family farm if a decision were made to monitor the performance and incomes of farms grouped by family status, it is not a particularly fruitful one at present.

3.9   Deductions from income

Attention has focused hitherto on the incoming elements contributing to the income of agricultural households, but a brief mention is necessary on the outflows which must be deducted in reaching estimates of their disposable income. The most important of these are current taxes on income and social contributions, which are often *quasi* taxes. In the UK farmers face essentially the same progressive system of income and profits taxation as other sectors of society, save for some concessions on the averaging of incomes across years (though there are other concessions on, for example, excise duty on diesel fuel, relief from rates on agricultural land and buildings, and favourable capital taxation provisions). In several other EU states this "normal" treatment of agriculture is not the case; for example in France, Belgium, Italy and Spain farmers in general are not taxed according to their actual income but on some flat-rate basis related to the size of holding (the *"forfait"* system) and in Ireland they are largely excluded from the tax net. This has an obvious impact on the marginal rate of tax on personal incomes relative to other households in the same countries. It also probably has some impact on the relative competitive ability of farmers from these countries in the single market for agricultural commodities, though no studies appear to have been undertaken on this issue.

However, even within a single country where the tax regime for incomes does not specially favour farmers, the incidence of taxation on them will not necessarily be the same as on other taxed units with whom income comparisons may be made. Later it will be demonstrated that, in many EU countries, agricultural households pay a lower proportion of their incomes as tax (plus social contributions) than do households in general, and that this is likely to reflect real differences in the effective rates. Part of this is explained by the fact that income from self-employment is taxed on a different basis from the income of employees; this helps explain why the UK system seems to work to the advantage of the farming community so that farmers appear to pay about the same proportion of their income in tax as do hired farm workers, although the average levels of income of the two groups are very different. In practice tax is not levied on all items that constitute income in the economic sense but on a subset and after the deduction of certain allowances. When attempting to make comparisons with other groups it is necessary to keep in mind any differences in the coverage; for example, certain living costs may have to be borne by non-farmers out of taxed income (such as the cost of childrens' ponies) whereas in practice ponies belonging to farm families use farm resources which are deducted from income in the estimate of tax due. Similarly, farm families may have greater opportunities for consuming directly part of the output of their farms businesses (as food) than do most other occupations.

Capital taxation is of importance to farmers because the land which they own often lifts their wealth to a level at which such taxes start to bite. The UK does not have a wealth tax, but where wealth taxes levied, as in the Netherlands, they must of course be deducted before disposable income can be calculated. In the British context discussion can be restricted to taxes which are applied when capital is transferred or sold. Although these are not taken into account when estimating disposable income on an annual basis, they must not be ignored in a longer term view of income. Capital gains are generally treated more favourably by the tax system than current income. This takes a variety of forms; not only are the nominal rates often lower than for income taxes (virtually a universal feature of tax systems) but tax is only paid on realisation and not as gains accrue, a deferment which further lowers the effective rate. Reduced real tax liabilities are a form of gain, and these can go on even in the absence of real gains in the value of land (Floystrup-Jensen and Dyreborg-Carlson, 1981). In addition, in the UK there are concessions for agricultural property and on gains which are reinvested in agricultural assets. Substantial allowances of tax-free gain on a farmer's retirement, plus a tax system which allows the cost of borrowing for land purchase to be treated as a cost in the calculation of taxable income, has meant that there has been a considerable incentive for farmers to arrange their businesses so that current income has been transformed into capital gain, principally in the form of land purchase and appreciation. In such an environment it is clearly necessary to encompass both current income and capital aspects, and in estimating the real income over a protracted period to take into account the taxes applied to each.

3.10 Wealth and economic status

So far the discussion has centred on personal income as the variable which determines whether a farmer and his family have a standard of living which can be considered fair or not. The definition of personal income cited earlier in this Chapter referred to changes in the store of property rights over a given period, and it is clear that real capital gains fall within the concept of income defined in this way. No account was taken, however, of the absolute size of those property rights - in other words, the wealth of the person or family was ignored. Personal income, in the Hicksian sense, is content to concern itself with the level of consumption that would be possible without diminishing the person's wealth. But this would give a false picture of the potential ability of the person to consume over his or her remaining lifetime. Take two individuals of identical income but one owning large amounts of saleable assets, the other none. Assume that the assets do not yield an income flow - perhaps they are in the form of paintings. The persons with the paintings is obviously in a very different position when it comes to being able, if the wish or need arose, to turn them into spendable money and thus into consumption goods. If the current income of both persons was low, to the extent that they fell below some arbitrary poverty line for income, society might feel that, while it wished to assist the one without assets, the owner of the valuable paintings was an entirely different case and capable of enjoying a perfectly adequate standard of living from his or her own resources. It is this sort of thinking that is behind the various qualifying tests which bar applicants from a range of welfare benefits in the UK if they have savings over a certain limit or property. What society is doing by these tests for assets is applying, in a rather crude way, a two-factor (income and wealth) criterion - not a poverty *line* but a poverty *boundary.*

Whether or not wealth is taken into account is of particular importance to agricultural households since it is common to find, in industrialised countries, farmers who have low current incomes yet hold very considerable quantities of wealth. Assessing the poverty position of farmers on current income alone is not very satisfactory if there are substantial differences in the wealth holdings between farmers and non-farmers. In the US, for example, the average net worth of farm families has been found to be nearly twice that of all families (Carlin and Reinsel 1973), a situation mirrored in the UK and Germany. Later estimates have greatly raised the relative position of farm families ("full-time" farmers to thirteen times and "part-time" farm families to five times the all-households American average) (Knudsen, O. *et al.*, 1990).

While acknowledging the deficiencies of adopting income as a single-variable indicator of poverty, there is an obvious convenience to a unified measure. One approach is to combine income and wealth into a single measure which reflects the potential spending power that comes from both; this is termed economic status. It depends on expressing the net worth of a person (or household), that is his value of assets minus his liabilities, in the form of an income-equivalent which can be added to the current income to give an overall figure. The initial work was not restricted to agriculture (Weisbrod and Hansen, 1968) but, as we will see in Chapter 6, application of the methodology has been taken up with important implications for farming families in the US, Canada, Australia and the UK. Here the logic behind the approach will be set out.

The underlying notion is that wealth has an income stream equivalent. This is commonly encountered with pension schemes linked with life assurance policies which pay a capital sum at retirement, and the beneficiary can decide whether to keep it as an addition to their wealth or to exchange it for an annuity - an income stream guaranteed for the rest of the investor's life. The size of the annuity will be dependent on three factors - the size of the lump sum invested (the wealth given up), the expected future life of the recipient, over which time the institution will be obliged to continue to pay annual amounts, and the rate of interest. (The formula linking the components is given in Chapter 6). The larger the initial wealth exchanged, the higher the rate of interest and the shorter the expected future life of the recipient, the larger will be the annuity. In this context wealth is understood to be net of outstanding liabilities - more properly described as net worth.

Expressing wealth of the agricultural population in terms of an income equivalent does not depend on farmers actually annuitising their net worths. As a concept the notion is independent of practice. There may be good reasons why few if any farmers would want to enter annuitising arrangements - their current incomes might be at such a level that there was no need to draw on their wealth in this way. Those in financial difficulties might prefer to consume their capital by extending their overdrafts which would give them greater flexibility in the amount of their net worths they chose to consume each year. It is not even necessary for financial institutions to exist which could perform the function. Practical use of annuitisation as a part of agricultural policy would, of course, require an institutional framework, but that is a matter for consideration in Chapter 6. Nevertheless the procedure makes certain assumptions that must be considered at this stage.

The period over which the wealth is annuitised is assumed to be that of its owner. Information on life expectancies of people by age, occupation group and other factors is available. The question is not an actuarial one, but rather whose future life is to be taken. For married couples who share a standard of living - though perhaps the income and wealth legally belong only one of them - a good case could be made that the life expectancy of the longer-lived should be the period chosen since the couple does not cease to exist until both are dead and therefore an income would be needed until then. Another assumption is that the wealth is freely at the disposal of the person or couple. In the calculation it is assumed that wealth is totally consumed by the end of the period, so that the successors of a person taking an annuity would not receive any of the wealth. Where wealth is not freely disposable, such as assets held in trust for someone else, these should not be included. Some owners of land might protest that, despite the legal situation of unencumbered ownership, they feel in some way to be stewards of their land for the following generations of their families. Come what may, they would never feel free to sell the land. Their wealth in the form of land is therefore not "real" wealth and should not be taken into account when assessing their economic status. The validity of this case can only be settled by how society as a whole views land. By the conventional definition, agricultural land falls firmly into the concept of personal wealth; the wealth of an individual is "his total stock of tangible or intangible possessions that have a market value. This implies that they must be capable of being exchanged for money or other goods, that is the ownership in them must be capable of being transferred" (Bannock, Baxter and Rees, 1978). In the estimates of economic status involving annuitised net worths it is normal practice to include agricultural land without any deductions.

Not surprisingly, the use of an economic status measure (income plus annuitised net worth) has a substantial impact on the level and distribution of incomes, with the effect particularly marked among the elderly where current incomes are low but net worth high. The effect for the entire US population was to increase the degree of inequality. Important for the study of poverty was the findings that the elderly constitute a smaller proportion of the poor when annuitised net worth is also taken into account (falling from 34 per cent of all poor families to 28 per cent) (Weisbrod and Hansen, 1968).

There are other techniques that could be explored, such as earnings capacity, which attempts to measure the ability of a household or family to generate an income if it were to use its physical and human capital at capacity (Garfinkel and Haveman, 1977). However, this concept does not substantially add to the understanding of incomes in relation to agricultural policy, though there is the suggestion that US farmers who are poor by the conventional money income measure have sufficient human capital to do better economically if they were willing to leave their farms.

3.11 Summary and conclusions

The first conclusion from this Chapter must be that the measurement of the living standards or incomes of the agricultural population in a way that is appropriate for applying the intentions of the Common Agricultural Policy is a complicated business. Among the problems to be faced are the decisions on what is the suitable unit to be assessed - the farmer or his household - and where the limits of the household come. Then there is the choice of what aspects to measure - the consumption flow from the household or the income flow to it. And if the latter is selected on grounds of practicality, care must be taken to embrace all the forms of income, both those which arrive in money terms and those which are in the form of goods and services. Many farmers or their households have occupations that are run in parallel with the holding, and a majority of these with other gainful activities are not primarily dependent on agriculture for their livelihood but are farmers because of the non-monetary flows of goods and services which go with the occupation of agricultural land.

The second is that, when assessing the economic position of farmers, it is necessary to go beyond the income from current farming activities and to consider the possibility of capital gains or losses and also their net worth. This is particularly the case when attempting to use the concept of a poverty line to distinguish between the poor and the non-poor. Conventional indicators largely depend on money incomes, but this is clearly unsatisfactory with the agricultural population, where low incomes are frequently found combined with substantial wealth.

Lastly, it will not have escaped notice that the discussion relating to low living standards in agriculture has drawn largely on material from North America. European literature is remarkably sparse on the matter of the household income of farmers. This is reflected in the dearth of data for EU countries, described in more detail in Chapter 6. The central concern of the CAP, now that production has reached surplus levels in most major commodities, is with the incomes of the agricultural population. Yet, as has been demonstrated in this chapter, there are many gaps in the theoretical work in this area. Furthermore, later chapters will show that the volume of empirical studies is inadequate to support such a costly and, today, constraining policy.

4 Indicators of Income from Agricultural Production

There is ample evidence from Chapter 2 that, when income is mentioned in official statements of the objectives of agricultural policy in industrialised countries, such as the European Union's 1957 Treaty of Rome and its *Agenda 2000* document of 1997, the prime concern in most cases is with the living standards of the agricultural population. The design and administration of agricultural policy will require information on livings standards, or incomes, to enable the extent of the problem to be assessed and the performance of policy to be monitored. There must be data relating to the problem in hand - quantifications of income which assist in the system of enquiry - and these data must bear a close relationship to reality to be of much value. Data is not the same as information; information implies not only the production of data but also its analysis and interpretation in the context of some problem. However, data form an integral part of the information required for agricultural policy directed at living standards.

In this chapter and the next we review the ways that income is measured in the context of agricultural policy. It will soon be obvious that emphasis in official monitoring by the EU up to the present has fallen almost completely on the income derived from agricultural productive activity (farming). While interesting and useful as part of our understanding of the changing nature of the industry, data of this sort are not capable of casting much light on the central issue of the living standards of the agricultural population. Very little data exist on the personal incomes of farmers; what is available in Member States is reviewed in Chapter 5. In Chapter 7 an explanation of this mismatch is offered. Nevertheless, because of their importance in the policymaking process, it is necessary to be aware of the production-related income indicators used by the EU in the context of the CAP and, from a national standpoint, those measures employed in the UK.

Incomes from farming can be studied at two levels - that of the whole agricultural industry (macroeconomic, or aggregate) or that of the farm (microeconomic, or individual). Aggregate estimates play a prominent role in CAP policy formation; as well as monitoring the past behaviour of the agricultural industry they are used in planning future attempts to shape farming. However, they are only concerned with the overall position. Farm-level results are necessary to give the detailed information of how incomes differ between farms of different sizes and types, levels of indebtedness and efficiency, ages of operators, degree of family operation and so on. This chapter firstly reviews the various aggregate indicators employed by the EU and UK, the general methodology underlying them and the pictures they describe. It then goes on to give a similar treatment to the microeconomic measures. Though falling short of the full information needed to service the income objectives of the CAP, the patterns that emerge are nevertheless of substantial importance to the way that this policy operates. Consequently the measures of income from agricultural production must first receive our attention.

4.1   Agriculture in the national accounts

Even in the absence of an agricultural policy with specific income aims, an account of the economic activities of the agricultural industry would have to be made. All industrialised Western countries feel the need to monitor the state of their economic systems. These contain an immense variety of economic flows and separate units, and the essential function of a system of national accounting is to reduce this complexity into a limited number of fundamental categories. A basic framework of national accounts was established by the United Nations in its System of National Accounts - SNA (UN, 1968, 1993) and has been adapted for the European Union in the form of the European System of Accounts - ESA (formerly known as European System of Integrated Economic Accounts) with a standard set of concepts, definitions, and rules of accounting for use across Member States (Eurostat 1979, 1995b). Part of this is the system of classification of economic activities (NACE Rev.1) that lists what is considered as agriculture and what belongs to other forms of production. The 1995 ESA, which followed from the 1993 SNA, contained changes that carry implications for the way that the agriculture industry is monitored. These have not yet been reflected in the structure of the accounts for the EU so far published that form the basis of much of the discussion presented here. Nevertheless, the new ways of aggregate accounting are due to be adopted by the EU in 1999 and will form the basis of published statistics for several decades, so it is necessary to review the essentials of the revised system; this is the subject of a separate section later.

Within this system of national accounts there are two types of current account that are of direct importance to the present study – accounts that deal with production activity, and accounts that deal with resources flowing to and from institutional units. For the first the economy can be subdivided into various types of production, of which the agricultural production is one singled out for special attention. As an historically important part of the economy of most countries - and especially so in the period of the Second World War and its aftermath when so much of the present accounting system took shape - it was an obvious choice to put agriculture in a category of its own. There was a pressing need to know what was happening to the output of this vitally important industry and its use of inputs. It is quite feasible from a technical standpoint to construct a production account for the agriculture branch of the economy, as its outputs are fairly easily distinguished from those of other industries and the inputs it uses can also be identified, though not quite so easily

However, the treatment of agricultural production within national accounts, while being consistent with that afforded to other industries, does not necessarily provide quite the sort of information that agricultural policymakers have wanted (or perhaps that statisticians thought was the most appropriate) for the monitoring of this industry and for assessing the performance of policy directed at farming. Consequently it has become customary to construct a separate account for aggregate agricultural production that differs in some respects from the treatment of agriculture in national accounts in order to make it more policy-relevant. For example, agricultural statisticians have chosen to include certain forms of production that are not considered as agricultural in national accounts (Christmas trees, on-farm wine making) and to exclude others (such as parkland upkeep on contract by farmers), and different conventions are applied to the coverage of food production in gardens (see below). Up to 1998 the basis of the agricultural production account was the "branch", whereas for other industries it was the "sector" (the concepts will be explained later). As an account that belongs to the family of national accounts but differs in known and specific ways from them, this agricultural account is termed a "satellite" of the national accounts. Such "satellites" are, in principle, capable of being reconciled with the main accounts using a "bridge" that contains figures for the items where treatments differ.

Eurostat publishes the production accounts for this branch separately (as the Economic Accounts for Agriculture (EAA)) for each Member State and for the EU as a whole. The United Kingdom does so independently on a national basis in its annual reports *Agriculture in the United Kingdom* and *Farm Incomes in the United Kingdom* (both HMSO). The OECD collects and publishes agricultural accounts for all its member countries using the same methodology as is applied in the EU. These specialist satellite accounts attract much more attention than the agricultural element in the national accounts proper. As part of these accounts it is possible to estimate the reward remaining to farmers for the factors of production they own and use in agriculture, and the income figures so derived form an input to decision-making in the CAP and in many national policies and is a major element in the analysis of the impact of policy on agriculture.

For the second account - the Distribution of Income Account - the economy is broken down into a number of institutional sectors, of which households form one, on the basis of their principal function. This household sector can be further subdivided into subsectors according to a classification of households into socio-professional groups, of which agricultural households can form one. This account shows, on one side, the resources flowing to households and, on the other, the claims on these resources, the balancing item being disposable income - the residual sum available for spending on consumption and for saving. There is an obvious overlap of the two accounts, and it might be expected that the aggregate income from agricultural production would constitute a major portion of the income of the agricultural household sector. However, the two accounts are distinct from each other, and the substantial divergence that occurs between them is a constant source of confusion. Within national accounts this part concerned with the distribution of income of households is relatively undeveloped. We will return to it in Chapter 5.

4.2　The production branch agriculture – methodology used up to 1998

Aggregate economic accounts for agriculture have been published within the European Union since 1964, and from 1969 onwards the six original Member States adopted the common definitions and procedures of the EU's Economic Accounts for Agriculture. In the UK the conceptual basis of aggregate economic accounting as applied to agriculture had its UK roots established over half a century ago in the spurt of statistical development that accompanied the Second World War; published results go back to 1937/38. There are small differences between the systems applied in the EU by Eurostat and in the UK by MAFF for national purposes (MAFF, 1984; Eurostat, 1992; (Hill, 1998b)) but the essential approaches are the same and are shared by the accounting systems of the USA and other OECD countries.

Fundamental to interpreting these accounts, as used up to 1998, is an understanding of the concept of the *branch agriculture* on which they were based. A branch is described as consisting of "groups of units of homogeneous production which are exclusively engaged in the production of a single product or groups of products" (Eurostat, 1979). The consequence of this approach may be summarised as follows:

- Within the ESA the branch agriculture account was compiled as if the country consisted of a single huge farm (the concept of the "national farm"). Sales and purchases from one farm to another farm were ignored, and output was only recorded where it left the national farm, such as when the legal ownership of grain or livestock passed at sale to persons or firms outside agriculture. The concept of the "national farm" is illustrated in Figure 4.1

- The branch account covered all agricultural products (of which there is a prescribed list in the EAA methodology) irrespective of what type of unit produced them. Thus, in addition to the production from commercial farms, the branch concept included the output from domestic gardens, allotments and from firms and institutions that were not primarily involved in farming, such as prisons and monasteries.

- Non-agricultural goods which might have been produced from farms and other units producing agricultural commodities were excluded (food processing, farm tourism etc.).

The value of output was (and still is) estimated from a variety of sources, but principally from data on the physical area of crops, combined with estimated yields, and numbers of livestock, multiplied by appropriate prices found from market reports and from the relatively small number of first users/purchasers (such as dairies). The values of inputs, such as feedstuffs, fertilisers and seeds, are derived principally from sales from other industries to agriculture, something possible because of the largely agricultural nature of many of these inputs (animal feedstuffs and agro-

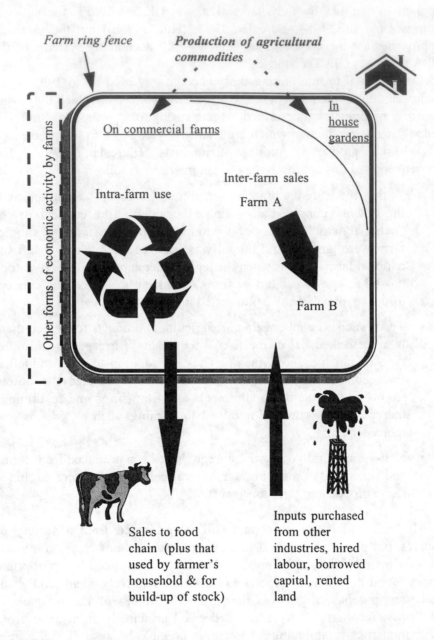

Figure 4.1   National Farm and the Agriculture Branch - the basis of EU aggregate economic accounts up to 1998

chemicals being mainly taken by farmers etc.). Data sources vary between countries; in the UK regular returns from manufacturers of agricultural inputs are used, and banks and mortgage institutions will provide the interest payments by farmers in total. The important point is that information used in building the account thus mostly comes from industry-level sources and not from grossing up the results of surveys of the practices of individual farms (though survey data will be used to fill in gaps). Labour costs are another good example; in the UK the national cost of hired labour is estimated from taking numbers of workers by category from the Annual Census of Agriculture and multiplying by annual average earnings found from the Wages and Employment Enquiry (MAFF, 1984).

The advantage of this approach is largely one of speed; the estimates of the aggregate value of outputs and costs of inputs can be more quickly to hand than if reliance were to be placed on surveys of sets of farm accounts, and for policy-makers rapid availability of estimates is important. Preliminary calculations of income based on aggregate accounts can be available in Eurostat before the end of the calendar year to which they relate. This timing should allow policy decisions on, for example, support prices to be made early in the following year, before all the farm-level plans for production are finalised.

The first part of the branch account as used before 1999 is fairly uncontentious; this is represented in the upper part of Figure 4.2. Terminology varied between the EU system and the UK, but the concepts were closely similar. The value of agricultural output was principally the amount sold from the national farm, but adjustments had to be made for items such as changes in the stocks of output on farms (grain in store for example) which represented sales not yet made, or changes in the stock of capital made directly by the farmer such as by increasing the size of his breeding herd. Output would be less than production because of physical losses in the system (in harvesting, transport etc.). Consumption of items produced on the farm but consumed directly by farm households also had to be taken into account. The result was Final Output. On the input side the expenditure of the national farm on purchases from other production branches of the economy was adjusted for changes in input stocks to give Intermediate Consumption. This was deducted from Final Output to give Gross Value Added, a term that reflects the addition to the value of inputs acquired from other branches of the economy brought about by the "fixed" factors of production (land, labour, capital and entrepreneurial talent) in

Sales of farm crops, horticulture, livestock and livestock products
  plus   Own account capital formation (breeding livestock and other)
  plus   Processing by producers
  plus   Value of physical change in output stocks and work in progress (closing stocks minus opening stocks)
  plus   Own consumption
  equals Final Output

  minus   Expenditure on intermediate consumption goods and services
  minus   Taxes linked to production
  plus   Subsidies
  equals Gross Value Added at factor cost (also called Gross Product in the UK)

  minus   Depreciation
  equals Net Value Added at factor cost (also called Net Product in the UK)

  minus   Rents paid
  minus   Interest payments paid (including loans for land purchase)
  equals Net Income from agricultural activity of total labour input (also called in the UK Income from agriculture of total labour input)

  minus   Wages and salaries paid (hired labour)
  equals Net income from agricultural activity of unpaid labour (the holder and his family)(also called Total Income from Farming (TIFF) in the UK)

In the UK a further deduction takes place
  Minus   Wages and salaries imputed to non-hired (family) labour other than farmer and spouse
  Equals Farming Income (a UK concept, not used by Eurostat)

Source: derived from Eurostat (1993)

Figure 4.2   The aggregate economic account for agriculture

agriculture. Adjustment to take into account subsidies and taxes linked to (and other assets) gave Net Value Added (NVA) at factor cost. This represented the return to the complete resource base in agriculture.

Net Value Added is a concept common to national accounting systems in all OECD countries. It is an important statistic when national accounts are compiled; NVA from agricultural activity represents the contribution that this form of production makes to the whole economy though, as was pointed out above, the detail of which activities are included when calculating NVA in the context of national accounts differs to some extent from that used in the Economic Accounts for Agriculture. In practice, the same basic data sources are drawn on, and frequently the same civil servants carry out the two calculations by following the different methodological rules. Agriculture's NVA would need to be calculated as part of national accounts even if there were no particular interest in it arising from agricultural policy.

4.3   The reward to farming entrepreneurship

Net Value Added from agricultural activity can be divided up in alternative ways to give measures appropriate to particular policy circumstances. Basically two approaches could be employed, one based on factor function and the other on ownership.

A thoroughgoing distribution by function, distributing NVA according to the contributions of land, capital, labour and entrepreneurship, would make charges for all the land, whether owned by the farmer or not, and for all the capital employed. Arguably the physical labour contributed by the farmer should also be charged for, leaving a residual which would be the reward for the risk and management input to agriculture.

The alternative is to distribute the NVA according to the ownership of factors. Farmers could form a particular sector of owners who, in reality, would receive rewards for the factors they owned not only in agriculture but also in other productive activities. To restrict coverage to only their agricultural factors would be to cut off part of the subject of their allocation decisions. Nevertheless, as will become clear, in practice factors in non-agricultural use are ignored and the division by ownership is confined to those used in agricultural production.

A number of attempts have been made to distribute agriculture's NVA by factor share. The EU at one time proposed a set of indicators in which deductions were made for the remuneration of the farmer's own capital and for his family's labour, leaving a residue (termed Net Operating Profit) which represented the return to entrepreneurship (Commission, 1982) (see Fig 4.3). As we will see later in this chapter, at a microeconomic level use has been made of a Labour Income concept by imputing a charge for all non-land capital, so that the residual represented a return to all forms of labour. Such exercises have not been pursued for long, since they depend heavily on imputing charges for land and capital owned by the farmer and his family and on the value of the labour provided by them. This labour income concept has been abandoned, largely over the choice of an appropriate rate of interest to use for imputing the capital charge.

Perhaps the most comprehensive exercise along the factor-reward lines was by Bellerby (1955, 1956). The reputation of this work as a piece of applied economic analysis is such that a description of its main features is called for. Bellerby in *Agriculture and Industry: Relative Income* (1956) attempted a functional distribution to achieve a return to the physical and entrepreneurial resources of farmers and their families - a concept for which he coined the term "incentive income". This was found "by estimating the total factor income of agriculture ..... and subtracting from it agricultural net rent, interest, the wages and salaries of farm employees, and the income of any independent agricultural personnel not ordinarily classed as farmers." Essentially this meant deducting charges for owned land as well as rented land, and for owned capital. Although imputing a rent charge for owned land, using existing rents as a yardstick may be not too difficult (it one formed part of the method of the UK's aggregate farming income calculation and still is used in the Farm Business Survey), Bellerby's use of an imputed capital charge is open to dispute, less on the logic of making such a charge than on the method of arriving at a particular figure.

The residue is the reward not strictly to risk-bearing, since a return to physical labour of the farmer is also included, but to the "human effort and enterprise" of the farmer "and any relatives actively engaged with him on the work of the farm". This family-unit of resource is justified by Bellerby on the grounds that "the relatives' income is often indistinguishable from that of the farmer, and as a rule they share with him both the risks and the responsibilities of the enterprise in some degree. Hence it is convenient, and seems not unreasonable, to regard them as part of the entrepreneur group" (Bellerby, 1956, p16). "The incentive income per man equivalent

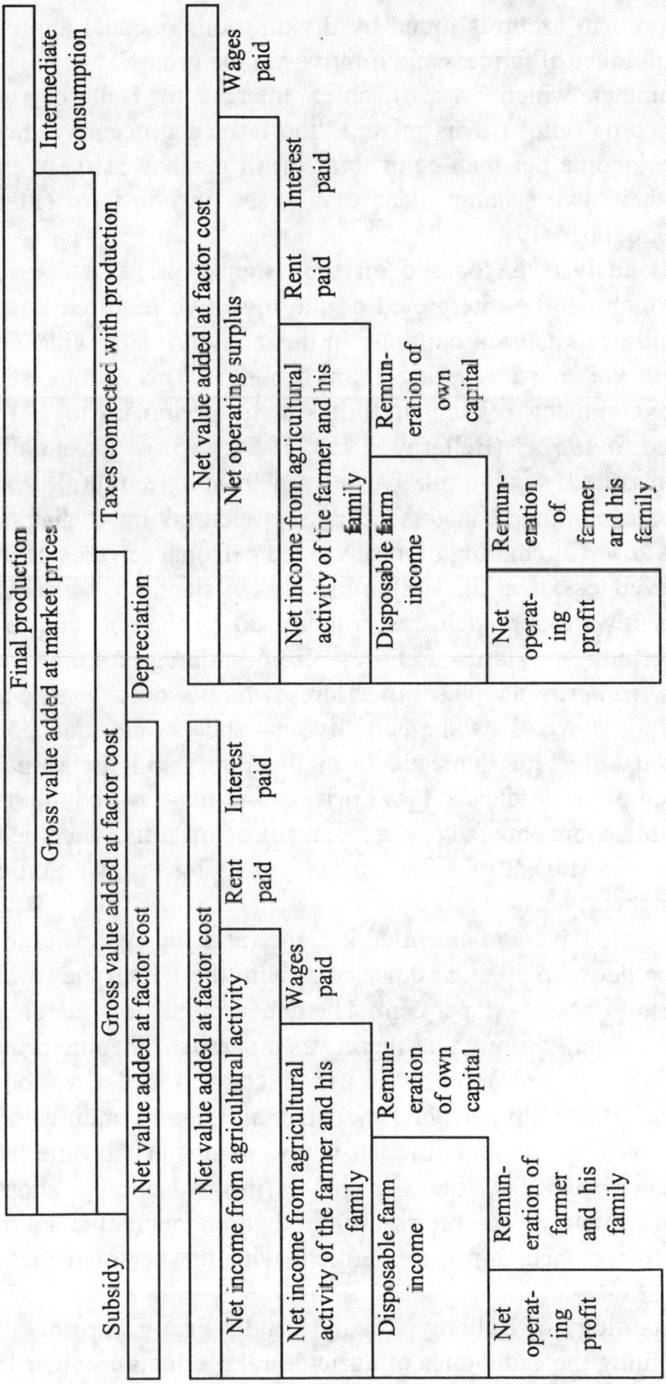

Figure 4.3 Scheme of income indicators proposed by the European Commission (from Commission, 1982) VI/308/82-EN (0082d)

of the entrepreneur group is found by dividing this residual aggregate by the adjusted number of farmers and relatives in the group."

The parameter which was of chief interest to Bellerby was the "incentive income ratio". This related "the farmer's incentive income to the incentive income per man-equivalent of all persons actively engaged, whether on their own account or as employees, in non-farm enterprise." (Bellerby, 1956, pp16-17).

Bellerby's analysis is focused on the "supply price" of agricultural enterprise, which can be interpreted as the incentive required by farmers and their families to enter or continue in this activity. His evidence was a statistical *tour de force* covering many countries in various stages of economic development, relating initially to the period up to 1936-8 but later extended to 1952-3 (Bellerby, 1953, 1954, 1955). Essentially what was being measured was the relative reward from agricultural production accruing to the combined factors of entrepreneurial input and operator labour. He was *not* attempting to measure the personal rewards of the farm families or, even less, their disposable incomes or standards of living.

The factor-reward approach was emphasised by the decision to ignore incomes accruing to farm families from non-agricultural sources. Nevertheless, Bellerby adopted procedures which would be expected to also appear in a study of standards of living - such as the inclusion of an imputed rental value for domestic farm dwellings and the valuation of own-consumption of produce at retail prices - but these were undertaken in order to reach a more satisfactory assessment of incentive income. For a similar reason the subject of different costs of living in town and country was also broached.

The unweighted average incentive income ratio for 1938 was found by Bellerby to be between 50 and 60 per cent, with the UK in the band 60-75 per cent and the USA 35-45 per cent. The generality of low factor rewards does not automatically imply that there was a *personal* income problem in farming, although it is clear from the introduction to Bellerby's book that its genesis was at least in part the low personal incomes endured by some sectors of the farming communities in many nations at the time the work started. Nevertheless, at times in his writings Bellerby adopted an interpretation which verges on assuming that the incentive income for agricultural entrepreneurship *was* identical with the personal incomes of farmers.

The methodology of Bellerby's analysis falls firmly into the group of studies examining the economics of agricultural production rather than the well-being of agricultural households. As such it is of reduced relevance to the current concern of policy which is directed at the social aspects of income in agriculture. In the economic conditions of the late 1990s these living standards are determined by important factors in addition to the average incentive income - and it is highly likely that in the UK at least this complexity has always existed. This in no way diminishes the significance of Bellerby's work as a classic of its time and as a repository of insights pertinent to the farming industry of the new millennium.

4.4   Derivation of income indicators from the branch agriculture account – methodology used to 1998

In addition to its role within national accounts, the concept of NVA within the production account for the branch agriculture is also the point of departure for a number of agricultural aggregate income indicators. It is increasingly recognised that no single income indicator is capable of reflecting all the aspects of agricultural production, and the EU, UK and USA each now have extended beyond calculating a single indicator (which carries the danger that it will be used in inappropriate circumstances simply because it exists) to the generation of a range to cope with differing statistical requirements (Hill, 1991).

NVA itself could be used as a proxy for the income derived from farming by independent farmers and their families if (a) all land was owned by them, (b) they borrowed nothing, and (c) they operated the farms totally without hiring in any non-family labour. This is far from reality, at least in the EU of the late 20th century. The residual income of farmers and their families from agricultural production will depend on how the NVA is shared (distributed) between the resources owned by the farmer and family and those owned by others. From the standpoint of an individual farmer his income will be after deducting the following:

- The cost of interest on the loans taken from banks and other lenders for agricultural purposes. Strictly, loans can only be taken out by institutional units (in the present context, households or incorporated business), not by UHPs which are not legal entities. Consequently, an assumption has to be made that the interest paid by an industry comprised of agricultural UHPs can be equated to that paid by farm households and companies for loans for agricultural purposes. From a theoretical standpoint it may be meaningless to draw a distinction between interest on agricultural loans and loans for other purposes, such as for consumption spending. In practice all interest charges are likely to be taken as agricultural and deducted.

- Rents paid to landowners for tenanted land. While the rent element attributable to the fixed assets associated with the land (including farm buildings) are deducted, this is not supposed to include any part of the rent pertaining to the domestic aspect of farm dwellings. Again, any partition of actual rents into the agricultural and domestic portions is likely to be rather arbitrary;

- The costs of hired labour, which will include wages paid plus the other costs of employing someone (employers' social contributions etc.).

Accounts for the branch agriculture usually therefore go a stage further by developing income indicators by deducting these items from NVA, although various combinations of deduction are possible and not all paid labour need necessarily be subtracted, giving rise to a range of indicators. When all three are deducted, the residual represents the reward to farmers and the other non-hired members of their workforce (in effect, their families) for their owned land, their owned capital, their physical labour and their managerial input. It is therefore a hybrid of rewards to each of the four economic factors of production (land, labour, capital, entrepreneurship) broken down along lines of ownership. In the EU terminology that was in place up to 1998 this residual was called *Net income from agricultural activity of unpaid labour*, an accurate but unpithy label, whereas the same concept in the UK nomenclature is termed *Total Income from Farming (TIFF)*.

An intermediate EU measure (*Net income from agriculture of total labour input*) deducted only interest and rent. This was supposed to represent the residual reward to all the labour in the industry although it was particularly difficult to interpret as it combined the rewards to hired labour with the mixture received by the self-employed households (Hill, 1991).

4.4.1 *Aggregate income indicators in the UK*

Five aggregate income indicators are currently published by the MAFF; Net Product (Net Value Added), Income from Agriculture of Total Labour Input, Total Income from Farming, Farming Income, and one (formerly two) cash-flow measure. The range was developed following discussion of a large number of possibilities put forward to stimulate discussion on the choice of appropriate measures for assessing trends in agricultural business incomes (Lund and Watson, 1981). The first has not usually received much attention since the main policy concern has been with incomes after the removal of expenses faced by farmers.

By far the longest established aggregate income indicator, and the one that has been given the greatest political attention, is Farming Income, although in the late 1990s emphasis has shifted to the Total Income from Farming (TIFF). Farming Income is the residue from NVA after deducting costs of interest on loans for farming purposes (but not those taken out explicitly for land purchase), agricultural rent payments and costs of labour. By convention, it is assumed that each farm has a single entrepreneurial household consisting of farmer and spouse (something that Chapter 5 will point out is increasingly challenged as unrealistic). Consequently, costs are imputed for the labour input of unpaid members of the family of farmers (it is assumed that no-one but family would work unpaid) and for other partners and directors; this treatment of unpaid labour is what distinguishes the concept of Farming Income from that of the Total Income from Farming. Farming Income was described by MAFF in the 1987 Annual Review White Paper as "The return to farmers and spouses for their labour, management skills and own capital invested after providing for depreciation" (HMSO, 1987).

Farming Income has undergone methodological modifications and in earlier guises was termed Net Farm Income; these changes have mainly taken the form of removing the initial convention of treating all land as if it were tenanted and charging a rent for all land, whether actually rented or owner-occupied (an acceptable simplification when land was predominantly tenanted, but not in the fourth quarter of the 20th Century when owner-occupation is dominant) and changing the accounting period to a calendar year rather than a harvest year (Outlaw and Croft, 1981). Bearing in mind that some discontinuity is involved (the new series is available from 1970), estimates of the aggregate income from farming in the UK are available from just before the Second World War.

4.4.2 Aggregate income indicators in the EU

Income indicators at European Union level have formed an integral part of the decision-making process for the CAP, of which the most notable in CAP history has been the fixing of support prices for farm products. Formerly an annual event at which the prices of all products covered by CAP regimes were set, from the mid-1980s onwards decisions have often taken place over a number of meetings of the Council of Ministers and have affected a run of years, particularly since the MacSharry reforms of 1992. There is no longer any pretence of automatically compensating the agricultural industry for any fall in income by raising prices according to some formula (the so-called "objective" income criterion). Nevertheless, there is a demand for background information on incomes that is both relevant to the objectives of the decisions and timely.

It would be possible to take measures of income direct from the absolute figures shown in the Economic Accounts for Agriculture that Eurostat publishes for each Member States and for the EU as a whole. However, difficulties encountered by some countries in providing data on a harmonised basis in time to inform the Commission when it was assembling its price proposals caused Eurostat to develop the so-called Sectoral Income Index (SII) to estimate the *changes* that have taken place in the income from agricultural production, with particular attention being paid to what has happened in the latest year. Changes rather than absolute income levels (which would imply comparisons between countries) seem to be the main area of interest of policymakers. As operated to 1998 this SII consisted of three indicators based on the EAA but that, for the most recent years, involved projections of various price and volume components using appropriate change indicators.

Results of the SII are presented in index form (with a recent three-year average set as 100), in real terms (that is, deflated) and expressed not as industry "global" figures (as in the UK) but on a "per caput" basis, that is, divided by the number of full-time labour equivalents (Annual Work Units - AWUs) estimated to contribute to the relevant economic aggregate (total labour input to agriculture, or input of labour from the farmer and family alone, see below). This is justified on the grounds that Article 39 of the Treaty of Rome refers explicitly to "increasing the *individual* earnings of persons engaged in agriculture" (Commission, 1982). Thus a movement in an indicator can come from a change in the NVA from agriculture, or a change in the volume of labour in the industry, or both. Though the reliability of the estimates of labour input has been questioned, particularly for some Member States (a new harmonised methodology for estimating labour input was published in 1997)(Eurostat, 1997a), it would seem that year-to-year changes in the Indicators are more likely to be explained by what is happening to aggregate incomes.

Three Indicators have formed the basis of the SII up to 1998 (Indicators 1, 2 and 3), defined as shown in Figure 4.4. The one that has attracted the most attention, was the longest established (in 1976) and felt to be the most reliable, was Indicator 1 (Net Value Added per Annual Work Unit - NVA/AWU). It must be born in mind, however, that a substantial portion of NVA does not stay as income for the farmer and his family but is paid off the farm for inputs, interest, hired labour and so on. NVA is therefore not a good proxy for changes in the income from farming.

In response to this criticism, from 1985 two additional indicators were published. Indicator 2 (*Net income from agricultural activity of total labour input* expressed per AWU of total labour) was found by deducting the paid costs of interest and rent from NVA. It was therefore the reward to the factor labour plus the capital and land owned by farmers and their families. When expressed as an average per AWU was thought to get nearer the residual incomes of the intended beneficiaries of the CAP, seen not just as farmers but embracing all the people engaged in agriculture. In the UK this was of dubious validity; the numerical importance of the hired work force in the UK and the different manner in which their earnings are determined makes any sort of averaging across all labour potentially misleading.

Indicator 3 went further by deducting the cost of hired labour to leave the reward to the farmer and his family for the factors of production they used in agriculture; as *Net income from agricultural activity of family labour input* it was divided by the amount of *family* labour input.

Results for each Indicator were available in preliminary form by the end of the calendar year to which they related, with revised figures being published in the following March (as Eurostat's annual Agricultural Income report, latterly termed *Income from Agricultural Activity*). They were in advance of the absolute figures published later for the EAA (at the end of the next calendar year). Any discrepancies between the changes in income predicted in the indicators and those that emerge from the absolute figures of the EAA were investigated and explanations sought. In practice, revisions tended to be predominantly in an upward direction, suggesting caution on the part of statisticians when producing their first estimates.

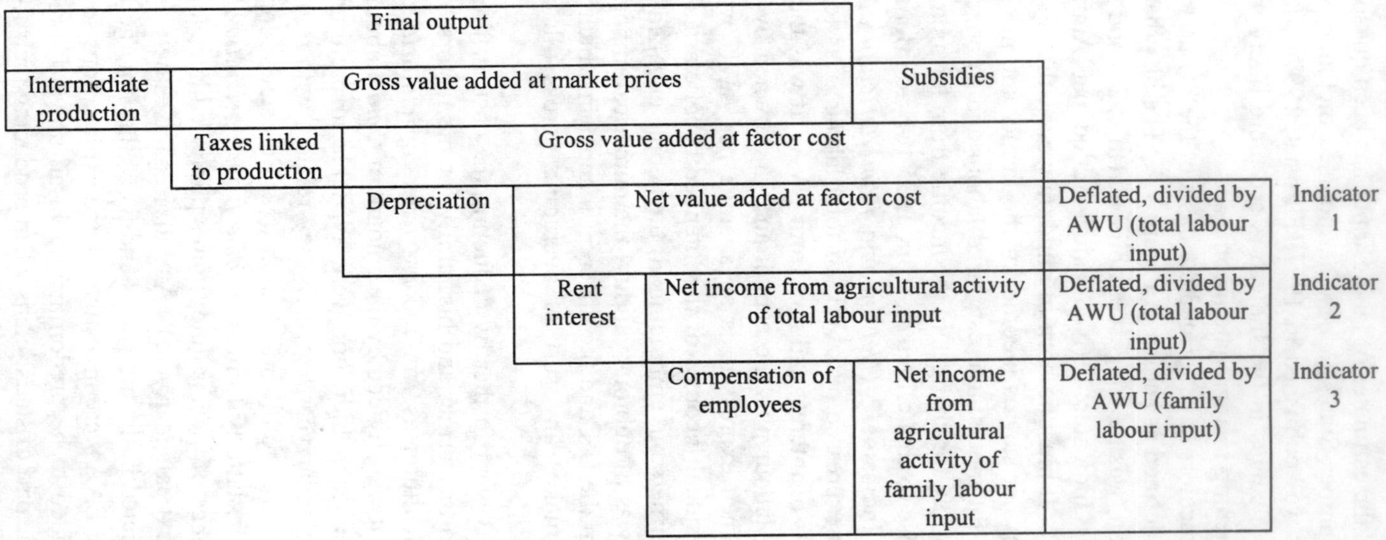

Final output					Indicator 1
	Gross value added at market prices				
		Gross value added at factor cost			
Intermediate production	Taxes linked to production	Depreciation	Net value added at factor cost	Deflated, divided by AWU (total labour input)	
	Subsidies				Indicator 2
			Net income from agricultural activity of total labour input	Deflated, divided by AWU (total labour input)	
		Rent interest	Compensation of employees	Net income from agricultural activity of family labour input	Deflated, divided by AWU (family labour input)
					Indicator 3

Figure 4.4 Derivation of Eurostat's Indicators of agricultural income

4.5 The new system (1999 onwards) for measuring the production activities of the agricultural industry

The methodology on which the EAA were built up to 1998, incorporating the concepts of the "pure" agriculture branch and the "national farm", described in 4.2 above, proved to be both practical, durable and accepted by users. A major factor contributing to its attractiveness to agricultural statisticians has been the relative ease with which much of the EAA, on both the output and input sides, could be built up without recourse to surveys of actual farm businesses. Such a method of calculation enabled an account to be constructed quickly, provisional NVA estimates being in hand at the end of the calendar year; timeliness of statistics is highly valued by policy-makers.

Nevertheless, the bases on which this version of the EAA rested have become increasingly unsatisfactory for the following reasons (after Eurostat, 1995).

- The use of the agriculture branch concept, comprising fictitious UHPs, was increasingly distanced from the reality of an industry comprised of production units that are engaged in a range of economic activities that are not all specified as agricultural on the NACE Rev.1 list.

- With the growth of non-agricultural activities, a practical consideration was that it became increasing difficult to identify and eliminate those elements of intermediate consumption and labour that did not relate to agricultural activity. To the extent that these could not be eliminated in pursuit of the pure branch approach, an overstatement resulted of inputs relative to outputs. This will have had an impact on the size of the residual reward from agricultural production and on the technical coefficients of performance (such as output per unit of labour input).

- The method for measuring output and intermediate consumption in the EAA, under the 'national farm' concept, introduced a further source of bias when calculating technical coefficients and value-added ratios and assessing their developments over time. For example, costs for items such as fertilizers or measures of labour input related to the total output of crop production, not only to the part which was sold outside the national farm.

Thus the use of the national farm concept precluded consistent comparisons of technical coefficients to be undertaken between agricultural sub-branches and between the agricultural branches of different Member States. It added a further complexity to the already intransigent problem of comparing the performance of agriculture and other branches of the economy; the accounts for agriculture have been on a different basis from those of other industries, requiring adjustments to enable them to be incorporated into national accounts.

An opportunity to confront these problems arose through the necessity of modifying the EAA to fall in line with the revision in the internationally-agreed methodology of national accounting, published as the United Nations' *System of National Accounts 1993* (SNA93)(UN, 1993) and, within the EU, as the (almost) fully compatible *European System of Accounts 1995* (ESA95)(Eurostat, 1996a). In 1997 Eurostat and the statistical authorities of Member States agreed on the changes that are necessary to make the EAA conform to the new framework. These have been incorporated in a revised EAA methodology (EAA97)(Eurostat, 1997b) which is to be implemented for EU agricultural aggregate accounting in 1999, initially for 1990 to 1997 but subsequently running back to 1973. There have been related changes to the industry classification system; the NACE Rev 1 is the new General Industrial Classification of Economic Activities and there is a CPA (Classification of Products by Activity) for use in input-output tables. Member States are expected to use the revised system for national purposes; in the case of the United Kingdom the new basis has been applied to national accounts generally in 1998, so UK-generated estimates relating to its agriculture are available one year before the EU system is underway. Equivalent changes in the system of accounting used in the USA are expected, though the timetable is not yet determined.

Readers only concerned with what has happened in the past, including the interpretation of the wealth of aggregate economic statistics that are already published, may not need to know how the EAA has adapted to the changing conditions surrounding them. However, for those who may be operating in the first decades of the 21st century, the next section considers the nature of the EAA to be applied from 1999 onwards.

4.5.1 Main features of the EAA97

First, a change of presentation has been made. In line with the SNA93/ESA95, the new EAA97 is split into series of three current transactions accounts (see Figure 4.5):

(a) The Production account, with its balancing item of Net Value Added;

(b) The Generation of Income account, with its balancing item of Operating Surplus (termed Mixed Income where unincorporated businesses are concerned because it includes the rewards both for self-employed labour and for capital (this term is used in the SNA93);

(c) The Entrepreneurial Income account, with its balancing item of Entrepreneurial Income (which is equivalent in the previous Eurostat methodology to Net Income from Agricultural Activity of Family Labour Input).

Production account	Generation of income account	Entrepreneurial Income account
Output *Minus* Intermediate consumption *Minus* consumption of fixed capital	Net Value Added *minus* compensation of employees *minus* other taxes on production *plus* other subsidies on production	Net Operating Surplus (Mixed Income) *minus* interest paid *minus* rent paid
= Net Value Added	= Net Operating Surplus (Mixed Income)	= Net Entrepreneurial Income

Source: (Eurostat, 1997b)

Figure 4.5 Revised Economic Accounts for Agriculture - Current transactions accounts

Within the conceptual framework of the EAA97 there is also a Capital account, not dealt with here because it cannot yet be compiled on a complete basis and because it attracts relatively little attention among policy decision-makers – a point taken up in Chapter 6.

For unincorporated farm businesses, the calculation of Entrepreneurial Income requires only deductions for interest payments and rents attributable to farming, though a separation of business expenses from non-production (consumption) payments may be difficult in practice, a problem that existed under the previous system. For farms arranged as companies, there are (in principle) deductions for all payments to their owners other than dividends. There is therefore a difference in the estimation of entrepreneurial income between that part relating to farms arranged as companies (corporations) and that part relating to unincorporated businesses (mainly sole proprietorships and partnerships); the composite estimate of entrepreneurial income excludes all rewards to labour and management in the former but includes those to self-employed (including family) labour in the latter.

Second, and more important than the change in presentation, are the revisions that concern substance. In addition to many adjustments to individual items (such as the timing of transactions, the calculation of own-account capital formation, and the inclusion of computer software as capital assets) there are some fundamental changes to the EAA with regards to the basic unit, the measurement of output, the method of valuation and to the calculation of capital consumption. These are described below.

4.5.2 *The basic unit under the revised system*

Under the revised EAA there is a change in the basic unit and hence in what constitutes the agricultural part of the economy (now termed the "industry"). While UHPs remain within the conceptual framework of national accounts, EAA97 follows the ESA95 in giving pre-eminence to a different concept - the Local Kind-of-Activity Unit (LKAU). Rather confusingly, the equivalent term to the LKAU in the SNA93 is the *establishment,* also adopted by the FAO in its *System of Economic Accounts for Food and Agriculture* (FAO, 1996) that is intended to be used primarily outside the OECD. The LKAU is itself a grouping, in a distinct unit, of production activities which predominantly (but not exclusively) fall into one class of the revised NACE, to which the LKAU is attributed.

The LKAU may include *secondary* activities belonging to other NACE classes if information if these cannot be separately identified from that on the main activity. These other activities may, and typically will, be connected with the main activity, but this need not be the case. Thus within the EU's EAA the output of the agriculture "industry" will in future come from two types of activity: (i) the agricultural activity of LKAUs, and (ii) the non-agricultural secondary activities of agricultural LKAUs, which cannot be separately identified (currently excluded from the "pure" branch that consists of UHPs).

This change broadens the coverage of activities in the agricultural "industry" compared with the present "pure" branch and might be welcomed on the grounds of greater reality. However, some caution is necessary. The first reason concerns the issue of what are and what are not separable activities. In many cases it will be possible to find on a single holding both an agricultural LKAU and a LKAU belonging to some other NACE Rev.1 category (or several LKAUs belonging to different categories). In distinguishing more than one LKAU on the same holding much depends in the new approach on the ability to separate in the data source the agricultural and the other activities, a somewhat loose criterion. As an additional condition, not stemming from the ESA95, Eurostat in consultation with Member States has stipulated that agricultural activity should *always* be separated from other activities when the agricultural activity would otherwise be a secondary activity (Eurostat, 1997b). Thus an asymmetric treatment is to be applied in which, while secondary non-agricultural activity can exist in an agricultural LKAU on grounds of inseparability, it is deemed that the reverse cannot occur. Furthermore, Eurostat and Member States have agreed *inter alia* that, within the EU's EAA, secondary activities should be covered only if they are of economic significance to a significant number of farms in specific Member States. These assumptions provide a degree continuity with the previous system in that all agricultural production is still covered in the EAA; none is "lost" to other industries as secondary activity, and what is regarded as a secondary activity is somewhat constrained.

Another ground for caution when considering the EAA97 is the decision, made largely for practical reasons, that agricultural LKAUs (and thus the agricultural "industry") should not include units whose sole purpose of production is for own-consumption and that fall below a certain size; this threshold is to be determined (as a default) by reference to the criterion for inclusion in each Member State's Farm Structure Survey

(FSS). In effect, this will exclude family gardens and allotments. While this simplification may be acceptable for current EU Member States, it is not necessarily appropriate in other countries where small units that produce exclusively for own consumption represent a significant proportion of aggregate food supply. It is unlikely therefore that this convention will be followed without some modification outside the EU (whose methodologies have often hitherto been taken as models) and it may even be inappropriate for use by some candidate countries where production from household plots may be substantial. It should be noted that, under the EAA methodology operated up to 1998 based on the "branch" concept for agriculture, output from gardens and allotments is included, so this change represents a small narrowing of coverage by the EAA97, though for the purpose of measuring agriculture's contribution to GDP in national accounts their output is currently excluded. Under the revised methodology of the ESA95 and EAA97, the exact reverse takes place; they are excluded from the "industry" of the EAA but are included in national accounts as agricultural LKAUs, no size threshold being applied in that context.

4.5.3 *Measuring output - replacing Final production with Total production*

The revisions to the EAA involve a change in the way in which the value of production is measured. Under the concept of the "national farm", only the value of *Final production* of agriculture was calculated, i.e. the value of the products that left the branch. Under the revised EAA97 an alternative measure of output, *Total agricultural production*, is to be used; this represents the total value of all agricultural products and includes production which is then used in a further agricultural process. The most important example of this is cereals and fodderplants used for animal feed.

When attempting to measure Total agricultural production there are theoretical issues to be faced and substantial practical difficulties in identifying and valuing intra-branch production. In the SNA93/ESA95 the general rule is that the output of an industry is to be measured as the sum of all the outputs of all the units of the industry (in the case of agriculture, all agricultural LKAUs), excluding the output used as intermediate consumption *within the same unit* (LKAU) and within the same accounting year. This means that sales of agricultural products direct between farms would be measured, but the use of agricultural materials produced on the same holding would be excluded.

However, in the methodology of the EAA97 this general rule is not followed. Rather, an approach to output is taken in which some of the intra-LKAU intermediate consumption is to be measured where this output *concerns two different basic activities* (the major example is products used for animal feed). The arguments for this departure from the strict conditions of the SNA93/ESA95 are that, *inter alia*;

- Production for intermediate consumption within the same LKAU is particularly significant in agriculture (even though it is far from unique to it);

- The LKAU could cover a very heterogeneous collection of different forms of production, though all agricultural;

- Adopting the SNA93/ESA95 rule would not adequately meet the aims for dropping the concept of the national farm, since much output is used within LKAUs rather than being sold between agricultural holdings;

- It would enable greater consistency with other statistics, such as those coming from the European Commission's Farm Accountancy Data Network (FADN).

While respecting the motives behind this aspect of the EAA97 methodology, there is an obvious danger that measuring intra-LKAU output and intermediate consumption could easily take on ridiculous proportions in processes that involve progressive stages, as are common in agriculture. Therefore the EAA97 specifies that in practice only the following items are to be covered: (a) animal feed products such as cereals, dried pulses, potatoes and oilseeds, and (b) some feed products which, though not normally marketed, are included "by convention" (hay, silage and other dried or preserved animal feeds), though in an early modification to the new methodology this has been extended to also include grazed fodder. In the UK feedstuffs where ownership moves outside agriculture but which is bought by other farms and used as intermediate consumption represented an addition to Final Output of some 5% in 1996, though this did not cover sales between farms or usage of own-produced materials (figures from MAFF).

4.5.4 *Valuation of output at basic prices*

The methodology of the EU's EAA used up to 1998 was based on valuing output at the "ex-farm" price. However under the SNA93/ESA95 all output, whether intended for sale, or stored for later sale or for any other use, is to be valued at its *basic price*. This rule is carried over into the EAA97.

The value of output at basic price is taken as;

> Value at producer price (price actually received by the producer, excluding invoiced VAT)
>
> *minus* Value of taxes on products (other than VAT)
>
> *plus* Value of subsidies on products

Thus, valuing output at basic prices requires the explicit treatment of taxes on products and subsidies on products; these represent the amounts due in respect of output for the year. This is in line with the general principle of the ESA95 that all recording should be on an accruals basis (amounts due rather than on the amounts actually received, which may be different in a particular period).

The main issue here is how subsidies are treated, and in particular what constitutes a "subsidy on a product" and what is an "other subsidy on production". After consideration of the aims of the various main forms of subsidy currently provided under the Common Agricultural Policy and the degree to which their payment is linked with the level of output, it has been decided, for example, that in the EAA97 both compensatory aid for arable crops and cattle premiums are to be classed as "subsidies on products" (and thus included within the value of output). In contrast, compulsory set-aside aid, not being linked to either production or products, is to be included within "other subsidies on production" (and thus not included within the value of output). Although this partition makes a difference to the calculation of value added at basic prices (the balancing item in the production account), it makes no difference to the calculation of Operating Surplus (or mixed income) or the Entrepreneurial Income of agriculture. This is because the "other subsidies on production" are included in the Generation of Income Account. Subsidies on investment in capital items are, of course, not included in these current accounts (though subsidies on interest are included as a current item).

4.5.5 Consumption of fixed capital

In the methodology used to 1998, the EAA stipulated that consumption of fixed capital must be calculated for all reproducible capital goods, with the exception of goods which have an indeterminate lifetime (such as roads and drainage) and "blocks of capital" such as orchards and herds of "capital account" livestock (EAA92, 122.2). Under the revised SNA93, there are no such exclusions; significantly, this implies that depreciation of breeding livestock is a form of capital consumption (SNA93, 6.185).

However, under the ESA95 a different view is taken, in which depreciation of breeding animals is to be specifically excluded (ESA95, 6.03). The EAA97, though conceding the theoretical need to cover such livestock (in line with the SNA93), followed the ESA95 line; while roads and plantations are now subject to consumption of fixed capital, this is not to be done for productive livestock (EAA97, 2.57.1 - 2.64.2). The case for exclusion on grounds of practicality and greater compatibility is not argued convincingly in the base documents (Eurostat, 1996a; Eurostat, 1997b). An asymmetry of treatment thus results; while own-account capital formation in breeding livestock is included in output, capital consumption is not deducted in reaching NVA. This implies that, within the EU, a bias will be introduced into the income results between Member States which reflects the extent to which their agricultural industries comprise production involving breeding livestock, detracting from the comparability that is supposed to be at the heart of the EU accounting system. On a wider scale, a disparity will open up between, on the one hand, the EU's EAA and, on the other, the general practice of countries that are intending to follow the SNA93 principles strictly. These include not only OECD countries that are outside the EU, hampering international comparisons, but also, on this issue, the UK in its accounts prepared for national purposes, risking confusion with the circulation of two sets of results.

Under pressure from several Member States, including the United Kingdom, in 1999 the EU committee responsible for the ESA reviewed its questionable decision on the treatment of capital consumption in the form of breeding livestock. Consequently, it is anticipated that a change will be made to include this item in national accounts for EU Member States at some stage. The methodology of the Economic Accounts for Agriculture can be expected eventually to fall in line, thereby removing this unfortunate disparity between the EU and the rest of the OECD. However, until this happens the figures published for the EU will suffer from this source of bias and will not be strictly comparable with those from elsewhere.

4.5.6 Changes to the indicators of "income" from agricultural production

A major function of the aggregate economic accounts for agriculture has been to form the basis of the calculation of a range of indicators of what can be loosely described as "income" from agricultural production. The three indicators currently in use within the EU were described above. It should be noted that all three are expressed per unit of labour input and thus will reflect both changes in the economic aggregates and in the volume of labour input to agricultural production. Taking account of movements in only one of the "fixed" factors is open to criticism on theoretical grounds (Hill, 1991) and, on practical ones, because of the less than satisfactory quality (at least in some countries) of the data on labour inputs

Of the three EU Indicators, Indicator 1 (based on NVA/AWU) is the longest-established (originating in 1976). A case can be made that the present Indicator 3 (introduced in 1985) is to be preferred as a proxy for the rewards remaining to farmers and their families for their productive activities in agriculture. However, a major difficulty is that, when attempting to calculate Indicator 3, the residual net income of *incorporated* businesses by definition does not have any units of non-hired ('family') labour input associated with it to include in the divisor. This asymmetry could be dismissed as not affecting the overall figures greatly when the output from incorporated businesses was an insignificant proportion of the total, but this simplifying assumption is no longer acceptable. Always questionable for the UK and the Netherlands (unless administrative adjustments were made to the status of directors), the problem has been brought to a head by the need to take into account the farming structure of the enlarged Germany, where the output from enterprises that are not close to the family farm model is significant. The prospect of accession to the EU by countries in Central and Eastern Europe has further underlined the necessity of a rethink.

Consequently, the EU has revised its indicators of income from agricultural production as part of the EAA97 methodology. Bearing in mind that the coverage of output and basis of valuation are both changed from the present system, and that other detailed alterations are taking place, the new indicators are as follows:

- *Indicator A Index of the real income of factors in agriculture per annual work unit.* This is calculated by taking the Net Value Added at basic prices that appears in the new Production account and adjusting it by adding "other subsidies on production" and deducting "other taxes on production", dividing by the labour input and expressing in deflated and index form.   Without these adjustments NVA (at basic prices) would be sensitive to the classification of subsidies as being "on products" or "other subsidies on production". Thus Indicator A is essentially the same as the present Indicator 1 and provides continuity with it, though the revised full name is a more accurate descriptor.

- *Indicator B Index of real net agricultural Entrepreneurial Income per unpaid annual work unit.* Entrepreneurial Income contains the same broad elements as the former "net income from agricultural activity of family labour input", though the label is now more appropriate. Hence Indicator B is essentially a continuation of the present Indicator 3, and will be retained for countries where agriculture is organised almost totally as unincorporated holdings.

- *Indicator C   Net Entrepreneurial Income of agriculture.* This aggregate is to be given in absolute terms, but may also be expressed in index form. The important point is that it is *not* calculated per unit of non-hired labour and so is suitable for uses involving countries where the output from corporate farms is an important part of the total.

Despite the revisions, it is clear that the approach embodied in each new Indicator remains essentially one of trying to gauge the rewards to a hybrid bundle of factors used in the production of agricultural commodities. The historic role given to the previous generation of production-based indicators is likely to secure a prominent position for the new versions that form part of the EAA97.

4.5.7　Comment on the changes

The changes to the methodology of the EAA, to operate from 1999, are a mix of welcome and less welcome features, and go beyond what would be required to provide conformity with the revised SNA93/ESA95. They involve replacing a concept (the "pure" agriculture branch) that was widely understood among statisticians - though perhaps less so among political decision-makers - by one of the "industry" that appears to be better at representing reality. Changing the basic unit to the Local Kind of Activity Unit (from the highly artificial Unit of Homogeneous Production) means that the coverage is no longer restricted solely to the production of a prescribed list of products deemed to be agricultural. However, the shift is only partial, since the LKAU is still narrower than the whole agricultural holding or business; in practice many farms will undertake forms of non-agricultural production that are integral to their existence as businesses but which are still excluded from the new approach. It must be recognised that the revised EAA approach does not enable the growth of diversification by farms that policy is attempting to encourage to be monitored.

This change to the basic unit of the EAA has also introduced an element of arbitrariness into the coverage, in that the account will now include non-agricultural production but only where this cannot be separated from agriculture in the data sources, a less than precise criterion. The previous system was clear on what activities should have been covered in the agriculture "pure" branch, even if making the calculations were often less than straightforward. Moreover, the stipulation in the EAA97 (going beyond the requirements of the ESA95) that agricultural production must not be permitted to form the secondary activity of a LKAU that belongs to some other industry, apparently to preserve a high degree of consistency with the previous "branch" approach, introduces an asymmetry in the coverage, even if it is not likely to be of great quantitative importance. The advantage of prescribing only minimal changes from the existing way in which the EAA figures are calculated, though avoiding discontinuities in statistics that upset policy-makers, may conflict with reality if farming (often only of an ancillary variety) is indeed the minor activity of a fully integrated business.

In short, the changes only very marginally widen the focus of the aggregate accounts beyond their traditional concern solely with the economics of and residual rewards from agricultural production. While the new system tackles some old problems with the EAA, it reveals some previously hidden ones and introduces some intractable new ones, with possibly an increased danger of misinterpretation.

4.6   Patterns in aggregate economic accounts for the agriculture branch

Though space has been given to considering the new methodology of the EAA, in reality long series on the new basis have yet to be calculated and published for the EU and its Member States. Consequently, the description of the development of aggregate incomes from agricultural production is better confined to the patterns seen in the old methodology that was operational up to 1998.

4.6.1 Historical development of the Farming Income indicator in the UK

Figures taken from the annual official publication *Agriculture in the United* Kingdom, its predecessor, the *Annual Review of Agriculture* White Paper, and MAFF's *Departmental Net Income Calculation – Historical Series 1937/38 to 1974/75* can readily demonstrate the major changes experienced by UK agriculture in the post-war period. In the following analysis monetary values have been taken after allowing for inflation (using the GDP implicit deflator). Some stitching together of series based in different years has been resorted to in order to create a time series extending over forty-five years, and during this period there have been some methodological changes which cause wrinkles in the indicators. In particular this applies to incomes before and after 1970. Nevertheless, broad patterns are revealed that are not sensitive to such statistical refinements.

The value of UK farm Gross Output: Gross Output is the aggregate value of agriculture including that output which is used within farms as inputs (for example, cereals retained on farms to feed animals or as seed) or sold between them without using an intermediary merchant (in other words, it never leaves the "national farm"). Gross Output therefore represents the physical activity that is generated from the resources in agriculture in a rather more complete way than does Final Output, which is calculated after deducting this intermediate output. However, the difference between the two should not be overstated; in 1993 the difference was only 3 per cent.

As long as an equivalent adjustment is made to inputs (in the UK terminology Gross Input being greater than Net Input by this same amount) the calculation of Net Value Added (Net Product) is unaffected.

When calculated using the prices of a single year, Gross Output can be taken as an indicator of the volume of output. From Figure 4.6 it can be seen that the *volume* of output from the UK agriculture showed a markedly consistent rise over the post-war period up to the mid-1980s, with the output at the end of this period being almost double that of the early 1950s.

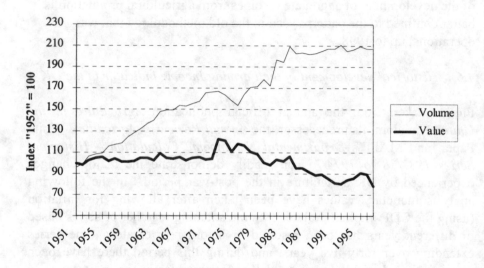

Figure 4.6 UK: Gross Output of agriculture: volume and real value, 1951-97

Output in the mid 1970s was below the longer-term trend, largely as the result of dry weather conditions; after that, the annual rise in output volume was, if anything, slightly faster until 1985, when a plateau seems to have been reached. However, the *value* of this output in real terms has not kept pace. Gross Output value was about the same in 1986 as it had been in 1952; this implies that the prices which were received by farmers for their produce fell between these years at about the same rate as physical output expanded. That is, the real prices received by farmers approximately halved over the period. The pattern is not uniform. Up to 1971 there was a slightly rising trend in the value of the industry's output; the early 1970s saw a substantial jump through increased prices (physical output hardly changed) brought about by a combination of UK entry to the European Economic Community, with the adoption of the CAP's higher market prices, and an international boom in the prices of primary commodities which had an impact on the domestic prices received by farmers.

Since the peak in 1973 the value of agricultural output has been in sustained decline, though with short periods above the trend; figures for 1998 are expected to show a further fall. This has happened despite a substantial displacement of imported food supply, with a consequential rise in the level of self-sufficiency, most notably since the later 1970s. The decline in output value is also despite the action of the CAP in supporting product prices. Without this support the prices of the given levels of production would have been lower, but it is difficult to assess the implication for the value of output because of the reduced physical production that lower prices would have called forth from farmers.

This contrast between movements in physical and value of output indicators should come as no surprise to anyone familiar with the basic demand characteristics of food in industrialised countries, as has already been outlined in Chapter 2. The particular circumstances of the UK represent only minor diversions from the generality.

Items leading from Gross Output to Farming Income Figures 4.7 and 4.8 show the aggregate economic account for the branch agriculture in graph form for the period from 1937 to 1997 (when the basis of the calculation shifted to new methodology). All items are expressed in real terms, that is after having been deflated, in this case using the implicit GDP deflator. The total height of the stacked lines in Figure 4.7 corresponds to Gross Output. As noted above, this rose substantially in the post-war period, steadied in the 1960s and, after peaking in 1973, has been in sharp decline, though with some reversal in 1993 to 1996, associated with the higher prices that UK farmers have received as a by-product of the decision that Sterling should leave the EU Exchange Rate Mechanism in September 1992 and a short-lived surge in commodity prices on international markets. Farming Income corresponds to the margin between the accumulated costs

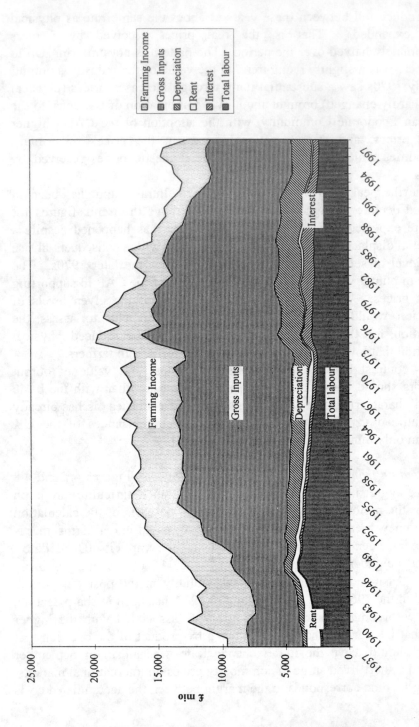

Figure 4.7 UK: Components of Gross Output in real terms, 1937-97, stacked presentation

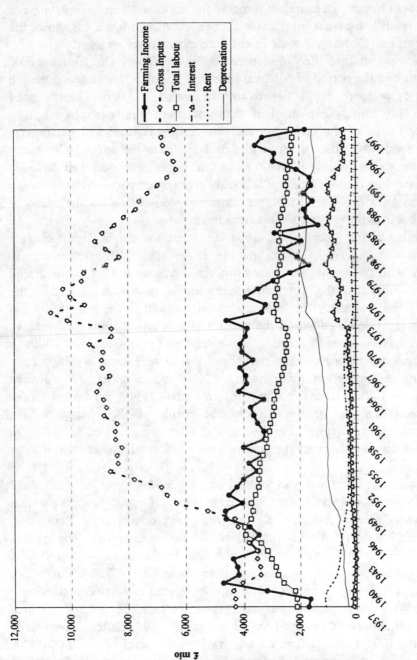

Figure 4.8 UK: Components of Gross Output in real terms, 1937-97, non-stacked presentation

and Gross Output. Because movements in individual components are not always readily apparent from a stacked presentation, Figure 4.8 shows the cost items and Farming Income in absolute terms in non-stacked form

It is evident that the large increase in the Gross Output from UK agriculture in the period of post-war recovery up to 1955 was accompanied by an even more rapid growth in the value of Gross Inputs used (presumably largely explained in terms of more inputs purchased from other branches of the economy, such as fertilisers, fuel and machinery, animal feeds and others). From the mid-1950s to the early 1970s these inputs increased broadly in line with output but a jump occurred in 1972-73. Since then the value of inputs bought from other parts of the economy has been on a declining trend, not as rapidly downward as the value of output but also mirroring its short-term deviations.

In terms of the other inputs, *labour costs* are the single largest charge; as shown in Figure 4.8 these include an estimated charge for family workers who do not have a contract of employment and for partners and directors other than the principal farmer (but not his spouse) based on the pay of hired workers. The total labour bill peaked in the late 1940s and were on a falling trend until the early 1970s when a temporary plateau seems to have been reached. However, in the 1980s and 1990s a continuing downward trend in the labour bill in real terms was apparent. *Interest charges* were a minor claim on Net Product up to 1970 but then rose, although they have fallen in real terms since 1990. *Rent costs* appear to have fallen, but this is largely the result of the change in the methodology which resulted in the national farm being treated according to its actual tenure rather than the previous convention which assumed it to be all tenanted.

Notwithstanding the fall in the real costs faced by agriculture since the early 1970s, the even faster decline in Gross Output has meant that aggregate *Farming Income*, the reward to producers for their own resources, has declined substantially over the post-war period. The level in 1970 was little different from its real value in the late 1940s and early 1950s, though over the two decades there was first a small downward movement followed by one of a similar rise. The unusual circumstances of 1973 saw a peak in income, but from then on a rapid decline set in which was only temporarily reversed by the events of 1992. After a short-lived boom, by 1997 Farming Income was back to the level of the late 1980s. Estimates for 1998 suggest a further fall of 46% from the year before, to an income in real terms smaller even than in 1937/38. However it must be borne in mind that changes have also taken place in the numbers of farms, farmers and farm households over this period which will have had an impact on the average income per unit, something that the EU Indicators, reported below, do allow for.

This decline is also reflected in the proportion of the value of output that remains to farmers as income. Figure 4.9 shows that, once the cost of purchased inputs and depreciation are deducted and all the claims of the non-farmer owners of land, labour and capital met, the residual Farming Income has since 1940 formed a declining share of the value of agriculture's Gross Output. Discounting the unusual conditions immediately before and during the War years, in the early 1950s almost 30 per cent of the value of output remained as Farming Income, but by the 1980s this had fallen to only about 10 - 15 per cent. Though the short-lived conditions of 1993-6 took it somewhat higher, by 1997 it was back within this range. A large part of this change has come about through a tendency to purchase more inputs from other industries, either to substitute for inputs from farm origins (fuel for tractors in place of horses bred and fed within agriculture) or as an addition to them. This is reflected in the persistent decline in Net Product (NVA) as a percentage of Gross Output, from over 50 per cent in the early 1950s to about 40 per cent in the 1980s. However, there was a large jump in the share of output retained as income in 1993 and 1994, again the result of the decision to leave the ERM and unusual world market conditions, and therefore unlikely to persist.

4.6.2 Eurostat's Indicators for the EU and UK

Eurostat's Indicators 1, 2 and 3 were defined above. The one to which reference is most frequently made in EU policy documents, such as the influential annual *Agricultural Situation in the Community* report, is Indicator 1 (NVA per AWU). In real terms its level for the EUR 15 as a whole over the 1980s and 1990s has shown a small upward trend; the annual increase between 1980-82 and 1990-92 was 1.4 per cent, increasing to 2.6 per cent between 1990-92 and 1996-98 (Eurostat, 1995a, 1999). There have been periods in which Indicator 1 has been almost static (1983 to 1988 and 1990 to 1993). Only in the three years immediately following the implementation of the 1992 MacSharry reforms was there any consistent rise. However, this picture of overall stability masks some quite diverse movements among individual Member States; some experienced substantial rises (Greece, Spain, France, Ireland, Luxembourg, Austria,

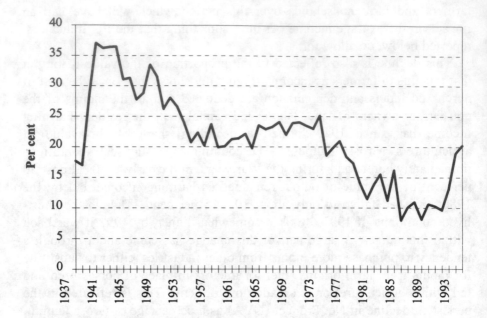

Figure 4.9 UK: Percentage of Gross Output remaining as Farming Income, 1937-97

Finland), Sweden suffered a fall, and others approximately maintained their long-term positions. Though half the Member States have seen peaks in Indicator 1 in the mid-1990s followed by declines, the sharpness of this movement has been most noticeable in the UK.

It must be borne in mind that Indicator 1 does not tell anything about the personal incomes of farmers in these countries, either in respect of movements or of levels, as it relates solely to agricultural production and ignores all other sources of income. It is even far from the concept of profit that farm operators would consider as coming from their agricultural activities since it is calculated before any of the costs associated with the "fixed" factors are deducted (rent, interest, wages of hired labour). Nevertheless, the Commission has seemed intent on promoting confusion by using Indicator 1 in contexts that imply that is *does* give a picture of farmers' personal incomes. For example, in its review of twenty years of European agriculture in the 1987 edition of *The Agricultural Situation in the Community,* the growth of agricultural incomes was shown in relation to those in the general economy using Net Value Added per Annual Work Unit as the agricultural parameter and Net Domestic Product per person employed as the general parameter (both at factor cost and in real (deflated) terms). The comment was offered by the Commission author that, while in the period 1965-75 the position of agriculture had improved more rapidly than in general, agricultural incomes had remained relatively stable since 1974. The income position of agriculture relative to the general economy was seen as having been favourable until 1979, but the situation subsequently changed considerably. From these statements the reader was led into making assumptions about the personal income position of farmers and non-farmers. This is not what the indicators are capable of showing. Still less do they reveal the household and disposable incomes of the groups. While the evidence on factor-rewards is of interest, its use in an income context is misleading and likely to lead to a misapprehensio of the personal income positions of the agricultural population in the EU. While a later, more detailed, analysis of the long-term trends in the income from agricultural production and their causes (Terluin, 1991) acknowledged the presence of other income received by people working in agriculture, it nevertheless again placed great emphasis on comparing the level of (gross) value added per work unit in agriculture with that achieved in the rest of the economy. There is a clear inference that, with reservations, this factor-reward ratio can be taken as a proxy for the relative income of the people engaged in agriculture.

A stronger case could be made for Indicator 3 being used to show what has been happening to the aggregate incomes that producers derive from agricultural production. Patterns for the EU and Member States are shown in Figure 4.10. Regrettably, the enlargement of Germany in 1990 to include the Länder of the former German Democratic Republic has presented statistical difficulties (in relation to family and non-family labour) so that the EUR 12 series for Indicator 3, which started only in 1980 when figures for Portugal were first available, terminates in 1992. Over this period there was no obvious income trend at EUR 12 level. However, since 1973 some individual countries have seen remarkable improvements (Greece, Spain, Ireland), some falls (Italy until about 1990), Denmark and (to a lesser extent) Portugal have witnessed great variation, and the UK saw a sustained decline followed after 1992 by a strong recovery and then another collapse.

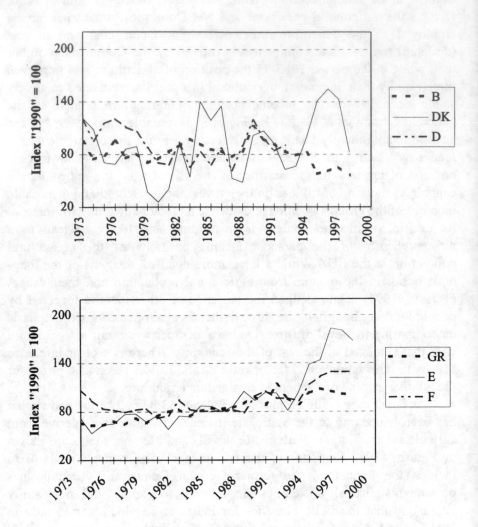

Figure 4.10   Eurostat's Income Indicator 3 (Net income from agricultural activity per unit of family labour input) by Member State. Index "1990" = 100

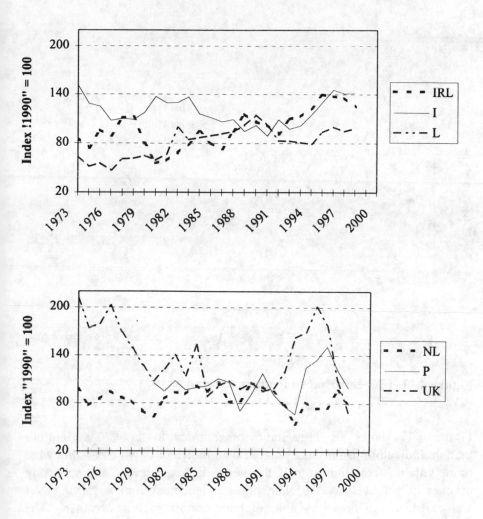

Figure 4.10 ctd

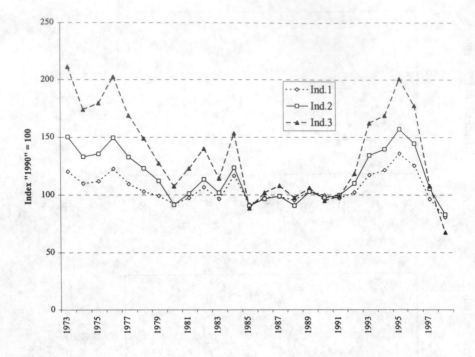

Figure 4.11 UK: Eurostat Indicators 1, 2 and 3, 1973-98

Figure 4.11 shows all three Indicators applied to the UK agriculture branch. Indicator 3 is far more volatile than Indicator 2, which is somewhat more volatile than Indicator 1, as would be expected if an increasing number of relatively stable elements are deducted from a varying Net Value Added influenced by unpredictable factors such as weather. The similarity between the movement in Indicator 3 for the UK and the Farming Income pattern in UK national accounts (Figure 4.8 above) is also hardly surprising; apart from being expressed per family labour unit, numbers of which have not altered to the extent seen in most other countries, the income definition is closely similar. (By 1998 the volume of family labour input in the UK had fallen to 74 per cent of its 1973 level. Elsewhere the fall had generally been greater. In Denmark and Luxembourg the family labour input had contracted to only one third. In Italy, the Member State with the largest volume of family labour (over a fifth of the EUR 15 total in 1998), it had shrunk by almost exactly half. Only in Greece, Ireland and the Netherlands were the 1998 inputs much more than 50 per cent of the 1973 level.)

4.6.3 Branch indicators in the United States of America

The OECD now collects and publishes sets of aggregate economic accounts for agriculture for its Member countries using, as a template, the methodology of the EU's EAA (OECD, 1992). Though the accounts are presented in such a way that Net Value Added could be used as an indicator of income, in practice the main income measure is Net Income from Farming, conceptually the same as the EU's Net Income from Agricultural Activity of Family Labour the UK's Total Income from Farming (TIFF). Figures are given in aggregate, not per unit of labour input or per farm. A review of patterns of the income from agricultural production shown in OECD statistics for all countries is beyond the scope of this book, though attention on what has happened historically in the USA is of special interest.

In the US the development of farm income estimates originated before the First World War, with figures derived from the 1910 Census of Agriculture being published in 1913. Accounts for agricultural production are drawn up by the Economic Research Service of the US Department of Agriculture, and elements from this are taken as the agricultural component in the National Income and Production Account, produced by the Bureau of Economic Analysis (BEA). The US agricultural accounts use the same concept of the national farm as did the UK and EU to 1998, though terminology is not the same; as in Europe, non-agricultural production undertaken on farms is excluded (with some minor exceptions). Currently the US has four indicators of aggregate agricultural income - Net Farm Income, Net Cash Income (with a related net cash flow), Net Business Income, and Production Transactions (Johnson, 1990). Some of these are also available on a state basis. In addition there are indicators of the incomes of agricultural households; these will be covered in Chapter 5. The main definitional differences among the US series concern whether or not the income and expenses associated with the farm dwellings occupied by farmer households are included, whether or not non-cash items such as depreciation and changes in inventory values are included, and who receives the net income (USDA, 1988). Net Farm Income (NFI) is the oldest and most widely recognised of the USDA income series.

Conceptually it is close to the Total Income From Farming of the UK. It differs in that *inter alia* the US concept includes an imputed rental value for the farm dwelling and deducts interest on land purchase loans. In the US the Production Transaction series ignores the imputed rental value of and the expenses associated with dwellings and provides a closer though less long-running parallel. Net Cash Income and Production Transactions were added as series as recently as 1980 in response to realisation that the established NFI did not reflect satisfactorily the changing economic situation of farming in the 1970s. Net Business Income came later - in 1985. All these new indicators have been estimated back to 1940.

Comparison with developments in the UK has been facilitated by a USDA decision to present its aggregate production accounts in a form compatible with that used by the OECD (which is the EU system), and to publish a long series on this basis, with Net Farm Income as the final line in the account.   Figure 4.12 shows the value of US final agricultural output and NFI, both after allowing for inflation, extending for well over a half-century; undeflated figures are available from 1910 but the index used for deflation (implicit GDP deflator) only goes back to 1929. Output value rose rapidly during and immediately after the Second World War and maintained a similar level up to about 1970, trending slightly upwards in the 1960s. Net Farm Income also jumped in the 1940s but from the early 1950s declined gradually as the rise in output was matched by increasing costs.   A sudden spurt in the value of output in the early 1970s was reflected in a peak of income followed by a subsequent fall until a plateau seemed to be established in the mid-1980s.

There is a clear similarity between the US income pattern and that noted above for the UK, with again the changes in output value explaining the short-term movements. Both saw a surge in prosperity during and immediately after the Second World War, though the decline to the 1960s was more marked in the US. The same peak in 1973 can be seen and also the subsequent steep decline accompanied by greater income instability, but the UK's boom period of the mid-1990s was not experienced in the US, hardly surprising given the pivotal part played by Sterling in the UK's situation. As in the UK, the residue remaining to agricultural producers from the value of their output has fallen steadily; Figure 4.13 shows that in the 1940s about half remained as Net Farm Income (in the UK it was nearer 40 per cent) but this shrank in the 1980s to well below 20 per cent (similar to the UK situation) before recovering to the low 20s in the 1990s.

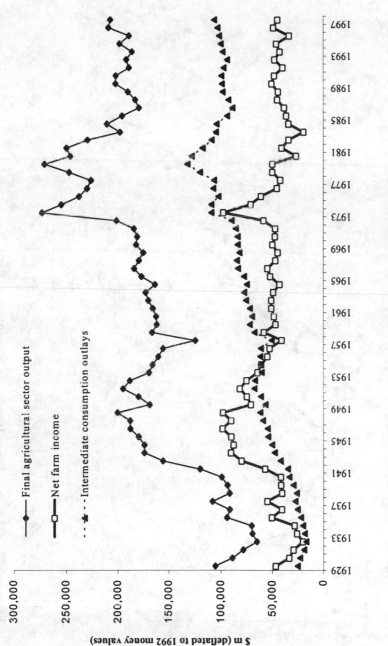

Figure 4.12   USA: Agricultural sector final output, intermediate consumption and Net Farm Income, 1929-98

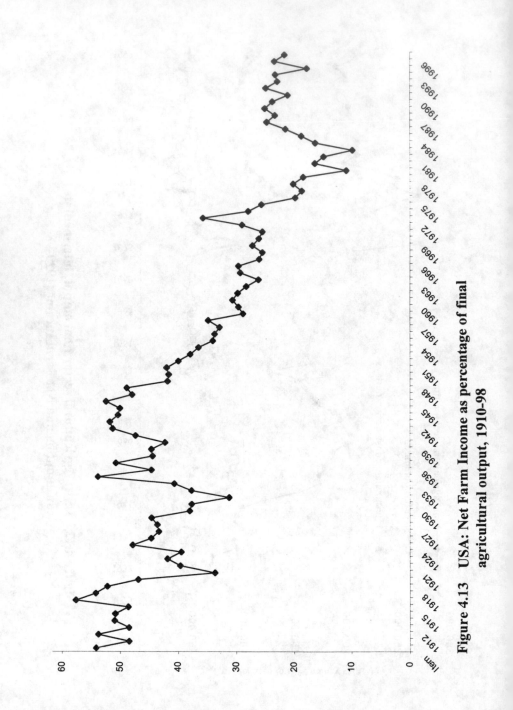

Figure 4.13   USA: Net Farm Income as percentage of final agricultural output, 1910–98

4.7 Official microeconomic information on the incomes from agricultural production - farm accounts surveys

Agriculture in all industrialised countries with capitalist market economic systems consists predominantly of small-scale producers. There may be certain commodities in which large units are responsible for the bulk of output and a few where economies of scale are evident and industrial-scale production, under public companies, has taken over from the traditional family farm. However, overwhelmingly farms are businesses which in terms of labour force, turnover, profits or even working capital (though not total capital if land is included) are small in comparison with other industries, except retail trade. This atomistic structure carries economic implications, as a myriad uncoordinated decision takers will be unable to influence the markets for their inputs or products - they will be forced into the role of price-taker in both markets - and will tend to suffer price cycles. The treadmill of technical advance will ensure that new profit-enhancing (or risk-reducing) innovations will be taken up, even if this expands output and pushes down product prices so that the pressure on the marginal farmer is exacerbated.

Yet within this atomistic structure there are wide variations in size and type of farming, management ability, regional conditions, business form and asset array. These force the commentator on agricultural policy to call attention to the diversity of incomes and to the distributional effects of any change in the industry, whether this be brought about by active intervention by governments or by events outside their remit, such as weather. This calls for a bank of data relating to individual farms and farmers. Such microeconomic data can form a rich resource for analysis; flexibility is a general characteristic and groups are usually capable of reclassification as the process of investigation proceeds and new questions are thrown up. Microeconomic data banks are, however, expensive to assemble and often suffer from delays between when policy questions are asked and when the data necessary to answer them are available.

The main form in which such microeconomic data are collected is from surveys of farm businesses. Official farm accounts surveys take place not only in all member states of the EU but in all non-EU European countries, North America and Australasia. Within the EU the coverage and conventions vary a good deal. However, a shared characteristic is that many confine themselves to data relating solely farming activities. Among the EUR 15, in only seven countries (Denmark, Germany, the Netherlands,

Austria, Finland, Sweden and the United Kingdom) does the official national farm accounts survey regularly collect data on income from non-farm sources. At EU level the Farm Accountancy Data Network (FADN, also known as RICA) builds on and draws from national surveys, but this too is only concerned with data on farming activity on the holding; attempts to add questions of a broader nature have met with resistance in some countries (especially France) where this is not established national practice. Nevertheless the importance of official farm accounts surveys for informing policy makes it necessary to examine what income information is available from them and what are the major patterns that emerge.

4.7.1 The United Kingdom's Farm Business Survey

We start with the UK's national farm accounts survey because it predated and in part set a model for the Community's data network. The official annual survey of farm businesses in England and Wales, called from its establishment in 1936 the Farm Management Survey, was re-titled the Farm Business Survey in 1986, its fiftieth anniversary. Parallel surveys, slightly predating the England and Wales FMS, are carried out in Scotland (Farm Accounts Survey) and Northern Ireland. Although the surveys are conducted independently in the four countries of the UK, there is a large amount of co-ordination and the methodologies are similar (Barnett, 1987). MAFF assembles data into a set for the UK as a whole. For practical purposes the surveys can be considered as parts of a single large survey consisting of some 3,900 cases (MAFF, 1994). Associated with the major survey are special periodic studies relating to particular farm enterprises or aspects of farming, such as the very small farm, agricultural contracting, or the economics of egg production. Since 1986 FBS results have been published in an official annual income report covering macro and micro estimates for the UK, but previously in separate volumes for the constituent countries.

It is worth noting the way in which this official source of information is organised and financed. In Great Britain data collection is not undertaken by the civil service but by universities and colleges as contractors for the relevant agricultural departments (MAFF for England, the Scottish Office Agriculture and Fisheries Department (from 1999 the Scottish Executive Rural Affairs Department) and the Welsh Office Agriculture Department (from 1999 the National Assembly for Wales Agriculture Department). This arrangement is in large part a product of the historical development of agricultural economics in the UK (Whetham 1981, Colman 1987). However it is also a legal convenience; under British legislation MAFF is empowered to collect physical but not financial details through official censuses and sample surveys, to which occupiers must respond. But a study of the business performance of farms inevitably involves both sorts of data. The legal prohibition is neatly circumvented by the use of the academic institutions as agents who then pass the data to government departments in an anonymous block. Thus it is impossible for any financial results for any holding to be identified by MAFF but the information which it contains can be used for policy purposes.

The universities and colleges (eight in England, one in Wales and the three sections of the Scottish Agricultural College) have autonomy on operational procedures, within the bounds required by the need for consistency (Sturgess, 1984), and in addition to passing data to MAFF, can analyse and publish reports on the farm businesses in their provinces.

According to the preface of the first FMS report, covering 1936 and 1937, the Survey was intended:

(a) To be of service to agriculture and to the State in the framing of public policy in regard to the industry,

(b) To supplement official statistics by collecting information annually of the capital, equipment and labour employed, purchases of requisites and sale of produce,

(c) To ensure that an adequate picture will be secured of the economic conditions of farming, of changes in output, costs, organisation and equipment,

(d) To enable co-operating farmers and others to increase their efficiency and to organise their farms on a more profitable basis,

(e) To supply the means for local and national research into the main economic problems of the industry.

Early in the life of the FMS four main objectives emerged, based on the above. Through the detailed monitoring of events the FMS was to assist in:

- The framing of national policy
- Improving efficiency of individual farms

- The conduct of local and national research

- Teaching (a later addition perhaps implicit at the outset)

These aims have been repeatedly affirmed by internal reviews, with the amplification that the Survey should be capable, as far as it is possible, of providing the data bank from which answers to the policy questions of tomorrow can be based.

Notwithstanding these aims and objectives, the FBS has been fundamentally a study of farm businesses and the business income they generate, *not* one which attempted an assessment of the incomes of farmers and their families. This is because it is designed primarily to "monitor year-to-year changes in incomes of farm businesses classified by type and size." "The emphasis throughout is on a comparison of results for the latest accounting year with that of an identical sample for the preceding year" (Sturgess, 1984). Hence, it has not been able to cast much light on the central issue of the incomes of the agricultural population. Up to 1988/89 no questions were asked on the income which the farm households received from off-farm sources, despite the influence that such income may have on the management or investment behaviour of the farm.

The concern of the FBS with monitoring the income from the *activity of farming* rather than the income of *farmers as people* is reflected in the nature of the sample and, most important, in the income indicators used. The sample represents not all farms, but only those estimated being capable of providing full-time employment for one man. Below this size many farms will have additional sources of income, but also many will not. In 1975 an official sample survey in England and Wales found that nearly half the occupiers below the threshold (then defined in terms of standard man days, 275 constituting a full-time farm size) claimed that they worked on their farms for not less than 40 hours per week and for not less than 47 weeks per year (MAFF, 1977). Another official survey of 1983, enquiring into the numbers of farmers (and spouses) with additional sources of earned income, found that about 60 per cent of farm occupiers below the FBS threshold did *not* have another gainful activity, and three-quarters of spouses did not (Eurostat, 1986c). Income from investments or pensions must help explain how the occupiers of these very small farms get a livelihood.

The income concept that has been used since the outset of the FBS as its main indicator of year-on-year change in farming conditions is Net Farm Income. In view of the attention given to the results by politicians, administrators and the media, it is worth mentioning the conventions adopted in its calculation. The main elements in Net Farm Income are:

Net Value Added (the value of sales less purchases from other firms, adjusted for own-consumption of farm produce, changes in the stocks of products and inputs, and after depreciation)
less
Rent (including an imputed rental value for land which is owner-occupied)
less
Labour costs (including an imputed figure for any unpaid family labour)
equals
Net Farm Income

The calculation of this indicator assumes, therefore, that all farms are tenanted and that all tenant-type assets are owned by the farmer (that is, there is no borrowing to finance them). In reality, owner-occupiers will not face an actual rent charge. On the other hand, both they and tenant farmers may be borrowers and have to make interest payments. Of course, any income from other sources is ignored. NFI is officially is described as "the return to the principal farmer and spouse for their manual and managerial labour and on tenant-type capital of the business" (HMSO, 1994). The conventions on tenure and interest were initially adopted in order to allow rented and owned farms, and indebted and non-indebted farms, to be grouped together on a comparable basis. For the narrow purpose of indicating short-term changes in profitability, NFI may be a workable concept. But it is patently inappropriate for indicating the level of personal income which operators receive, even that part which comes from their farm business.

Additional indicators were introduced into the 1987 FBS report - termed Occupier's Net Income and Farmers' Flow of Funds (a cash flow measure). In essence, Occupier's Income is calculated in a similar way to Net Farm Income, except that notional rental values are not deducted for owned land. Interest on farming loans is subtracted (net of any interest receipts) but those specifically for land purchase are not. The flow of funds indicator covers, in addition to the farm's cash flow from the current account, expenditure (net of sales) on fixed capital, changes in net borrowing, and resources introduced by the farmer and spouse from outside the farm business. The total flow of funds figure "represents the total funds ... which are available to the owners of the farm business for consumption purposes, off-farm investment, tax and national insurance payments, private insurance premiums, the reward of other unpaid labour... and any other private payments" (HMSO, 1987). However, this is not the full picture of the income situation of the farmer as this list might suggest because, although some funds which farmers and their spouses have from non-farming sources may be reflected in the flow estimates where they are used to finance investments on the farm, there could well be additional consumption and saving that totally escapes the partial net of the FBS. Currently a range of four income estimates are published; Net Farm Income, Occupier's Net Income, Cash Income and Cash Flow from Farming Business (MAFF, 1994).

4.7.2 *Farm Accountancy Data Network (FADN or RICA)*

At European Union level the farm accounts surveys of all the Member States are brought together under the co-ordination of the agricultural Directorate-General of the Commission (DGVI) as the Farm Accountancy Data Network (FADN), also known by its French acronym RICA. This was established in 1965 "with the specific objective of obtaining data enabling income changes in the various classes of agricultural holding to be properly monitored" (Commission, 1982). The justification for FADN was rooted in policy, in that "...the development of the Common Agricultural Policy requires that there should be available objective and relevant information on incomes in the various categories of agricultural holdings and on the business operation of holdings coming within categories which call for special attention at Community level"(EEC Regulation 79/65). FADN is therefore not a single survey but is an amalgamation of national surveys carried out by Member States. In some countries these predated RICA, as in the UK, but in others they were started from scratch. The nature of FADN is in part a reflection of the approaches inherited from these pre-existing surveys. Ways of collecting the data vary from country to country, but there is a fundamental harmonised methodology which applies to the concepts of income employed and, increasingly, to the selection of the sample (Commission, 1989).

Selection of the FADN sample was originally limited to holdings on which the day-to-day management was in the hands of a single farmer or manager, which had a labour input equivalent to at least one Annual Work

Unit (with some national exceptions) and whose main activity was agricultural production for sale (Commission, 1985a). The sample was therefore intended to consist of commercially-operated farms where the holding contributed the main source of living; this implies a discrimination against part-time farmers in the sample, but this was justified by the belief that "main-living" farms constituted the most important target for agricultural policy measures, an interpretation which should not go unnoticed. However there seems to have been a revision of this thinking, and from 1982/3 selection thresholds have been made only in terms of size in Economic Size Units (which are based on Standard Gross Margin).

There is a minimum size threshold that varies between Member States, reflecting their different farm size structures as shown in the periodic EU Farm Structure Survey. In particular, Belgium and the Netherlands have imposed size thresholds that exclude many holdings that would be eligible for inclusion in FADN in the other Member States.

Consequently, while the overwhelming majority of farming activity falls within the FADN field of observation, only about half the Community's agricultural holdings are represented. In 1988 FADN's field of observation covered 95 per cent of all Standard Gross Margin (EUR 10) but only 56 per cent of holdings (and therefore of holders) which appeared in the Community's Farm Structure Survey. Though numerically important, holdings below the threshold contribute very little in terms of agricultural activity. In Italy and Greece, where the official percentages of holdings covered were 54 per cent and 53 per cent respectively, it is thought that the coverage of holders is even lower, because some are so small that they fall below the size for qualification for inclusion in the Structure Survey (Hill and Brookes, 1993).

Altogether the FADN sample consists of about 60,000 holdings (EUR 15), corresponding to just over 1 per cent of all holdings within the FADN's field of observation. The sample is stratified by economic size (in European Size Units), by farming type and by region and all published results are weighted appropriately. In the strict sense, the sample is not random, since it is drawn from holdings that keep accounts and participation by farmers is voluntary. However, the representative nature of the sample is under constant scrutiny.

Another feature of the sample is that its composition changes a little from year to year as holdings enter or leave the survey. There are good statistical reasons why a turnover is required; the experience in some national surveys is that the greater information that becomes available to co-operating farms enables their performance to improve so that they are no longer typical of the generality of farms. Part of any difference in results from year to year can be laid at the door of this changing sample, though the impact is unlikely to be substantial in countries where FADN is well established and the sample is of stable size. Nevertheless, the gradual drift up in average size must be borne in mind when interpreting income movement over time.

A comprehensive set of data relating to many aspect of the farm business is collected. The items are specified on a standard Farm Return, which is established in Community legislation and published as section III of the *FADN Handbook*. Though having the advantage that Member States are obliged to provide this data, the legal basis of the Farm Return makes any major changes to it a cumbersome process. Currently data are collected covering the physical and value details of animal and crop output, the costs of crop variable inputs (such as seeds and fertilisers), of animal feedingstuffs, labour, interest and land charges, details of spending and receipts from livestock, deadstock and machinery, the debt situation, grants, subsidies and Value Added Tax (VAT). The data relate to the whole farm, so that, for example, it is not at present possible to allocate the input of fertiliser between the various crops on the holding and to calculate measures of enterprise profitability. This severely limits the ability of FADN to monitor the impact of the CAP's main policy instruments - the regimes to support the market prices of single commodities.

The data collected relate only to farming activity on the holding. For the FADN the borderline between agricultural and non-agricultural is based on the standard industrial classification used within the EU. Agricultural activity is deemed to include agricultural contracting (primary stage activity, such as ploughing and harvesting for other farmers). Thus, if the resources of the holding are used in on-farm food processing, manufacturing or any other non-farming activity which contributes to the income of the farmer and his household, these are not covered in FADN. This exclusion also applies to any building activities which the farmer may undertake himself rather than by employing a builder. A small exception applies to farm-based tourism and forestry, but these are included within FADN only where they are connected with the farm business. Similarly, FADN does not collect information on any off-farm activities which the farmer of his family may engage in (as hired workers or as self-employed), or on pensions, property extraneous to the agricultural holding, personal taxation or private insurance.

FADN's main income measures are Farm Net Value Added, expressed per farm or per Annual Work Unit (FNVA/AWU) (that is, per full-time person equivalents working on the farm) and Family Farm Income (FFI), per farm or per Family Work Unit (FFI/FFI). Figure 4.14 shows how these are calculated.

NVA is the difference between the value of farm output and the variable inputs purchased from other sectors of the economy, after adjustment for subsidies and taxes on production and for the consumption of capital (in the form of a depreciation allowance). Produce consumed by the farm household is valued as part of output. Changes in stocks of output and inputs are taken into account. As a concept it is close to Net Value Added as used in the aggregate Economic Accounts for Agriculture, though there are differences in detail. FNVA is the sum that is available for rewarding all the fixed factors of production, that is, all the labour, land and capital used on the farm irrespective of who owns them. As with the macro-indicator, the reason why an Farm NVA per AWU is used without distinguishing between farmer labour and hired workers seems to do with interpretation of the intentions of Article 39 of the Treaty of Rome as relating to all agricultural workers (employed, self-employed and family help). It seems highly unlikely that such a measure when applied in the UK at group average level can adequately provide this information.

FNVA is capable of being distributed in a variety of ways. In the earlier phase of the FADN attempts were made to calculate a *Labour Income* by deducting costs for all other inputs, including imputed rents for owned land and a notional interest charge for the working capital of the business. Such calculations were eventually abandoned because of the difficulties of settling on the levels of imputed costs (Hill, 1991).

As a measure of income, FNVA falls short of what most farmers would perceive as their profit because no deductions are made for interest payments on loans, for rents on tenanted land and for the cost of hired labour. In the early stages of FADN some Member States experienced difficulty in obtaining reliable information on some of these fixed factors, particularly interest payments, so FNVA was the most convenient common measure which could be adopted.

With the passing of time, FNVA has tended to be replaced as a measure of income by Family Farm Income (FFI), a concept first used in the 1984 report on incomes covering the years 1978/9 to 1981/2. This is the residual remaining to the farmer and the other unpaid labour of the household *after* the deduction of interest payments, rent payments and the

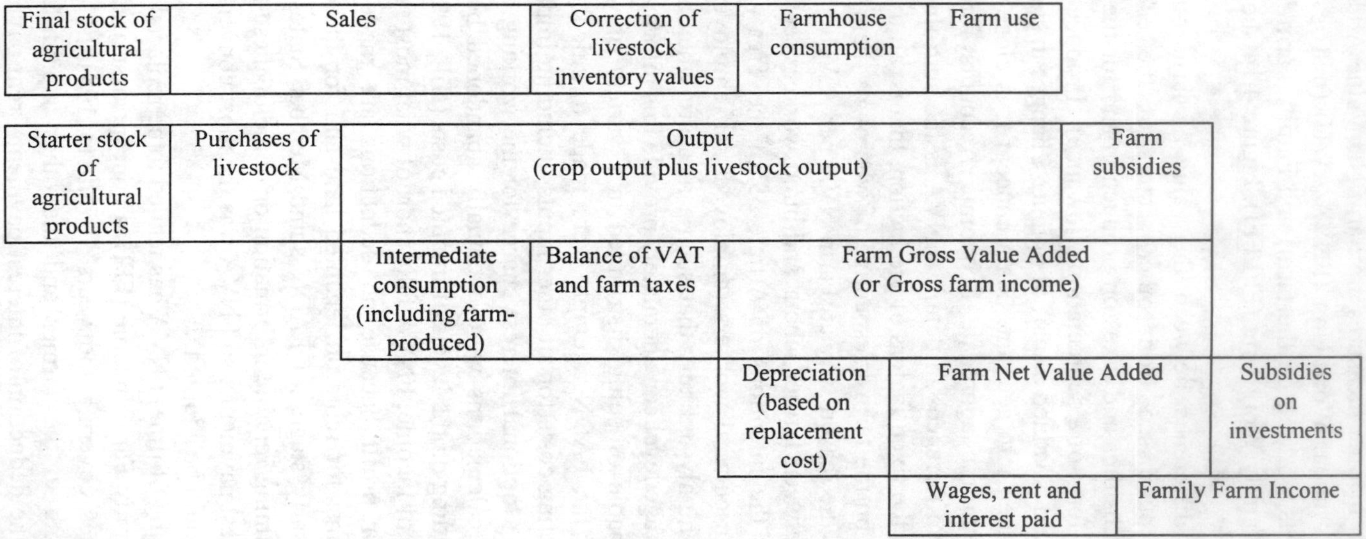

Final stock of agricultural products	Sales	Correction of livestock inventory values	Farmhouse consumption	Farm use
		Output (crop output plus livestock output)		Farm subsidies
Starter stock of agricultural products	Purchases of livestock			
	Intermediate consumption (including farm-produced)	Balance of VAT and farm taxes	Farm Gross Value Added (or Gross farm income)	
			Depreciation (based on replacement cost)	Farm Net Value Added	Subsidies on investments
				Wages, rent and interest paid	Family Farm Income

Figure 4.14 The calculation of income indicators in the FADN
Source: based on Commission (1988) *Agricultural Situation in the European Community, 1987 Report*

costs of hired labour. It represents the reward to the farmer and his family from using their owned land, capital and labour input in agricultural activity on the holding. In practice it accords broadly with the notion of profit from farming which is available for consumption spending, for saving and investment or for other calls on personal income (such as taxation).

Of course, there may be other income sources which contribute to this spending and saving, but they are not derived from farming the holding and are therefore outside the coverage of FADN. Capital gains (and losses) on land and other assets do not form part of FFI, though they too might be considered as elements in the long-term rewards from farming and might form the basis of borrowing for consumption and investment purposes.

Again, FFI is often expressed per annual work unit of unpaid (family) labour (FFI/FWU), including the farmer, in order to reflect the varying amounts of such labour used. As long as its definition is borne in mind, FFI is a very useful measure on two counts; first, it represents what would generally be accepted as being income derived from farming and, second, by excluding the hired labour force, it covers only those people whose welfare the CAP is in practice primarily aimed - farmers and their families.

FFI is similar in definition to Operators' Net Income used in the UK's FBS, with the notable exception that FFI includes the return to all the unpaid labour of the farmer's family, whereas in the UK a charge is imputed for any labour coming from members other than the farmer and spouse, and there are differences in the treatment of interest on land purchase loans. FFI is also conceptually close to Eurostat's aggregate Net Income from Agricultural Activity of Family Labour Input (re-titled Entrepreneurial Income in the EAA97) and, when expressed per unit of family labour input, to Indicator 3 (Hill and Brookes, 1993). A number of additional income indicators have been proposed and investigated (Hill, 1991).

4.8   Patterns observed in Farm Accountancy Data Network results

Results from the FADN are not published with the regularity of Eurostat's aggregate Indicators. In part this reflects the status of FADN as primarily a tool to inform policy-makers in the Commission and under the control of the Directorate-General for Agriculture rather than as part of the EU's statistical service. Reports appear only periodically, concentrate on figures for a single year or a very short series, and the figures are somewhat historic, a drawback of this survey approach which is dependent on the speed of the slowest Member State in supplying data, which then has to be checked and assimilated into the database. The report that appeared in 1993 covered incomes in the year 1990/91 and selected results from the preceding four years (Commission, 1993). A very brief presentation is given in the European Commission's annual *The Agricultural Situation in the Community (latterly the European Union)* report, and there have been special publications that take a somewhat longer-term view of the results (Hill and Brookes, 1993). From 1988 summary results have been available on the internet (under the *Forum* section of the European Commission's part of the *europa* site).

Very valuable compensating virtues, however, are that FADN results are in absolute quantities (with incomes expressed in ECUs, not indices) and that the basic data permits a multitude of analysis which is useful in different ways to policy-makers and policy analysts. This includes comparisons of income levels between Member States, something that is usually avoided as being *non-communitaire*. Two terms are used in this context, *disparity* and *dispersion*. The former is concerned with the differences in average levels of income when farms are grouped by country (or region), by type of farming or by size. *Dispersion* is concerned with the variation found within groups, that is the extent to which individual farms are distributed around the average.

Only a small selection of the most significant patterns in FADN results can be presented here (based on Commission, 1993; Hill and Brookes, 1993). These use Family Farm Income per farm and per Family Work Unit as the income measure, as this is generally recognised as being superior to NVA as a proxy for the income from farming.

4.8.1 Differences in income between countries and regions

Great disparity exists between countries in the absolute levels of Family Farm Income (FFI) per farm business and rankings were very similar at the end of the 1980s to what they were at the beginning (see Figure 4.15, in which comparisons are made between 1981 and 1989 using the ECU values of the latter year). At one extreme, in 1989 the Netherlands had an income per farm business almost four times in the EUR 12 mean. At the

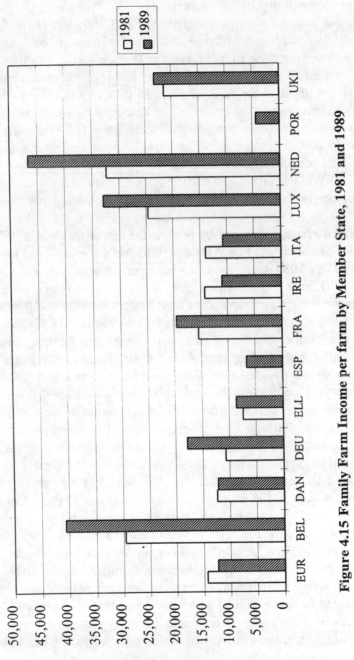

Figure 4.15 Family Farm Income per farm by Member State, 1981 and 1989

other was Portugal, with an income per business only a third of the mean and one eleventh that of the Netherlands.

On the basis of income per person (FFI/FWU) the Netherlands again emerged with the highest income, followed by Belgium, both having levels at least three times the EUR 12 average (Figure 4.16). Portugal again had the lowest income. France and Germany had levels between one third and one half greater than the EUR 12 average, Ireland was close to the average, and Italy was somewhat below. The disparity between the highest and lowest average incomes per person (Netherlands and Portugal) was about eleven to one, the same as when expressed on an income per business basis. The particularly low usage of family labour in Denmark (averaging only 0.8 FWU per farm) was sufficient to raise its ranking from seventh on an income per business basis to fifth when expressed per Family Work Unit.

When farms are grouped by regions the disparities widen. The highest incomes per person (FFI/FWU) over all FADN regions (and single-region countries) in 1989 were found (in descending order) in the Champagne-Ardenne (France), the Netherlands, Niedersachsen (Germany), Belgium, Nordrhein-Westfalen (Germany) and Eastern England, all with incomes 2.7 or more times the EUR 12 average. This list is very similar to that for 1981, when the highest levels were found in Eastern England, the Netherlands, the Champagne-Ardenne of France, Northern England, Belgium and the Ile-de-France. At the other extreme, in 1989, were eight regions with incomes less than half the EUR 12 average (Makdonia-Thraki in Greece, Galicia and Asturias in Spain, Campania in Italy, and four of the five regions of Portugal, the exception being the Alentejo e do Algarve). Lowest incomes in the Community were found in the Galicia region of Spain, but the next four poorest regions were all in Portugal.

Taking the extremities dramatically illustrates the magnitude of the differences seen in the income situation of farmers in the Community; the average absolute income per person in the highest income region (Champagne-Ardenne in France) was twenty-two times greater than that in the lowest income region (Galicia in Spain). However, there is considerable overlap of regional income among Member States. Even in countries where the national average income per person is not high, there are likely to be some regions which perform comparatively well. Of all the countries in 1989, only Greece and Portugal did not have at least one region whose average FFI/FWU was above the average EUR 12 position.

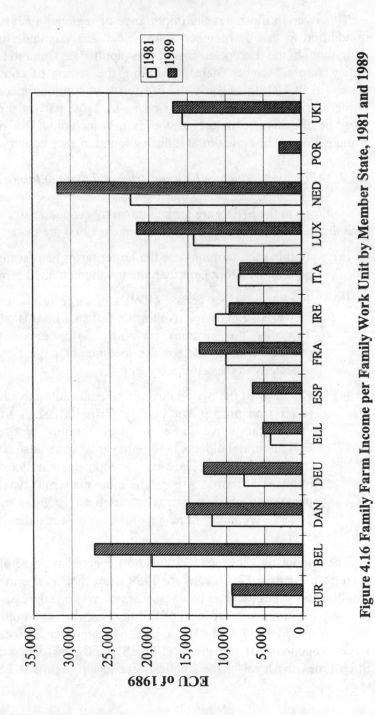

Figure 4.16 Family Farm Income per Family Work Unit by Member State, 1981 and 1989

This overlap illustrates the importance of regional analysis of incomes in addition to that by Member State. Such analysis underlines the point that, though the European Union has applied a Common Agricultural Policy across Member States, including the setting of common support prices (in ECUs), this clearly did not result in common income levels for farmers in different parts of the Union. A large part of the explanation must be the diverse nature of the farms, including the size and type composition of the agricultural industry found in each country.

4.8.2 *Differences in income between sizes and types of farm*

When farms in the FADN are broken down by economic size and farming type the main conclusions (Hill and Brookes, 1993) are that:

(a)   Within each farming type the larger farms had far higher incomes per Family Work Unit than the medium or small farms.

(b)   The incomes per person (FWU) of large farms appear to have increased slightly relative to those of small farms over the 1980s. Typically the incomes of small farms remained steady or declined a little whereas the incomes of large farms improved, especially in the last three years.

(c)   For most of the period covered, the absolute incomes per person (FWU) on pigs and/or poultry farms (all sizes together) were clearly far above those of other farming types Incomes on horticultural holdings and vineyards were also comparatively high. Each of these, however, accounted for only relatively small numbers of farms. Among the more numerous types, the income per person on dairy farms was noticeably greatest. Mixed and general cropping farm incomes were consistently below the average.

The relationship between income and the economic size of farm can be seen from Figure 4.17. Results for 1989 show that, as one moves from the smallest to the largest farm businesses, there was a progressive increase in not only the group average level of FFI per business, as would be expected, but also in FFI per Family Work Unit. Income per business among the largest (open-ended) size group (100 ESU and over) was almost twenty-three times the level in the smallest size group (below 4 ESU). On the

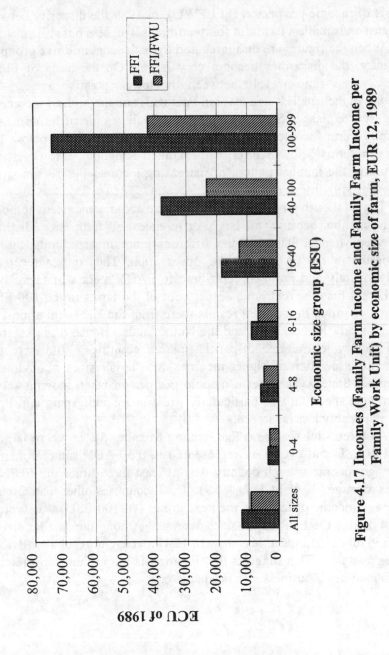

Figure 4.17 Incomes (Family Farm Income and Family Farm Income per Family Work Unit) by economic size of farm, EUR 12, 1989

basis of income per person (FFI/FWU), in 1989 the disparity between the largest and smallest farms, at fourteen times, was less but still substantial.

When the figures are disaggregated by both economic size group and by country, the disparities become very large. On the basis of FFI/FWU, there was a ratio of 1:40 between the lowest positive average income (found in the smallest size class in Portugal) and the highest income (in the largest size class in Spain, though for a small sample of farms). Average Family Farm Income was negative in Denmark for farms below 16 ESU and for farms below 8 ESU in the United Kingdom. However, in both countries the familiar pattern of increasing incomes per person with farm size was still observed.

The relationship between economic size and income needs to be treated with caution because of large differences in farm size distributions between Member States and the different minimum size limits (thresholds) of farms in the FADN field of observation. Thus only Greece, Spain, Ireland, Italy and Portugal contribute to FADN's class of farms below 4 ESU. At the other extreme, 83 per cent of the farms in the 100 ESU and over size group in the 1989 results were from the UK (with almost a third of the total), France, Italy, and the Netherlands. Hence it is perhaps more satisfactory to examine disparities *within* countries. But here too the general association of higher incomes with larger sizes is obvious in all Member States. The rise in income per person when moving across the farm size spectrum was particularly great in Ireland, Spain and Portugal, but noticeably less in Greece.

An interesting feature is that, among Member States where large farms of 100 ESU and over were represented in the FADN sample, their group average income in each country was at least three times the EUR 12 all-sizes average (9,305 ECU in 1989). In all countries other than Greece, the average income of farms in the next group (40-100 ESU) was typically at least double the EUR 12 all-sizes average. Among the smaller sizes, only in Belgium did farms of less than 16 ESU manage to reach the EUR 12 all-sizes average. This suggests that location is not a handicap in achieving high incomes if business size is adequate.

4.8.3 Dispersion of incomes

The final aspect of income differences to be explored in this chapter concerns the dispersion of incomes of individual farms within groups. There is interest both in the way that incomes are dispersed between income levels and in the way that this dispersion is changing over time. One commonly heard assertion is that incomes in agriculture are polarising, with an increasing proportion of farms having either very low or very high incomes. For example, Dancey (1983), taking evidence from the UK's FBS, has predicted that the wide gap between the efficient best (however defined) and the rest could well increase, and concluded that "one could foresee this increasing polarisation amongst farm businesses leading to the need to develop very different technologies applicable at the upper and lower ends of the spectrum".

Figure 4.18 shows the distribution of farms represented in the FADN field of observation according to the level of income (FFI/FWU) for 1981 and 1989. To facilitate comparison, incomes for 1981 have been expressed in the money values of 1989. Because the inclusion of Spain and Portugal in 1989 influences the distribution, EUR 10 is illustrated for both years. There were large numbers of farms with low incomes and a progressive decline in farm numbers as higher incomes were reached. In part, the distribution is a result of the choice of intervals between the income groups; there is a greater degree of subdivision at lower levels and the class at the top of the income spectrum is open-ended. This choice does not undermine the general conclusion that, in the EU, there are relatively few farms generating high incomes and many more generating low ones.

A surprising feature is the close similarity of the distributions of income in 1981 and 1989. For EUR 10 the percentage of farms in each income band remained unchanged or shifted by not more than two percentage points. However, it would be unwise to conclude too firmly that polarisation has *not* taken place. Other influences must be borne in mind. For example, in the intervening period there were some changes in methodology relating to sample coverage, and the number of sample farms in FADN in the EUR 10 Member States increased by almost half (48 per cent) which, despite weighting, may have had some influence. For some countries 1989 was a more prosperous farming year than average for the late 1980s. These factors may have masked any longer-term changes in

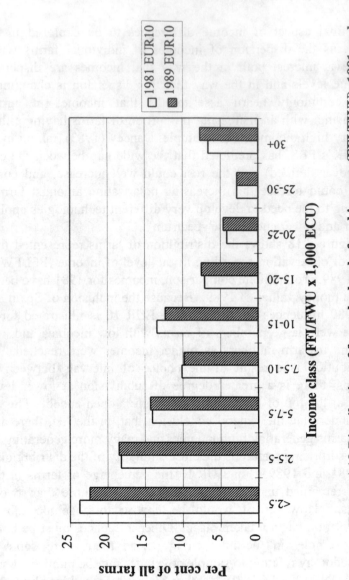

Figure 4.18 Distribution of farms by level of real income (FFI/FWU), 1981 and 1989, EUR 10

the levels and distribution of real incomes. Nevertheless, these two years do not offer any *prime facie* evidence that there *has* been polarisation of farm incomes within the FADN's field of observation.

Adding the substantial number of farms in Spain and Portugal has only a modest impact on the distribution for 1989, with the main effect at the low end of the income spectrum. The share of farms in the lowest income class (less than 2,500 ECU) rose from 22 per cent (EUR 10) to 29 per cent (EUR 12) when these countries were included, with very small reductions in the percentages in each of the higher income bands

Figure 4.19 illustrates the distributions of income within three Member States selected to give rather different forms of distribution; incomes for 1981 and 1989 are both expressed in ECU of 1989. In Greece incomes were largely confined to the lower end of the income spectrum, with only 3 per cent of farms having levels of FFI/FWU above 15,000 ECU in 1989. In contrast, high income dominated the situation in the Netherlands, even in 1981; in 1989 farms with incomes of over 30,000 ECU in the Netherlands accounted for almost half the EUR 12 total in that group. The United Kingdom had an unusual bipolar income distribution, very similar in both 1981 and 1989. About one quarter of farms had very low positive, or negative, levels of FFI/FWU and one fifth very high incomes. There was a fairly even spread across the remainder of the distribution but with a further concentration in the 10,000 to 15,000 ECU band.

A more sophisticated approach to measuring income distributions, using later FADN data (1994-95), found that the Mediterranean countries typically had the largest proportions of farms with low incomes from farming (FFI per holding, rather than per FWU as used in the above analysis)(Allanson, 1999). The northern countries had the highest proportions with high incomes and average incomes that were larger. Nevertheless, among countries such as Denmark and Netherlands the incidence of negative incomes from farming implied that, from a welfare viewpoint, the northern situation is not necessarily to be preferred. Of course, for many households with a low income from farming there may be other sources of income that should be taken into account when making welfare judgements, a point returned to in Chapter 5.

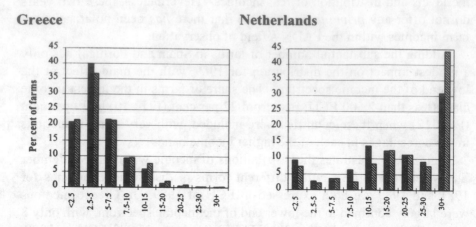

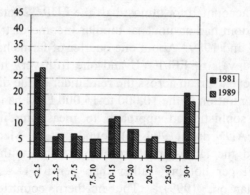

Income class
(FFI/FWU x 1,000 ECU)(1989 ECUs)

**Figure 4.19 Distribution of farms by income class (FFI/FWU)
for Greece, the Netherlands and the United Kingdom,
1981 and 1989**

4.8.4 *Location of high income and low income farms*

Another aspect of dispersion which is of relevance to agricultural policy is the location of farms where incomes are particularly low or high. Such information can be useful to decision-makers in any attempt to be selective in support. It is clear that cases of income extremities are not evenly spread throughout the Community. In 1981 almost half the total number of low income farms (with FFI/FWU of less than 2,500 ECU) were to be found in Italy (46 per cent), followed by Germany (17 per cent), France (15 per cent) and Greece (10 per cent). The proportion of low income farms in Italy was also greater than its share of all FADN farms. The Member State with the greatest number of high income farms (with FFI/FWU more than 30,000 ECU) was France, followed by the Netherlands, Italy, the United Kingdom and Germany. Although the Netherlands accounted for only 3 per cent of all FADN farms in 1981 (EUR 10), 16 per cent of all farms with incomes per person over 30,000 ECU were found there. A similar situation existed in Belgium; with only 2 per cent of farms, Belgium had 8 per cent of the high-income cases.

The entry of Spain and Portugal into the Community substantially altered the distributions; Figure 4.20 shows how farms with low and high incomes were distributed among Member States in 1989. Portugal and Spain were the countries with the second and third largest concentrations of low income farms (after Italy); together these three accounted for over two-thirds of all FADN farms with incomes per person of 2,500 ECU or less. If low levels of FFI/FWU are associated with household income problems, it is clear that these farms in these countries should receive appropriate assistance. However, Spain also had about as many high income farms (with FFI/FWU of 30,000 ECU or more) as Germany and the Netherlands, and substantially more than the UK. France and Italy remained the countries with the greatest numbers of high income farms.

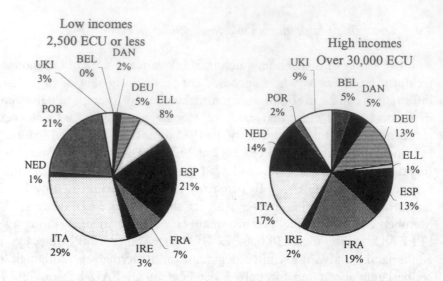

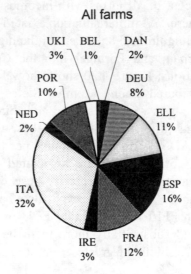

**Figure 4.20 Distribution by Member State of farms with highest
and lowest incomes per person (Family Farm Income
per Family Work Unit), 1989**

4.8.5 Incomes averaged over three years

Incomes in the FADN are measured over the period of a year. Chapter 3 suggested that this was not entirely appropriate in an industry subject to random effects of weather and other natural phenomena, and that consideration should be given to averaging over a short run of years. Years of particularly low incomes do not necessarily indicate a permanent income problem. Conversely, Murphy (1984) has noted the inability of cereal farmers in Eastern England to remain in the top income group. In Germany evidence suggests that a period of three years is appropriate for reducing random variation (Cordts *et al.,* 1984). Special analysis of FADN data, using a constant sample, has found that the average income of low income farms in the 1987 FADN (FFI under ECU 5,000) was raised by 31 per cent when their three-year average income 1987-89 was measured, though this improved income was still not high compared with the income generated by the more successful farms in the survey (Hill and Brookes, 1993). In some countries the effect was spectacular; in Belgium a small average negative income of this group (FFI - 933 ECU) was turned into a positive one of 13,446 ECU and in the Netherlands the change was from - 12,269 ECU to 3,895 ECU. While in line with expectations, these modest explorations require further development of a technique that enables constant samples to be drawn with greater ease.

4.9 Summary and comment

The two approaches to measuring the income from agricultural production described above - the aggregate branch agriculture and surveys of farm business accounts - should be complementary. However, within the EU's official agricultural income information system there are differences between the aggregate Economic Accounts for Agriculture (EAA) and the microeconomic Farm Accountancy Data Network (FADN / RICA) in terms of coverage (the first measuring all agricultural activity, the latter only that on commercial farms), year ends and definitions that prevent their integration. Changes made in 1997 to the EAA's basic unit to small extent narrow the gap in terms of the coverage of activities. Rather surprisingly, results from the two have rarely been compared, one possible reason being the delay with which farm survey results are published. (for such an exercise see Hill and Brookes, 1993). Policy-makers will naturally be most interested in the figures for the most recent period, which only the macroeconomic results can supply. However, part of the explanation lies in their separation in the present institutional structure. The aggregate income measures are the responsibility of Eurostat in Luxembourg and are seen as part of the EU's statistics, with a commitment to regular publication. FADN is supervised by the Commission's Directorate-General for Agriculture (DG VI) in Brussels and is seen more as an internal tool to aid its policy deliberations; there is not the same commitment to publication either in terms of resources or time schedule. However, in the late 1990s when making reference to the composition of the EU's economic statistics on agriculture, both Eurostat and DG VI have listed FADN / RICA as part of the Union's statistical system (see for example the papers in (Hill, 1998a)), suggesting that some of the old intellectual division is being eroded, though the administration remains separate.

In some countries a more complete macro-micro integration is achieved (for example, Denmark and the USA), providing a powerful tool for investigating the problems of agricultural change and policy monitoring, while in the UK an explanation for differences between macro and micro sources has been offered (Lund and Watson, 1981). However, this present inability to integrate must be seen as a weakness in the agricultural information system of the European Union.

Of greater interest in a policy context are the results that emerge from these two systems of income measurement. A prominent feature is the diversity of income situations seen between EU Member States. An overall view of the average incomes from agricultural production in each country and developments seen over the 1980s has been synthesised by Hill and Brookes (1993) and is presented in Figure 4.21. Three characteristics of the "income problem" are tackled - the level of income, the variability of income and the direction of change - over the decade using Eurostat's Indicator 3 and the similarly defined Family Farm Income per Family Work Unit of the FADN. These show widely varying characteristics, with some countries experiencing high yet rising average incomes (Netherlands, Luxembourg) while others had low and falling ones (such as Portugal). The high inter-year variation of Denmark was unique. Diverse experience within a single policy framework has also been pointed

Member State	Change *(a)* "1982" to "1989"	Variability *(b)* 1981 to 1989	Level *(c)* 1989
Belgium	Intermediate	Low	High
Denmark	Rising*	High	Medium
Germany	Rising	Medium	Medium
Greece	Rising	Low	Low
Spain	Rising	Low	Low
France	Intermediate*	Low	Medium
Ireland	Rising*	Low	Medium
Italy	Falling	Low	Medium
Luxembourg	Rising	Low	High
Netherlands	Rising	Low	High
Portugal	Falling	Low	Low
United Kingdom	Falling	Medium	Medium

(a) Change: Rising = increase in Indicator 3 greater than EUR 12 average (10.2%); Intermediate = increase in Indicator 3 in real terms but below EUR 12 average increase; Falling = Indicator 3 falling in real terms
* indicates where there a substantial differences between trends as shown by FADN and Eurostat. Only three years are available in FADN for Spain and Portugal.
(b) Variability: High = MacBean Index of both income measures over 20%; Medium = MacBean Index of both income measures 10% to 20%; Low = MacBean Index of both income measures below 10%
(c) Level: High = both income measures above 150% of EUR 12 average; Medium = intermediate category; Low = both income measures less than 75% of EUR 12 average

Figure 4.21   Synthesis of main income characteristics over the 1980s, by Member State. Family Farm Income per Family Work Unit (FADN) and Indicator 3 (Eurostat)

out for the UK by Furness (1982, 1983) who drew attention to the wide disparities of income between farm businesses of the same type in each constituent country of the UK and the dissimilarities in the patterns of income over time. Such differences pose further questions about why they occur and whether the existing policy measures are appropriate for tacking the underlying problems.

Another feature of the results is the diversity of incomes on farms of different sizes and types. The almost universal finding that incomes from farming per person engaged (FFI/FWU) are higher on larger farms points to the crucial role that structural change can play in solving income problems. If the alleviation of low incomes is a priority, then from the results given here it would appear that CAP support resources should be channelled primarily towards Italy, Portugal and Spain, since these countries contain about seven out of ten of the low income farms in the European Union. And the finding that income averaging over three years reduces the numbers of low income cases points to the need to take a longer view of income and to distinguish between those farms where incomes are persistently low and where assistance may be required from those who experience occasional low incomes but for whom no policy action is necessary

Of course, the measures of income examined in this chapter are restricted to income coming from farming. They take no account of other sources that may contribute to the livelihood of the farmer and his family. As will be seen in the following chapter, this other income can transform the situation of agricultural households and can radically alter the perception of the income problem facing agriculture, perhaps to the extent that there may be no real income problem at all. The fact that the European Union's official farm-level income monitoring system ignores such off-farm income and that, until very recently, there has not been any aggregate information for Member States must stand as an indictment of the EU information system. Though income results that relate to agricultural production have a part to play in shaping agricultural policy, they clearly fall far short of providing a picture of incomes that is satisfactorily complete.

5 Incomes of Agricultural Households

5.1 Introduction

It was established in Chapter 2 that the central objective of the European Union's Common Agricultural Policy (CAP) was, in the words of the Treaty of Rome, to "ensure a fair standard of living for the agricultural community", a phrase echoed in the *Agenda 2000* package agreed by Member States in 1999. From the outset of the CAP there has been recognition of the interaction of agriculture with the rest of the economy, especially the local economy in rural areas. This means that the inflow of resources to many agricultural households is likely to include income gained from non-agricultural activities as independent (self-employed) operators or dependent (waged) employees. To these sources of income from economic activity could be added other forms of income, including welfare transfers such as pensions received by elderly farmers (important in some Member States) and receipts from property (interest and rents).

The EU's Farm Structure Survey has shown that about one third of farm holders have another gainful activity, to which when assessing the importance of these linked sources should be added the work of spouses and other members of farmers' households in activities off the holding. The use of farm resources in forms of production that are not strictly agricultural (such as food processing, tourism and provision of environmental services) is encouraged as one way of enabling farmers to cope with the economic situation facing the agricultural sector and with the changes to the CAP that are intended to make production more sensitive to market conditions. Off-farm occupations appear to be of increasing importance to farm families, and since 1988 part of the enlarged Structural Funds of the European Union have been used for promoting such broadening of the industrial base in areas selected for rural development assistance. The reforms to the CAP introduced in 1992 and the further revision made in 1999 seem likely to accelerate this diversification of income sources among farm households.

The consequence of these forms of non-farm income is that the living standards of agricultural households cannot be described satisfactorily by only measuring the incomes they receive from farming.   For many households with farms the income from non-farm sources may be the major source.   The indicators of income from agricultural production, described in Chapter 4, are increasingly recognised as being unsuitable for the central purpose of assessing the need for a policy directed at living standards and the effectiveness of instruments designed to bring the income objective about.   Indeed, their use may lead to policies that are wholly inappropriate.   In Chapter 3 it was suggested that, among the alternative proxies for the standard of living of the agricultural community, the most practical were measures relating to the total personal income of households, covering income from all sources, not only that coming from farming.   The concept of disposable income was particularly appropriate as this made allowances for current taxation and other outgoings over which the household had no discretion.

This chapter examines the available information on the total and disposable income of agricultural households in the European Union and other OECD countries and interprets the results within a policy context. Special attention is given to developments in information taking place within the EU, as these mark a major statistical advance that could have profound implications for the way that the CAP is operated.

As with the information on incomes from agricultural production, statistics on personal incomes of agricultural households come both in aggregate form, relating to the entire subsector of households in this and other socio-professional groups, and also as microeconomic, household-level results. We start with the former.

5.2   National accounts and the households sector

The national accounts of all the industrialised market economies that are touched on in this book are based on the System of National Accounts of the United Nations (United Nations, 1993) which provides guidelines for all countries throughout the world.   The European System of (national) Accounts (the ESA), which is based on the SNA, provides the framework for national accounting both for Member States and for the EU as a whole (Eurostat, 1979, 1995).   The harmonised approach enables the accounts of Member States to be compared and aggregated.

Mention has been made (in Chapter 4) of the aggregate production account within the ESA, of which that part covering the activities of the agriculture branch of the economy has been developed into the satellite Economic Accounts for Agriculture. The other account within the national accounting framework of the EU which is relevant to income measurement in the present context is the *Distribution of Income Account of the Households Sector*. Households form one of a number of institutional units, grouped according to their principal function. In the account for the households sector, on one side are the resources flowing towards households (from independent and dependent activity, from property income, welfare transfers and so on) and, on the other, are the payments which households are required to make (including taxes and social security contributions). The residual in this account after all claims on income are met is Net Disposable Income.

All countries in the European Union with the exceptions of Greece, Ireland and Luxembourg now construct distribution of income accounts for their households sectors as a matter of routine.

Within the SNA/ESA there is provision for a further sub-division of households into socio-professional groups. Though not specified in the methodology, one of these groups could consist of agricultural households. However, this has not as yet been developed by most Member States. Until the publication of the third edition of the ESA in 1995 even the basis by which households were to be subsectored into socio-professional groups was not set out in any detail. Consequently at present only three of the fifteen EU Member States (Germany, France and the Netherlands) regularly disaggregate and publish nationally household sector accounts broken down systematically into socio-professional groups, of which agricultural households form one, within the frameworks of their national accounts. In the case of the Netherlands these take the form of a related set of Socio-Economic Accounts - SER (Huigen, Van De Stadt and Zeelenberg, 1989: Kuipers, 1994). Even so, these three countries use different bases for grouping households. Outside the EU, complete disaggregation of the household account into socio-professional groups is not common practice either. The USA goes part way in disaggregating by estimating the incomes of its farm household sector and deducting this from estimates of total personal incomes to achieve figures for all non-farmer households. The US data are useful because of the long time series available. In the UK no comparable macroeconomic estimates are available.

Recently in the EU an extension of the breakdown of the household sector has taken place within the domain of agricultural statistics (rather than that of national accounts) as part of Eurostat's initiative to produce estimates of the overall income situation of agricultural households, termed the Income of the Agricultural Households Sector (IAHS) statistics (formerly known as the Total Income of Agricultural Households (TIAH) statistics). The IAHS statistics represent, in effect, an anticipation of a more general disaggregation of the households sector account which is proposed within the programme of development for national accounts following the application of the 1995 ESA. The aim is to construct for each country a Distribution of Income Account for agricultural households, and for other socio-professional groups where possible, in order to estimate aggregate Net Disposable Income for these households; results are to be generated in aggregate and on a per unit basis (per household, per household member and per consumer unit). Using these accounts, comparisons can be drawn with the income situation of all households and, where the data exist, with other socio-professional groups. The account for agricultural households also allows the composition and distribution of their total income to be examined.

In this sector approach some conceptual problems (described later) are encountered because agricultural households are engaged both in consumption activities and in production, no separation being made in the ESA Distribution of Income Account. On a more practical level, it is important to realise that in the Distribution of Income Account all the resources flowing towards agricultural households are covered, not just the rewards from farming. Drawing up the Account presents more data problems than are encountered by the aggregate account for the branch agriculture, since the economic activities of agricultural households extend well beyond the limits of agricultural production. Many of the aggregate data sources (such as the interest paid or received by banks) will not keep separate records of the amounts paid or received from agricultural households; a variety of sources have to be used to build up the income picture. Thus there is not such a clear borderline between macroeconomic and microeconomic approaches as was found in Chapter 4, because information from surveys of households will be used both to distribute economic aggregates between different groups of households and, where other information is not available, as primary data sources.

5.3 Aggregate statistics on the total income of agricultural households (IAHS statistics) in the EU

The potential importance to the CAP of Eurostat's new IAHS statistics requires some aspects of their methodology to be noted before commenting on the results. It is also worth noting the objectives set by Eurostat for these statistics; these are to generate an aggregate income measure for the following purposes (Eurostat, 1990b):

- Monitoring the year-on-year changes in the total income of agricultural households at aggregate level in Member States;

- Monitoring the changing composition of income, especially the proportions of income from the agricultural holding and from other gainful activities, from property and from social benefits;

- Comparing the trends in the total income of agricultural households per unit (household, household member, consumer unit) with that of other socio-professional groups;

- Comparing the absolute income of farmers with that of other socio-professional groups, on a unit basis.

When considering income statistics of agricultural households and other socio-professional groups within the national accounts framework, key issues that must be borne in mind are the definitions of income, of a household and, perhaps the most important of all, of what constitutes an agricultural household. For specific policy purposes it may be desirable to use other concepts, in line with the principle that the choice of any indicator should depend on the problem in hand.

5.3.1 Definition of net disposable income

The main income concept used in the IAHS statistics is net disposable income. The way that this is defined is shown in Figure 5.1. It should be noted that this concept includes not only income from other gainful activities, but also from pensions and other forms of transfer. The value of farm-produced goods consumed by agricultural households and the rental value of the farmhouse are treated as positive components of income. Elements deducted include current taxes and social contributions.

(1) Net operating surplus from independent activity
      a)   from agricultural activity
      b)   from non-agricultural activity
      c)   from imputed rental value of owner-occupied
            dwellings
(2) Compensation to members of agricultural households as
    employees, from agricultural and non-agricultural activity
(3) Property income received
(4) Non-life insurance claims (personal and material damage)
(5) Social benefits (other than Social benefits in kind)
(6) Miscellaneous inward current transfers

(7) *Total resources* (sum of 1 - 6)

(8) Property income paid
(9) Net non-life insurance premiums
(10) Current taxes on income and wealth
(11) Social contributions
(12) Miscellaneous outgoing current transfers

(13) **Net disposable income** (7 minus 8 - 12)

(14) Social transfers in kind
(15) Net adjusted disposable income (13 plus 14)

Figure 5.1   Eurostat's IAHS statistics: definition of net disposable income

Some features of the definition are worthy of note, since lack of awareness may mean that results are misinterpreted. Many of these reflect the macroeconomic origins of the methodology; though there are proposals to adopt a definition that is more in line with a microeconomic concept of income that would *inter alia* ease interpretation and enhance harmonisation between Member States, published results are on the basis of the definition shown in Figure 5.1.

First, in the flow of resources to agricultural households, the reward from independent activity (self-employment) is shown in the form of operating surplus (net value added by production minus costs of hired labour). Rent and interest costs (property and entrepreneurial income paid) are deducted later, among the list of negative items. However, in practice many Member States deduct these two at the level of Item 1, showing what is in effect a net income figure. The end result in terms of Net disposable income is the same, but there are implications when looking at the composition of total income.

Second, accident insurance premiums and claims (receipts) are shown as separate items. This may seem strange, but is explained by the fact that the Distribution of Income Account for households, as part of the ESA, has to record flows between all the various sectors; one of these is the Insurance Enterprises sector. On the negative side, at the individual household level insurance premiums would normally be regarded as a cost to be deducted before the calculation of disposable income, but receipts from claims, especially for the replacement of assets destroyed by accident, probably would not. This is a specific example of a general point; in microeconomic approaches some items would not normally be regarded as elements in the calculation of disposable income although they appear in the list in the macroeconomic approach. Macro/micro disparities are a familiar problem to national accountants (Ruggles and Ruggles, 1987).

Third, in the IAHS methodology all interest charges are treated as negative items, whether the borrowing is for business purposes or to finance consumption goods. This reflects the dual role of agricultural households within the ESA as both production and consumption units. Again, a family budget approach might accept the former as being a cost associated with independent activity, but would probably claim that payment of interest on consumer borrowing should be made out of disposable income, and not treated as a cost in its determination. However, even if the methodology required a distinction between the two, for agricultural households it may be impossible in practice for surveys to separate them in any meaningful way because of the close association of business and personal wealth.

Net disposable income should not be interpreted as bearing a direct relationship with standard of living for reasons put forward in Chapter 3 (including the lack of adequate identification and valuation of income from the farm taken in kind, the exclusion of capital gains and the setting aside of the wealth of the household). No account is taken (at present) of the consumption of goods and service provided by the state without direct cost to the individual, such as public health care or education. In the revised version of the IAHS methodology (Eurostat, 1995b) which reflected changes in the 1995 ESA (Eurostat, 1995a), there is provision for the concept of Net adjusted disposable income, the nature of the adjustment being social transfers in kind, which include *inter alia* publicly provided education and health services. This concept is intended to improve the comparability of disposable income figures over time and space, such as between countries, between socio-professional groups and between time periods that include changes in the extent of public sector activity. However, results are not yet available on this on the new basis.

5.3.2 Definition of a household

In the IAHS statistics, households are defined as in national Family (Household) Budget Surveys. Though not completely harmonised, the definitions of household employed in Member States typically include all members who live under the same roof and share meals. A household can consist of a single person. Large groups of persons living together in institutions (religious houses, universities etc.) are normally excluded. It is important to note that households of farmers, defined in this way, may include persons who contribute no labour input to the agricultural holding. These individuals may or may not have other occupations or sources of income. Their treatment reflects the consumption orientation of income measurement in the IAHS methodology. In contrast, some of the assistance given by the CAP under structural aids adopts a narrower view of the household, comprising only those members of the family working on the holding, or only the individual. These various approaches to the size of the unit over which income measurement takes place are not necessarily in conflict. Aids directed at those engaged in agriculture will, understandably, not wish to consider people who do not work in agriculture. In practice, it is felt that very few people who are members of agricultural households would contribute zero labour input to the farm at times of labour shortage, such as harvest, even if they held full-time jobs off the farm. As noted in Chapter 3, a case could be made that, for the purpose of income measurement in the context of the CAP, it might be preferable to adopt a unit narrower than the dwelling household, comprising only individuals who unambiguously pool income and expenditure (typically a couple and dependent children, and excluding financially-independent adults who happen to live uner the same roof), though this is not technically possible at present.

5.3.3 Definition of an agricultural household ("narrow" definition in Eurostat's IAHS statistics)

The most significant part of the target IAHS methodology, and one which can have a substantial effect on the results, is the system used for classifying households as agricultural or belonging to some other socio-professional group. For the purpose of classification in IAHS statistics, households are allocated to socio-professional groups on the basis of the main source of income of the reference person (typically the head of household or the largest contributor to the family budget). This system allows a complete and consistent allocation of households to occupation groups for the purpose of drawing comparisons. Thus an agricultural household is one in which *the main source of income of the reference person is from independent activity in agriculture.* Some Member States, that cannot at present use an income criterion for household classification, substitute the main declared *occupation* of the reference person. This system could be considered as inferior from a theoretical standpoint to one based on the income composition of the entire household (which is the one recommended under the 1995 ESA) but for most countries it is far more practical.

In the context of the IAHS statistics this definition of an agricultural household is sometimes labelled "narrow" since it excludes those households which operate a holding but where farming is not the main income source of the reference person (or the person's main occupation). Of course, when measuring household income the incomes of all members are summed, but these additional incomes are not considered at the classification stage.

Under any "narrow" definition of an agricultural household there is the possibility of substantial year-to-year changes taking place in the numbers of households, and this could make income results difficult to interpret. An income-based system which only looks at figures for a single year is likely to result in many temporary reclassifications at the margin due to the fluctuating nature of farm incomes. Not only will the number of agricultural households change; their average income will be affected, though it is not clear if this results in an overstatement or an understatement of the position relative to that of a more consistent group of households (Hill, 1995). IAHS methodology encourages the use of classifications involving the averaging of incomes over time. While at present income measurement systems are rarely set up in ways which enable this to be carried out formally, in practice an element of informal averaging seems to take place in most Member States. For example, when information on the main source of income involves some subjective judgement by administrators (such as is used in the UK by taxation authorities in allocating self-employed taxpayers to trade groups according to their normal main income source) a form of averaging is already being employed.

Even if the effects of short-term fluctuation in the income of farming on the numbers of agricultural households are smoothed out, the households which are covered will not form a constant group over time. In the long term numbers will be expected to fall, in line with the historic pattern. If the policy interest were to trace the development of income of people who *started* any given period as members of agricultural households, some attempt would have to be made to retain these in the group. For example, the households which are most successful in diversification into non-agricultural activities can be expected sooner of later to fall outside the agricultural group (defined in the "narrow" sense) and to join some other. Under the present statistical arrangement, farmers who face a fall in their income from farming will eventually be excluded from the agricultural category as their welfare transfers grow in relative importance. Thus when commenting on income developments over time, changes in the composition of the group of agricultural households must be borne in mind.

It should be noted that households headed by hired workers in the agricultural industry are not included within the agricultural household group under any of the classification systems put forward. In practice, only farmer-households are covered. The unification of Germany in 1990 has created a statistical problem in that the people that work on the large farms arranged as forms of co-operative do not fit the model of a self-employed farmer that lies behind the IAHS statistics (and many others); this issue remains (1999) to be resolved and the results for Germany only relate to the former FRG.

When comparing households in different socio-professional groups according to their levels of disposable income, there appears to be no strong reason why restrictions should be placed *a priori* on the selection of groups. Though there may be a particular policy interest in seeing how the incomes of agricultural households compare with, for example, the incomes of small retail traders, there is little inherent reason why their potential spending power should not be compared with household headed by employed persons, or by persons who are retired or mainly dependent on social transfers for their income. Real differences in costs of living (especially of housing, food and transport) may require caution when drawing inferences about relative potential consumption levels, but this also applies to many other forms of comparison (such as disparities in the costs faced by rural and urban households, which may be large). These cost differences are not in essence related to the manner in which the income is generated. Nevertheless, when interpreting comparisons it should be borne in mind that the income from farming differs in its economic characteristics (including risk) from, for example, income from employment, and that satisfactory data are often less easy to obtain for income from self-employment, not least because the concept of income is more complex and involves the identification and evaluation of a greater volume of items which are taken as income in kind.

5.3.4 Definition of an agricultural household ("broad" definition in Eurostat's IAHS statistics)

For some policy purposes it may be desirable to treat all households with which a holding is associated as "agricultural". In certain countries (Greece, for example) such an approach may have little meaning; small holdings operated on a part-time basis and associated with large families whose members are predominantly engaged in urban jobs will not produce meaningful information on the income situation of the agricultural community. Though the main focus of attention of IAHS statistics remains the "narrow" approach to what constitutes an agricultural household, at the request of the agricultural Directorate-General of the Commission (DG VI) supplementary sets of results using a "broad" definition have been calculated, though for only a few countries and for single years. An agricultural household is included under this "broad" approach if *any* member of the household has some income from farming. By subtraction it is possible to throw light on the income situation of those households with agricultural holdings which are not primarily dependent on farming for their livelihood (those households which fall outside the "narrow" but inside the "broad" approaches). In practice, the information on these "marginal" households is particularly illuminating and leads to major questions about who are the intended beneficiaries of the income support aspects of the CAP.

5.4 Results from statistics on the total income of the agricultural households sub-sector in the EU

IAHS statistics covering all fifteen EU Member States have only recently appeared (Hill, 1995) though are now published annually (Eurostat, 1997c; Eurostat, 1998). At present countries differ widely in the number of years covered, degree of disaggregation of the households sector and the extent to which results are integrated with national accounts. At one extreme is Germany, with annual figures for the period 1972-93 broken down within the framework of national accounts into socio-professional groups of which agricultural households form one; extending the series to later years is presently hampered by problems of applying the methodology to the agriculture structure in the part of Germany the comprised the former GDR. At the other are those countries for which only a single year is currently represented, such as Ireland (1987) and Luxembourg (1989), or a larger number where comparable figures for non-agricultural households are not broken down in detail. Sets of results have already been provided by the Member States that joined the European Union in January 1995. Both Finland and Sweden have traditions of income measurement and monitoring at the household level (covering the whole population) and have used methodology for agricultural households that is in close accordance with the IAHS target; Austria also has an established system for measuring the overall income of its farms but not yet have comparable figures for other socio-professional groups.

Detailed descriptions of the findings from IAHS statistics appear in Hill, 1995, 1999 and in Eurostat publications (Eurostat, 1997c; Eurostat, 1998). Here only a summary can be given. Full harmonisation in methodology has not yet been achieved among Member States and gaps in the data exist. Results should therefore be regarded as indicative and, in the case of some countries, experimental. Nevertheless, even when these caveats are taken into account, the findings are of great relevance to agricultural policy within the EU.

5.4.1 Numbers of agricultural households

It is clear that the number of households that satisfy the IAHS definition of an agricultural household (that is, where farming is the main source of income of the reference person, typically the head of household) is much smaller, in most countries, than the number of holdings shown in the Farm

Structure Survey. This is apparent from Table 5.1, where a common year has been chosen. For EUR 12 the number of agricultural households was less than half the number of holdings. In some countries (notably Denmark, Italy, Spain and Portugal) the relative numbers of agricultural households were particularly low, implying that on two-thirds or more of holdings there were no households whose reference person (head) had farming as the main income source (or occupation). This finding is of obvious significance to the CAP with its declared intention of benefiting the agricultural community.

However, the correspondence between holding and household is not exact, and on some (typically large) holdings there may be more than one agricultural household. This and other technical factors help explain why in the United Kingdom the numbers of holdings and agricultural households were almost the same, despite the known existence of many smaller holdings where there was no household that satisfied the definition of being an agricultural one.

Because of this, a preferable approach is to compare the numbers of households that satisfy the "narrow" definition with those of households where at least one member has *some* income from farming (that is, the "broad" definition). This also throws some light on the households that are outside the former definition but inside the latter, which might be called "marginal" agricultural households. Only seven countries can provide such information at present (Denmark, Germany, Greece, Ireland, Netherlands, Finland and Sweden), and mostly for only single years spread from 1988 (Germany) to 1995, (Denmark), so the findings must be interpreted with caution.

While in each country the use of the "narrow" definition reduces the number of agricultural households compared with the number that qualify under the "broad" definition, the extent varies substantially. The number of "narrow" households as a percentage of "broad" households ranges (in ascending order) from 33 per cent in Denmark (1996), 41 per cent in Ireland (1987), 53 per cent in Finland (1992), 57 per cent in Sweden (1992), 58 per cent in Germany (1983), 60 per cent in the Netherlands (1988) and 65 per cent in Greece (1994). Further consideration of the incomes of these "marginal" agricultural households is given below.

In countries where IAHS results are available for a run of years, it is clear that the number of agricultural households has been in decline. In Germany (as constitued before October 1990) the fall was from 349,000 households in 1984 to 261,000 in 1993 (-25 per cent, or an annual change

Table 5.1   EU: Comparison of numbers of agricultural holdings with numbers of agricultural households (IAHS "narrow" definition), 1987

Member State	Agricultural holdings x 1 000	Agricultural households x 1 000	Households as % of holdings
Belgium	93	66	71
Denmark (1989)	81	28	35
Germany	705	319	45
Greece	953	393	41
Spain	1,792	505	28
France	982	660	67
Ireland	217	85	39
Italy	2,784	646	23
Luxemb'g (1989)	4.0	2.7	67
Netherlands	132	92	70
Portugal	636	191	30
U.K.	260	261	100
Sum of the above	8,639	3,249	38

Notes:

(i)   Not all Member States are fully harmonised on the IAHS definition of an agricultural household. For example, France classifies according to the self-declared main occupation of the reference person (rather than main income), which is a subjective judgement that may include both time and income components. In the Netherlands, an agricultural household is one in which the main income of the entire family is from independent agricultural activity.

(ii)   An agricultural holding may have no agricultural household associated with it, one or more than one (such as on large farms where there are several households headed by self-employed farmers, who may be partners).

(iii) The UK is unusual in that its number of holdings and agricultural households coincide; though there are many holdings (mainly small) without an agricultural household, there are many others (usually larger holdings) with more than one. The number of agricultural households in the UK is taken from the Survey of Personal Incomes. This probably under-estimates the real number because it does not cover farmers whose farms are arranged as companies.

Source: 1987 Farm Structure Survey and Eurostat's IAHS database.

of −3.2 per cent) against an overall rise (+13 per cent) in the total number of private households. In France numbers fell even faster, with a fall of more than a quarter (-27 per cent, or −3.9 per cent annually) in the number of agricultural households in the seven-year period 1984-90 against a background of a 7 per cent increase in the total number of households. Over the following five years the fall was even faster, the number of agricultural household numbers shrinking annually by −5.5 per cent against a background rise (for the entire 5-year period a 25 per cent fall against anall-households 7 per cent rise). In Portugal the fall in agricultural household numbers between 1980 and 1989 was 37 per cent (-4.9 per cent per year). Interpretations of income movements over time must recognise that the composition of the agricultural households group is not constant but changing and contracting. (Over the same periods the declines in the total labour input to agriculture, measured in Annual Work Units, were somewhat smaller than the change in household numbers; Germany -14 per cent, France -20 per cent for the first period mentioned, and Portugal -30 per cent (Eurostat, 1997a)).

5.4.2 Composition of income of agricultural households

In all EU countries, agricultural households ("narrow" definition) are recipients of substantial amounts of income from outside agriculture. Typically only about a half to two-thirds of the households' total income comes from farming, though there are substantial differences between Member States and resulting from using alternative systems of household classification (see Figure 5.2). In the years shown (three-year averages ending in the latest available year or, where this is not possible, two-year averages of single years), countries in which substantially less than half of the total household income came from farming included Germany, Finland and Sweden. At the other end of the spectrum, with more than two thirds coming from farming but still with a substantial minority of their income coming from other sources, were the Netherlands and Austria.

This finding amply demonstrates that the overall income situation of agricultural households cannot be described satisfactorily by considering only their income from farming. It should be borne in mind that households where farming is not the main income source of the household reference person (or in some Member States, the main occupation of the reference person) have already been excluded from the IAHS statistics. Thus Eurostat's Indicators 1 to 3 relating to the branch agriculture, and the

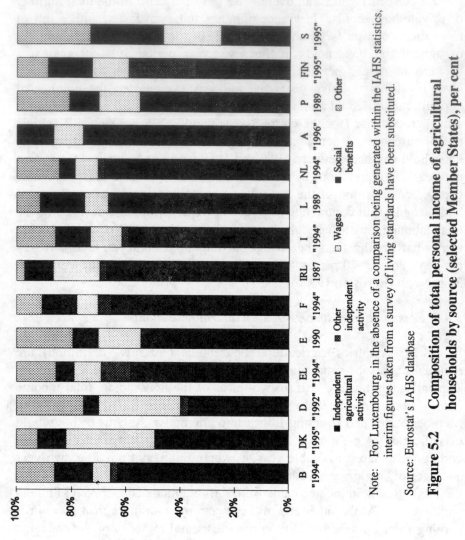

Note: For Luxembourg, in the absence of a comparison being generated within the IAHS statistics, interim figures taken from a survey of living standards have been substituted.

Source: Eurostat's IAHS database

Figure 5.2   Composition of total personal income of agricultural households by source (selected Member States), per cent

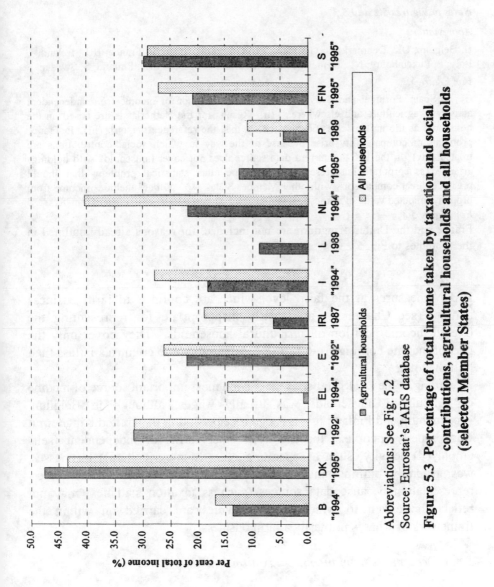

Abbreviations: See Fig. 5.2

Source: Eurostat's IAHS database

Figure 5.3 Percentage of total income taken by taxation and social contributions, agricultural households and all households (selected Member States)

Notes to Figures 5.2 and 5.3

Abbreviations

B, Belgium; DK, Denmark; D, Germany; EL, Greece; E, Spain; F, France; IRL, Ireland; I, Italy; L, Luxembourg; NL, Netherlands; A, Austria; P, Portugal; FIN, Finland; S, Sweden.

For Figure 5.2

(i) In Spain, Portugal and Sweden there is no subdivision of income from independent activity in agriculture and elsewhere. (ii) Results for the Netherlands are based on the household as the unit of classification (rather than the reference person). (iii) In France problems of comparability arise because of the way in which social contributions are treated. (iv) In the UK the current data source does not cover households with holdings arranged as corporate businesses, and there are other statistical problems that should preclude direct comparisons with other Member States. (v) "Other" includes income from property, imputed value of domestic dwelling, and other miscellaneous current transfers.

For Figure 5.3

France and the United Kingdom are not included, for reasons already outlined in the footnotes to Fig. 5.2.

FADN measures at the farm level which are confined to farm business activity (see Chapter 4) are clearly inappropriate for representing the overall income position of agricultural households. They cover only the part of income coming from farming, which in some countries is less than half the total.

According to the IAHS statistics the second most important source of income of agricultural households was usually wages, although in Belgium, Luxembourg and Finland it was social receipts and in the United Kingdom it was property income. Income from other forms of independent (self-employed) activity, such as operating other (non-agricultural) businesses, was generally unimportant, though there may have been some under-representation because data sources (such as taxation statistics) may not reflect the extent to which other activities are carried on within the framework of what is primarily a farm business.

5.4.3 Deductions from income - taxation and other items

Countries also differ in the amounts of household income taken in taxation and other deductions (see Figure 5.3), so the same average total income figure can imply different levels of disposable income in different Member States. At one extreme in the IAHS statistics are Denmark, Germany and the Netherlands, where more than a quarter was taken in the latest year for which results are available, and at the other Portugal and Greece, with less than 10 per cent. Of course, these differences reflect national policies on taxation for which there may be a counter-provision of goods and services in the form of social benefits. Only some of these are at present captured in the measurement of disposable income. For example, the provision of individual non-market goods or services (such as education and health services) is not currently covered (though it will be if the concept of *Net adjusted disposable income,* provided for in the IAHS methodology is adopted). Consequently the net effect on consumption is impossible to assess without detailed information. Differences in the taxation load may carry implications for the competitiveness of farmers from different countries in a single market, and have longer-term impacts on income, for example by influencing farmers' abilities to reinvest in modern technology. However, these issues go beyond the limit of the IAHS statistics, which simply establish that differences exist within the European Union in the shares of income taken by these items.

Another general finding is that the proportion of total income taken by current taxes and social contributions is lower (often much lower) among agricultural households than among households in general in each country. Despite the frequent assertion that farmers are treated preferentially by taxation regimes, and the few known examples of taxes where this is the case, no conclusions can be drawn as to the relative burdens of taxation without much more information on the levels and distributions of income, and details of the tax regimes applied to income from self-employment in general and agriculture in particular *vis-à-vis* income from employment and other sources.

5.4.4 Stability of income of agricultural households

The IAHS statistics show that, in all the EU countries for which comparisons over time are possible, total household income is more stable than is the income from farming alone. This is reflected in Figure 5.4, where, over the various periods illustrated, the percentage change in total income is smaller than that derived from farming. Various pieces of evidence show that non-agricultural income (taken all together) is less variable from year to year than is farming income (though this is not a condition necessary for total income to be more stable). Disposable income seems to be somewhat less stable than total income. A variety of factors is operating here, including the way that taxation is levied. The conclusion is that year-to-year changes in agricultural income, such as are

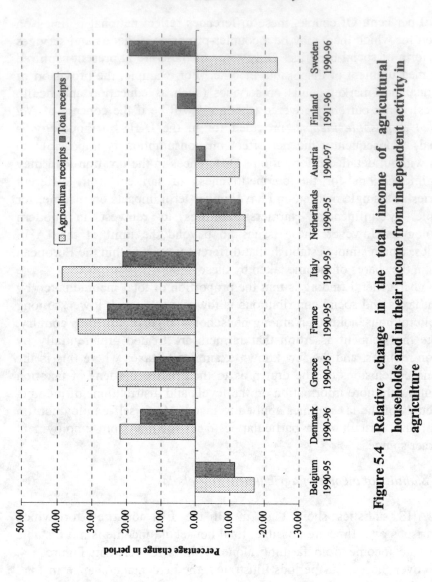

Figure 5.4 Relative change in the total income of agricultural households and in their income from independent activity in agriculture

shown by Eurostat's Indicators 1 to 3 for the agriculture branch of the economy and the farm-level measures from the FADN (see Chapter 4), should not be taken to imply equivalent movements in the total income of agricultural households. These are likely to be smaller. The point can be best illustrated in detail using results for Germany, though the longer-term income movements there may not be representative of other countries in the EU. Figure 5.5 traces income developments for agricultural households from 1973 to 1993, in deflated money values per household. It shows, separately, income from farming, income from other sources, total income, deductions made in order to calculate disposable income, and disposable income.

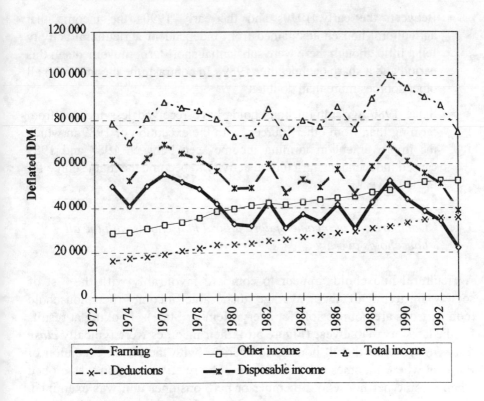

Figure 5.5 Germany: Income per household by source. Agricultural households, 1972-93, deflated DM ("1990" = 100)

The following observations may be drawn for Germany:

- Non-agricultural income (per household) has added a degree of stability to the total income situation of Germany's agricultural households which, in proportional terms, has been less variable than the income from farming alone;

- Even after the deduction of taxes and other negative items from the total, the average disposable income of agricultural households throughout the period was substantially greater than their income from farming alone. Disposable income appears to have been more stable than agricultural income, though less so than total income;

- Between the early 1970s and the early 1990s the income that agricultural households gained from independent agricultural activity fell a little, though there were substantial short-term movements in this period and a sharp decline after 1989. In contrast, the income from all other sources more than doubled

- Since 1980 agricultural households have received less income from farming than from other sources, with the exception of 1989 in which the improvement in farming income seen between 1987 and 1989 caused independent agricultural activity to become the main source for the latter year.

5.4.5   Comparisons of income of agricultural households with the all-households average

Agricultural households appear to compare favourably with the rest of society in terms of their average disposable incomes per household (comparisons are not possible for every Member State). Looking at results for the latest available year (Figure 5.6), their incomes were typically *close to or higher than* the all-household average, with the single exception of Portugal where incomes were far lower. The relative position was eroded when income per household member or per consumer unit was examined. Nevertheless, on all three measures (per household, per household member and per consumer unit) agricultural households had incomes above the national averages in Denmark, France, Ireland, Luxembourg and, most notably, the Netherlands. However, more detailed comparisons, in which non-agricultural households were subdivided into occupation groups, showed that agricultural households on average usually had incomes lower

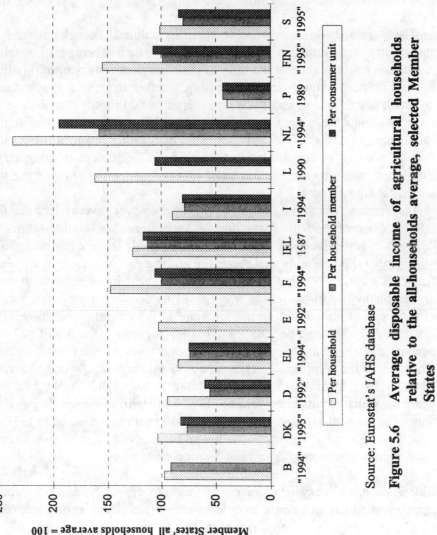

Source: Eurostat's IAHS database

Figure 5.6 Average disposable income of agricultural households relative to the all-households average, selected Member States

than households headed by other self-employed reference persons (Hill, 1995).

These results do not suggest that agricultural households are a particularly disadvantaged group in terms of their average disposable incomes, a major finding in the light of the objectives of agricultural policy in the European Union. In investigating whether there is a low income problem, other factors need to be considered, including the distribution of incomes around the group mean. And it should be recalled that, despite the stabilising influence of income from sources other than farming, the relative position of agricultural households can be subject to quite large short-term variations, so caution must be exercised when considering the results for single years.

In Germany, which has information extending over several decades, the relative disposable income situation of agricultural households seems to have deteriorated over time. The average disposable income per household of agricultural households was above the all-household average in all years from 1972 until 1991, but with a narrowing gap. In 1992 their income dipped below the all-household average. This does not necessarily mean, of course, that agricultural households are in poverty and should receive assistance. In France a decline from 1970 is suggested (though there have been changes in methodology that dictate caution in drawing conclusions). However, in the comparable series from 1984 there was a strong recovery in the relative income position of agricultural households in the last two years for which results are available (1989 and 1990) to a level 23 per cent above the national average, very similar to the position indicated in 1970.

5.4.6 Income situation of "marginal" households

Reference has already been made to the numbers of households where some member has an income from independent activity in agriculture (that is, from farming) but where farming is not the main income source of the household reference person. Among the Member States where information is available, in Denmark and Ireland such households are relatively numerous, accounting for well over a half of all households with some farming income (67 per cent in Denmark in 1996 and 59 per cent in Ireland in 1987); they constituted 47 per cent in Finland (1992), 43 per cent in Sweden, 42 per cent in Germany, 40 per cent in the Netherlands (1988) and 35 per cent in Greece (1988). Perhaps of even greater importance are the income characteristics of these "marginal" households and the impacts they have on average income levels when a "broad" definition of an agricultural household is adopted. Table 5.2 shows the average disposable incomes per household of three groups of agricultural households - "broad", "narrow" and "marginal" - in index form, with the all-household figure set at 100.

Table 5.2 Number of households and indices of average disposable income for three groups of agricultural households. Denmark, Germany, Greece, Ireland, Netherlands, Finland, Sweden
All households = 100

	Denmark (1996)	Germany (1983)	Greece (1994)	Ireland (1987)	Nether-lands (1988)	Finland (1992)	Sweden (1992)
No. agricultural households (x 1 000)							
"broad"	64	613	615	207	136	139	94
"narrow"	21	353	398	85	87	73	54
"marginal"	43	260	217	122	49	65	41
Disposable income per household (index)							
All households	100	100	100	100	100	100	100
Agricultural households							
"broad"	101	110	114	105	210	124	81
"narrow"	107	101	86	127	267	131	79
"marginal"	98	123	166	89	108	116	85

Notes:

The definitions of the three groups of agricultural household are:

"narrow" - main source of income of the reference person is independent activity in agriculture.

"broad" - where any member of the household has some income from independent activity in agriculture.

"marginal" - households which satisfy the "broad" definition but not the "narrow" definition.

Source: Eurostat IAHS database

In Denmark, Ireland, the Netherlands and Finland the average incomes per household of the "marginal" households were smaller than those of the agricultural households defined in the IAHS "narrow" way; in the other countries in Table 5.2 they were above it. In Ireland "marginal" agricultural households appeared to be a relatively low-income group, with incomes below the all-households average. However in Germany (as constituted before the enlargement of 1990) and Greece they appeared to be a relatively high income group, with an average disposable income per household that was not only larger than that of agricultural households defined in the "narrow" way but was also substantially above the all-households average. In Finland "marginal" households had incomes below those covered by the "narrow" definition but were still substantially above the all-households average.

Such diversity (further ones are revealed by incomes per household member and per consumer unit, not elaborated here) among only seven countries points to the need for sets of income results to be available for both "narrow" and "broad" (and "marginal") agricultural household groups in each Member State. The differing social, economic and agricultural structures seem likely to require countries to be considered individually and quick generalisations are to be avoided, at least until more comprehensive information is available.

However, a characteristics shared by all the countries from which evidence is available so far is that only a small proportion of the total income of these "marginal" household comes from farming. In Germany only 5 per cent of their income came from farming (1983), in the Netherlands 8 per cent (1988, but based on operating surplus), in Finland 11 per cent (1992), Ireland 14 per cent (1987), and in Greece 17 per cent (1994). In Denmark 20 per cent of total income came from farming in 1996; these marginal households had a disproportionately high level of interest payments in 1995 compared with those that satisfied the "narrow" definition. Both characteristics reflect the unique extent to which inter-generational sales of land plays a part in the process of succession in Denmark, together with the borrowing that goes with them and the necessity faced by operators and/or their spouses/partners to take off-farm jobs to service the interest.

It follows that changes in the income from independent agricultural activity have a relatively small impact on the total income of these "marginal" farming households; their overall position is more likely to be affected by changes in the economy in general (as these impact on wages, often the major source of income) and policy on social benefits (another major source). Support of farming incomes through such instruments as raising the market prices of agricultural commodities is therefore not likely to be an appropriate way of improving the income situation of these households. Neither would the reduction of support be expected to impact much on their total incomes.

Finally, compared with their substantial numerical importance, "marginal" households were responsible for only a disproportionally small percentage of aggregate farming income. Figure 5.7 shows that, for most of the countries shown, these households received only a fifth or less of the total income earned by all households from farming activity. Germany was in an extreme position with, in 1983, the 42 per cent of its households with agricultural holdings that were classified as "marginal" only receiving 8 per cent of the total income generated. Only in Denmark, with its unique agricultural finance structure linked to inter-generational land transfers, were these households responsible for more than a third of all the income generated.

These characteristics of "marginal" households suggest that the decision by Eurostat to exclude them from statistics on agricultural households and to concentrate on those for which farming was the main income source (at least of the household's reference person) was reasonable. They are little dependent on farming and appear to be far from the sorts of households that the designers of the CAP had in mind to benefit. Furthermore, even for policy issues concerned with agricultural production the results imply that they should be given only light attention; though the link between income received and the value of output or value added is not a direct one, it would be expected that the group that only earns a small proportion of income would be making only a small contribution to total ouput. However, the lack of information for the United Kingdom about its agricultural households is particularly unfortunate, as many of its largest farms are operated by persons who have substantial business interests off the farm; the inclusion of such households in the "marginal" group could cause the general picture to change.

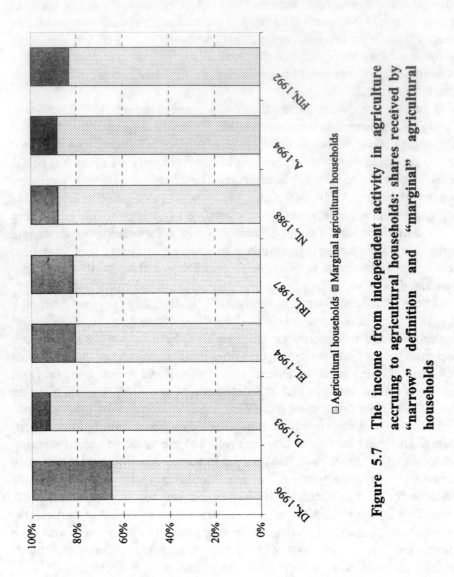

Figure 5.7 The income from independent activity in agriculture accruing to agricultural households: shares received by "narrow" definition and "marginal" agricultural households

5.5   Sector-level results for the United States of America

Within its system of national accounts the USA estimates the disposable income of households, but does not currently attempt a complete disaggregation of its household account into socio-professional groups. However, estimates have been made using aggregate methodology of the income of the farm and, by deducting these from figures for all households, some comparison is possible between farmers and the rest of society. There has been a recent change of approach, and emphasis is now given to microeconomic methodology (described later). Notwithstanding this shift, the superseded aggregate calculations allow an assessment of farmer household incomes from 1934 to 1989 population (two overlapping series), a much longer period than is available elsewhere.

The farm population in the USA can be defined in various ways (Banks and Kalbacher, 1981; Banks, Butler and Kalbacher, 1989). These include households where one member is employed primarily as a farmer (2.2 million households in 1983), those where at least one member of the household received some self-employment income from farming (2.0 million households) and where the household was resident on a farm (1.8 million households). In total the number of farm-related households (covering all three criteria) was 3.6 million households. Surprisingly, no attempts seem to have been made to define the farm population in terms of the main income source of the entire household, or of a reference person.

In the longest-established USA series on the aggregate income of farm households, these were defined in terms of *residence*. This series ran from 1934-84; the methodology is described in USDA (1969). Farm households were thus those which lived on farms. A farm was (and is) defined as an establishment from which $1,000 or more of agricultural products are sold or would normally have been sold during a year. The income figures thus represented the total flow of income to resident farm operators for their capital, labour and management, and all the non-farm income earned by farm residents; these included resident farm workers, but the farm wages of non-resident workers (and operators who do not live on farms) were excluded. The farm (resident) population thus encompassed some self-employed operators who would be excluded under European classification because they are not primarily dependent on their farm for their livelihood. Personal taxes and similar social contributions were deducted in arriving at disposable income. The basic data were collected primarily through the Census of Agriculture, carried out every four or five years, with estimates for years not containing a Census being made on the basis of other indicators (a "Benchmark-Mover System"), the provisional estimates being suitably corrected at the next Census.

This traditional USA definition of the limits of its farm population implies that agricultural policy, or at least parts of it, has been concerned with all producers who generate significant quantities of marketed output, whether or not they have other income sources, and some hired workers (in reality likely to be family members too).

In Figure 5.8 the aggregate personal income of the farm resident population (before personal tax and non-tax payments were deducted but with social insurance contributions removed) is shown for years 1934-83 after adjustment for inflation. This income arose from both farm and non-farm sources. It is evident that total real personal income was much higher in the 1940s and early 1950s than before or after, with the exception of 1972-74. Even discounting these exceptional years, total personal income seems to have been in decline from about 1970. Most of the ups and downs of income were due to that part coming from farming. Non-farm income showed a steady rise in real terms from 1934 to the early 1970s, with the suggestion of a fall-off in the 1980s.

Income from non-farm sources contributed a rising proportion of the aggregate personal income of farm resident households. Up to 1965 the income from farming exceeded the income from non-farm sources, but from 1966 onwards non-farm income became the major source, with the former dominance only reappearing in the exceptionally prosperous period for US farming of 1972-74. In the first three years of the 1980s the non-farm income of the farm (resident) population exceeded its farm income by over 50 per cent. However, these estimates do not allow for changes in the numbers of people comprising the farm population.

Perhaps surprisingly, the income surge of the early 1970s was not reflected in a rise in the proportion of tax take, a feature reflecting the tax system and the ability of farmers to plan their purchases of capital to minimise tax liability. Before 1941 tax took less than 5 per cent of personal income; by 1942 it had jumped to over 10 per cent and from then on took a gradually rising proportion of income, peaking at just over 15 per cent in 1981.

Comparisons of income levels and income movements of the farm (resident) and non-farm populations are given in Figure 5.9. Here incomes are expressed in real terms (deflated by the Consumer Price Index,

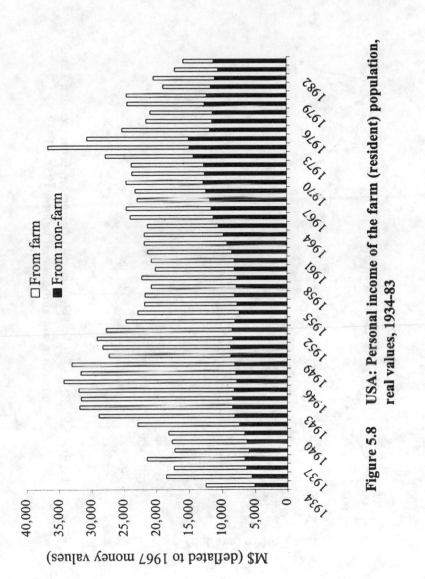

Figure 5.8   USA: Personal income of the farm (resident) population, real values, 1934–83

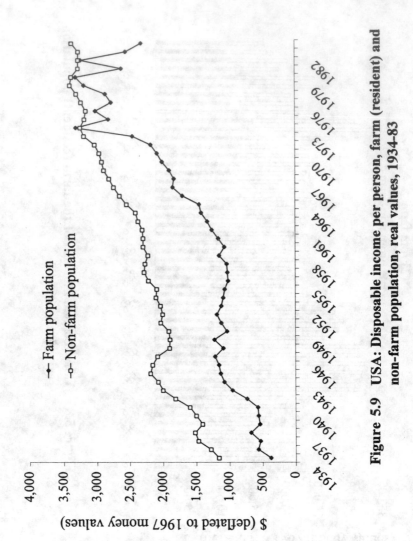

Figure 5.9 USA: Disposable income per person, farm (resident) and non-farm population, real values, 1934–83

1967=100) and per person (not, it should be noted, per household) to allow for changing numbers in the two sectors. The per person disposable income of the non-farm groups shows a fairly steady rise over the half-century from 1934, though the effect of the Second World War on raising income in the short term is evident. Incomes of the farm (resident) population also rose in the War but did not suffer the same retrenchment in the late 1940s. However, neither did they exhibit the same steady growth in the 1950s as was felt elsewhere.

From about 1960 the per capita disposable income of the farm (resident) population increased at a faster rate than for the non-farm sector. Up to then the absolute level of income had typically been about half that of the non-farm population (and 50 per cent in 1960), but the 1960s saw a rapid improvement in the farm position to 70 per cent in 1970 and, exceptionally, in 1973 the per capita farm population income was greater than the non-farm figure. The later 1970s and 1980s were marked by substantial fluctuations in incomes, with a trend downwards, especially in the period 1981-3, so that the relative position of agriculture seems to have worsened. It should be noted that these absolute income figures do not take into account any differences in the costs of living between the two groups; it is usually felt in the US context that these are lower in rural than urban areas (estimated by Ghelfi (1988) in Wisconsin at 3 per cent less).

In addition to this historical information on farm residents there is a newer aggregate-based series relating to the incomes of families (households) of farm operators, running from 1960. Although it was terminated in its original manifestation in 1989 on the grounds of growing methodological deficiences (Ahearn, 1996), as will become apparent, its successor allows a degree of continuity from 1960 to the present. This aggregate-based series permitted comparisons to be drawn between the incomes per household of farm operators and other households; the farm operator is the individual generally responsible for day-to-day management decisions. It is important to note that the coverage extended to all farms, not only those where farming was the main source of livelihood; in the terms used in Eurostat's IAHS statistics, this would approximate to a "broad" definition of what constitutes an agricultural household. Only one operator was assumed per farm, and in the case of partnerships with equal status, the elder was considered as the operator; in reality there were about 1.1 households per farm unit. In most cases the nominated operator would be the owner of the farm business. Unlike the first series described above, operators who did not live on the farm were included - these comprised about one fifth of the total (Gardner, 1992) - and farm workers who were not also members of the operator's family were excluded.

A debate largely within the USDA, initiated in 1980, led to a change in the indicator of the total income accruing to agricultural households. The new measure, "Total cash income of farm operator households", was thought to be the most appropriate concept to provide "an approximate measure of the aggregate financial well-being of farm operator households" (USDA, 1988, p16). As the label implies, only cash income was considered, and no allowance was made for the value of farm produce consumed by the family, the imputed rental of the dwelling, or changes in stocks. On the outgoings side no deductions were made for either capital consumption or the purchase of capital equipment or spending on the farmhouse. The thinking behind this change reflects some of the points made in Chapter 3; that capital spending is in the short run something that is within the discretion of the farmer and could be deferred, the resources going to consumption spending instead. And however valuable the farmhouse as a place to live for which others might be expected to pay a rent, an imputed value cannot be spent in the local supermarket. Also, from a practical standpoint, the imputed rental value of owner-occupied housing was not counted in the measurement of the incomes of non-farm households. Compared with the previous series, the incomes of farm households were improved by some 11 percentage points under the new measure, though the movements over time were very similar (Gardner, 1992).

Estimating these household income series for farm operators involved making additions and adjustments to the net farm income figure calculated within the aggregate economic accounts for agriculture. However, the fact that not all the aggregate net farm income was received by farm operators, that non-farm income data related only to one household per farm, and other data complications, caused the USDA to cease making estimates based on aggregates in 1989. From 1988 the greater flexibility and distributional possibilities afforded by a farm survey approach has been preferred; national estimates of household income are grossed up from the sample of farms in the Agricultural Resource Management Study (formerly called the Farm Costs and Returns Survey) and compared with all-households figures derived from the Current Population Survey. The concepts of income (cash less depreciation) are consistent in the two data sources. The detailed analysis that this microeconomic data source permits are dealt with later in this chapter. Here the grossed up figures are used to complete the picture for the sector as a whole, carrying the series from 1960 to the present, though caution should be exercised at the point of methodological shift.

Figure 5.10 shows, in real terms, the average total cash income (less depreciation) of farm operator households, the part coming from farming, and the US all-households average from 1960 to 1997. Figure 5.11 contains the ratio of (cash) income per household of farm operator households and other households. It is clear that US farm operator households have shared in the general rise in real incomes over the last three decades, but that they are mainly dependent on their non-farm income for this. Farm incomes were still depressed in the early 1960s (as in Figure 5.8) but, nevertheless, there was a rapid convergence of the incomes of farm and non-farm households. The early 1970s saw farmers' incomes substantially above those of non-farm households, followed by a deterioration and a further surge to finish the late 1980s about one fifth higher. Other data sources seem to support this picture (Ahearn 1986, 1990). In the 1990s there has been a return to broad parity; a breakdown by source showed that farming constituted only 13 per cent of household income between 1991 and 1997, ranging from 17 per cent (1992) to 10 per cent (1994). This relative lack of dependence on farming helps explain the comment of one distinguished analyst on the income situation of farm households in the USA that "It is hard to conclude that a sector-wide farm income problem exists any longer". (Gardner, 1992, p82). This assessment covered a wide range of farm family situations, and is based on a rather broader concept of an agricultural household than is used in Eurostat's IAHS statistics, but there is obvious similarity in the general tenor of his judgement to what has been observed in the EU.

5.6   The need for microeconomic data and potential data sources

Chapter 2 found that there are three major strands of policy concern relating to incomes in agriculture. These are of poverty in agriculture, comparability of rewards with other parts of the economy, and income stability. While some light can be thrown on these issues using aggregate, sector level income results for agricultural households and other socio-professional groups, all three require a bank of microeconomic data on the personal incomes of farmers if they are to be properly explored. Taking an overall view, studies of the overall income position of farmers or farmer

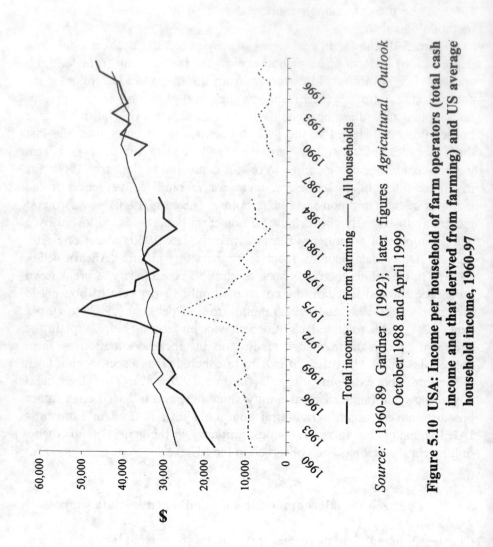

Source: 1960–89 Gardner (1992); later figures *Agricultural Outlook* October 1988 and April 1999

Figure 5.10 USA: Income per household of farm operators (total cash income and that derived from farming) and US average household income, 1960–97

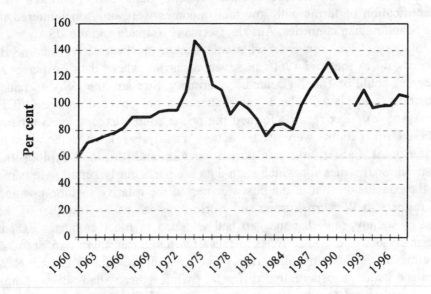

Figure 5.11 USA: Income per household of farm operators relative to all households, 1960-97

households that draw on microeconomic data are not common, and are restricted to a small range of countries where there is a tradition of measuring personal income in addition to that generated by the farm business.

In 1964 the OECD examined the issue of low incomes in agriculture. An important piece of information it attempted to collect from the twenty-two countries that took part concerned the incomes that farmers received from other sources and which might compensate for low earning from farming. To its concern it found that:

> ...In most countries, the information available does not give a precise indication of the farm income situation. Farm families cannot be accurately classified according to their level of income; data on income received from non-farm sources are particularly deficient. These limitations are a serious handicap in devising suitable policies and in assessing the results of measures taken; attention should be given to improving the situation (OECD, 1964, p.7).

Although scraps of information about off-farm activities could be found for most, sets of microeconomic income data that permitted the identification of farms with low total incomes were only encountered in the Scandinavian countries, Austria, Germany, Canada and the USA.

Slattery (1966) reviewed what was known on the relative income of farmers up to the mid-1960s in seven countries where data on personal incomes could be found (Denmark, Germany, Sweden, the USA, Canada, Australia, and New Zealand – the latter two not covered by the OECD work above). Tax records formed the prime source except for Germany where farm accounts were used. Slattery's analysis related to the average incomes of farmer and non-farmer sectors and did not explore the distributional issues for which such data are particularly suited. He came to the conclusion that in the post-war period the relative income position of farmers in Western Europe and North America was below that of the rest of society, and that the gap had widened in most countries except Germany and the USA. Even in these two countries there had been no decline in the absolute disparity. The position in Australia and New Zealand was substantially different; while there had been some deterioration up to the 1960s, the incomes of farmers here were still approximately comparable with incomes elsewhere in the economy.

This part of Chapter 5 examines what recent information is available in Europe and elsewhere. In the European Union this turns out to be virtually nothing in a harmonised form at EUR level. Despite the passing of three decades during which the CAP with its increasingly important income objective has come to dominate the agricultural policies of Western Europe, the list of EU Member States with satisfactory micro-data on the overall income of their farming households in the 1990s is almost unchanged from that found by the OECD in the 1960s; only Ireland and the Netherlands have been added to Slattery's list. The absences of countries of such major importance to the CAP as France, Italy and the UK are particularly regrettable. Furthermore, no progress has been made is putting what exists at national level, patchy as it is, on a common methodological basis that would permit comparison and aggregation. This must represent a substantial failure on the part of the official statistical services to provide the data necessary to the monitoring of the CAP's central agricultural policy objective.

The paucity of the situation at EU level obliges us to look at national results in Member States and in other OECD countries in the expectation that patterns found there are likely to apply more widely. The OECD has recently reviewed microeconomic income sources as part of its studies on farm household income, labour flexibility and structural adjustment (OECD, 1995). In the EU the general state of data provision is unsatisfactory but is mitigated by individual examples of countries with adequate data. In particular, Scandinavian countries have a history of building up income statistics by drawing on and integrating tax and other registers, and the accession of Sweden and Finland in 1995 considerably reduced the information deficit. As will become apparent, information on the broader income situation of farm households is often more available among non-EU Member States. However, international comparisons of income findings are very difficult because of many disparities, particularly in their definitions of farm households and in the breadth of coverage of members within the household. The conclusions from the OECD on the findings from this review will be returned to later.

5.6.1 Types of data sources

Microeconomic information on the personal incomes of farmers in industrialised countries comes from data gathered in three main ways - from surveys of farm accounts, from household budget surveys in which farmers form one of several socio-professional groups, and from taxation records where self-employed farmers can be identified as a trade group within the industrial classification. In addition, there are various other sources, regular as in the case of the annual microcensus in Germany and claims for income support under welfare programmes in Ireland and France, or occasional like the investigation of farming households in 1978 by CEPS (Hill, 1988)(Brangeon, Jégouzo and Roze, 1991)(Jégouzo, Brangeon and Roze, 1998). Occasional data also come from special studies that involve looking at the incomes of farmers, such as surveys of farm business structure (Harrison, 1975), of part-time farmers in the UK by Gasson (1983, 1986) and, of a more qualitative nature, the large-scale multi-country study of farm household adjustment in Europe undertaken by the Arkleton Trust (Bryden *et al.*, 1992) and its national offshoots (for example (Eboli, 1996) for Italy and (Shucksmith *et al.*, 1989) for the UK). Here emphasis is given to the regular sources.

Farm accounts surveys take place in all EU Member States and many other OECD countries. Accounts surveys are important for EU policy purposes because they are undertaken either by or for governments and form part of the official data set on agriculture; each country has at least one survey that contributes to the European Commission's Farm Accountancy Data Network using a harmonised methodology. The quality of the information is generally high because of the way in which the sample is selected and data are collected (Commission, 1989). However, as suppliers of data on the total income of farm households they are of limited potential. As was pointed out in Chapter 4, FADN does not require from its contributing national surveys information beyond that related to the farm business. A few national surveys go beyond these narrow limits and regularly collect data on the farm household's non-farm income; among the EUR 15 countries this only applies to Denmark, Germany, Netherlands, Austria, Finland and, since 1989, the United Kingdom (though in the latter's case using a banding system rather than precisely determined and verified figures). The Scandinavian countries have for some time adopted a broader approach though in Sweden questions on non-farm income were dropped for the survey in 1990, a change associated with reforms in agricultural policy towards a less regulated approach (only to be reversed shortly on joining the EU and adopting the CAP). Where farm accounts surveys take a narrow perspective, whatever their relevance to the problems of farming at the time they were set up, they are now of limited capability in providing answers to many of the policy questions of the 1980s. Nevertheless the FADN and the national surveys that contribute to it appear to be the most likely option for further development by the addition of questions related to off-farm income and other aspects of the household that are of increasing relevance to explaining their farming decisions and of establishing their economic well-being.

Family (household) budget surveys take place in all EU countries and are moving towards a common methodology (Eurostat, 1978, 1980, 1981, 1990c, 1993). One of their prime purposes is to provide information for the weighting of price indices, and emphasis has traditionally fallen on the expenditure side. The amount of information collected on incomes has gradually been expanding, though there is variation in the amount of detail between countries. This flows from the fact that income data are collected primarily to obtain a classifier for the study of patterns of consumption rather than to study income in its own right (Eurostat, 1993). Nevertheless, in countries with a substantial proportion of their population still engaged in agriculture these surveys are a potentially valuable source of information on the total income of farmer households. In the UK the number of farmer households is too small for its household budget survey to be regarded as a reliable source of data but in Ireland and Germany such surveys are extremely important and provide the sorts of information that modern policy demands.

The main disadvantages of household budget surveys are, first, that they are expensive to carry out, with the result that they are conducted only occasionally - typically at 5 to 7 year intervals. This creates the problem of how their findings should be updated in non-survey years. Analysis of the mass of data also tends to be rather dated when it is published. These surveys are therefore best at providing detailed information when time is not of the essence. Second, the reliability of data on incomes is not high (see, for example, the case of Greece in (Sarris, 1996)). This comes from the under-representation of self-employed households in voluntary surveys (there may be difficulty in making contact and a high non-co-operation rate), and also the understatement of real income levels from self-employment. This may not be deliberate but arise from the uncertainly which households have about the amounts they are earning, even of what constitutes income (Martin *et al,* 1996; van der Laan, 1999). In agriculture the problems may be exacerbated by systems of national taxation that, in many EU countries, still do not require farmers to keep accounts. In the Commission's Agricultural Situation in the Community report of 1980 only 15 per cent of EUR 9 holdings kept accounts, with book-keeping being the norm only in the Netherlands, Denmark and the UK. (The percentages were Germany 9, France 5, Italy 8, Netherlands 98, Belgium 8, Luxembourg 11, UK 83, Ireland n.a., Denmark 70).

An important example of an attempt to use household budget surveys to identify poverty was the general micro-based research study of poverty published by Eurostat in 1994 (Hagenaars, de Vos and Zaidi, 1994). Both income and expenditure approaches to assessing poverty were considered, using poverty lines set at various national levels. However, the usefulness in a CAP context is reduced, firstly, by the amalgamation of the households headed by farmers with those headed by agricultural workers. Secondly, the authors conceded that the quality of the survey-based income data was frequently poor; in that self-employed people typically understate their incomes, the degree of poverty will be overestimated. For farmers, data on expenditure might also be highly misleading as to real consumption and standards of living. The percentage of the households of agricultural workers and farmers shown to be in poverty in each of the EUR 12 countries was typically higher than that of other economically active household groups but lower than the unemployed and of a similar order to the retired. By way of example, in France 25 per cent of the agricultural group were in poverty (below half the arithmetic mean national household expenditure, corrected using a modified OECD equivalence scale), compared with 11 per cent of private sector manual workers, 8 per cent of other self-employed, 22 per cent of retired households and 35 per cent of the unemployed. However the problem of data quality, and some surprising internal inconsistencies, suggest that study's figures should be treated with great caution.

In an attempt to circumvent the problem of unreliable survey income information for farmers, the latest Irish household budget survey for which results are published (1987, the 1994 survey is still being processed) used as agricultural household cases holdings that were already co-operating in the Irish farm accounts survey (Hill, 1988). In Germany, incomes are estimated indirectly by summing consumption spending with the level of savings.

Related to the household budget surveys in approach is the *European Community Household Panel (ECHP)*, a survey involving periodic revisits to a panel of households. This was initiated in 1993 with the intention of establishing a European database of comparable statistical information for all Member States (EUR12) on the income and living conditions of households. The first main survey took place in 1994, with a sample of some 60,500 cases. It was anticipated that about 3,300 would turn out to be agricultural; in the UK the sample of 5,000 households was expected to yield about 100 farm households. In reality, the first round of the ECHP threw up fewer than 2,661 cases in which the head of household (or the reference person) was returned as self-employed and had agriculture as their broad industry group. In Germany there were 25 households with such a reference person and in the UK 61 cases; only in Greece, Ireland and Portugal were there more than 300 (Eurostat, personal correspondence). Subsequent survey rounds are likely to see shrinkage in the panel's size. The number of cases corresponded to less than 1 per cent of agricultural households estimated in the IAHS statistics, and less than 0.5 per cent in countries other than Ireland and Luxembourg; in contrast, the EU's Farm Structure Survey aims for a minimum sample of 10 per cent in order to catch the diversity found in this industry, although in practice this sometimes falls to 3 per cent. Consequently, the sample is too small for the ECHP to be useful in throwing light on the income situation of agricultural households in the EU as a whole. In addition, the ECHP is expected to suffer from the same well-known problems as household surveys in its attempts to gather reliable income data from self-employed people, especially those in agriculture.

Taxation records, another potential source of microeconomic data on total personal incomes, have their usefulness hampered in many EU countries by farmers not being taxed on their actual incomes but according to some standard - typically dependent on farm area - or by their falling below the tax threshold; Belgium, Greece, Spain, France, Ireland, Italy and Portugal are particularly affected this way. Assessment on an actual income basis can only happen if the farmers keep accounts for their businesses, and for the EU as a whole this seems to be still very much the exception. Taxation records typically reflect tax conventions on matters like capital allowances, offsetting losses and so on, and these may not accord with the treatment appropriate for assessing personal incomes in the context of agricultural policy. There may also be under-reporting. Where tax is assessed on the basis of an accounting profit this is often done in arrears, unlike other forms of income that are taxed in the year in which they are earned, and there are problems of aligning information on self-employment income with statistics on other income. Comparison of the income of farmers with other sectors of society using tax data also has to contend with the problem that, even if all the farmers are caught by the tax net, this will not be the case for many low earners in other socio-professional groups.

A summary of the available data sources on the overall income situation of agricultural households in EU Member States is given in Figure 5.12 (from Hill, 1988, (OECD, 1995; OECD, 1997) and updated). This indicates the potential for exploring personal incomes in each country. For many sources regular or periodic reports are published based on the data, but this is by no means universal. The ability to draw upon data for analytical purposes is considerably enhanced in countries where it is legal for statistical authorities to make links between the various data sets (tax returns, agricultural census, population census, other administrative records etc.) using some sort of personal identifier, such as an individual's national insurance number; countries that may do this include the Scandinavian group, where statistical registers on income are built up from several sources in this way, and Canada. The political acceptability of making direct links for individual cases between existing

EU Member State	Farm accounts survey	Family (household) Budget Surveys	Taxation records	Other
Belgium		But few agricultural cases	But income not on an accounting basis	
Denmark	Accounts of the Farmers' Association (16,000); Smallholders' Association (4,600); Institute of Agricultural Economics (1,800)	But few agricultural cases	Income Statistics Register System (tax based combined with agricultural statistics register)	
Germany	Test holdings (11,000)	Survey of incomes and expenditure (5-yearly)	3-yearly	Annual population microcensus
Greece	Not normally covered, but a pilot survey made in 1992	But difficulty with incomes from self-employment	Farmer coverage small	
Spain		But difficulty with incomes from self-employment		
France		Some 500 farmer households covered.	Two levels of sample enquiry (general and agricultural) but incomes mainly not on an accounts basis. Special study in 1990.	Special 1978 farm survey (CERC)
Ireland	Not normally covered, but linked with the Family Budget Survey in 1987	1,300 farmer-households in 1987 survey. Income data good. Repeated 1994.	Farmers not well represented	Social assistance records

Derived from Hill (1988), OECD (1995, 1997) and updated

Figure 5.12 Sources of microeconomic data on the total incomes of agricultural households: EU and selected other countries

Figure 5.12 continued

Member State	Farm accounts survey	Family (household) Budget Surveys	Taxation records	Other
Italy		Continuous, with many agricultural cases, but income data not of high quality		Bank of Italy survey of households
Luxem-bourg	Special questions added in 1989 only	But few agricultural cases	Most farmer's incomes not on an accounts basis	Poverty survey of households (CEPS)
Nether-lands	Formerly two annual surveys; one used to build the national production account (3,000 cases), the other part of FADN (1,500 cases); now combined.		An annual panel study, the Personal Income Distribution Statistics	
Austria	Sample of 2,500 holdings	Only carried out once every 10 years		
Portugal		Difficulties with income from self-employment	Few farms are covered	
Finland	Profitability Study of Agriculture (FADN Finland) (1,000 holdings). In principal the entire household is covered.	But from 1994 the sample is being reduced	(a) Agricultural Enterprise and Income Statistics (10,500 cases in 1999) with data taken from tax forms; (b) Income and Taxation Statistics for the Finnish Farm Economy (formed by combining administrative registers); (c) Income Distribution Statistics (tax based) covering all households, with 700 agricultural cases	

Figure 5.12 continued

Member State	Farm accounts survey	Family (household) Budget Surveys	Taxation records	Other
Sweden	Farm Economics Survey (JEU) with 600 holdings, but questions about non-farm incomes dropped in 1990		(a) Taxation Statistics of Agriculture (DU), historic series ended in 1993 (2,700 cases 1991); (b) Survey of Income Distribution (HINK), taxed based, covering all households, about 600 agricultural cases in 1992, 199 in 1997; (c) Annual taxation statistics for the whole population, farmers identified 1991, 1992, 1996, 1997.	Family Resources Survey (new 1996); too few agricultural cases
United Kingdom	Non-farm income of farmer and spouse covered from 1988/89. Income banded. Current data not regarded as of high quality.	But few households headed by a farmer (about 60)	Agricultural cases (less than 2,000) taken from the Survey of Personal Incomes (from tax records of self-employment income). Farmers with businesses run as companies not covered.	
Other Countries				
USA	Farm Costs and Returns Survey (USDA) (usable sample about 12,000 farms)(now called the Agricultural Resource Management Study)	Money Incomes of Households, Families and Persons in the US	Inland Revenue Service (IRS) data on those filing Schedule F.	Census of Agriculture / Current Population Survey (few agric. cases)
Canada	Farm Expenditure and Income Surveys/ Farm Financial Survey/ National Farm Survey	Survey of Consumer Finance	Taxation Data Programme	

Figure 5.12 continued

Country	Farm Accounts Survey	Family (household) Budget Survey	Taxation records	Other
Australia	Austrian agricultural and grazing industries survey (AAGIS) ("broadacre" industries) Australian dairy industry survey (ADIS)			Henderson Poverty Enquiry (1973)
Japan	Farm Household Economic Survey			
Mexico		Household Budget Survey identifies "rural" households, and the money incomes of those employed in different sectors		
New Zealand	Surveys on a sectoral basis: NZ Meat and Wool Board's Economic Survey/ NZ Dairy Board			Special 1992 national survey covering pastoral and horticulture, aimed at off-farm income
Norway	Survey of accounts of "commercial" farmers whose main income source is farming (sample of about 1,000). Agricultural activity should be at least equal to 400 standard man-days.	Yes, but few agricultural cases	Survey of farmers' income and wealth based on taxation records and an annual sample survey of agriculture/ Income and Property Statistics – tax-based survey of income and wealth covering the whole economy	
Switzerland	Survey of full-time farmers (sample about 3 500); only 27% of farms are covered.			

data sets varies widely; in Norway statisticians are required to explore this possibility before additional surveys can be contemplated, whereas in the UK it is prohibited.

5.7 Country studies using microeconomic data

The remainder of this Chapter reviews published information from microeconomic sources on the personal income of farmers, concentrating on the distributional issues that only this type of data can illuminate. The EU Member States are considered first, as these form the focus of the present study. Only eight of the fifteen EU countries appear to analyse and regularly publish information from microeconomic sources, five of the EUR 12 (Denmark, Ireland, the Netherlands, Germany and the United Kingdom, though the last suffers severe data problems) and the three countries that joined the EU in 1995 (Austria, Finland and Sweden). Other countries may have occasional research studies that throw light onto the income situation of agricultural households, but regular statistics of an official or semi-official nature, produced by government institutions and based on public sector data, will probably be more highly influential in decision of public policy towards agriculture. We move then to North America, where microeconomic data is well-established, and Australasia. More importance is attached to the identification of enduring findings in the statistics than to how up-to-date they are. Despite the material's fragmentation, there is much in common in the patterns thrown up.

5.7.1 The United Kingdom

The UK forms a convenient example of a country where relatively little is known of the total income of its farming population. There is a household budget survey, but the sample contains only about 60 cases of households headed by self-employed persons working in agriculture, forestry and fishing - far too small to give statistically reliable results. A *Family Resources Survey,* also covering all household types and first mounted in 1994/95, has similarly produced insufficient agricultural cases, despite steps having been taken to boost the agricultural component. The only two regular data sources containing numbers of cases approaching the adequate are taxation statistics and the official farm business survey, though both have substantial deficiencies in terms of providing a comprehensive picture.

The annual *Survey of Personal Incomes (SPI)* is drawn from taxation records held by the Inland Revenue. The SPI does not cover the same set of cases each year; a fresh sample is drawn annually. Tax cases are classified to agriculture or horticulture based on the Inland Revenue's Trade Classification. Up to the 1990/91 year of assessment these cases were those in which self-employment (independent) income from agriculture or horticulture usually constituted the main or principal additional source of *self-employment income* of single persons or husbands or the main source of self-employment income of wives. Since then, husbands and wives have been treated separately and included in the analysis only if they *as individuals* have a main or principal additional source of self-employment income deriving from agriculture or horticulture. It should be noted that the classification system does not make use of a comparison of the income coming from independent activity in agriculture with total income, but only with that part coming from independent activity in all industries. Some discretion is used by tax authorities in allowing for fluctuations in the income from farming before a household is reclassified. The SPI contains about 1 per cent of agricultural cases.

Information from this source was first published by the Ministry of Agriculture in the 1986 edition of its *Farm Incomes in the United Kingdom,* the annual national report on incomes, and the period covered now extends from 1977-78 onwards. However, the change to a system of independent taxation of individuals (rather than treating married couples as a single tax case) from the 1990-91 year of assessment means that figures published for 1990-91 and subsequently are not comparable with those for earlier years.

The SPI has been the subject of attention of researchers both in the government service (Lund and Watson, 1981) and independent (Hill 1984, 1987). The main advantage is that income from all sources is covered, even that which is taxed at source such as interest on building society deposits, and the amounts coming from a range of sources can be identified separately. The disadvantages arise mainly from technicalities associated with the data source; tax records are not designed primarily for studies of income. At present the drawbacks are that:

(a) The sample does not include farmers whose businesses trade as companies and who technically are employees of their own companies, although they could possibly be selected if they have other self-employment income from agriculture. These are important in the UK context. According to ministry sources, in 1990 just under one quarter (23 per cent) of the Net Operating Surplus of UK agriculture was estimated to have been generated on corporate farms; the proportion was very similar in 1984. Evidence from a range of sources points to these farms as tending to be found disproportionately frequently among the larger size-groups but, despite their size, the overwhelming majority would also be owned and managed by families. The omission of the households associated with these farms is a significant gap in the SPI coverage which, probably, means that the operators of high-income farms are insufficiently represented in the results.

(b) The unit over which measurement is taken is the tax unit, not the entire household. In the earlier part of the series couples were treated as single units, but the change to independent taxation has reduced the usefulness of this source. Technical problems preclude the aggregation of the returns of individuals living at the same address.

(c) Information given in national publications is on the basis of years of assessment, not the year in which it was earned; for income from self-employment this has corresponded to farming profits earned in a previous period (typically profits for the calendar year 1990 will be assessed in the 1991/2 tax year) whereas any income from employment or investment will be assessed in the same year that it is earned, giving a mix of accounting periods and a substantial lag in the case of self-employment income. Adjustment to a calendar basis is possible, and this is the form in which data are passed to Eurostat for use in IAHS statistics. The recent change to taxation on a current year basis (from 1998/99) may, in future, assist in this respect.

(d) The income concepts are those of the taxation system and use fiscal conventions for the treatment of depreciation and losses; this, and problems over the allocation of allowances between farmers in businesses arranged as partnerships, makes a simple reconciliation with alternative income estimates in national and sector accounts impossible at present.

Within the confines of these limitations (which may be partly overcome in the next few years), some pertinent observations may be made using results from the SPI. Income from independent activity in agriculture and horticulture formed just over half the total income of agricultural cases, varying over the period 1980-91 from 54 per cent (1981) to 62 per cent (1984). The second largest source in each year was investment income; the share of total income from this was at its greatest (29 per cent) in 1991. The main change seen with the switch to independent taxation seems to have been a drop in the share of income coming from "other earnings" (that is, mainly wages) and a rise in the share of income from property. Deductions are not available adjusted to a calendar year basis. However, reference to the unadjusted figures in national publications finds that, in the taxation years 1978-79 to 1991-92, tax took from 17 per cent (1988-89) to 24 per cent (1981-82) of total taxable income.

The nature of the data source permits disaggregation according to level of income. Again using the unadjusted figures, under the previous system when couples were taxed together, farming was found to be somewhat more important for middle income bands than for incomes at either of the extremes. Under the system of independent taxation, it can be shown that in 1990-1991 income from self-employment in agriculture and horticulture was relatively less important in the highest income band (the 2 per cent of cases with incomes of over £50,000), where it accounted for 32 per cent of total income, compared to over 60 per cent in the other income bands. Half of the total income of these high-income cases came from investments. Cases at the other end of the income spectrum, where taxable income was less than £5,000, were far more numerous (42 per cent of cases); the share of their income coming from investments was lowest (16 per cent of total income) but they were relatively more dependent on pensions (10 per cent of income). The importance of pensions declined as higher income bands were reached.

Developments over time are best described using incomes per tax case, but this is only appropriate up to 1988. Figure 5.13 shows movements in the components of total income (in current £ per tax case). No consistent differences are evident in the growth patterns of the various income components. By 1988 total income had risen to 221 per cent of its 1980 level in nominal terms; the smallest rise (to 183 per cent) was shown by investment income, but this had fallen from a higher figure (231 per cent of the 1980 level) in the previous year. The largest rise (to 282 per cent) between 1980 and 1988 was seen in the income derived from self-employment in other trades. In no year in this period did the average nominal income from self- employment in agriculture and horticulture fall from one year to the next, though there was a slackening in the rate of increase between 1982 and 1983. This corresponded with falls in income from wages, from pensions and, in particular, from investment, so that total income per case fell, though how much of this can be attributed to sampling error is not clear.

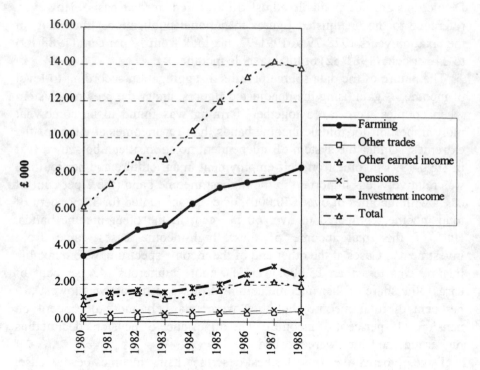

Figure 5.13 **UK: Development of income per case in the Survey of Personal Incomes where agriculture or horticulture is the main or principal additional source of self-employment income, 1980-88**

Table 5.3 UK: Income distributions of farmers according to partial and total income measures, 1982/83

Income	Self-employment income		Earned income		Total income	
£000s	cases (x 1,000)	Per cent	cases (x 1,000)	per cent	cases (x 1,000)	Per cent
Negative/ nill	30	1	21	8	5	2
1 < 2	62	24	57	22	33	13
2 < 4	64	25	61	24	62	24
4 < 6	38	15	38	15	48	19
6 < 10	35	14	44	17	55	22
10 < 15	15	6	21	8	27	11
15 < 20	5	2	6	2	11	4
20 < 30	5	2	5	2	8	3
30 +	2	1	2	1	5	2
Total	255	100	255	100	255	100

Source: derived from SPI Public Use Tape, given in Hill (1987)

On occasion the Inland Revenue has made available a public use tape of the SPI for individual years, permitting a flexible analysis of what cases are considered as agricultural (Hill, 1987). Using this it has been possible, for the year of assessment 1982/83, to narrow the definition of farmer to only those cases where both members of a couple have agriculture as their main self-employment income source, or where it is the major source for one and the other has no self-employment income. These form the basis of Table 5.3 in which the distribution of incomes is shown based on three types of income; that from self-employment (very largely from agriculture), all earned income (self-employment and as employees), and total income including pensions and investments. The distributions that are revealed underline the importance of including non-farm incomes in an assessment of the position of farmers. On the basis of their business incomes alone, 36 per cent of cases fell below an income of £2,000. Taking other forms of earned income into account reduced the proportion to 30 per cent, while including all other forms of income reduced it dramatically to 15 per cent. Obviously, to take only the self-employment earnings from agriculture is to risk a serious misrepresentation of the real income position

Comparison of the taxable incomes of farmers with other members of UK society is complicated by the different timings of the assessment of self-employment and employment earnings. However, one attempt for the late 1970s (Hill, 1984) found that farmers formed a rising proportion of cases as the higher income bands were reached. In the range of taxable income £1,000 to £8,000 agriculture and horticulture cases represented 1 per cent of all cases, and this increased progressively to 7 per cent of cases in the band of incomes of £20,000 and over. This is not the sort of characteristic that would be expected if low incomes were a feature of the farming community.

Turning to the other sources of data in the United Kingdom, the Farm Business Survey casts light on some important distributional issues. Only a flavour of the information available can be given here. Though covering the great majority of agricultural activity, the FBS is not necessarily representative of households that operate farms, or even those whose main incomes come from farming, because of the imposition of a minimum economic size threshold designed to restrict coverage to "commercial" farms. From the accounting year 1988/89 the FBS has included questions on income from employment and self-employment away from the farm and unearned income from investments, pensions and social security payments (including child benefit, family credit and other cash welfare payments); in 1997/98 about 2,700 of the 3,500 farms in the UK sample supplied this data. Income generated on the farm from activities that are not closely related to agriculture, and for which the employed resources of the farm business can be separately measured (such as tourist accommodation, catering and rural crafts), is included in "Other on-farm income". Scrutiny of the results, including comparison with the taxation statistics and other concerns with the sample of respondents, suggests that the FBS findings should be treated with caution. At this stage not too much should be attributed to short-term changes between years. However, they provide some interesting indications of a qualitative nature not available from elsewhere.

In England 57 per cent of farms reported some other income to the farmer or spouse in 1997/98 (69 per cent in 1992/93) (MAFF, 1994, 1999). The average off-farm earnings was £4,900 (£4,700 in 1992/93) compared with a cash income from farming of £16,500 (£21,700 in 1992/93). However, off-farm sums were unevenly distributed, with only 12 per cent of farms receiving more than £10,000 in both years. In both of these years on average in England about half of the off-farm income came from employment and self-employment off the farm, and half from other sources, including pensions and property. In Scotland and Wales the proportions of farms with some other income in 1997/98 (1992/93 in parentheses) were 65 per cent (56 per cent) and 53 per cent (48 per cent) respectively. Average off-farm incomes per farm in Scotland was £6,000 (£4,000 in 1992/93) and in Wales £4,200 (£2,700). Across Britain average off-farm income was generally lowest among dairy farms and was highest among English cereal farms and Scottish mixed farms.

There is some evidence that large farms in England differ somewhat in their income composition from those elsewhere in Great Britain, though low response rates throw doubt onto the representativity of the replics. In England in 1997/98, large farms recorded the biggest average off-farm incomes, followed by small farms, with the lowest levels found on medium-sized farms. In Wales and Scotland, however, the lowest levels were found on large farms and the highest on small farms, than on medium-sized farms,

In Northern Ireland (where off-farm income averaged £4,100, with 15 per cent earning more than £10,000) it was clear that in 1997/98 on cattle and sheep and mixed farms the income from farming was very low or negative, and without these off-farm sources household income would not have been positive.

Finally, for England and Wales some fragmentary information on incomes has emerged from studies of part-time farming (Gasson 1986, Hill 1987). The sample was drawn from holdings which reported that the farmer or spouse had some gainful activity in addition to the farm; this meant as self-employed or as employees, and did not cover any investment income that may have been present. The evidence suggested that there was no simple pattern of substitution of farm for non-farm income or vice versa; high non-farm earnings were found both with high and low farm earnings, though there was a tendency for high non-farm and low farm figures to be associated. Of particular interest were those households claiming low incomes from *both* sources; some 10 per cent claimed they received less than £2,000 from the farm and less than £2 000 from their other activity, so that their combined income was less than £4,000. Seven out of every ten of these were on holdings which, according to standard labour figures, were too small to occupy a man full-time, which suggests that policy aimed at low incomes in agriculture should not ignore the holdings that are considered to fall below the full-time threshold. These low income holdings formed a higher proportion of holdings either side of this threshold than of the very small holdings or those capable of occupying two men or more. This supports the belief that income problems are felt most acutely among farms that are on the margin of full time occupation, too large to allow the occupier to have another full-time job yet too small to generate a satisfactory income from full time farming.

5.7.2 Denmark

We turn next to the information on the personal incomes of farmers in the countries with which the UK shares the Common Agricultural Policy. Denmark is perhaps the most interesting point of departure, because it is relatively well endowed with microeconomic data. However, it should not necessarily be treated as typical, because the tradition of selling agricultural land and buildings to the next generation on retirement by the operator has created a situation where the level of borrowing and interest payments is exceptionally high (by EUR 15 standards) and where off-farm jobs are frequently taken by younger farmers and spouses to help meet these commitments (Commission, 1992; OECD, 1998). This in turn impacts on the (net) income levels from farming and on the types of enterprise that are pursued. We have already noted that this situation produces low numbers of households classified as agricultural in Eurostat's sector-level IAHS statistics (where net income from farming is the main income source of the reference person)..

There are several primary data sources in Denmark. An annual Income Statistics Register is kept, based mainly on tax information and covering all sources of income and deductions; agricultural households selected from this form the basis of Denmark's contribution to Eurostat's IAHS statistics. Farm accounts information is published by the Farmers' Association and Smallholders' Association relating to their members, and this covers both the income from farming and from other sources. The State Institute of Agronomy conducts an annual survey that covers just under 2,000 holdings, drawing its sample from the register of account-keeping farms made up from the two associations already mentioned. This sample contributes to the European Commission's Farm Accountancy Data Network (FADN/RICA) but goes further in the information it collects and publishes. The reliability of the sample means that the survey findings can be grossed up to national levels, and these estimates are compatible with the national accounts for the Danish agricultural industry. The holding size threshold for inclusion is 5 hectares, and at least half the holding's standard gross margin has to come from agricultural and horticultural production, two criteria which cut out what might be considered as non-commercial farms. The incomes measured included those accruing to the spouse but not other family members; in Denmark agricultural households are typically one-family and consisting of parents and dependent children so this use of a narrow definition of a household is not considered a problem. All forms if income and deductions are covered, but the account is carried down further to distribute disposable income between that used for consumption spending and for saving, something that is rare among farm accounts and in aggregate measures.

The first valuable insight provided by Denmark relates to consumption spending. It has been argued earlier that this may be a preferable parameter to income for the purpose of monitoring the standard of living of the agricultural population, preferable even to disposable income. Figure 5.14 clearly shows that, on the basis of group averages, consumption expenditure of farm households is more stable over the years than is disposable income. Current income (from self-employment, employment, pension and supplementary benefit) and disposable income followed similar patterns, most of the change being attributable to the income from farming. In years when consumption spending exceeded disposable income, dis-saving took place; when disposable income was greater than consumption, positive saving took place. The main point is that, on this evidence, fluctuations in disposable income, in turn more stable than the income from the farm alone, are not reflected in the short term directly in the amounts that farm households spend on consumption. Caution should therefore be exercised when commenting on annual movements in disposable income, as they do not lead to adjustments in living standards. However, there is a suggestion in the movements of average income in Figure 5.14 that periods of falling or rising incomes are reflected in small adjustments to consumption spending.

The other valuable insight comes from analysing farms by size. Table 5.4 shows farms in 1991-92 grouped by two size measures - area and economic size (although, in contrast to the above, all farms in the survey are included here). Overall, farming accounted for 48 per cent of total income, followed by employment income (28 per cent) almost equally contributed by the farmer (15 per cent) and others in the household (13 per cent, mainly the spouse). The farm's relative contribution was tiny on the farms with the smallest area but increased across the size spectrum. When ranked by economic size (based on Standard Gross Margins) the smallest farms made a loss from their farming, but the share from this source again increased with size. Put in another way, when ranking farms using either size measure, on about four farms out of ten (the smallest) farming contributed less than one sixth of the household's total income.

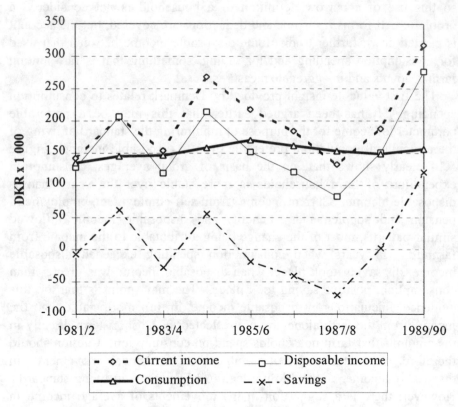

Relates to farms of at least 1,800 hours labour per year.
Deflated to 1990 DKR values

**Figure 5.14   Denmark: Real income per full-time farm, 1981/2-
1989/90**

Table 5.4 Denmark: Income characteristics of farms grouped by size (utilised farm area in ha and economic size in ESU), 1991/92

Size	Proportion of all farms	Farm income	Total income	Disposable income	Farm income/ total income
	Per cent	DKR per farm (x 1,000)	DKR per household (x 1,000)	DKR per household (x 1,000)	Per cent
Area (ha)					
5-10	16	3	237	143	1
10-20	24	39	270	146	15
20-30	17	119	308	153	39
30-50	21	229	401	177	57
50-100	16	408	583	230	70
Over 100	5	788	1059	263	74
Economic size (ESU)					
Under 8	20	-9	262	151	n.c.
8-16	18	12	244	131	5
16-40	26	93	284	133	33
40-100	27	329	476	193	69
Over 100	9	811	1028	364	79
All sizes	100	187	391	173	48

Source: Denmark Institute of Agricultural Economics, reported in OECD (1995)

Earlier analysis (Hill, 1989) reported that the holder's contribution from off-farm earnings declined with increasing farm size but the income of the rest of the family (mainly the wife) was fairly constant across the size bands. Welfare payments (pensions and daily allowances) were more important among small farms. Though the income from farming increased strongly with farm size in Table 5.4, impact of non-farm income was to substantially lower the disparity of income between the large and small farms. Disposable income was very similar up to 30 ha, and when economic size was used the occupiers on the smallest farms had average disposable incomes that were higher than those occupying larger farms, even though the farm made a loss.

Once again the importance of non-farm income to the smaller, low-income farm is apparent and the inappropriateness of using the income from farming as an indicator of the total agricultural household income is exposed.

Denmark's farm survey data show that other sources of income vary between farming types, as in the UK and many other countries. Taking just the three major types, covering 66 per cent of all farms, income from the farm was least important among cereal farms (13 per cent of total income) but was higher in mixed farming (32 per cent) and highest in dairy farming (72 per cent). These characteristics are probably explained by the phenomenon already referred to above; that young Danish farmers and their spouses tend to work off the farm to meet interest charges, and cereal farming is more compatible with regular absence from the farm than is dairying.

Analysis based on the age of the head is similarly affected heavily by the issue of intergenerational transfer of land. Households on farms headed by young farmers obtained a somewhat larger proportion of their income from off-farm sources (52 per cent, compared with the all-household average of 48 per cent) but this fell away sharply among the oldest farmers (aged 65 years and over), with 26 per cent. Analysis for 1995 of the families on farms that were "full-time" (in the sense that they required an estimated labour input of at least one annual labour unit) found that, though the elderly farmers produced a much smaller operating surplus from their farms and also earned less from off-farm wages and salaries, they enjoyed a much greater disposable income than younger families because of the lower interest payments they faced (40 per cent of gross income for the over-60 years group compared with 67 per cent for the under-30 years group) (Eurostat, 1999).

5.7.3 Ireland

Ireland in many ways forms a sharp contrast in its economic and agrarian structure with the UK and Denmark. Within EUR 12 Ireland has the third highest proportion of the employed population engaged in agriculture, hunting and fishing (in 1997, 10 per cent against a EUR 15 average of 4.6 per cent, with only Greece's and Portugal's being larger). In 1991 family farm households accounted for 16 per cent of all households in the state

(CSO, 1998). Agriculture generated only 3.4 per cent of Ireland's GDP at market prices (1997) which, when ranged against the population proportion, is suggestive of an income problem in farming. Its Net Value Added per Annual Work Unit in agriculture was 82 in 1996-98 compared with a EUR 12 figure of 100 ((Eurostat, 1999)); the UK equivalent income indicator was 124. Its average size of holding in 1993 was 26 ha, and this has changed only a little since 1975, in contrast to the rapid structural change witnessed in many other EU countries.

Ireland has a farm accounts survey (National Farm Survey with some 1,500 cases) but this does not normally cover incomes of the farmer from non-farm sources or personal taxation details. Irish farmers are mostly in practice outside the tax net, so tax statistics on their incomes are not available. However, Ireland has a Household Budget Survey, conducted at about 7- year intervals; results from the surveys in 1973, 1980 and 1987 surveys have been published, but those from the 1994 survey are not yet available. Ireland provides one of the few published surveys (others being Germany and Denmark) in EUR 12 which looks at farmer households in terms of their expenditure as well as their income. It could therefore be a valuable source of information for policy directed at the living standards of farmers and their families.

Total household income in this survey covers not only cash income from all sources and the value of farm produce consumed in the home (at retail value) but also the value of non-cash benefits, such as medical, educational, housing and social welfare benefits and subsidies such as those on food and transport (Higgins, 1986). The acknowledged difficulty of measuring the incomes of self-employed farmers was got over, in the 1980 survey, by requiring the medium to large farm encountered (those over 12 ha.) to keep detailed farm accounts over one year. In the 1987 survey this was rendered unnecessary by selecting agricultural cases from households already taking part in the National Farm Survey. Households are classified according to the occupation of the head of the household; thus farmer households are taken as those where farming is the main occupation of the reference person (though for the 1987 survey alternative criteria can be used). The detail with which income information is collected enables the relative importance of the various income components to be assessed for different sizes of farm and for a range of income indicators to be used, of which Disposable Income per household is the most interesting.

In the 1987 survey income from farming constituted just under half (49 per cent) the gross income of farmer households (less than in 1973 and 1980), income from employment 22 per cent; most of the rest came from state transfers. Wide differences were seen between sizes of farm in the level of dependency on state transfer payments; on small farms (under 30 acres) these transfers (mainly old-age and retirement pensions) constituted over a third of total gross income (40 per cent). These payments reduced the relative income gap between the small and large farms; average income from farming in the smallest and largest farm bands was in the order of 1 to 10, total direct income after the inclusion of other earned and direct income in the ratio 1 to 4, gross income after taking into account state transfers about 1 to 2. Non-farm incomes did much to compensate for the increasing inequality in the profits from farming which developed in Ireland·after its entry to the EC (Pratschke, 1984). The Household Budget Survey found that income support programmes had played an important part in maintaining the household incomes of those in the lower income deciles. This was especially so in less favoured areas where state transfer payments made up 44 per cent of the total income of farm households and only fell below one third of total income in the top decile. The resulting picture is of a farm sector whose incomes were particularly vulnerable to changes in government policy on poverty and to the ability of government to continue funding such transfers.

The HBS permits some comparison between the incomes of farmer households and other sectors of Irish society. The 1980 HBS found that the direct income of farm households was lower than other groups in rural areas but the inclusion of state transfers reduced the size of the gap. When tax and social insurance were also taken into account, the effect was to make the disposable income of farmer households very similar to that of agricultural workers and to put it above the all household average. The figures also showed that the tax burden on farmers was noticeably lighter than on other employed sectors; only 6 per cent of their gross income went in this way as opposed to 14 per cent for agricultural workers. In the 1987 HBS, though farmer households had total incomes very similar to the all-households average (including levels of state transfers that were also close) the lighter tax burden meant that farmer households enjoyed an average disposable income some 27 per cent higher than that of other households in rural areas, 8 per cent higher than urban households, and 12 per cent higher than the national average.

The Irish data also permit the possibility of farmer/non-farmer comparison on the basis of spending on consumption rather than on incomes. In some ways this is a preferable way of comparing the relative welfare positions, as long as the households have similar compositions. In 1973 consumption expenditure by farm households was on average only 80 per cent of that of urban households, and was particularly low for 2, 3, and 4 adult households, perhaps reflecting the age structure of rural households with only adults present, but it may also reflect under-employment on farms and therefore low per capita incomes (from NESC, 1982). There is also the question of the relative cost of consumption goods, especially housing which was estimated at IR£4.1 per week for urban households (9 per cent of expenditure) against IR£1 for farm households (3 per cent). It may be recalled that in the USA the poverty line for farmers is set at 85 per cent of the general level to reflect the lower living costs. Overall the conclusion (NESC, 1982) was that the welfare of farm households in 1973 was below that of urban ones. However, in 1987 average total household expenditure of farmers was higher than that of other rural households and 94 per cent of that of urban households (though the average household size, at 3.89 persons, was larger than urban households with 3.45 persons and the national average of 3.51). Farmer households spent more than other rural households or urban households on most items except housing and fuel and light.

No firm conclusions can be drawn from these consumption figures in the absence of information on savings. If farm family preferences were such that they saved a higher proportion of their income than non-farm households, then consumption expenditure would appear to under-value the welfare of the former relative to the latter. Saving levels would also reflect the differential living costs. These caveats underline the conclusion of Chapter 3 that comparing incomes or expenditures of farm families with other groups as a way of indicating comparative welfare is a highly complex matter.

5.7.4 Germany

In Germany information on the incomes of households headed by self-employed persons in agriculture is collected as part of the 5-yearly general Income and Expenditure Survey and has been used to study income levels and distributions (Wolleb, 1989). In 1985 the average disposable income of farmers' households was very close to the national all-households average (DM 3,734 and DM 3,707 respectively), though their median income was more than a fifth higher (DM 3,567 and DM 2925 respectively). Their average (and median) disposable incomes were below those of other self-employed, non-manual and civil servant groups, but above those of households headed by manual workers and pensioners. However, farm household incomes were more evenly distributed than those any other group, with a Gini coefficient of 0.21; the all-household figure was 0.35, other self-employed 0.27 and manual workers 0.22).

Annual data comes from the official farm accounts survey for Germany comprising, as far as the western Länder are concerned, some 11,000 "test holdings". This survey covers income from the holding received by the farmer and spouse and other family helpers and, in addition, collects information on non-farm income, though the coverage of this source for other family members is considered as incomplete - a situation shared with the comparable surveys in Finland and the USA. Three income measures are used, firstly profit ignoring all non-farm income, secondly all earned income and, thirdly, total income including social transfers.

The German Ministry of Agriculture uses a classification of holdings operated by households into three groups - "full-time" (in which the operator-and-spouse's earnings from off-farm sources are less than 10 per cent of total income; "part-time" (Type 1) holdings are those with substantial off-farm earnings (10 - 50 per cent of total income); "part-time" (Type 2), or "spare-time", holdings are those where the farmer-and-spouse earnings from gainful employment come mainly from off-farm sources. In the first two types the operator will be predominantly occupied on the farm, though the basis for classification does not take time allocation into account, despite the terms used. The farm income for classification purposes is not the actual income but an estimated one based on standards reflecting the holding's cropping and stocking and size - this gives a more stable classification over short time periods than if actual incomes were used. In 1991/92, 65 per cent of the total number of German holdings above 1 hectare were "full-time" in this official classification, 7 per cent were "part-time" (Type 1) and 28 per cent "spare-time" (Type 2). Typically the "spare-time" holdings are much smaller than the other two categories; even excluding those below 1 hectare gave a "spare-time" average size of only 5.3 hectares, against a "full-time" holding average of 26.6 ha and "part-time" average of 15.8 (figures for 1986).

Over time a polarisation has been occurring, with a concentration into farms where the income is very largely farm-derived or the "spare-time" holdings whose income is predominantly from off-farm sources, and with a corresponding shrinkage in the importance of "part-time" holdings where the farm still provides the main income but other sources form 10 to 50 per cent of the total, a phenomenon noted in many countries where records of multiple-activity farm households are available (OECD, 1978).

When farms are classified on this income-composition criterion it is not surprising to find that "full-time" farms received the bulk of their income from the farm, but even so in 1991/92 nearly 10 per cent of their total income came from non-farm sources; this share was quite stable across the size spectrum of full-time farms (figures given in OECD, 1995). However, of greater significance is the evidence that the low levels of farm profit found on "part-time" and "spare-time" farms is no guide to the total incomes of these groups. The average disposable income of "part-time" farms (Type 1) was 28 per cent higher than the "full-time" all-size average (Table 5.5). Even on "spare-time" (Type 2) holdings, with very low incomes from farming, the average disposable income was 8 per cent higher than the "full-time" average and substantially above that of small "full-time" farms. Far from being cases of particular hardship, farms where there are additional income sources seem to be rather well off; this mirrors the findings in Eurostat's IAHS statistics for Germany given earlier. Lowest total incomes were found on small full-time farms, a common finding among countries. Analysis of farms in size groups irrespective of their income status seems not to be published.

Mention should be made here of the requirement within the legislation for a comparison to be drawn on the basis of microeconomic data from the test holdings (farm accounts survey) of the income position of farmers. This takes the form of a comparison of the profit (plus a 35 per cent addition to allow for consumption of own production) on full-time farms only with the earnings received by other business proprietors (also adjusted for management and interest elements). The resulting difference is referred to as "income disparity". Apparently this system has fallen into disrepute, and it is not difficult to see why. The comparison only refers to two-thirds of the farmers in Germany and is made on only part of the income received by agricultural households. Nevertheless, its existence must be acknowledged.

Table 5.5 Germany (western Länder): Income characteristics of farms grouped by income status and size (utilised farm area in ha), 1991/92

Status and size	Per cent of all farms	Farm income	Total income	Disposable income	Farm income/ total income
	%	DM per farm (x 1,000)	DM per household (x 1,000)	DM per household (x 1,000)	%
"Full-time"					
Area (ha)					
Below 10	3	35	40		88
10-20	8	35	39		90
20-30	14	42	47		91
30-40	14	45	50		90
40-50	9	54	60		91
50-100	16	71	78		91
Over 100	2	126	137		92
All sizes	65	48	53	39	91
"Part-time" (Type 1)					
	7	37	67	50	55
"Spare-time" (Type 2)					
	28	9	64	43	13

Source: derived from *Agrarbericht* (1992)

5.7.5 France

France has no regular and reliable source of microeconomic data on the overall income situation of its agricultural households. Information comes in the form of a special survey, conducted in 1978 but with the report only published in 1991 (Brangeon, Jégouzo, and Roze, 1991). Despite drawbacks to the methodology and the passage of time, in the present climate of greater interest in the overall income of farm households this remains the "least bad" microeconomic data source. Three groups of households with farms were distinguished according to the occupation of the head; principally a farmer (69 per cent of households), secondarily a farmer (13 per cent), or retired (18 per cent). Though low or negative farming incomes were particularly common among the latter two groups, their average total incomes per consumer unit were higher than that of the households headed by a principal-occupation farmer; average incomes per unit were FF 21,417 for the principal-occupation group, FF 31,534 for the supplementary occupation group and FF 24,361 for the retired group. Even among the principal-occupation group, only 13 per cent of households were solely dependent on farming for their income; more than half (55 per cent) were mainly dependent on non-farm income.

Though low farm incomes did not necessarily put the household into poverty (because of non-farm income), about one quarter of households headed by a principal-occupation farmer were below the poverty line (less than 50 per cent of the whole-population average disposable income per consumer unit). These poor households were concentrated among the small and medium farms. At the time, among the very small farms (below 20 ha equivalents of wheat) over half (52 per cent) of the household heads described themselves as principally a farmer; at least half of these "small peasantry" families were not below the poverty line. The authors of the report were aware of the transitory nature of low farm incomes, that their coverage of income was less than complete, and that low incomes in agriculture may represent less stress than outside. They also point to the many changes which have taken place in France since 1978 and the need for more recent results not limited to one year.

In an attempt to study the question of income distributions in agriculture, with particular attention to the incidence of poverty and of high incomes, the same team drew on tax survey data covering all types of household for 1990 (Jégouzo, Brangeon and Roze, 1998). For studies of high income, tax data were used, as numbers of cases in the family budget survey were too small for statistical reliability. (As noted earlier, tax data for France is not particularly appropriate because of the way in which taxable income is estimated and recorded, particularly for low income farm households, though this does not mean that the data are not used, for example in France's contribution to the study of trends and distributions of income in a number of EU Member States which identifies farmers as a separate occupation group (Wolleb, 1989)). Some 7 per cent of farm households were found to be among the top decile of incomes per consumer unit. For the study of low incomes, household declarations to the family budget survey of income for the twelve months of 1994 were taken; as all households were covered, comparison by socio-professional group was possible. On the basis of incomes declared, just over a quarter of farmer household were deemed to fall below the poverty line (set at half the median income per consumer unit), far more than the all-household average of 10 per cent though a little less than the 28 per cent for the group comprising agricultural workers and non-skilled workers. Perhaps surprisingly, a somewhat lower proportion of households of retired farmers (20 per cent) were deemed to be in poverty than among the households of economically active farmers. However, the public body responsible for the statistics (INSEE) was concerned that the self-employment income was under-reported, levels of farm income being lower than those indicated by the EU farm accounts survey FADN (RICA in its French acronym).

Some credence is given for the caution afforded to self-declared incomes by the fact that very few farmers had received benefits under the guaranteed minimum income provision (RMI) introduced in 1988, only about 1 per cent of farmers over the years 1992 to 1996 compared with 2.5 per cent for the population in general. It might be noted that in 1996 there were twice as many hired agricultural workers in receipt of RMI than farmers; this is in sharp contrast with Eurostat's labour input statistics show that they provided only about one fifth of the labour input (Eurostat, 1997a). This situation strongly suggests that in France poverty is much more prevalent among hired agricultural workers and among self-employed farmers (a finding previously noted in (Hill, 1988)). Hired workers are not, however, usually seen as the targets of the EU's Common Agricultural Policy.

5.7.6 Some other EU and EEA countries

Brief mention can only be made of some other EU countries. *Finland* and *Sweden* have particularly good data sources and a history of interest in income distribution issues in their period before adopting the CAP. National legislation in both countries required explicit comparisons between the incomes of farm households and other groups, and information sources were developed with this in mind. In *Finland* the Income Distribution Statistics (largely tax-based) indicated that the primary income of farmer households (that is, those headed by a farmer) per consumer unit in 1986 was only 71 per cent of the corresponding income of industrial workers, but this was raised to 95 per cent when disposable income was considered (Puurunen, 1990). This combined effect of transfer income and taxation was particularly noticeable among small farms. Comparison with other small-scale entrepreneurs (enterprises with less than 5 persons), often a preferred yardstick, found that the primary income per economically active person in farmer households averaged 68 per cent of that of these entrepreneurs, but disposable income was almost the same (96 per cent). Improvements in the relative position of farm households from the 1960s to the 1980s primarily were due to increases in the amounts coming from non-agricultural income sources.

Finnish data from the Income Distribution Statistics show that the distribution of incomes among farmer households is made more equal when the view of income is broadened to include income from property and transfers, and that the incidence of taxation and other deductions further serves to reduce inequalities. (Ylisippola, 1989 quoted in Puurunen, 1990). The following Gini-coefficients applied for 1986 at household level:

- Primary income (from self-employment and employment) 0.29
- Factor income (primary income plus interest and rents) 0.27
- Total income (factor income plus welfare transfers) 0.24
- Disposable income (total income less taxes) 0.22

Interestingly, the distribution of disposable income was substantially more even when calculated per consumer unit (coefficient of 0.12). Compared with households of economically active persons in general, the incomes of Finland's agricultural households appear more unequally distributed, with a skew to lower incomes. However, the distribution of disposable income of other small entrepreneurs was *more* uneven than among farmer households.

In *Sweden* explicit comparisons of income of farmer households with other households were made during the 1980s (up to 1987) as a basis for the negotiations on agricultural prices. This form of comparison was abandoned as part of the agricultural policy reforms of 1990. However, this illustrates a situation where attempts were made to put farmer households and others on the same statistical base by adjusting income data. The intention was to indicate the potential standard of consumption for farmers and other groups in society. The agricultural households in the sample were selected in a special way to satisfy agricultural policy makers and were limited to holdings in the size group 20-100 hectares of arable land (354 cases in 1987). In order to make a more complete comparison of the incomes of employees with those of farmers and other entrepreneurs, some adjustments were carried out, including changes to agricultural income to allow for investment requirements and to housing benefits. The amount of tax was corrected to correspond to the adjusted income level. Table 5.6 shows the "comparable incomes" (disposable income per household) of married/cohabiting persons for the years 1980 to 1987. On this basis, the average income of farmer households was in each year below that of both groups selected for comparison. Furthermore, the relative position of farmer households appeared to have deteriorated over the period.

Table 5.6 Sweden: "Comparable incomes" of farmer households and other selected groups, SKR (nominal) per household

Year	Farmers (a)	Workers (b)	Salaried employees (c)	(a) as % of (b)	(a) as % of (c)
1980	64,600	78,400	87,400	82	74
1981	73,800	85,300	93,900	86	79
1982	81,000	92,300	103,300	88	78
1983	78,400	100,300	111,800	85	70
1984	91,800	110,100	120,700	83	76
1985	91,600	121,400	133,000	75	69
1986	94,700	127,600	141,400	74	67
1987	103,100	137,900	155,200	75	66

Source: Joint Council for Economic Studies in the Food Sector

A pilot study in *Greece*, based on the FADN/RICA farm accounts survey, found that non-farm incomes contributed to the smoothing of income inequalities, though there was difficulty in collecting reliable data on income from financial assets and for family member other than the farmer and spouse (Efstratoglou, 1994).

The *Netherlands* has both farm accounts surveys (formerly two separate ones, now integrated) and tax statistics that can be used to monitor the overall income situation of agricultural households. In measuring non-farm income each restricts coverage to the farmer and spouse but, given the structure of households in the Netherlands, this is unlikely to affect to a major extent the distribution patterns. The survey of farm accounts used in national accounting, formerly undertaken by the Central Bureau of Statistics, took cases from holdings which used accountants; small holdings (those below about 14 European Size Units) and very large holdings were omitted. The use of a fairly high lower threshold (the UK contemporarily used a threshold of 8 ESU for its Farm Business Survey) was important as there were likely to be more subsidiary off-farm activities among those holdings which were excluded. Neverthele ss, the results showed the same (by now familiar) pattern of greater importance of non-farm income among the smaller farms; in 1982/3 this fell from 28 per cent in the smallest to 10 per cent in the largest categories. Off-farm income seemed less volatile than that from the farm, and the tax and welfare system operated, as one might expect, so that disposable income formed a higher share of total income among the small-size/low-income groups.

The Agricultural Economics Research Institute (LEI) also conducts an annual survey (which forms part of RICA) and publishes information on the basis of the "average holding"; this takes into account the rising average size of holdings. In 1991/92 the proportion of total income coming from off-farm sources fell from 35 per cent among those below 40 Netherlands Size Units (NGEs - based on gross standard product values) to 14 per cent for farms over 110 NGEs; the all-farms average was 22 per cent. Variation was seen among farm types; off-farm income was most important among arable farms (33 per cent)(OECD, 1995). In 1983/4 the average farm family paid almost 20 per cent of its income as income tax and public insurance premiums, a share fairly stable over the preceding fifteen years and implying parallel movements in total and disposable incomes. Compared with other groups in Dutch society, this proportion seemed rather low; the explanation appeared to lie in the fiscal possibilities for pension planning, wages paid to the wife and other provisions. The amount of savings that farm families were able to make was also comparatively high, though it was difficult to distinguish satisfactorily between purely personal savings and that necessary to finance the longer-term viability of the business by compensating members who leave the family farm and to enable the transfer to the next generation. All in all, it appeared that "Compared to fellow-citizens, the average Dutch farm family has a fairly reasonable standard of living" (Poppe and Zacharieasse, 1986).

In *Austria* information on poverty among farm households has been gleaned as part of a national study that covered all types of household, based on the 1984 consumer survey and a microcensus on household incomes in 1989 (Steiner and Wolf, 1996). Using a poverty line set at half the average weighted household income, 22% of people living in household headed by farmers were below the threshold, compared with 13% for households in general, 12% for household with other self-employed heads and 14% for worker households. Farmer households contributed 13% of all poverty cases. However, the method of assessing total household income for farming households that gave rise to these figures was indirect, involving comparisons with the living standards of salary and wage earner households, and must therefore be treated with caution. Information on farmers' total incomes based on direct measurement comes from farm accounts surveys. In 1983 the share of total income accounted for by income from the farm was 72 per cent on full-time farms but only 14 per cent on part-time farms (Niessler, 1986). On full-time farms (in a labour-input sense) the proportion from non-farm sources has been increasing, especially among those in high mountain areas. Government transfers are divided into those for farming purposes and those of a social nature, with the latter being the more important. The share of these transfers has been rising, and was up to 24 per cent of total family income of full-time farmers in high mountain areas. Taking all full-time farms together, of the 28 per cent of family income was not from the farm, 12 per cent was from non-farming (non-governmental) income, 4 per cent from transfers for farming purposes and 12 per cent from social transfers.

In contrast with what is found in Germany, the average total income of part-time farm families in Austria was slightly below that of full-time farmers, but the distribution was relatively homogeneous. However the distribution of their incomes from farming was extremely unequal, with about one in five making a farming loss. Among full-time farms there was a high degree of inequality in total income, the mean of the top decile being 13.7 times the mean of the bottom decile (Gini-coefficient 0.334). Observation of incomes over long periods shows that in Austria the degree of disparity had been growing, and was especially noted after the late 1970s. Important for policy purposes was the finding that the dispersion of income from the farm was softened by income from non-farm sources, a situation similar to that noted above for Finland.

Though *Norway* decided in 1994 not to join countries Finland, Sweden and Austria in their move to full EU membership, it remains part of the European Economic Area (EAA) and shares the Scandinavian tradition of interest in household-level income studies and the data collection systems needed to support them. (It also shares the tendency to regard the concept of income from self-employment as something measured before the payment of interest charges, a fact that hinders some international comparisons). If anything, concern with the living conditions of farmers has increased since 1995 and the policy changes that have shifted the income aim of policy from a specific target to fostering conditions for a "robust" agriculture. Data are collected from farm accounts surveys, but the richest source appears to be the various data banks that draw on tax records and other administrative material. There is a liberal attitude to using personal identifiers to collate information. These sources are used not only to shadow the sector-level IAHS statistics of EU countries but also to investigate distributional characteristics. Much of the recent work has yet to appear (in English). An analysis of agricultural families in the farm accounts survey with two adults for incomes earned in 1997 found that, when ranked by level of household net income, the families with low income from agriculture had relatively large incomes from other activities, the consequence being that average total income was remarkably constant across the deciles up to decile 8. Operating surplus from agriculture was negatively correlated with other forms of income except for interest received, the largest negative correlation being with (off-farm) wages(Hegrenes, 1999). Perhaps this also explains the finding (from tax data) that the total income in 1994 was quite even across the spectrum stretching from those that worked few hours on the farm or many (Statistics Norway, personal communication). Total income tended to be highest among families with heads aged 45-59 years and with those having tertiary education (where much was contributed by off-farm wages and salaries); this analysis covered all farm families, not only those with farming as their main income. Rather surprisingly, the tailing-off seen among the group of farmers aged 60 and over was not seen, or to such a marked extent, among the population in general. Another interesting finding was that farmers (males aged 30-59) who had an off-farm occupation tended to record a lower total income than those people who were full-time in that other occupation, irrespective of the nature of that occupation (grouped into three; professions, services, or primary, construction etc.), though the difference was smallest in the third (manual) group which had the lowest total incomes. One interpretation of this might be that higher-earning professionals living on farms are taking their rewards as environmental benefits. Comparisons over time suggested that, though households have increased the amount of time they spend working off the farm, the amount used on the farm has barely changed. Part of this probably comes from spouses increasing their participation in the labour market, but there is some indication of Norway's farm households being on an upward-sloping labour supply curve (Bjornsen, 1999). In a study that traced the income, consumption and savings behaviour of a panel of farms over a long run of years (1976-1997), Sand (1999) showed a the steady rise in consumption spending, a trend that was quite stable in the face of fluctuating disposable incomes. In addition, it was apparent *inter alia* that the propensity to consume differed between types of income, being higher among off-farm income and subsidies than on the inherently less stable income from farming, a finding in line with the notion of Friedman (1957) that the propensity to consume out of an income stream was inversely related to its volatility (and hence its riskiness). The possibilities for analysis offered by such rich microeonomic data sources will hopefully encourage the development of similar resources in EU Member States.

5.7.7 The United States of America

In sharp contrast with most of the EU, the USA is well provided with data on the total income of farm operators through a combination of its Census of Agriculture, conducted every four or five years by the US Department of Commerce, and its annual Agricultural Resource Management Study - ARMS (called up to 1995 the Farm Costs and Returns Survey - FCRS), conducted by the Economic Research Service (ERS) of the US Department of Agriculture. Another source is the Current Population Survey; this found that in 1976 only 30 per cent of families with some farm income (positive or negative) were dependent on farming for more than half their income (Banks and Kalbacher, 1981). The US Department of Commerce also collects income and employment data for individuals related in some way to a farm business (Money Income of Households, Families, and Persons in the United States), including a series of non-farm employment data for people who live on farms. There are also data series available on those whose principal occupation is operating or managing a farm and those who receive farm self-employment income. The former series omits those operators for whom farming is not their main occupation; the latter omits farm operators of incorporated farms and includes landlords who rent farmland on a share rental basis. The fact that none of the available series purely captures any of the contributors to agricultural production (operators, workers, landlords, other claimants of residual income) is seen as a serious drawback to their usefulness (Ahearn and Lee, 1991). However, these sources seem plentiful compared with the paucity in the EU. A series of publications has dealt with the distributional aspects of the total income of farmers and their households using these sources (see for example USDA, 1984; Ahearn *et al.*, 1985, 1993).

Attention here focuses on the Agricultural Resource Management Study (ARMS)/ Farm Costs and Returns Survey (FCRS). Since 1988 this has been the prime source of information on farm household incomes, and raised estimated based on data from it have displaced the former indirect way of producing figures for the agricultural household sector. Initiated in 1985, the FCRS replaced previous surveys. This change mirrored an increasing awareness of the importance of the distribution of income to agricultural policy, and that this required a large, statistically representative micro-data base that could be used to produce results raised to national levels. Furthermore, it needed to adopt a methodology in common with the aggregate accounts of the branch agriculture to allow integration with the macroeconomic parameters (Baum and Johnson, 1986). In 1986 enumerators contacted over 23,000 operators for information on their 1985 costs and returns, and usable data were obtained from some 14,000. The usable sample size is now about 9,000 farms (1996). Farms are classified into size groups based on the value of their (expected) sales, and information on the income of operators from farm and non-farm sources by farm sales class is available from 1960 (based on the old methodology) (USDA, 1988). The ARMS/FCRS consists of multiple versions; since 1988 the Farm Operator Resource (FOR) version has been dedicated to collecting special data on farm operator households (Ahearn *et al.* 1993)

The large volume of data generated from the ARMS/FCRS on the economic well-being of farm operator households has given rise to a weighty publication devoted entirely to this topic (Ahearn, Perry and El-Osta, 1993); subsequent updatings of its tables are available on the internet. On a smaller scale, results relating to the households of farm operators forms a chapter of the annual *Family Farm Report to Congress* (Sommer, 1998) and in *Rural Conditions and Trends* (Bowers, 1997). Tables 5.7 and 5.8 extracts some of the most relevant to this study related to household income level (1992) and to farm size for two years (1988 and 1992); farms in the ARMS/FCRS are classified into size groups based on the value of their expected sales.

Only a few findings from the plethora of tabulations can be touched on here. Characteristics seem quite stable in successive yearly data from the ARMS/FCRS. Small farms dominate the numbers of operator households with low farm incomes, but size is no reliable guide to their total household income.

First, off-farm income is important as an income source, accounting for 89 per cent of household income of farm operator households in 1995. Within this total, wages and salaries contributed 53 per cent, off-farm business income 13 per cent, interest and dividends 8 per cent, and other off-farm sources 16 per cent. Farming only provided 11 per cent. Only 20 per cent of farm operator households in the 1990 and 1992 FCRS received more from their farm than from off-farm sources.

Second, when operator households are ranked by their total household income (Table 5.7) a wide spectrum of income levels is encountered. About one in five has a household income of less than $10,000 and a quarter more than $50,000. Those with negative household incomes seem to have characteristics that set them aside from the rest of the income groups; they have substantial off-farm income but this is overwhelmed by large losses suffered in their farming activities which in terms of farm size are quite akin to those of the households with the highest incomes. In the two classes with the low but positive household incomes, losses from farming are more than offset by other income. The households with the highest incomes not only have substantial incomes from farming (and produce nearly half of all agricultural output) but they also have the greatest average incomes from off-farm sources, a characteristic of which seems to be the surplus generated by off-farm businesses. There is also a relationship with age; apart from the those with negative incomes, the proportion of household headed by someone over 65 years declines as the higher household incomes are encountered.

Table 5.7 USA: Characteristics of the income situation of farm operator households ranked by household income, 1992

	Household income class					
	Negative	$0- $9,999	$10,000- $24,999	$25,000- $49,999	$50,000 and over	All households
Per cent of farm operator households	6.4	12.0	26.5	31.3	23.8	100.0
Percentage headed by person 65 years or older	22.7	40.5	35.0	19.9	11.2	24.5
Operator major occupation (per cent):						
Farming	86.2	73.2	57.3	44.7	44.5	54.1
Other than farming	13.8	26.2	42.7	55.3	55.5	45.9
Average income per household ($)						
Farm income	-35,274	-3,100	-225	3,249	26,919	7,180
Total off-farm income	10,117	8,513	17,103	31,794	82,312	35,731
Business income	1,459	625	1,270	3,522	26,200	7,837
Wages/salaries	5,046	3,414	8,734	20,796	40,478	19,185
Interest and dividends	1,427	617	1,333	2,150	5,933	2,603
Other	2,186	3,857	5,767	5,327	9,701	6,106
Household income	-25,564	5,766	17,616	35,914	117,524	42,911
Per cent where actual value of farm income exceeds off-farm income						
	0.0	22.0	17.3	18.2	28.8	19.8
Economic size of farm (sales class)						
Less than $50k	54.5	80.8	82.9	76.6	60.6	73.5
$50k - $249,999	35.4	17.3	15.6	20.8	27.0	21.4
$250k - $499,999	7.0	1.9*	1.5*	2.6*	7.1	3.2
$500k and more	3.2	*	*	*	5.3	1.8
All sizes	100.0	100.0	100.0	100.0	100.0	100.0
Total value of agric. production (%)	12.2	6.0	12.5	21.5	47.8	100.0
Sample size	1,314	1,012	2,051	2,676	3,798	10,851

* Adjacent categories are combined due to disclosure requirements

Source: 1992 Farm Costs and Returns Survey, all versions

Table 5.8 USA: Characteristics of the income situation of farm operator households ranked by farm size, 1988, 1992

Income in $ x 1,000

Characteristic		Farm size (sales class)				
		Less than $50K	$50K to $249	$250K to $499K	$500 K and over	All sizes
Per cent of farm	1988	71.9	22.0	4.2	2.0	100.0
operator households	1992	73.5	21.4	3.2	1.8	100.0
Per cent of operators	1988	26.7	11.9	8.6	8.8	22.4
aged 65+	1992	28.1	15.2	10.0	14.1	24.5
Farm income per	1988	-3	16	53	118	6
household ($'000)	1992	-2	20	46	149	7
Per cent with	1988	67.7	24.4	20.3	21.0	55.3
negative farm income	1992	63.2	24.1	20.9	16.7	52.6
Off-farm income per	1988	37	22	26	33	33
household ($'000)	1992	40	22	20	43	36
Per cent reporting	1988	95.9	82.8	78.9	73.4	91.9
some off-farm income	1992	96.9	84.6	79.6	72.2	93.2
Total household	1988	34	38	79	151	39
income ($'000)	1992	38	42	65	192	43
Per cent with	1988	6.4	14.3	13.1	16.3	8.6
negative household income	1992	4.7	10.6	13.9	11.2	6.4
Per cent of households with income below poverty line						
(a) based on farm income only	1988	93.2	40.5	28.0	24.1	77.5
(b) based on total income	1988	22.0	22.5	17.9	20.0	21.9

Source: extracted from (Ahearn, Perry and El-Osta, 1993 and updated)

Third, off-farm income is significant across the farm size spectrum. While in the 1990 FCRS farm income rose sharply with farm size, off-farm income did not vary to the same extent. It was greatest in absolute terms among the smallest and the largest farms (sales class $500,000 and over), and even among the latter it contributed more than a fifth of total income (almost a fifth in 1995). It could well be that the methodology employed (which assumes one operator household per farm) understates the extent of off-farm income on large farms (Ahearn and Lee, 1991).

Fourth, and related to the above, low farm incomes are not necessarily linked with low total incomes. About half the US farms make a loss in any one year, but most have off-farm incomes that offset their farm losses. The average total income of those families reporting a farming loss in 1990 (55 per cent of the total farm numbers) was still $29,390, three quarters of the figure for all farms. Using the 1984 FCRS, Ahearn *et al.*, (1985) have shown that when households are ranked by farming income, as might be expected, the highest total family income median was found on the farms with the highest farm incomes, but at lower farm income levels the median total income was broadly similar irrespective of farm income. Earlier studies have found that a slight "U" shaped pattern was perhaps present, with the farms generating small positive money incomes having median total incomes a little lower than the rest; this ties in with what was observed when farms were arranged by sales class (above) and with the remarks about low-income farms in the UK. When classed by the sources of non-farm income, those with incomes from wages and other self-employment earnings had the highest median total income and those whose additional source was welfare payments was the lowest.

When farms are grouped by sales class (in contrast to income level), on over two thirds of the smallest farms the income from farming was negative in 1990. However, the total income of the operator households was positive and far more satisfactory. A similar but more subdivided analysis for the 1981 survey found that the average total income of operators with farms with sales smaller than $5,000, which accounted for over a third of farms by number, was only exceeded by the 10 per cent largest farms.

Fifth, the smallest farms had the lowest percentages of households with negative total incomes. Again a more detailed breakdown of the 1984 FCRS found that among farms with less than $10,000 sales only 12 per cent had negative overall incomes, compared with 17 or 18 per cent in all the classes above this size (Ahearn *et al.*, 1985). Perhaps unexpectedly, about one fifth of households tend to fall below the poverty line irrespective of the size of farm (this line is set at a positive income level). It may be that some of these cases on large farms are more able to withstand the low income, and no distinction is drawn between cases of occasional and more permanent low incomes. Nevertheless, in the USA no simple link exists between farm size and poverty.

Sixth, the total incomes of farm operator households are more unequally distributed than are households in general in the USA (with a Gini coefficient in 1990 of 0.64 compared with 0.43 for all households). A higher proportion of farm operator households were below the poverty line than all US families (21.9 per cent and 10.7 per cent respectively) and also more were recipients of very high incomes (6.3 per cent and 4.3 per cent) (Department of Commerce, quoted in Ahearn, Perry and El-Osta, 1993). Incomes were less unequally distributed among the small farms than in other farm sizes.

Although the above analysis is detailed, comparison with findings in the EU, particularly with those using Eurostat's concept of an agricultural household, is hampered by the coverage in the US statistics of all occupiers of farms, whether or not agriculture is their main source of income or occupation. Ahearn and Lee (1991) have gone some way in selecting households that are more in line with Eurostat's definition by publishing an analysis of the incomes and other characteristics of farms in the 1986 FCRS which fell into four groups. These are where:

(1) The operators' major occupation was not farming and the household was not dependent on farm income; (these accounted for 33 per cent of all FCRS farms - but only produce 5 per cent of national production).

(2) The operators' major occupation was not farming but the household was dependent on farm income; (4 per cent of households, 8 per cent of production).

(3) The operator's major occupation was farming, but the household was not dependent on farm income; (22 per cent of households, 11 per cent of production).

(4) The operator's major occupation was farming and the household was dependent on farm income (40 per cent of households, 76 per cent of production).

Only the second and fourth groups would be classed as agricultural households in Eurostat's IAHS statistics, though European equivalents of all four combinations were encountered when definitions were discussed in Chapter 2.

Whereas only 5 per cent of operator households in group (1) fell below the official poverty line, 58 per cent of group (2) were in poverty, 28 per cent in group (3) and 33 per cent in group (4). It is clear that the first group, which probably accounted for 40-50 of US farms, though having low farm incomes (average loss of $2,700) had the second highest average total income ($46,000) thanks to substantial off-farm income. Group (2) was a small section of the farm household sector, and consisted of two distinct types - large and successful grain and livestock farms with operators whose main occupation was off the farm, and households with small livestock farms that earned low returns and which include operators with low-paying off-farm jobs. Group (3) was also heterogeneous. Group (4), which could be considered the most uncontroversially labelled as agricultural households, was more homogeneous. Average total income ($70,000) was the highest of the groups, about nine-tenths coming from farming. Nevertheless, one third of Group (4) households were below the official poverty line; these were less likely to participate in government programmes, were smaller (60 per cent with sales below $40,000 as opposed to 20 per cent for those not in poverty) and were more likely to be livestock producers than those above the poverty line.

As noted earlier, when considering the entire farm operator household sector, the ARMS/FCRS is now the basis of data used to compare the incomes of farm households with those of US households in general (a more detailed comparison with selected socio-professional groups does not appear to be made). It found that, in 1993, when both farming income and other sources were taken into account, farm operator households averaged an income 97 per cent of the national all-households average. In 1995, when the average was 99 per cent, medium sized farms tended to have lower household incomes (74 per cent of the national average for the sales class $50,000 – $99,999) than farms in the adjacent size groups which were both above average; farms in the largest class ($500,000 and over) had household incomes over four times the national average. This overall position was sufficient for the ERS to declare (for 1993) that farm operator household income compared favourably with the national position. However, the judgement should be made with caution as the distributions were somewhat different; rather more farm operator households than the average had incomes below £10,000 (19 per cent compared with 14 per cent) and slightly less had incomes of $50,000 or more (25 per cent compared with 29 per cent).

This sort of information is vital to an agricultural policy that has a social aim of raising incomes of farm families and is looking for indicators. It supports the earlier observations of Larson that researchers can

> ... demonstrate that the notion of family farm income being closely tied to size of farm business is no longer valid. The number of persons dependent on farming as a primary source of income is now a relatively small proportion of all people with farm earnings. A significant change in the economic conditions of the farming sector may mean only a minor change in income of many people engaged in farming (Larson 1975).

5.7.8 Canada

Income studies in Canadian agriculture have a substantial literature, facilitated by an unusually rich store of data. Some comes from farm accounts surveys, and the first major exercise of this sort (the 1958 Farm Expenditure and Income Survey) took care to cover both farm and non-farm income sources in order to give a comprehensive picture of the distribution of income (Fitzpatrick and Parker, 1965). The statistical framework of Canada is such that it is possible, and legally permitted, to link the population census with the census of agriculture. Some association has also been made between the census of agriculture and tax returns (taxfiler data), though the taxfiler population cannot be related directly to that of the agricultural census. In addition there is the household budget survey, called the Survey of Consumer Finance. All this means that Canada has probably the most flexible data sets relating to income at the micro level of any country. To further improve the utility of data, in 1991 Agriculture Canada launched its Farm Level Data Project, "aimed at providing the data necessary for monitoring the financial position of farm businesses; assessing the impact of changing policies, programs and economic conditions on them; and administering and evaluating agricultural programs" (Statistics Canada, 1993). An essential component of this is the Whole Farm Data Base, which brings together in an integrated way farm-level data from the Taxation Data Program, the National Farm Survey, and the Farm Financial Survey.

The tax data show that over time off-farm income has been gaining importance. For "farmers" (individual taxfilers whose major source of income is from farming, although those with any income from farming can also be selected) off-farm income rose from about 15 per cent of total income in the late 1940s to almost 50 per cent in the 1980s (Bollman and Smith, 1987). Off-farm income growth in absolute terms was much more consistent than that of income from the farm (Chase, 1980). For three decades the growth had come mainly from off-farm work, but after the mid-1970s it came from increased investment income (Bollman and Smith, 1987). In 1991 and 1992, off-farming accounted for 58 per cent of the total income of agricultural households in taxfiler data. The main component of this off-farm income (almost half) was wages and salaries.

Farm size in Canada is usually measured by the value of gross sales (revenue). Brinkman (1980) classified Canadian farmers on this basis into "hobby farmers", "limited resource farmers" who were "serious" farmers but who were limited by small farm size, low output and generally poor management, and the "commercial" farmers. When related to tax information, among those taxfilers who had farms that could be uncontroversially labelled as commercial undertakings (revenue of $50,000 and over), non-farm income still on average contributed about one quarter of current total income. Smaller commercial farmers seemed to have a similar or somewhat greater dependence on off-farm income. The limited resource group (revenue $10,000-$24,999) received a larger proportion from off-farm sources, and the 1970s saw a rise in this from about one third to about two thirds of total income; at least half of these farmers had a non-farm job. On average, the group of "hobby farmers" made a loss from farming, yet in terms of total income the levels they enjoyed were greater than any other size of farm other than the largest commercial ones - something also noted earlier for the US. Even for the "limited resources farmers" off-farm income did much to compensate for their low farm incomes. However, lowest total incomes were found on these small farms, a characteristic also apparent in the mid-1980s (Bollman and Smith, 1987). Another similarity with findings in the USA was that, when farmers were grouped by level of gross self-employed income using taxfiler data for 1990, there was a distinct "U" shape to their total incomes. Farmers in the smallest self-employment gross income class on average reported a net loss on their farming operation. Nevertheless "In general the total income was the highest for the operators of small farms and very large farms." (Culver, O'Connor and Yap, 1992).

Later results, for 1992, do not cover the farms with very small revenues (the Tax Data Program only includes families involved in a single unincorporated farming operation with a total farm revenue of $C10,000 and over) but show a similar pattern in group average incomes for the larger sizes (Table 5.9). Among the smallest farms covered, that represented over a quarter of the total farm numbers in the field of observation, farming generated very little income and was of little importance to their total incomes, most of this coming from off-farm sources. Farming rose in relative importance as size increased, contributing over two-thirds among the largest farms. However, in absolute terms the greatest amounts of off-farm income came at the two extremities of the farm size spectrum. Off-farm income tended to be less prevalent among some farm types (such as dairying, with 33 per cent of total income in 1991) and higher among others (such as cattle rearing, with 84 per cent (79 per cent in 1992)).

Table 5.10 shows that, overall, about 5 per cent of farms in Canada had negative total incomes in 1992. However, as in the USA, this was not confined to the small farms; even 4 per cent of the largest farms shown had negative incomes (Yap *et al.*, 1995).

Canada's Survey of Consumer Finance enables analysis to be conducted on a family basis as well as for individuals, and for alternative definitions of a farmer or farm family to be used, from a broad one of where any non-zero income from farming is reported by a member of the family to narrow ones where farming is the main income source; occupation criteria can also be employed. As might be expected, income from non-farm sources was found to be more important for family units than for individuals. In 1986 less than one third of the average total income of farm families (meaning all those with some income from farming) came from the farms (Bollman and Smith, 1987). Criticism that the overall figures could be unduly affected by families in which there were no "real' farmers were countered by only looking at situations where there was an individual who stated that farming was his/her major occupation or major source of income. Among the former the relative importance of income, from the farm and from other sources was very similar to the overall trend. Among the latter farming income was relatively more important in the family total in the 1960s and fell to little more than half in the mid-1980s

The use of tax and consumer information for farmers and non-farmers also permits some general conclusions on the relative income position of

Table 5.9   Canada: Income characteristics of farms grouped by revenue class, 1992

Size	Proportion of all farms	Farm net operating income	Off-farm income	Total income	Farm income / total income
Revenue class	Per cent	$ per farm (x 1,000)	$ per farm (x 1,000)	$ per farm (x 1,000)	Per cent
$ x 1,000					
10-25	28	0	30	30	2
25-50	22	6	25	31	21
50-100	24	16	17	33	48
100-250	21	35	15	50	69
250-500	4	64	20	84	76
500 l	1	83	31	115	73
All farms	100	16	22	39	42

Note: Net operating income is before depreciation charges. Total income is the sum of off-farm income and farm net operating income

Source: Statistics Canada: Whole Farm Data Base

Table 5.10   Canada: Distribution of total income of farms grouped by revenue class, 1992

Revenue class	Total income of operators					
	Below 0	$1 - 10K	$10K - 25K	$25K - 50K	$50k +	All
	Number of operators (x 1,000)					
$10-25K	4	12	24	19	7	65
$25K-50K	3	8	21	15	5	53
$50K – 100K	3	7	20	22	6	57
$100K +	3	4	19	32	20	78
Total	13	32	84	87	38	253
% of total operators	5.0	12.5	33.1	34.5	15.0	100.0

Source: Statistics Canada: Whole Farm Data Base

the farm sector. The incomes of farmers and farmer families as defined above for tax statistics and the consumer survey were compared with incomes of the rest of the Canadian economy in Bollman (1980), Bollman and Smith (1987) and (Davey, 1996). Comparison at this level concentrated on money income only; nevertheless this was adequate to establish broad movements over time if not relativities in an absolute sense.

First, all measures indicate a substantial and rapid improvement of the farmer position relative to the rest of society in the early 1970s (see Figure 5.15). Full comparability was reached or exceeded by all groups except individuals who declared their main occupation was farming, and taxfilers whose major source was farming. The position was then broadly maintained by family units to 1987 but relative income then deteriorated, falling to 87 per cent in 1990 as the result of a fall in farming incomes, although off-farm income continued to grow in nominal terms (OECD, 1995). Nevertheless, in 1990 farmers had total incomes that compared favourably with most other self-employed people; among the nine groups in an analysis of taxfiler data farmers came third highest, after "professionals" and "commission earners" (Culver, O'Connor and Yap, 1992).

Second, the farmer/non-farmer gap was smaller with broader definitions of what constitutes a farmer or farm family. Obviously, this implies that incomes from off-farm sources (which disqualify the individual from a narrow definition of "farmer") were typically higher than farm incomes.

Third, the farmer/ non-farmer gap was smaller when families were compared rather than individuals. Thus it appeared that secondary family members contributed relatively more to family income among farm families than among non-farm families. One factor explaining this is the larger average size of farm families.

Fourth, the Canadian data permit estimates of the proportion of farmer families that fall below the low income "cut-off" which is used in poverty studies; this is adjusted for family size and is defined separately for rural households. On this basis, poverty has declined. (Figure 5.16). The proportion of farm families with incomes below the low income cut-off fell dramatically from about 40 per cent at the start of the 1970s to 14 per cent in the mid-1980s. However, it was still somewhat higher (by 2 per cent) among farm families than amongst all families in Canada. When farms were grouped by gross sales quartiles in 1985, the highest

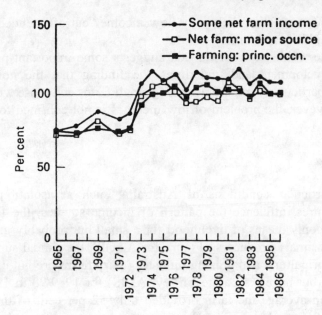

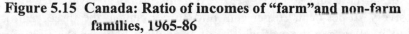

Figure 5.15 Canada: Ratio of incomes of "farm"and non-farm families, 1965-86

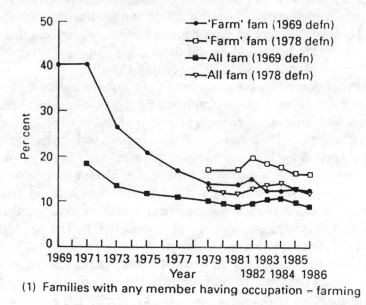

(1) Families with any member having occupation – farming

Figure 5.16 Canada: "Farm" families below the low-income cut off, 1969-85

proportions of farms falling below the low income "cut-off" tended to be amongst the middle sized farms.

To conclude, evidence from Canada suggests some important patterns of income development and underlines the finding that the non-farm component is particularly important among small farms and those with low incomes. However, the problem of low incomes is not confined to small farms.

5.7.9 Australia

While the particular conditions of Australia, such as isolation from population centres, influence the pattern of income sources, the farm is clearly not the only means of livelihood for a small but probably growing proportion of primary producers. Figure for AAGIS, the annual survey of farms in the agricultural and grazing industry (dairy farms are not covered in this survey, but have a separate survey, ADIS) for 1989/90 to 1991/92 indicate that on average the farm provided only 52 per cent of the total income of farmers and spouses. However this proportion varied widely (successively 70 per cent, 26 per cent and 36 per cent in the three years), reflecting a collapse in the profitability of agriculture between the first two years combined with relatively stable off-farm incomes. Overall, the level of total household income of farm households was 89 per cent that of the average Australian household for the three years, but this contained a fall from 139 per cent in 1989/90 to 60 per cent in 1990/91.

Results for Australia have a number of particularly interesting features. First, Australia offers a rare example of the use of a constant sample of farms in a study to monitor changing patterns of income, though this is by now quite elderly. Data relating to the same 5,644 primary-producer taxpayers (excluding hunting, fishing, trapping and forestry) over the period 1968/9 to 1972/3 displayed a pattern of change similar to that of seen in cross-sectional data from the US and elsewhere, in that non-employment income (wages and salaries) increased consistently while farm income fluctuated considerably (Tubman, 1977). The percentage of primary producers reporting wage and salary income rose from 23 per cent to 27 per cent in the short period covered. Other later evidence on family farms (not using the same sample) confirms the widespread nature of other income sources; in 1984/5 on 27 per cent of family farms the farmer or spouse earned some additional wages or salary (Males and Poulter, 1987). When all sources of income were added, the farm was on average responsible for 72 per cent of total income, wages and salaries 11 per cent, off-farm investment 14 per cent and direct government payments 3 per cent. These income figures related solely to the farmer and spouse and did not consider the incomes of other family members. The proportions of farms on which one or both members of the farming couple worked off-farm was highest on horticulture and wool farms (35 and 41 per cent respectively) with an all-type average of 27 per cent. Couples involved in off-farm work tended to be younger and better educated, but the farms also tended to be significantly smaller in terms of area and capital, suggesting that there may be some necessity for off-farm income to provide an adequate livelihood.

Australia is also interesting in that it has conducted a specific study of poverty among farm families. This took the form of a farm household survey carried out in 1973 by the Australian Bureau of Statistics (ABS) for the Henderson Poverty Inquiry (Vincent, 1976). It established its own poverty line for farm families, 20 per cent lower than for other sectors of society to allow for differences in living costs. Households falling below this line tended to be occupied by old farmers, frequently single person households, and of small farm size. Many low-income farms (including those somewhat above the poverty line) had only a marginal involvement in farming in terms of the proportion of their income that came from the farm. Considerable numbers had substantial reserves of net wealth, posing a low income/ high asset paradox. However, of particular importance for the present study was the finding, using a follow-up study of tax records, that low incomes are transitory for a large majority of farm households, and it is therefore foolish to categorise on the basis of incomes in a single year alone, as is common in income distribution studies. Over the period 1968/9 to 1972/3 almost half the cases studied (47 per cent) had fallen below the poverty line at least once in the five-year period, but only 9 per cent had been below it in 4 or 5 of the years. Put another way, on a single year basis between 17 and 23 per cent of farm households were in poverty, but taking the period as a whole only 4 per cent were below the poverty line for the whole period. This suggests that a distinction must be made between the core of farm households that are in a persistent low income situation and those who suffer temporary low incomes. While the former are likely to constitute a welfare problem requiring some intervention with public funds, the latter are not. It may even be inappropriate to use the term "poor" in the context of the temporary low incomes, though how low incomes have to fall and for how long before government action is justified is, of course, a matter of political judgement.

5.8   Summary and conclusions

Households headed by farmers are not solely dependent on agriculture for their livelihoods. They frequently have income from employment, from property, from pensions and other income sources. Not all of this is freely disposable, and account has to be taken of taxation, social payments and other deductions.

Information on the overall income position of agricultural households is far less well established in the EU than that on the income from agricultural productive activity (see Chapter 4). Provision exists within the framework of national accounts for Member States to disaggregate their households sector account into socio-professional groups, of which agricultural households could form one. This would allow comparisons of levels of income between farmer households and other occupations on a harmonised basis in Member States and allow changes in the composition of this income to be monitored. Until recently only Germany, France and the Netherlands (through its Socio-Economic Accounts) have taken this approach. However, the development of Eurostat's Income of Agricultural Households Sector (IAHS, formerly the TIAH) statistics has extended this range of countries, and now all EUR 15 Member States generate estimates for the aggregate disposable income of their agricultural households, although for some (particularly the United Kingdom) the methodology is capable of much improvement. Most (but not the UK) also produce comparable figures for other socio-professional groups, or all households together.

Though results are not fully harmonised, and the coverage in terms of year and degree of detail varies, the following features can be identified from the aggregate figures.

- The number of agricultural households (defined as those where the main income of the reference person comes from farming) is substantially smaller than the number of households where there is some income from farming, and generally smaller than the number of agricultural holdings. Where data exist over time, absolute numbers of agricultural households have been falling, in some instances very rapidly;

- On average, households with an agricultural holding but where farming is **not** the main income source of the reference person appear to derive little income from self-employment in agriculture.

- Agricultural households (defined as above) in all countries are recipients of substantial amounts of income from outside agriculture. Though typically about a half to two thirds of the total comes from farming, there are large differences between Member States and some between years;

- The total income of agricultural households is more stable than their income from farming alone. Non-agricultural income (taken together) is less variable from year to year than is farming income. Disposable income seems to be less stable than total income, but the relationship between the two depends on a variety of factors, including the way that taxation is levied.

- Countries differ in the share of income taken from agricultural households in taxation and other deductions, so the same average total income figure can imply different levels of disposable income in different Member States. Within individual countries, agricultural households tend to pay a lower share of their total income as taxes and social contributions than the all-household average;

- Agricultural households in the EU have average disposable incomes per household that typically compare favourably with the all-household average and in some countries is substantially above it. The relative position is eroded or reversed when income per household member or per consumer unit is examined.

Regrettably few EU countries have information by which the distributional aspects of incomes can be explored. Data sources vary widely, although they tend to be of three forms - farm accounts surveys, household budget surveys and tax records. National farm accounts surveys in many countries (Belgium, France, Spain, Greece, Ireland, Italy, Portugal) normally restrict their field of interest to the income from the farming activity alone; this is also true of the EU's Farm Accountancy Data Network that builds on these surveys. Household budgets are held typically only every five to seven years; in northern Member States there are few agricultural household cases and in southern ones the quality of income data is not good. Taxation sources are not a useable data source on incomes in the many countries where farmers are taxed on a flat rate rather than on their actual incomes or where farmers are poorly covered by the tax net for a mix of technical reasons. Consequently, among the EUR 15 countries only five – Denmark, Germany, the Netherlands, Finland and Sweden - can be described as reasonably well provided with microeconomic data on the overall income situation of agricultural households which allow detailed study of income distributions and offer the possibility of comparison with the income situation of other groups of households.

An overall picture of distributional characteristics of the incomes of EU farming households is thus only to be gained by stringing together fragments of information from disparate sources for Member States and by drawing on more complete data from other countries, notably the USA and Canada. This is enough to show that there are differences between countries that reflect, *inter alia,* their varying social, demographic, economic, geographic and cultural conditions as well as the conventions used to measure farm size and incomes. Nevertheless, common threads run through the income evidence, threads which are of the utmost importance to agricultural policy (OECD, 1995). In addition to the characteristics already revealed by the aggregate statistics the following are apparent:

- When farms are ranked by size, as would be expected, the income from farming (per farm, which for simplicity is often assumed to correspond to per household) increases across the spectrum, although the relationship may be affected by the measure of size that is used. The pattern of non-farm income and total income is not so straightforward. Non-farm income tends to be greatest in absolute terms among the smallest and largest farms, though its relative importance declines across the size spectrum. When farm income and non-farm incomes are combined, there is a tendency for total incomes to rise with farm size, but the smallest farms do not always have the smallest average total incomes.

- Non-farm income transforms the income situation among small farms, so that on average their total incomes are frequently satisfactory. There is some suggestion that lowest total incomes are associated not with the smallest farms and those generating the smallest incomes from farming but with those somewhat larger, typically those which are too large to be operated on a part-time basis but too small to generate an adequate income from farming to support a household.

- The wide disparity of incomes found if only the income from farming is considered is made substantially more homogeneous once the non-farm incomes are taken into account. The tendency for the disparity of farming incomes to widen is to some extent modified by the growth of non-farm incomes, though the evidence is not clear-cut.

- The impact of non-farm income is not uniform across the enterprise types, and this is reflected in regional differences (though other factors may be at work here too, such as the availability of alternative employment opportunities). In particular, dairy farming is relatively labour-demanding and exacting in timeliness, restricting the capacity for off-farm activity, so that the total income of farm households may be low, even where farming incomes are relatively high (as in the Netherlands). Conversely, the total incomes of large crop farms are often high because other activities are carried out in parallel, though this form of farming may not be particularly profitable. However, the direction of causality is not always clear. Instances can be found in which cereal production is adopted in place of livestock on relatively small farms because of the need for the household to earn off-farm income to meet interest charges (associated with succession) that could not be serviced from the farm business however organised; cereal farming, possibly depending heavily on contractors, makes this possible..

- When farm households are grouped according to the age of the reference person (typically the head of the farm household) up to a certain age, total income rises with the farmer's age, peaking between the age of 40 and 50 in Germany and Sweden, a little earlier in Denmark (35-45 years) and a little later in the US (45-55 years). Thereafter, total income declines.

- There is a suggestion that income disparities among agricultural households are wider than among households in general. Consequently, adequate average incomes among agricultural households may be consistent with greater relative proportions of farm households that fall below a given poverty line.

- Low total incomes in one year may be transitory. A distinction should be made between those farm households where incomes taken over a run of years may be satisfactory, though single years may be low, and the smaller number of those who face a more permanent income problem. In those few instances where information exists, it is clear that farmers' consumption expenditure is more stable from year to year than is their income, again pointing to the need in a welfare context to look at incomes over a longer period.

In the light of these findings it seems incontrovertible that, in assessing whether the "fair standard of living of the agricultural community" mentioned in the Treaty of Rome and *Agenda 2000* is being approached, it is necessary to include all forms of income flowing to that population. Low incomes cannot be assessed on one part of income alone, especially as the income from farming seems to be a particularly unreliable guide to total income on small farms where income problems could be most anticipated. And the comparability of the incomes of farmers with those of other groups in society cannot be judged in the almost total absence of reliable statistics.

Some commentators suggest that even a more complete income account for farmer households is inadequate for appraising their economic status. The wealth position must also be considered before it can be decided whether they form a group for which merit special treatment from public funds. This is the subject of the next chapter.

6 Wealth

Wealth is a shadowy but potent component among the factors that determine the position of the agricultural community within society. Wealth is important because it gives rise not only to income in a variety of forms but also because it provides security, freedom of manoeuvre, and economic and political power. Within society as a whole wealth seems to be much more unequally distributed than income and has a major influence on the overall degree of inequality (Atkinson, 1980). The importance of wealth as a contributor to the economic welfare of farmers cannot be denied, yet it rarely receives a mention among agricultural economists. Rural sociologists have been more aware of its significance because of its strong social and political associations. Property confers rights which are legally or socially determined, and a broad view of the agricultural scene would need to take account of both those that are primarily economic and form part of personal wealth and those which belong to other facets of reality and are studied by other disciplines. How property ownership is regarded is an important part of any study of social inequity. "This is not only in the obvious sense that the distribution of material resources will in large part determine the character of that society's economic and political life, but also in the sense that such conceptions serve as important legitimising ideologies buttressing the stability of social life" (Newby et al., 1978).

As in the earlier treatment of income, here we are concerned with the economic attributes of wealth and its relationship with agricultural policy. Even more than with current income it is necessary when considering wealth to be aware of the social and political connotations. Economics views reality from a particular standpoint, and no single aspect reveals the whole. Nevertheless, an economics approach has much to offer, even though its tools have rarely been employed for the study of wealth and agricultural policy.

Chapter 3 established that not only are *changes* in the wealth position in the form of capital gains a proper component to be included in estimates of personal income - though the precise way in which they are to be taken into account is open to question - but that the *absolute level* of wealth itself is a determinant of economic status. In matters of agricultural policy almost all attention is focused on income and little if any on the assets held by farmers. Here we are concerned with the empirical evidence on the wealth of farmers and their households and an attempt will be made to assess the significance that a greater attention to this wealth could have on the shape of EU policy.

It is commonly believed that farmers live poor but die rich. There is some truth in this assertion, at least for land-owning farmers in post-war Britain. A common pattern is for the wealth of farmers to increase with age up to a plateau; in contrast, incomes first rise and then decline as old age is reached. Reasons for this are considered later. Much of this wealth is passed to succeeding generations, with important consequences for the distribution of assets in society. It is also held, and with greater statistical backing, that attempts by government to support the incomes of farmers are capitalised into land values, a phenomenon which results in landowning farmers and landlords benefiting through capital gains, though this is probably not the intention, but with little improvement in incomes remaining ultimately to those without owned land.

In this Chapter an attempt will be made to present the asset position of farmers to parallel that of incomes described in Chapters 4 and 5. Once again it will be necessary to draw a distinction between, on the one hand, the balance sheet of the agricultural industry and of farm businesses, of which a good deal of data exists though of questionable validity, and on the other hand the personal wealth of farmers and their households, of which very little is known at either sector or individual levels. Yet it is clear that the wealth of the farming population is of importance in a welfare context - or so it might seem to an objective observer. Whatever the income situation, would a sensibly organised CAP redistribute income from relatively poor consumers to farmers who were relatively wealthy, as seems presently the case? The absence of adequate information on the personal wealth of the farming community can in part be blamed for the perpetuation of a policy which, in broad outline, manages to achieve such a topsy-turvy redistribution.

6.1 Wealth and property rights

In Chapter 2 the wealth of an individual was defined as his total stock of tangible or intangible possessions which are capable of being exchanged for money or other goods. In an agricultural context this embraces not only physical items such as farmland, buildings and livestock, but also rights to fish and shoot, business connections and goodwill and personal skills which, in the relevant market, could be sold. A creation of the CAP is wealth in the form of rights to produce or to receive payment linked to production. Principally in the form of milk quotas introduced in 1984 - licences to produce which can be transferred, though not perhaps with the legal clarity of similar quotas in Canada – these now extend to entitlements on numbers of some other types of livestock.

A rather special position is reserved for land, the asset which is the prime feature of farming and farmers. In the eyes of the law in the UK wealth in the form of land is not the land itself but rather the bundle of rights which are associated with the land. Individuals can own rights or interests in land. A variety of rights can exist concurrently; the right to occupy, the right to receive under the CAP forms of support – such as arable area payments – that are deemed to go with occupation, the right to occupy at some future date, the right to take rent from the land, the right to the capital value on sale, the right to determine when and to whom the land shall be transferred (or rather some of the rights associated with it. Freehold is merely a form of tenure which happens to confer a particularly wide range of rights held (Forse, 1979; Shoard, 1980). Under the "fee simple" conditions, the freeholder may bequeath his rights to whom he pleases without restriction and, if no will is made, the land is held for the benefit of his spouse and heirs. Wealth from land, then, arises from the value of these rights.

This system of ownership of rights, not of the land itself, is the product of long history. Ownership rights in pre-capitalist England were often conditional on performing some social function, they tended to be rights over certain aspects of the property (such as revenue flowing from it) and were frequently not freely disposable (Massey and Catalano, 1978). Gradually the limited range of rights broadened, so that it has become natural to think of the land itself as being the property. Other rights associated with land exist in the UK alongside those of the freeholder, like common-land rights (principally involving rights to graze animals), those to fish, to extract water or minerals and the right of passage over land. The value of a freeholder's bundle of rights, or the value of his wealth in this form, will be affected by concords and conflicts (both actual and potential) between rights within and outside his direct control, and by public actions to restrict the exercise of rights or to take some of them away.

The protection and enforceability of rights over land form part of the legal framework of the nation, but this framework is not immutable.

Changes can be made with the intention of promoting the national interest. The owners of land rights have generally had to accommodate these changes without compensation. Before the Second World War much housebuilding in the UK took place on farmland in ways that, in retrospect, were neither visually nor socially desirable. Since the 1947 Town and Country Planning Act the right to develop agricultural land has rested not with the freeholder but with the State, needing the permission of the democratically-elected local planning authority. Another example of a legislative change of rights was the Agriculture (Miscellaneous Provisions) Act of 1976 which extended rights of succession to members of the family of tenant farmers, seen as a group who were disadvantaged in that they could be removed from a farm which in practice they had long farmed even though their elderly father (or mother) had nominally been the tenant. However, this change was not a move towards a Pareto-type optimum in that the right of the landlord to take possession and re-let the farm to whom he pleased was curtailed without compensation. Subsequent changes in the legislation (Agricultural Holdings Act of 1984) restored the right of landlords to take possession at the demise of a tenancy for new lettings but did not take away the rights of succession of existing tenants' families. Giving the right of succession increased the wealth of tenants, since a tenant with potential successors would have required a greater compensation from his landlord in order to quit than before the 1976 legislation, though it is difficult to assemble empirical data on the magnitudes involved.

Of the rights associated with land, perhaps the most important for the long term welfare of the agricultural population is the ability to pass it to others. In this, land is no different from other personal assets. The right rises to special prominence when land is passed from one generation to another of the same family. The relative importance of inheritance among top wealth leavers appears to be greater in agriculture (with forestry and fishing) than in any other industrial group (Harbury and MacMahon, 1973). Its significance has grown now that UK farming consists primarily of owner-occupiers (Northfield (1979) suggested that two thirds of land in Great Britain was held in this way) and when the capital requirements are such that entry to the occupation of farming is virtually confined to members of existing farming families. Contrary to popular belief, the family is more important to the inheritance of land among large farms than among the small (Gasson *et al.,* 1988), and families seem to have coped remarkably well with capital taxation aimed at breaking up large accretions of wealth by taking advantage of legal devices to circumvent their impact (Commission, 1981).

6.2 Valuing wealth

Two essentials for evaluating the wealth of the agricultural population - and here the term is broadened to include all owners of assets used in the industry - are a system of valuation and information on the pattern of ownership. The valuation of wealth in money terms can take one of two broad approaches. The first values assets according to the price they would fetch if sold on the open market, and this can be labelled "realisation value". In the case of machinery this would correspond to the salvage value which could be raised by sale; for land it would be its sale price. The second is to value the assets as they appear to the person who currently possesses and uses them if they remain in his control, termed "going concern" or "use" value. For machinery this could be the cost of acquiring a replacement machine. For land it might be taken as the net income flow generated by the land and capitalised into a single figure - the "worth" of land as an income-generator. The two approaches are likely to give different results. With durable productive assets like buildings or machinery there will be a divergence between acquisition and disposal values, and this disparity has been used as part of the "asset fixity" theory to explain the cause of the global farm income problem and, in particular, why the supply of agricultural products is more responsive to rising than to falling product prices.

In general, it seem that "realisation" values lie below "going concern" values. This applies not only to durable assets themselves but to claims over them; shares in a family business may be worth more to their present (family) holders than the price obtainable on the market (Atkinson, 1975). This difference applies in an extreme form to the value of pension rights or interests in discretionary trusts where the right to an income flow cannot be sold and so has zero realisation value yet is worth much more than zero to the beneficiary.

Agricultural land is different from many other forms of wealth in that its realisation value is typically considerably *above* its value as a generator of current income in the hands of its present occupiers. This manifests itself in the despairing comments of potential new entrants that land is far too expensive for an aspiring farmer to borrow all he needs at current interest rates to set himself up as an owner-occupier. This is by no means a new phenomenon; entry by purchase has almost always been expensive (Northfield, 1979). Land prices are determined in a marginal market in which only a very small percentage of the land changes hands in a year - typically one to two per cent in the UK and even less in some other EU states. In the UK the market for vacant possession land is dominated by existing medium and larger farmers wishing to expand. Not only does this category of purchaser have economic advantages in terms of economies of size - so that, for example, they are capable of spreading fixed costs over a larger acreage than they at present command so that a higher price can be justified - but the taxation system has worked in a way that has encouraged them to buy. Interest charges are deductible from revenue when calculating taxable income, and this applies to borrowings not only for the financing of current farming activities but also for land purchase. This makes borrowing particularly attractive for farmers with high marginal rates of personal taxation. These will tend to be the larger farmers. Inflation further reduces the real burden of interest. The upshot is that in the post-war period in the UK the real rate of interest for farmers paying tax at the standard marginal rate, after taking into account inflation, was *negative* for most years up to the end of the 1970s (Burrell, Hill and Medland, 1987). For farmers facing higher tax rates the real "cost" of borrowing would have been even more negative. These conditions encouraged borrowing by the tax-liable farmer, typically the medium and larger ones. Expansion in area being a goal of a majority of farmers (Harrison, 1975), this borrowing has naturally expressed itself in terms of marginal land purchases. Only since the early 1980s has the control of inflation in the economy coupled with higher rates of interest charged by lending institutions turned the cost of borrowing into a positive figure.

In the post-war period land prices increased faster than inflation up to 1980, giving landowners real capital gains and further stoking the desire for the prosperous farmer to buy land. The price of land is determined not only by the present and expected income flows associated with it (and the rate at which these are to be discounted) but also by the expected changes in capital values (Higgins, 1979). In the UK, and almost universally in developed countries, capital gains are taxed at lower rates than is current income (OECD, 1979). There is thus an incentive to turn farming profits into capital gains, and borrowing for land purchase has been the favoured way of doing so. Though the falling real land prices experienced in the UK since the start of the 1980s no doubt substantially reduced the attractiveness of marginal purchases, it has by no means totally extinguished the economic rational under particular circumstances. There are in addition the personal motives which urge expansion - the desire to set up a son as a farmer, the sign of success that an enlarging farm displays, the social and political power that larger-scale landownership brings - and these remain. The element of a greater controlling role is interesting; a person may strive to become more wealthy "for the sake of increasing his control *per se* of the economic institutions of a capitalist society, and for the sake of the various satisfaction..... which such control brings over and above (that) derived from the expenditure of income from this capital" (Vickrey (1947) in Atkinson, 1975). Many examples of this sort of behaviour can be found among farmers.

The principle of wealth evaluation adopted here is that of realisation value. Not only is data usually in this form, but it appears that the economic power that wealth implies is measured in its most potent form by the magnitude of the direct purchasing power into which the wealth can be converted. Realisation value is the basic approach taken in the taxation of capital in the UK. Nevertheless, use value has at times been built into the legislative framework of policy instruments; for a time in the life of UK Capital Gains Tax the value of tenanted farmland was set for the purpose of calculating tax liability at a multiple of the gross rent, generally achieving a lower figure than the valuation at market prices.

6.3 Estimating the net worth of the agricultural industry and farm businesses

To establish the wealth position of the agricultural community requires information on its net worth. This is obviously not the same as the equity of the agricultural industry, because not all agricultural assets (and liabilities) are owned by farmers and, conversely, farmers may be holders of non-farm assets. However, the two will be related. The intention here is not to review the complete equity situation of agriculture but rather to investigate those aspects which are of relevance to the welfare of the agricultural population. The key features are:

(a) The assumptions that are made when estimating balance sheets for the agricultural industry and for farm businesses, and the link between these and the balance sheet for agricultural households and companies

(b) The way agricultural net worth has changed and the extent to which this has come from capital gains, and

(c) The implication of the net worths of farmers for their economic status.

In Chapters 4 and 5 it was found that estimates of the income of the agricultural industry (based on the somewhat artificial concept of the agriculture branch of the national economy) were available as a matter of routine in industrialised countries, but information on the personal incomes of farmers (the agricultural household sector comprising real institutional units) was rarely estimated. Much the same occurs with wealth. Balance sheets for the agricultural industry and for farm businesses (showing assets, liabilities and the resultant net worth), though drawn up on a rather artificial basis, are much more readily available than is information on the net assets position of farmers and their households as a sector of the community or as individuals.

6.3.1   The basic units to which balance sheets relate

Balance sheets set out the values of assets and liabilities belonging to institutional units at particular times. As conventionally calculated, the asset side is valued mainly in terms of the market prices of capital items used in agricultural production where such markets exist, and on other bases (such as costs of production) where this is not possible. A central point is that only real institutional units have legal status and are therefore capable of ownership of assets or of incurring debt. While analysis can take either an aggregate or disaggregate approach, the units to which the basic data relate must still be institutions in the economic sense.

In all Western countries agricultural production takes place in units that, in terms of numbers, are predominantly operated as unincorporated businesses, in which the legal responsibility is that of individuals (mainly sole proprietors and partners without limited liability). In the EU the Farm Structure Survey (FSS) records whether the holder of an agricultural holding is a "natural person" (mainly individuals and partnerships but with various other inclusions that differ between Member States) or a "legal person" (Eurostat, 1986). This implies that the former comprise unincorporated businesses operated by individuals or jointly by individuals (often labelled as being operated by 'households'), with no separate legal entity. The unincorporated business is not itself an economic institution; the individuals that operate the business take this role. The others (mainly incorporated businesses) have separate legal status, and the decision-maker is a director and/or salaried manager.

The FSS shows that in 1987 98.6% of EUR12 holders were "natural persons" (UK 92.7%)(Eurostat, 1991). However, the FSS is not a satisfactory guide as to composition of agricultural business by type of legal status and understates the part taken by businesses with separate level entities. This is because some countries (including Germany, the Netherlands, the United Kingdom) for the purpose of the FSS treat certain types of company as if they were natural persons. The case made for the UK is that such arrangements are used characteristically for the incorporation of family businesses (Eurostat, 1986), with the implication that they behave as partnerships, with no additional access to management or capital that incorporation might be expected to bring when used in other industries, an observation with some empirical support (Harrison, 1975).

As balance sheets can, strictly, only be drawn up for real institutional units, the attempt to produce an aggregate balance sheet for the agricultural industry, defined in national accounts as consisting of fictitious units (Units of Homogeneous Production or, from 1999 in the EU, as Local Kind of Activity Units) which are exclusively (or, when using LKAUs, almost exclusively) concerned with the production of agricultural commodities, involves assumptions and partitions. Typically, the approach taken when presenting a balance sheet for the agricultural industry is essentially similar to that of the "national farm" used in the production account (Hill, 1998), since only the assets and liabilities that are assumed to be directly linked with agricultural production are included. There are, however, important differences in coverage that mean that the industry balance sheet does not relate directly to the "national farm". This concerns, in particular, dispute over whether the value of tenanted land should be included, a matter of great relevance to the size of the stock of capital in many OECD countries.

In the conventional way of calculating balance sheets, the value of both owner-occupied and rented land (at market prices) is included; this implies that, for the purpose of drawing up the balance sheet, landlords of let farmland form part of the agricultural industry. This is in contrast to their treatment in income measurement for the industry, where landlords are excluded from the group to which the residual reward from agricultural activity accrues (rent being treated as a cost). A respectable case can be made that landownership (the provision of land, whether for own use as an owner-occupier or by others as tenants) is not part of agricultural production. This was long the stance adopted by the UK over the treatment of loans for land purchase, interest on which was not deducted in the estimation of aggregate Net Farm Income. If this argument is accepted, then it would be logical to exclude the market value of *all* land from the industry balance sheet. The current position adopted in the EU (and thus by the UK) in its current aggregate accounting procedure is that landownership of owner-occupied land is assumed to fall inside the boundary of agricultural production but not the landownership of tenanted land. Thus there is an inconsistency between the composition of the agricultural industry for income measurement and balance sheet purposes and the two accounts do not strictly relate to each other. An income measurement that was consistent with the balance sheet coverage would not charge a rent for tenanted land as this would represent a transaction within the border of the "national farm" between one type of agriculturalist (tenant farmers) and another (owners of let land).

On the liability side, even totals before dividing up are not always secure. A good deal of uncertainty has always surrounded the true size of informal credit between family members (Harrions, 1975), and it is believed that official statistics for southern EU Member States often miss informal intra-family credit arrangements and underestimate the real level of borrowing, thereby distorting the differences between them and the northern countries. Another understatement of liabilities probably exists with respect to the liabilities of landlords, representing a further inconsistency in the present balance sheet at industry level. If the agricultural assets of landlords letting land to tenants are deemed to be part of agriculture, then a symmetrical treatment would require the inclusion of all the borrowings of these landlords where these could be linked to land purchase, though this is unlikely to happen in practice.

However, a simplistic view that agricultural assets and liabilities of real institutional units can be separated off from other assets and liabilities is rather unsatisfactory both from a theoretical and a practical viewpoint. The widespread and increasing nature of pluriactivity involving agriculture suggests that this farm/non-farm separation is a growing problem and introduces a substantial artificial element, especially in countries such as the UK where the running of other self-employed business activities in parallel with farming is a major form of pluriactivity. Where an institutional unit owns both agricultural and other assets, decisions about issues such as patterns of use, investment programmes and borrowing will be taken in light of the total fund of capital under the single control. Only in very peculiar conditions would decisions about agriculture be taken in complete isolation from their wider context. The argument that the decisions of agricultural households should be considered in the round is usually made in terms of current economic activity and incomes (for example, (Nakajima, 1986; Phimister, 1993; Schmitt, 1989)) but this also applies to capital. By making separations there is a danger of creating an "artificial" balance sheet that may be misleading in terms of what it purports to represent. On the liabilities side the fungible nature of lending means that any division into agricultural and non-agriculture is likely to be arbitrary. Even dedicated loans from institutions whose specific purpose is to fund agricultural investments (such as the Agricultural Mortgage Corporation in the UK) may indirectly find themselves providing finance for other sectors in which farmers and landowners have interests. Banks may have data on lending to people they class as farmers and the purpose put forward for that lending, but it is impossible to distinguish a loan for purely production purposes from one for personal consumption (especially for items which cross the divide, like farm cars).

Even if the objections on theoretical grounds are set aside, on a practical level there will be problems of drawing up a balance sheet that relates only to agricultural assets and liabilities. While farm livestock and most field machinery may be incontrovertibly and exclusively agricultural in nature, some assets (such as farm vehicles and the domestic buildings) may serve both farming (production) and consumption functions. In the face of a probable lack of data on the respective uses the allocation to farming may be only a rough approximation. Similarly, any attempt to partition the assets of businesses that engage in activities covering more than agricultural production (for example, ranging from farmers who use some of the domestic dwellings on their farms to provide bed-and-breakfast accommodation for tourists, to large-scale vertically integrated poultry units that both rear the chicken and process them into frozen food) will rather arbitrary choices. Of particular and increasing relevance in the UK is capital in the form of surplus farm houses and cottages that are let to people who do not work on the farm as the need to house farm labour contracts; in industrial classification this corresponds to the provision of housing services, so these houses should not, in theory, be included in the stock of farming capital. A division of liabilities will need to be even more dubious, and rules of thumb may be used, such as treating all liabilities of farm operators as if they were agricultural in nature (a typical solution to the problem which probably overstates the extent of agriculture's indebtedness) or some allocation according to the purpose put forward to the lending institution.

6.3.2 Additional problems at the level of the farm business balance sheet

The inclusion of land among the assets of agriculture raises some particular difficulties. At microeconomic level only the value of owner-occupied land is included among the business assets (opening a gap in terms of coverage between macro and micro balance sheets) but even the patterns of ownership of this land may be highly complex, making it difficult to draw a sensible boundary around the farm business. Among families running unincorporated farms and who own their land, it is not uncommon to find a partnership, such as between a father and son(s), that may constitute the business entity, and this partnership may technically rent land from the father who retains sole ownership of this asset.

In the case of the UK it is far from clear what legal basis is used to categorise the extent of the business assets; a farming partnership of a father and son may constitute the legal entity as far as the business is concerned, and this partnership may technically rent land from the father who retains sole ownership of this asset. To ignore the value of the land because it did not form part of the business assets might be legally correct but would distort the measurement of the real capital base which could be called on for business purposes, such as collateral for borrowing or to cover farming losses. Only slightly more complex is the common UK situation where a farm's land consists of parcels owned individually by the farmer, his spouse and other members of the family, with perhaps some also owned jointly, the pattern reflecting the way in which the farm has been put together over the years by purchase and inheritance and by decisions to pass part of the land to the next generation. When land is held by trusts or similar legal devices, the *de facto* ability of the farmer to exercise the normal rights, such as disposal, may not be transparent (Commission of the EC, 1981). Such situations make for difficulty in establishing the assets side of the farm business balance sheet.

In the case of farming companies, typically owned and run by members of the same family and functioning much as if they were unincorporated businesses, the assets of the company will be clearly bounded in the eyes of the law. However, this precise legal situation may not be one that makes much sense in terms of assessing the resource base on which the farm could draw in practice. Where the company relates only to the operating business and does not own land, renting it from individual members of the family (a common UK arrangement) who may also be directors of the farming company, the exclusion of the land asset will again give a partial and distorted picture of the net worths of the business and to the financial ratios that may be indicators of its economic performance and viability.

To sum up, attempts to construct a balance sheet for the agricultural industry and for individual farm businesses involve making rather heroic assumptions about the separability of farming from other activities, assumptions that are increasingly under question given the recognition of pluriactivity and multiple income sources among many farm households. The division between agricultural and non-agricultural assets and liabilities is problematic and in many circumstances highly artificial. The consequence is that neither the full asset position nor (probably) the full liabilities of these households are fully captured, and much of relevance to explaining the behaviour of the farm businesses and farm families is left out. Factors relating to the non-agricultural balance sheet items of households and firms (such as a drop in the market value of equities or rise in the value of off-farm domestic property) that might be expected to impinge on decisions relating to farms are currently ignored. Farms with apparently poor economic performance and dangerous capital ratios can be viable if there is an adequately supportive larger capital base, and apparently healthy farm businesses in strong capital positions can collapse if the non-agricultural balance sheet deteriorates; in such circumstances the income and capital aspects closely interrelate. And the net worths of farmers and their families cannot be compared with those of other members of society and policy decisions taken relating to their relative economic status, using a methodology that systematically excludes contributions from items that lie outside the deemed boundaries of their agricultural activities.

6.4 Examples of published "industry" and "farm business" balance sheets, net worths and capital gains

Despite the objections raised, balance sheets are calculated and published by official statistical authorities that purport to show the capital position of agriculture as an industry and of its component farm businesses. These are used as one way of assessing the economic health and prosperity of farming and to look for situations in which its viability is under threat. At present aggregate balance sheets do not form part of the EU's range of harmonised agricultural accounts, though there are plans to move in this direction. Consequently, attention will be focused on the balance sheets of the agricultural industries of the UK and USA. At a microeconomic level farm balance sheets form part of FADN/RICA, and parallel survey information is collected in other non-EU countries as a matter of routine. These will be commented on later when describing the distribution of net worths. A useful starting point is the balance sheet of farming in the UK.

6.4.1 The balance sheet of UK agriculture

Estimating the net worth of the UK agricultural industry depends on satisfactory specifications and measurement of both the assets and liabilities used in farming which, as the discussion above has outlined, is far from simple. Official estimates of the agricultural industry's balance sheet are available only from 1970 onwards; these are presented in Figure 6.1 after the removal of the effects of inflation. It is evident that the pattern of the industry's Net Worth has followed closely that set by the value of land and buildings. Liabilities were somewhat higher in real terms in the 1980s, but the main explanation for changes in Net Worth is on the assets side. Twin peaks in the early and late 1970s have been followed by a decline in Net Worth in the 1980s but with a partial recovery in the first half of the 1990s. The total Net Worth figure for 1993 was somewhat lower than that for 1970. Assets other than land and buildings formed 37 per cent of total assets in 1970 and 1993 (years of low land prices) but only 24-25 per cent in 1973 and 1979, high land price years. From 1993 there were large rises in land prices, reflecting the improved profitability of farming following the withdrawal of Sterling from the European Union's Exchange Rate Mechanism and the consequent upward adjustment in national support prices (which are set in ECUs). Prices of land with vacant possession in England increased by 31% in real terms

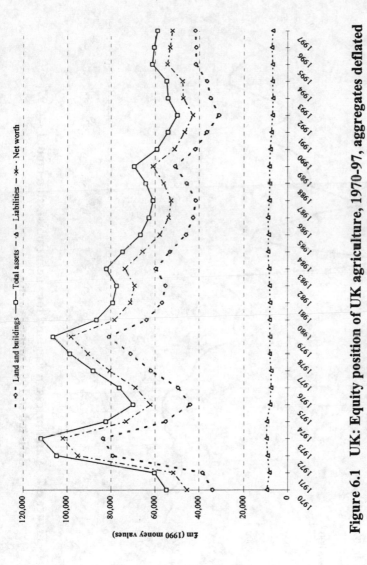

Figure 6.1 UK: Equity position of UK agriculture, 1970-97, aggregates deflated to 1990 money values

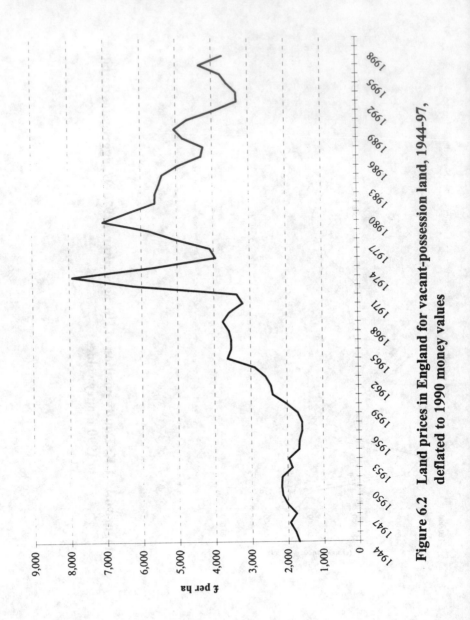

Figure 6.2 Land prices in England for vacant-possession land, 1944-97, deflated to 1990 money values

between 1993 and 1996. The turndown in the land market in 1997 is consistent with the sharp fall in farming incomes and further falls were to be expected in 1998 (Figure 6.2). However, the industry's net worth was still higher in real terms in 1997 than it had been in 1970.

For years before 1970 published estimates were occasional and made by a variety of sources - usually commercial banks (see CAS, 1978 and EDC for Agriculture, 1977a). Lack of information on the changing Net Worth is unfortunate since the period from the Second World War up to 1970 was one of greater stability during which the net worth of the industry was almost certainly rising steadily, especially in the 1960s, whereas the years since 1970 have been marked by instability. The problem in making estimates for this earlier period lies with poor information about liabilities. Evidence on the level of borrowing before the 1980s suggests that it was relatively stable, even declining in the 1960s (in 1975 prices estimates are for 1953, £2,924m; 1963, £2,967m; 1974, £2,211m; 1980, £2,352m (Burrell, Hill and Medland, 1987)). Therefore when attempting to see which way net worth altered before the 1970s, it is not unreasonable to look at the movement in the land market as a proxy for directions of change, as shown in Figure 6.2. The conclusion is that from the late 1950s to the start of the 1970s there were real increases in net worth arising from land appreciation.

The official estimates for land and buildings incorporated in the estimates quoted above exclude the value of residential housing on farms, in line with what is treated as agricultural. However, these are usually thought of as an inseparable part of the property, sold together with the land and buildings used for production. According to Johnson (1987), including houses raised the total asset value in 1986 by 20 per cent and lowered the liabilities-to-assets ratio from 18 per cent to 15 per cent. This distinction has particular relevance for the 1980s when land values were falling but domestic house prices continued upwards. Even in the mid 1990s, after the general decline in domestic property prices, farm houses often commanded exceptionally high prices when sold off. Asset values include both tenanted and owner-occupied land, and the drift in tenure towards owner-occupation will itself have resulted in some rise in the aggregate value because of the higher market value of land with vacant possession (and substantial capital gains to farmers buying as sitting tenants). The value of milk quotas is included by implication in the prices of the land to which it relates, and is therefore a contributor to capital gains and losses, but a separate valuation is probably needed now that quota is seen as a private asset marketable in its own right (such a view is not shared universally among EU Member States). The introduction of payments per hectare on land used for cereals, oilseeds and protein crops as part of the reforms to the CAP started in 1992 also implies the creation of an element in the value of land that could be increased, scaled down or removed by administrative action under political pressure. However, in both of these instances the market value of land incorporates the perceptions by farmers of the likelihood of policy changes, though this could change rapidly in the light of what they see as shifts in the attitudes of agricultural ministers and the Commission to the permanence of quotas, area payments or other similar quantitative restrictions on production.

6.4.2 The balance sheet of USA agriculture

Information on the assets and liabilities of US agriculture is more detailed and covers a longer period, being available on an annual basis from 1939 to the present, unpublished estimates having been made back to 1910. From the 1940s to the late 1960s the real value of the total assets used by US agriculture rose steadily and with only occasional temporary reversals. Rising real estate values (land and buildings) was obviously the main cause. Liabilities fell a little in the 1940s but increased subsequently, though at a rate much slower than asset values. The outcome was a rising level of proprietors' equity (net worth). In Figure 6.3 the balance sheet of US agriculture is presented in real terms (expressed in 1990 $ values) for 1970 onwards after the exclusion of the domestic assets and liabilities - this is in line with the earlier stance taken in UK official statistics. When the effect of inflation is removed the trend is clearly one which resembles that suggested for Britain. The 1970s saw an acceleration in asset values until 1980 after which there was a sharp drop in both the total value of assets and in net worth, exacerbated by liabilities that continued to rise until the mid 1980s. The change from 1980 to 1985 represented a rise in ratio of total debt to total assets of from 19 per cent to 30 per cent. Net worth ("equity") bottomed in 1986 and was followed by rising real estate values and declining debt. By 1989 the ratio had fallen back to 20%, a level that has not been subsequently exceeded (18% in the years 1995 to 1997).

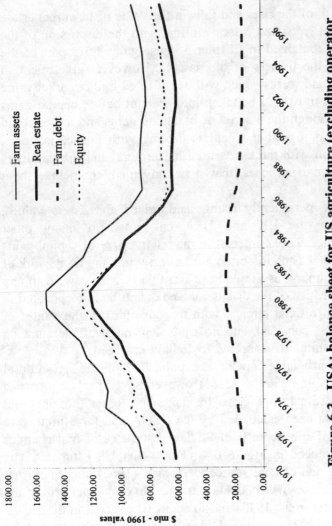

Figure 6.3 USA: balance sheet for US agriculture (excluding operator households), 1970-97

6.4.3 *Capital gains at the industry level*

Much, though not all, of the rises and falls in the value of farm real estate constitute real capital gains and losses. In line with the discussion of the concepts of income contained in Chapter 3, these gains form part of the personal income of the owners of the assets. However, investment in additional buildings and works which will be reflected in the market value of agricultural assets must also be taken into account before capital gains can be estimated. Though the magnitude of capital gains and losses could have been considered in earlier Chapters dealing with farmer incomes, their close association with the assets used by farmers, and the liabilities incurred for operational purposes, that it is convenient to include them here.

In the 1970s the persistently rising land prices and assets values, described above for the UK and USA but noted in many other industrialised countries, awoke interest in the relative size of capital gains to current income. Gains and losses do not fit easily into the framework of national current accounting as they do not form part of the reward to any productive activity. Much of the discussion and quantification appeared in academic rather than official circles; with the downturn in the values of farmland attention has subsided, and no equivalent body of literature on the implications of capital losses seems yet to have emerged.

For the UK no official estimates are published of the agricultural branch's aggregate capital gain or loss. However, several other countries make such official estimates. Figures for gains and losses (nominal and real) in the *USA* have been calculated by the USDA and for a time were shown in the annual Farm Sector(*sic*) Review; estimates of real changes from 1960 are reproduced in Figure 6.4. For earlier US estimates it is necessary to turn to non-official sources. Hoover (1962) suggested that real capital gain on farmer-owned assets was equal to only 2 per cent of the total income of farmers in the 1940s and to about 10 per cent in the 1950s. Estimates by Bhatia (1971) produced higher figures for the 1950s and 1960s, amounting to more than 50 per cent in some years. Those by Melichar (1979) were accompanied by the comment that "over the two decades preceding 1972 real capital gains averaged about one-third of net farm income." Throughout the 1970s real gain took place and at rates which exceeded Net Farm Income. Bringing the various estimates together suggests that capital gains started to become important in US agriculture in about 1968; from then on real estate started to yield more substantial and

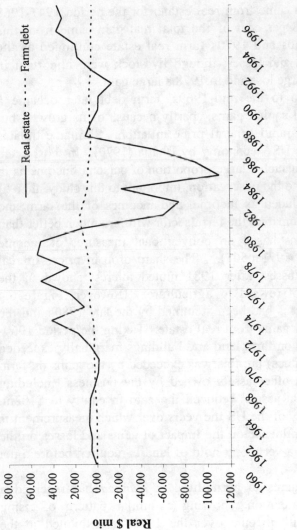

Figure 6.4   USA: Estimates of capital gains and losses on real estate and farm debt, 1960-97

regular gains than in the earlier post-war years and these gains were at levels which had only been seen occasionally before (1950, 1956 and 1958). Most of the gain came from real estate; for the period 1947-1968 Bhatia estimated that 88 per cent of the total real gain came from this source. In the late 1960s and 1970s farm real estate continued as the primary source of gains and losses, though livestock were important in 1974 by contributing a large loss and in 1978 a large gain.

Unlike the period up to the mid-1969s, farm debt later became a significant source of real capital gains, partly because of its growth, but mainly because of more rapid general price inflation. Similar estimates were made for the entire USA economy by Bhatia (1970). In most years capital gains did not form such a large proportion of personal income as in the farm sector. This led to the observation, important to this study, that "if all capital gains are included as income, and incomes of the farm and non-farm sectors are compared, the farm sector will fare much better than what similar comparisons based on conventional measures of income would indicate" (Bhatia, 1971 p505). The sharp drop in prices of real estate, and the capital losses, after 1981 muted interest shown in the literature in this form of reward to agriculture. However, Figure 6.4 demonstrates that the losses had been stemmed by the late 1980s and the 1990s saw further capital gains from real estate. Taking the period 1960-97 as a whole, real gains on farm land and buildings marginally exceeded losses ($32m. in 1990 values) but this was exceeded by the gains on farm debt ($166m); losses on other assets owned by the business (including stored crops and financial assets) reduced the gain in equity to $182m. Clearly, within the history of the US the years over which measurement is made can have a major influence on the impact of gains and losses on the overall rewards, and that a very long hold of land is required before a net gain may be seen.

The size of capital gains to agriculture in *Canada* has received a substantial amount of attention, showing a similar pattern of rising importance compared with income over the 1970s as exhibited in the neighbouring USA (Brinkman, 1980; Chase, 1980). Though only covering gains from real estate (that is, not dealing with other physical of financial assets), estimates starting in 1960 show that capital gains occurred, especially after 1973, a year in which current income rose substantially, almost doubling and remaining at the increased level. Real gains in the earlier period (1960-72) were noticeably more variable than current income, with capital losses occurring from 1967-71, mirroring a similar movement in the US. Nevertheless, from 1960-72 real capital gains averaged 25 per cent of income. After 1973, gains assumed a much greater importance in relation to current income and in four of the last six years of the 1970s they exceeded net farm income. However, within Canada there was evidence of sizeable regional variation, an element which could hold substantial consequences for agricultural policy (Huff and MacAulay, 1973)

Denmark is unusual among EUR 15 member states in that it has published estimates of capital gains and losses as part of its annual official survey of the agricultural industry. Figures for 1981/82 to 1986/87 are shown in Table 6.1. These estimates take account both of changing asset values and of liabilities, and are expressed in real terms by adjusting according to the general level of prices. The heavily indebted nature of Danish agriculture makes the inclusion of gains and losses on financial assets particularly important. Though the estimates are restricted to the assets and liabilities of "active" farmers, a comparison of the gains and losses with current income shows the implications of taking both into account when assessing the year-to-year change in economic status of farmers. Capital gains are far more volatile than current income, in some years substantially adding to current income and in others, when losses occur, largely wiping it out.

Table 6.1 Denmark: Real capital gains and losses in agriculture, 1981/2-1986/7 Mio DKR

	1981/2	1982/3	1983/4	1984/5	1985/6	1986/7
Farm real estate	-12.6	-6.6	10.3	7.5	22.6	-2.6
Other assets	-0.5	0.7	0.3	-0.7	1.4	-4.4
Liabilities	4.1	-2.6	0.0	2.1	-5.2	9.5
Real gains total	-9.0	-8.5	10.6	8.9	18.8	2.5
Total current household income	8.9	13.0	10.5	16.7	15.4	15.8

Note: Total current household income includes non-farm income and is net of transfers and interest payments but before the deduction of taxes.
Source: *The Danish Agricultural Economy*, Autumn 1987.

Sweden has a history of estimating capital gain, including those on agricultural real estate and liabilities (Gulbrandsen and Lindbeck, 1973). Over the period 1954-66 real gains in agriculture about doubled, with half coming from the declining real value of liabilities. In 1966, the trend-adjusted capital gains were equivalent to 43 per cent of farmers' income. In 1982-86 (annual) changes in the real value of assets that were not subject to capital gains tax (such as falls in the value of debts) were in the range SKR 20,000 to 30,000 for farmers but were SKR 7,000 to 13,000 for workers and white-collar employees. However, gains on the remainder (real estate, shares etc.) that were taxed became increasingly negative, for farmers increasing from SKR -7,000 to -60,000 and for the comparison group from SKR -2,400 to -13,900. Changes in real estate values were negative in most farm size groups during the whole of the 1980s. Overall capital losses (on all assets and liabilities) were negative in the early 1980s and in 1985. Any such calculations are, of course, sensitive to the indices used for the various types of assets.

One of the few attempts to study the effects of capital gains on the *United Kingdom* farming industry was made by Hearn (1977), though it is now rather dated (Table 6.2). Two series of real gains were calculated, one deflating by the Retail Price Index and the other by the Index of Equity Prices, so that gains could be viewed from either the consumption of the investment viewpoints. In practice the two series were closely similar. Only gains on real estate were included, in line with the UK convention of treating nominal gains on other assets as part of operating gains, that is as part of farm income. Gains on liabilities (that is, the decline in their real value associated with inflation) were not covered, an omission of significance towards the end of the series. Bearing this in mind, the figures show that real capital gains were generally greater in the latter part of the period than in the former. However, the degree of stability, as measured by the coefficient of variation, was greater in the 1960s than in the 1970s. Taking the pattern of land prices in the years after Hearn's figures end, in which the level in 1993 was very similar in real terms to what it was in 1970, it could be anticipated that the large gains to the agricultural industry in the early 1970s would have been more or less completely eroded by the early 1990s.

A good case can be put that capital gains and losses should be looked at over a run of years; land is normally treated as a long or medium term asset. Taking periods of five and ten years, Hearn showed that from 1950

Table 6.2 UK: Real capital gains on agricultural real estate, 1950-74

£ million (1950 prices)

Year	Deflated by index of retail prices (1950 prices)	Deflated by index of equity prices (1950 prices)
1950	91	91
1951	114	122
1952	-107	-135
1953	92	109
1954	-95	-87
1955	96	81
1956	-27	-26
1957	73	68
1958	40	39
1959	186	133
1960	35	21
1961	168	100
1962	108	72
1963	245	151
1964	351	210
1965	101	67
1966	32	22
1967	231	152
1968	232	113
1969	-35	-18
1970	-225	-140
1971	290	167
1972	2210	1074
1973	982	602
1974	-1086	-1320

Source: Hearn (1977)

to 1974 capital gain formed an increasing part of the overall reward to owner-occupiers, a pattern mirrored in the US, Canada and Sweden. Over the 1950s average annual gains were 21 per cent of disposable farm income, over the 1960s 90 per cent and between 1970 and 1974 110 per cent. For landlords, with the exception of the early 1950s, capital gains were more than twice the level of average net rents. This suggests that the landlords who remained in agriculture were prepared to regard capital growth as the chief financial reward to ownership. For both categories, it was apparent that capital gain should not be ignored either as an influence in business decisions and resource allocation or in consideration of welfare.

6.4.4 Farm-level business balance sheets

Although balance sheets that purport to relate to farm businesses are, as a concept, seriously flawed, nevertheless it is worth noting some of the findings in surveys that attempt to calculate them. Many countries' national surveys, and the EU's FADN, measure the levels of assets, liabilities and net worths of farms in their samples by making some simplifying assumptions that mirror those of the national farm; assets deemed not to be agricultural, whether found on or off the farm, and liabilities deemed as non-agricultural are not brought into the assessment of the balance sheet for the "farm business". In principle there should be no problem in establishing distributions of farms by level of asset value or net worth, though it must be borne in mind that the samples typically exclude many small units that contribute little to national production but nevertheless represent a significant proportion of the people engaged in farming. Such analysis is rarely carried out, even in the United States where attention is more frequently focused on differences in averages between states and regions (Weldon *et al.*, 1993). In practice, publications concentrate on the levels of indebtedness (distribution of farms by total borrowing or by the ratio of their liabilities to assets) and on measure of vulnerability that combine income flows with capital sheet ratios.

Perhaps the most important finding from balance sheets in the present context is that agriculture's characteristic of a striking diversity is again exhibited. While assets, dominated by real estate, would be expected to reflect the diversity of farm sizes, the pattern of debt is more surprising. The consequence is that the distribution of net worth does not necessarily mirror that of total assets, though they might be expected to be close. Harrison (1975) found, on a sample of English farms in 1969, that liabilities were very unevenly spread. At a time when the indebtedness of farmers averaged 10.7%, over a half of all farms (55%) had no liabilities other than the short-term deferments of payments to the end of the month normal in commerce. Two thirds of all borrowing was accounted for by only 5% of farmers. The heavily indebted ones (with liabilities more than 30% of assets) tended to be full-time operators of working farms, aged in their 40s, tenants and recent entrants. Later results for the farms covered by the EU's FADN found that, in 1989 the community of twelve countries, three quarters of farms had liabilities of 10% or less of their assets, and only one farm in ten had liabilities above 30%. This sort of distribution was also found for 1981. A disproportionately large share of the heavily indebted farms were found in Denmark, reflecting the atypical method of intergeneration transfer of property found there (parents selling to successors supported by special financial institutions).

Harrison (1975) produced raised estimates of the farming net worth of farmers in England and a distribution by size of net worth, drawing comparisons with the wealth holdings of the rest of the community. These data are very out-of-date but are unlikely to understate the relative position of farmers in the 1970s and later because a substantial rise in the price of land took place after the estimates were made. In 1969 the 1 per cent most wealthy farmers (taking only their farming assets and liabilities) held 12 per cent of farming's total net worth. The top 5 per cent accounted for 30 per cent of the total. Comparisons with other parts of society are notoriously hazardous, but given that both Harrison's estimates for farming net worth and those of the UK Inland Revenue for all wealth holders ignore the value of state and private pensions and do not properly deal with personal assets and consumer durables, they are of broadly similar coverage. With that in mind, it was evident that the net worth per person in the farming community (farmers and their dependent adults) was substantially above the general level even when consideration is restricted to their farming assets (and liabilities). Some 16 per cent of the farming community had net worths above £20,000 (current prices) whereas only 1.7 per cent all wealth holders were above this level. A later comment on the wealth position of UK farmers (Peters, 1980) indicated that all the owner-occupied farms in the 1977-78 Farm Management Survey in the UK, even those in the small farm group (275-599 Standard Man-days, corresponding to the one-to-two man farms) had net worths which put their occupiers among the richest 6 per cent of the population, and occupiers of most sizes and types of farms were in the top 2 per cent or less. However, these comparisons, that only consider agricultural property, are unsatisfactory because they are based on a unit – the agricultural business – that is somewhat artificial, as it ignores the other resources which many households that operate farms have and the influence that these have on the economic situation of farm families.

6.4.5 *Capital gains at the farm level*

At the farm level capital gains and losses have direct repercussions for a range of behavioural issues. They carry influence on production and investment decisions within the farm business and on the consumption levels of the farm operators. They affect savings, with a higher propensity for farmers to save from gains as opposed to current income (Bhatia, 1972). One important repercussion of capital gains is probably a changed attitude towards risk among owner-managers resulting from enhanced personal wealth. According to Hearn (1977), farmers who had experienced gains could be expected to take on investments and enterprises of higher risk characteristics and thus have a different farming pattern from those who had not. As discussed earlier, capital gain can be turned into spending power in a variety of ways, including borrowing on the strength of an improved equity position and the avoidance of having to make provisions for pensions out of current income. In the UK farmers have differed widely in the ways that they view capital gains as benefiting their abilities to borrow, with small farms tending to stress the greater credit that gains enabled them to raise more so than medium or larger farmers with stronger income positions (Hearn, 1977). Capital gains are also a factor causing farmers to stay in the industry or to quit; anticipation of rising land prices and the preferential taxation given to capital gains, especially on retirement, has been seen as a substantial brake on structural change to a farm size pattern more in accord with the technical and economic conditions of the present (Hearn, 1977; Perry *et al.,* 1986).

In the US Gardner (1975) estimated incomes of farmers including unrealised capital gains in a "normal" year. As reported in Chapter 3, this resulted in a substantial reduction in the number of farm families which fell below the poverty line. Harrison (1975) looking at capital gains in England through a survey of farms found, perhaps not surprisingly with hindsight over a long period of rising land prices, that the total capital gains which had accrued were by no means equally shared among farmers but had gone to those who had owned the most land and to those who had owned it longest. Also, farmers had not reacted in identical fashions even though they may have faced identical gains both in total and in time. In the USA there were regional differences in equity gains and losses that could be linked to income expectations flowing from policy decisions on commodity support programmes, implying that some types of farm were affected more than others (Weldon, Moss and Erickson, 1993). A less intuitive finding comes from Hearn (1977) who calculated the value of gains for the UK over the period 1950-74 and found that, at the individual farm level, capital gains were more important compared with current income among large farms than among small ones. This was because of differential rises in the price of land and because of lower incomes per acre among larger farms. In this case, including capital gain with current income had the effect of increasing the inequality in the distribution of income.

Findings concerning capital gains are usually made using data related to the farm business. Of course, if the farm operator and his family also hold other (non-farming) assets, capital gains and losses on these will carry implications for what happens on the farm and on consumption patterns. For example, a collapse in the value of off-farm assets would be likely to have a dampening effect on the willingness to make high risk decisions in the farm's use of capital. Hence, as with balance sheets, it is desirable to have information on gains and losses based on the household unit that could put the farm business in its broader context.

6.5   Balance sheets and net worths of agricultural households

6.5.1 Some theoretical issues

The conclusion of the discussion above is that balance sheets of farm businesses as currently drawn up, at the levels of agricultural industry or individual farm business, are flawed and form a very imperfect guide – possibly a misleading one - to the wealth or net worths of farmers and farm households or to their capital gains and losses. A preferable approach would be to base balance sheet statistics on real units (households that operate farms and incorporated agricultural businesses). This is particularly appropriate for the many policy questions that require microeconomic data for answers, such as trying to establish how many low income farmers also suffer from low net worths. For farms operated as unincorporated businesses this implies that the measurement of assets and liabilities would encompass all the assets held by their operators, not only those concerned with agricultural independent activity (self-employment) but also those in other forms of economic activity, financial investments and personal property. Liabilities would include all forms of loans made to the operators.

However, it is by no means certain *whose* balance sheets are to be measured, summed and analysed to achieve an aggregate picture or to show the distributions within it. The first issue concerns the individuals who comprise the household unit. Assets and liabilities may be held jointly or by individuals in households. But, as with measurement of disposable income, it usually makes sense to assess across the whole of the household unit that stands ready to pool resources for major decisions. Though in some circumstances a separation of assets owned by spouses is no doubt maintained (property rights involving land are usually clear), on balance an amalgamation of the two represents a more realistic situation. While this pooling might be extended to any assets held by dependent children, it does not necessarily embrace other adults who may be resident in the same dwelling. In many cases is seems likely that the capital pool and the income pool will comprise the same people.

The second issue concerns which households are to be included in the measurement of assets and liabilities. They might include all those households where at least one member is involved in operating an unincorporated business that undertakes some form of agricultural production, either alone or in combination with other forms of production. To do so would include many for whom farming is only very small-scale and where it represents only a minor part of their total economic activities (with considerable overlap among these two categories). While this might indicate the depth of the fund of capital on which agriculture might draw, it is by no means certain that this represents the most meaningful coverage in the context of explaining behaviour and of policy interest. Narrowing this "broad" coverage down poses a set of questions similar to those faced when Eurostat developed its statistics on the income of the agricultural households sector (IAHS) referred to in Chapters 3 and 5 (Eurostat, 1996; Hill, 1996). A case could be made that a similar set of responses should be sought in the case of assets and liabilities.

For the purpose of measuring disposable income of agricultural households in the EU, the agricultural community has been defined by Eurostat as those households where independent activity in agriculture (farming) is the main income source of the household reference person (normally the head of household). In that statistics have a policy context, and that a case could be made that agricultural policy is aimed primarily at this agricultural community, then it makes some sense to take this group as the one for which the balance sheet is to be established. Landlords who had no direct farming businesses would not be included, as rent is considered an income from property and not from economic activity (in the sense that self-employment is). This, however, is not the only view possible; for example, it might be suitable in some circumstances to select households of producers above a certain threshold of agricultural output, irrespective of whether agriculture is their main activity. Or, those whose main assets are agricultural could be selected.

Third, there is the issue of assets held in trust. These legal devices are employed so that, by sacrificing a degree of personal control, accretions of wealth can achieve preferential taxation treatment that, in particular, enables a more complete inter-generation transfer of wealth and the benefits that this wealth brings. This raises the issue of how that wealth should be valued in a household-based balance sheet; while not strictly personal property of individual household members, to ignore it would be to seriously misrepresent the possibilities that exist for drawing on the funds.

Fourth, there is the issue of the appropriate treatment of farm businesses arranged as companies. In line with the treatment given to households, a broad approach would include the capital position of all business that engage in agricultural production, whether or not it is the main activity. A more selective approach would mean that an explicit criterion had to be applied to what constitutes an agricultural business; it is possible to classify businesses into industry sectors according to their main activity. However, a high proportion of farm businesses arranged as companies are, *de facto*, very similar to partnerships in their underlying family ownership and management, having adopted this form largely for fiscal convenience. In such circumstances the legal distinction between business and private assets becomes less meaningful. Possibilities exist for cross-financing and movement across the business boundary, so that the personal wealth of director-shareholders and the balance sheet of the business are not essentially independent. In such circumstances an argument might be forwarded that the two should be combined, treating such the directors of such companies as if they were partners, along the line argued by the UK for their treatment as partnerships in structural statistics, mentioned earlier. (It is also worth noting that FADN, in selecting its sample of farm businesses, makes no explicit reference to whether the farm is unincorporated or incorporated, and assumes that the accounts for the latter can be drawn up as if they were unincorporated for the purpose of estimating income).

Thus, though it seems that balance sheet statistics built on the agricultural household unit and incorporated farm business could more accurately service the needs of policymakers and analysts, the stage of conceptualisation is by no means complete.   Important theoretical questions remain to be discussed before an operational methodology can be laid out.

6.5.2   Empirical evidence - household sector balance sheets

At present there is no attempt within the EU's statistical system to calculate balance sheets and net worths for the agricultural households sector, though the possibility exists within the national accounts framework and especially in that of the System of Economic Accounts for Food and Agriculture (SEAFA) put forward by the FAO which gives prominence to accounts that build on the household as the basic unit.

To find an example that takes this approach at aggregate level one has to turn to the USA and its Sector Balance Sheets at State and US levels. These are built up mainly using aggregate information (in contrast to the survey-based estimates discussed later). Although emphasis now falls on US agricultural balance sheets that take only agricultural assets and debts into account (see *6.4.1*), another series was formerly published that included "operator households". In essence this also included estimates of the assets and debts relating to the domestic aspects of the farms. On the asset side this meant that the value of the houses occupied by farm operators was included, as were the private shares of farm cars and trucks. It was intended also to include financial assets held by the operator household. On the liabilities side borrowings for private purposes were included, such as for operator housing. Though not now published, the facility to make such calculations appear intact. However, the coverage of non-farm assets was generally not thought to be complete (US Department of Agriculture – private communication); not all the assets owned were covered, such as other business real estate or holiday homes, one factor perhaps explaining why publication does not now take place. It is worth noting that the coverage of households is a "broad" one, in that all operators of farms are included, whether or not farming is their main source of income or represents their main stock of assets.

Perhaps because of the less than full measurement of non-farm assets, the differences in published figures between the series including and excluding "operator households are not large in relation to the total sums involved and the relationships between assets and liabilities are little altered", as the following figures for 1985 show (Table 6.3). Nevertheless this flexibility of presentation is advantageous when attempting to distinguish the branch of the economy designated agriculture from the sector of the population consisting of agricultural households.

Table 6.3 USA: Balance sheet for US agriculture, 1985 (billion $)

| | Operator households | |
	Included	Excluded
Real estate	607	560
Livestock	46	46
Machinery and vehicles	98	92
Crops	37	37
Household equipment and furnishings	26	-
Financial assets	53	37
Total assets	867	771
Real estate debt	105	97
Non-real estate debt	100	94
Total debt	205	192
Equity (Net Worth)	662	579
Debt/Assets (%)	24	25
Debt/Real estate (%)	17	17
Debt/Non-real estate (%)	38	45

Source: Economic Indicators of the Farm Sector 1985, USDA

6.5.3 *Empirical evidence – microeconomic data*

The EU is very poorly provided with statistics on the balance sheets and net worths of agricultural households. Evidence is fragmentary and suffers from poor comparability over time and space. In particular, what is considered as a farming household varies widely and probably makes a large impact to the results. However, the findings are sufficient to establish that farm households, as a group, hold significant amounts of assets outside the farm business and have relatively large net worths compared with other groups in society. This sort of information has obvious potential significance to agricultural policy and underlines the need for statistics to be developed in this area. The following gives a flavour of the situation.

A survey of farms in England in 1969 (Harrison 1975) found that, in addition to the farming capital they owned, 14 per cent of farmers (corresponding to 11 per cent of farms, the difference being explained by some farms having more than one business principal) had assets outside farming equal to at least 50 per cent of their net worths as farmers. About one third of these farmers farmed only in a small way (in terms of farm assets) but for the rest farming was by no means an insignificant activity. No comparable survey has been conducted since this information was gathered, so the extent of the present divergence of personal wealth from farm business assets in the UK is difficult to judge. There are a few pointers from information on part-time farming and from income tax records. About one third of farmers covered in the UK Structure Survey in 1989 had another non-farm gainful activity off the farm, probably nearer a half if spouses were included. A principle form this takes for the farmer is self-employment in some other business run in parallel with the farm; this implies the ownership of some non-farm business assets, but their extent is not known. Another fragment of information relates to income from rents and investments accruing to farmers in the Survey of Personal Incomes (MAFF, 1994 and similar annual publications); in the tax years since 1977-78 investment income for the tax cases classed as agricultural or horticultural accounted for between 18 and 29 per cent of their total taxable income. Grossing up these receipts according to expected yields to achieve a valuation of the assets which generated the investment income would of course be possible but might be wide of the mark unless the types of holdings could also be ascertained. However, the income streams are sufficient to show that these assets held outside the farm business are not insignificant for farmers as a group.

As noted above, for the most part commentators on the UK situations have had to work only with information solely about the assets and liabilities of the farm business. Though this sort of partial indicator is far from satisfactory in establishing the relative wealth position of farmers, it is the only approach available at present in the UK. It is adequate, however, to suggest that as a group UK farmers are among the wealthiest sectors of society (see *6.4.4* above). For more detailed information one has to look outside the UK.

Among EU Member States *France* provides a rather more precise indication of the relative wealth of its farmers in the form of 1992 study by INSEE that covered the wealth of all types of household (Jegouzo, 1998). This was based on declarations by households, rather than data collection by experts, so some under-recording is likely; aspects of human capital and pension rights were not covered. On this basis it was found that in 1992 the average household headed by a farmer had gross assets double that of households headed by other self-employed and salaried people (1.956,000 F compared with 969,000 F). The relationship between net worths was expected to be similar. When households were classed into deciles according to level of (gross) assets, farm households rose progressivly in relative importance as the more wealthy households were encountered, in the lowest decile of wealth farm households formed less than 1% of all households, yet in the higher two deciles they represented 9% of the total (overall farm households formed 4.5% of total numbers). The French study also suggests an important feature of wealth distribution; whereas among incomes in agriculture it is frequently found that low incomes are frequent and high incomes less numerous, the situation is reversed when wealth is concerned. Compared with the rest of society, wealth in agriculture is relatively broadly shared among farm families (a point also made for the UK by Harrison). Almost half of all the agricultural households (49%) were to be found among France's most wealthy fifth (that is, in the top two deciles of household wealth). A number of factors were associated with high wealth, important among which was inheritance from previous generations of farmers. In *Germany* agricultural households owned about three times the average amount of capital (304 per cent); though much more wealthy than wage-earners (56 per cent of the all household average) they were exceeded in holdings by other self-employed households (477 per cent) (Gebauer, 1982). As elsewhere, much of the wealth of these agricultural households consisted of real estate.

For a statistical system that attempts to cover the overall assets and liabilities of farm households one again has to turn to countries outside the EU. Two examples have come to light. In *Norway* balance sheets are drawn up annually for households grouped by the socio-professional status of the main income earner. Thus the coverage of farmers approximates to the "narrow" definition used in the EU's agricultural household sector statistics (IAHS statistics - see Chapter 5); those whose main income is from another source, such as many who would be regarded as hobby farmers, are not included. Unfortunately, in the published tables (available on the internet) farmers are not shown separately but are grouped with other self-employed people working in the primary sector. The presence of forestry and fishing households limits the usefulness of the statistics in their present form. Also, the value attached to agricultural land in these balance sheets probably understates to a significant extent what it would fetch if sold, though the heavily regulated nature of the land market makes valuation difficult. Some other assets are also subject to non-market pricing rules. Despite these drawbacks, it is worth noting that in 1997 the average published net worth of these primary sector households was more than three times that of the average Norwegian households (Kr 544,943 compared with Kr 131,267), and more than 50 per greater than that of households headed by other self-employed people (Kr 356,109). In addition to the real estate and production assets they owned (Kr 706,814), primary sector households held financial assets of Kr 464381, of which a little over half was bank deposits. A failure to take into account these other assets would have made their debt-asset ratio much worse; total debt represented 98 per cent of land and productive assets but 56 per cent of total assets (including durable consumption goods).

The other example is the *USA*. There the Agricultural Resource Management Study (ARMS) - formerly called the Farm Costs and Returns Survey – attempts to gather information on the non-farm assets and debts of all household members as part of its data collection. This large-scale national survey of farms thus has a somewhat broader coverage of assets than the Sector Balance Sheets referred to above (which did not cover all forms of non-farm wealth) but is similarly concerned that with the quality of the answers received (USDA, personal communication). In particular, the coverage of adult household members is imperfect, both in terms of their incomes and their assets. Nevertheless, results are considered sufficiently robust to provide the basis of the comparisons between the wealth of farm households and other groups that are published in the thrice-yearly *Rural Conditions and Trends* and for incorporation into the sections concerning farm operator households in the annual *Family Farm Report to the Congress*.

In the *USA* the average full-time farmer in 1988 had a net worth of $1,016,000; it should be noted that "full-time" in this context is a measure of farm size (sales of $100,000 and over). In contrast, all-households average (in 1986) was $78,734 with about half of all households being worth less than $32,677. Such figures led Knudsen *et al.* (1990) to conclude that "The average full-time farmer has a net worth almost 13 times greater than that of the average American family, and a net worth over 30 times greater than half the families of America. Even farmers in the part-time, $40,000-$99,999 sales class have a net worth of $426,487 - over five times greater than the average American family". In another analysis, and without applying a size criterion, it was found that the average farm equity of households where agriculture was the main income source and where farming was the main occupation of the operator (which accounted for 40 per cent of all farms in the 1986 Farm Costs and Returns Survey) was $319,690. Even where agriculture was *not* the main family income source and where farming was *not* the main occupation of the operator - a combination which accounted for 33 per cent of farms - the average equity was $139,546, double the national all-households average (Ahearn and Lee, 1991). Cross-sectional analysis of the 1990 FCRS by age of holder found that farm net worth increased sharply with increasing age up to the 45-54 age band and stabilised thereafter (though both farm income, off-farm income and total incomes all peaked at this band and declined among older groups)(Ahearn *et al.*, 1993). In 1990 the average farm operator household had net worth of $411,681m more than four times the all-household figure of $92, 017. By 1995 things had changed a little; the average net worth of household operating a farm had fallen back to $366,300 (of which non-farm net worth contributed $61,600), those with commercial farms (sales class of $50,000 and over) average $576,400 and those with a non-commercial farm $293,800. In contrast, the all-households average had increased to $205,950 though this was still lower than the farm operator households, even those with non-commercial farms. However, the average for all households with a self-employed householder was $731,500 (Sommer, 1998; USDA, 1997). Clearly the superior wealth of US farm households is subject to quite swift erosion, presumably linked to movements in land prices.

6.6   Implications of wealth held by farmers

Given that farmers and their households appear to be relatively wealthy compared with society in general, though the information on which this judgement is based leaves much to be desired, one might wish to question some of the issues associated with such a situation. For example, why is it that the wealth of farm families is often large in comparison with their incomes? Does wealth itself constitute a factor contributing to the economic status of farmers, and how might wealth be taken into account in assessing the need for any policy action to improve their standards of living?

6.6.1 Live poor, die rich

There is a paradox in the fact that in many industrialised countries farmers whose low incomes are a cause for concern and the reason for government intervention in support of them are frequently holders of wealth which is substantial and typically above that of non-farmers. In the USA in 1986, the average farm equity of farm operator households whose incomes fell below the income poverty line was substantially above the all-households average net worth (Ahearn and Lee, 1991). Among the farm households in poverty, more than half consisted of families where the head's main occupation was as a farmer and where the main income of the household came from farming; these had an average farm equity (net worth) of $238,640, over three times the national all-households average. A high ratio between wealth and income for all farmers was also found in Australia; one study (Stoeckel, Cuthbertson and Curran, 1974) found a ratio some 4 to 5 times higher for farmers than for non-farm families. In Britain the case for increased support of incomes has often incorporated references to the low income in relation to assets (for example see de Paula, 1973). Though often thought of as a product of the agricultural support policies of the post-war era, there is evidence that in a longer historical perspective land has frequently looked expensive in relation to the income it could generate (Northfield, 1979).

Several explanations can be put forward for this phenomenon (Sexton and Duffus, 1977; Harrison, 1975). The capital-intensive nature of the farming industry has arisen in part because of the inelastic supply of land and the tendency of the support of product prices to be capitalised into rising land prices and real capital gains (discussed below). Part of the explanation relates to a market which, at least in the UK, has been dominated by expanding farmers who could justify high-priced land purchases. In that land prices have risen and carried the wealth of farmers along with them, this process is unplanned and shows farmers to be passive beneficiaries, a situation underlined by the finding that the indebtedness of farmers in the UK is inversely related to the time elapsed since they bought land and the erosion of debts by inflation. (Harrison, 1975). Similarly, analysis of the FADN EUR 12 sample for 1989 showed that the ratio between liabilities and assets declined progressively across the age spectrum, and the percentage of (pre-interest) income absorbed by interest payments among holdings headed by a farmer aged over 65 years (7 per cent) was about half that of those under 45 years (Hill and Brookes, 1993).

Another explanation is the possible preference for asset holding on the part of farm families. In Australia Stoekel *et al.* (1974) have suggested that this may be due to the requirement for farmers to provide a large portion of their resources they need in retirement from their own assets compared with non-farmers who would normally be covered by superannuation schemes. It may also reflect a desire to pass physical capital to the next generation, more so than in other sections of society where human capital (in the form of spending on education) is shown a higher preference. A more likely explanation, put forward for the UK but probably generally applicable (Harrison, 1975) is that farmers' horizons are frequently limited to farming, so that investments tend to be made on the farm or at least in farming, such as by buying more land. Investment possibilities off the farm tend to be ignored or treated as too risky; one effect of this is to exacerbate the demand for land and hence raise its price. Information on investment income of British farmers suggests that not all are discouraged from off-farm investments, but these farmers may be those whose origins are not among the traditional working farmer group or whose main source of income is not the farm.

A further line of explanation comes from the patterns of income and wealth associated with the life cycle (Gasson *et al.,* 1988; Ahearn, Perry and El-Osta, 1993). There is evidence of an inverted-U shape in the age-earnings profile for farm operators whereas the net worth profile is either fairly flat or rises with age to a plateau. This combination tends to exaggerate the high asset values in relation to income of farmers at the end of their lives - the adage of live-poor/die-rich most naturally applies to the combination of income and wealth found among the elderly. In Australia the ratio of net worth to income of farmers over 60 years old was found to be between two and four times that of farmers aged between 30 and 40 (Sexton and Duffus, 1977) and was a feature encountered across several types of farming. A similar but less extreme pattern existed in the US for 1990, the ratio between net worth and (total) income among farm operators of 65 years and over being about ten to one, whereas among operators of less than 35 years it was about six to one (reported in OECD, 1995).

A word of caution is needed. When analysis takes place of farms broken down by the age group of the farmer, it is almost always according to that of the sole or principal farmer or occupier on the holding (see, for example, the analysis for the EU's FADN in Hill and Brookes (1993) and the USA's FCRS in Ahearn, Perry and El-Osta (1993)). This simplifying assumption that each farm has one family and one farmer is coming under increasing challenge, particularly for socio-economic studies (Boxley, 1989). There seems to be an increasingly common practice to involve younger generations in the business as partners, more so than in the past. This inevitably clouds the influence of age as a factor effecting the income as the younger person takes a more prominent role in the management of the farm business, often initially with responsibility for technical aspects but progressing to financial aspects of perhaps a single enterprise (Hastings, 1984).

The high wealth-low income combination, particularly found among elderly farmers, should concentrate attention on how wealth enters into the assessment of economic status and the criteria for public support. It may suggest ways in which wealth can be drawn on to provide current spending power, avoiding the transfers for other sectors which most other policy mechanisms entail.

6.6.2 *The economic status of farmers*

In Chapter 3 it was argued that the economic status of an individual, that is his potential consumption of goods and services, was related to both his current income and to his net worth. Wealth represents potential spending power, and two individuals with the same current income but different amounts of assets will have different consumption possibilities. In order to express income and wealth in a common measure the usual approach is to calculate the annuity value of net worth, that is an annual income stream of equivalence to the lump sum. This is added to conventional income to give a parameter of the total flow of economic services at the command of the consumer unit. The method was expounded by Weisbrod and Hansen (1968) in general form and later applied with particularly telling results in agricultural contexts.

The determinants of this income-equivalent are the amount of net worth (NW), the life expectancy of the recipient (n) and the rate of interest (r). The three are linked by the following formula (from Weisbrod and Hansen, 1968):

$$\text{Annuity value} = NW \times \frac{r}{1 - (1-r)^{-n}}$$

The shorter the expected life and the larger the sum annuitised, the larger will be the income stream equivalent. Normally the life expectancy would be that of the wealth owner, but in the case of couples it is not unreasonable to use that of the person expected to live the longer. This was discussed in Chapter 3. So too was the objection that some portion of the wealth is not really "owned" but is only held in stewardship for future generations and so cannot be used as a base for estimating consumption potential. However, when applied to agricultural land there seems little to justify this special treatment as land clearly forms part of the marketable assets of its owners and, whatever their intentions to pass it onto their children, represents potential spending power. Such arguments would not be accepted for the general exclusion of wealth from capital taxation (or of income from personal taxes) although it must be conceded that the preferential treatment in legislation often given to agricultural land has in part been won by using such a line of argument.

Applying the technique to farmers in the US for 1966, Carlin and Reinsel (1973) found that the distribution of well-being among farm families became more equal when annuitised wealth was added to current income to give a joint measure, and that disparities between the farm and non-farm sectors were narrowed as the position of the farm families improved. Similar results were reported for farm families in North Carolina for 1970 (Gardner, 1972). In Australia investigations into the poverty of farmers in three regions of Victoria (Vincent, Watson and Barton, 1975) found that the numbers of families falling below an income-based poverty line was substantially reduced if annuitised wealth was also considered. In Canada the method was applied at aggregate (agricultural household sector) level (Chase, 1980; Chase and Lerohl, 1981) using a range of interest rates, based on farm credit rates in the private and public sectors, and several life expectancies. The estimates relate to a time when capital gains were being received, and the conclusions were that over the period 1967-77 net worth constituted a rising proportion of the total economic well-being (status). In 1967 the average farm annuity added approximately 47 per cent total economic well-being (farm and non-farm income) and in 1977 the figure was 57 per cent.

However, the problem of using the above formula in order to assess economic status is that it provides only a notional measure of economic welfare. Chase and Lerohl pointed out that current annual income must be independent of net worth in order to add the two streams, something they achieved by removing the reward to land and capital from their estimates of the income from farming. Attempts at evaluating economic status at household level have to tackle the problem that farmers cannot in practice realise annuities based on net worths without losing the assets which form the basis for their current income. This is not the case when other forms of personal wealth are considered, with the notable exception of owner-occupied housing, where the income in kind would be lost on sale. However modification to the methodology are possible which allow for the retention of a current income-earning capacity. These are attractive for consideration because they are less open to criticism of being unrealistic and, moreover, they indicate channels by which the wealth of farmers may be released in practical agricultural policy aimed at income support. Farmers are free to sell up and exchange the proceeds for annuities, formally with financial institutions or informally by making assessments of their own life expectancies and consuming accordingly, but it is clear that this is not a common practice, at least in the UK and north America. In Denmark the custom of retiring farmers selling their land to the next generation (rather than making an outright gift) is one step in this direction, but such a system is exceptional and only applies when land is relinquished; methods of farm take-over in the EU are reviewed in Cornet *et al.,* (1991).

Two principle ways of expressing the income equivalent of net worth while retaining agricultural assets to generate current income present themselves. The first is a forward sales contract arrangement under which a farmer mortgages his property in exchange for an annuity based on the net worth of the property, but the mortgagee only assumes title to the property after the death of the farmer. Under this arrangement the value of the assets to the mortgagee, and thus the sum on which the annuity is based, is not the current sale price of the assets but rather the price at death of the farmer, discounted to the present. Several approaches to estimating this discounted land value are possible; for Australia Sexton and Duffus (1977) assumed that present land values were solely determined by future farm income flows so that the present value of a future land value could be found by deducting the discounted income flows to be received over the expected life of the farmer. When factors other than farm profits determine land prices, as in the UK, it might be preferable to make assessments of the likely future land prices and a rate of interest on alternative investment opportunities to discount these values to the present. In the Australian example the annuity value was added to the sum of the current incomes of all family members, including off-farm earnings, investment income (from other property, which did not enter the annuitisation) and non-taxed types of income (child allowances and so on). An arbitrary interest rate of 6 per cent was used.

The results of including a forward-contract annuity arrangement on the number of Australian farms deemed to be in poverty was marked. The proportion of families in the dairy sector with incomes of less than $4,000 in 1974 fell from 19 per cent to 5 per cent. In the dried vine fruit sector the fall was from 25 per cent to 14 per cent and in the apple and pear sector from 29 per cent to 9 per cent. When classifying by age of farmer, though reduction in the proportion of low status were observed among all groups, consistently high reductions were in evidence among families having a household head of retirement age (60 years) and over. In the dairy sector 30 per cent of families with a head of 60 years old were below the arbitrary $4,000 line on a current income basis, but only 1 per cent after annuitised net worth was included. If a practical scheme for exchanging net worth in the form of land were implemented, it would clearly have greatest significance among the older farmers.

The other land-retaining alternative, in countries which have a cash tenancy system, would be to sell the land on a sale-and-leaseback arrangement, remaining in occupation of the farm but paying a rent to the new owner. An estimate for the UK (Hill, 1982) assumed that owner-occupied farmers sold their land at prevailing tenanted-land prices (rather than at vacant possession prices) and annuities were calculated on the sums realised. For farms in the 1977-78 Farm Management Survey adding an annuity for the owned land raised the all-farm level of income by one third and lifted about half the farms with incomes below an arbitrary £2,000 to above that line.

6.7 Conclusion

There is no doubt that any full assessment of the economic position of farmers and their households should take into account their wealth. This applies both to the absolute level of wealth (as it affects economic status) and changes in wealth, in the form of capital gains and losses, which form part of personal income but are not usually included in income accounts compiled as part of the official statistics on agriculture because they do not arise directly from production activity. When farmers have the ability to switch between the alternative ways in which their net accretion of economic power is manifest - as current income or as wealth - any partial measure of the overall position will risk a misrepresentation of the real situation. The relative high wealth-to-income ratios found in agriculture afford particular opportunities for the transformation of income into forms that minimise taxation and therefore make the inclusion of capital aspects of unusual importance.

Including capital gains with current income has a substantial effect on the income position of farmers. Up to the 1980s current incomes from in the UK were enhanced by capital gains on agricultural assets. Subsequently a fall in the price of land probably resulted in notional capital losses, though land prices surged upwards between 1993 and 1996. However, the fact that land is normally treated as a long-term asset means that only a small proportion of landowners will have suffered capital losses on their acquisition prices. In the USA the persistent rise in land prices also reversed over the early 1980s but from 1986 farm equity recovered to approaching that of the late 1970s as farmers reduced debt and asset values stabilised. Again, short-term losses can be an unsatisfactory indicator of the longer period trend. Though the relevance of capital gains and losses will vary (their magnitudes can shift alarmingly, and sometimes they will run counter to movements in current income and sometimes with it) and they are largely beyond the influence of the individual farmer, they nevertheless constitute one form of economic reward. Furthermore, agricultural and other policies can have an impact on capital gains that measures based on current income from agricultural production – the conventional measures of farming prosperity – very largely miss.

The economic status of farmers, particularly the elderly ones, are altered in a major way if the command over goods and services resulting from their net worths is also included. The proportion suffering poverty is greatly reduced, though there will be some remaining, principally those without owned land. For policy-makers not only is the magnitude of the poverty problem transformed, but ways of aiding low income households become apparent which are based on enabling farm households to make liquid the assets which they control as an alternative to supporting their incomes. Any comparisons with the economic position of other parts of society, a central feature of agricultural policy, would have to ensure that the means existed by which the fuller treatment of farmers expounded here could also be applied to the other occupation groups.

Evidence used here from the UK, German and USA data sources represents little more than an ill-documented perception of the wealth of farmers in industrialised countries and how it compares with other groups in society. There is, first, a need for the development of a methodology for the measurement of wealth of agricultural households. Central theoretical issues would need to be resolved, such as what constitutes an agricultural household. The resolution of such issues would not appear more difficult than the similar tasks already achieved in the area of income measurement for the agricultural households sector. Next, there would remain the critical issue of whether data could be collected on a household basis to allow such balance sheets to be built up. For EU Member States that already have good data in the form of administrative registers, this might already be feasible. For others, particularly in countries such as the UK which lack a central statistical department with the legal authority to bring together the disparate data that already exist, new data sources would need to be developed. In the UK the Farm Business Survey is possibly the most attractive option for short-term development. It already collects limited information on non-farm income, which indirectly provides elementary indications of assets held outside the farm, and would be a starting point for widening the cover of liabilities. However, the difficulties that measurement might pose should not obscure the deficiencies of the present approach and the direction in which methodological improvements should be made.

7 Information and Policy

7.1   Introduction

This final Chapter looks at the way in which information on the income and wealth of farmers is taken into account when shaping agricultural policy within the European Union. The main thesis of this book is that within the CAP incomes are not assessed in a way that is appropriate to the fundamental needs of policy in the 1990s and beyond. This also applies in the UK, the USA and many other industrialised countries. Furthermore, with few exceptions, the necessary information is not available by which a policy aimed directly at enabling agricultural population to enjoy a fair standard of living, as prescribed in the Treaty of Rome and restated in *Agenda 2000*, could be designed and monitored. Wealth, as it relates to the economic status of farmers and their families, is almost totally ignored.

The present system of using partial indicators of income as a proxy for the well-being of farmers (only that arising from agricultural activity) in reaching policy decisions has fostered a system of support that is ineffective at securing the main income aims and one which at the same time generates unwanted levels of production. This level of production represents a burden on society in terms of the wasteful use of resources, budgetary problems within the EU and likely social and environmental costs. A reorientation of policy involving the identification of low incomes in agriculture and the adoption of measures that aim at alleviation without stimulating aggregate supply has long been overdue (for example, Commission, 1994; Ockenden and Franklin, 1995). The *Agenda 2000* revisions of 1999, though carrying a stage further the change of support mechanism from market intervention to forms of direct payment introduced in the 1992 MacSharry reforms, aimed to create a more competitive agriculture by exposing them to more realistic market prices, and rewarding them for the provision of other output, in particular environmental services. Yet the means chosen to "compensate" agricultural producers for these changes (mainly arable area payments and premiums per animal on livestock) have ensured that the misplaced obsession of the CAP with agricultural production has barely been shifted. Yet attempts to reform policy radically, towards one that gives income support only to farm families that would otherwise have a standard of living that was inadequate (while still paying for environmental and other services "blind" to the social needs of recipients) have faced inertia in the policy-making process sufficient to prevent a major change. Even if the will were there, the lack of reliable data on the total incomes of farmers poses a substantial bar to assessing the feasibility of schemes which aid the incomes of farmers more directly and with greater discrimination. Nevertheless, there is mounting impatience with the unsatisfactory nature of the income support role of agricultural policy, certainly among commentators on the CAP and politicians not closely wedded to the agricultural lobby. This will require information not yet collected as part of the EU's monitoring of agriculture. We examine the possibilities for improving the statistics and the implications of a reform of agricultural policy in the UK and the EU that attempts in a more direct way to approach the income aims of the CAP.

7.2 Current measurement practice

As was seen in Chapters 4 and 5, incomes in agriculture can be approached from two directions, each of which can be viewed at two levels - in aggregate and at the level of the individual. The first direction is the agricultural production approach, which envisages income as the residual reward to factors not compensated in other ways from the activity of producing agricultural commodities; these factors typically comprise the entrepreneurial input of the farmer and spouse and family members who are not paid a wage, their physical labour, capital and their owned land. Within the EU statistical system the aggregate Economic Accounts for Agriculture (EAA), which looks at the whole agricultural branch of the economy (under a newly revised methodology, the agricultural "industry"), and the farm-business level Farm Accountancy Data Network (FADN/RICA) both belong to this approach. The other approach is to assess the incomes of a sector of society, agricultural households; this involves making a decision on what distinguishes an "agricultural" household from any other and is typically reached on the basis of the proportion of income coming from self-employment in farming, or on the amount of time the head of the household spends in farming. Most, though not all, the income of agricultural households will come from agriculture. Though the income of the agricultural household sector, or at the micro level the individual household, is the more appropriate parameter in the context of agricultural policy which is aimed primarily at the living standards of those engaged in this activity, the former production branch approach is the one which is by far the more commonly employed. This mismatch between policy aim and statistics used to monitor and shape policy is a crucial flaw in the information system and is a major element contributing to the poor performance of the CAP in tackling basic problems of the agricultural industry and of its creating new ones, such as surpluses.

Evidence from the branch approach shows that in the UK and the USA since the Second World War the aggregate income from agricultural activity has been under long-term downward pressure. This is not surprising in the historic setting of a static demand and a rapidly rising supply that typifies developed industrial countries. Short-term phenomena, such as the fillip provided to UK incomes by the increase in CAP support prices following Sterling's withdrawal from the Exchange Rate Mechanism in 1992 and the benefits of transitional accession arrangements to Spain and Portugal, should not obscure the universality of the squeeze on aggregate income and the consequences for farm-level incomes unless adequate structural adjustment takes place. The EU's system for monitoring incomes at the farm level (the Farm Accountancy Data Network) shows that, while in the short and medium terms when raised to national level, average farm incomes broadly follow the patterns in aggregate income indicators, there are substantial divergences between farms of different enterprise types and size and among individual farms within the same type/size combination. Consequently, changes in the aggregate income figure are not necessarily mirrored by changes at the farm level, and even the direction of income shifts may be contrary to that experienced by large numbers of farmers.

7.2.1 *Interpretation of production indicators*

Among the users of information, changes in income from agricultural production, at all levels of aggregation, are frequently interpreted as indicating parallel movements in the welfare of farmers. Evidence presented in this book (Chapter 5) should be enough to dispel such a simplistic interpretation. The presence of other income adds stability to the incomes of agricultural households and transforms the absolute levels. It greatly improves the position of farm households relative to other households; as a group, farmers do not appear to be a particularly disadvantaged part of society and the opposite seems be nearer the truth.

Perhaps this interpretation of production-related income measures is an echo of their origins. At the inception of the UK aggregate agricultural (branch) income calculation it was the incomes of farmers rather than the industry income which seems to have been the prime interest. According to one of the staff closely involved at the time (Kirk, 1964) the calculation which started in 1942 under the prompting of Lord Robbins was undertaken because of interest in the effect that product price increases, made *ad hoc* on purely commodity considerations, were having in raising farmers' incomes. Potential tax revenue was an important underlying motive. The estimates could only be undertaken at the time using a macroeconomic approach. The calculations found that income had indeed increased some fourfold since 1938. In subsequent years this aggregate figure became an integral and closely watched item in the Annual Review and Determination of Guarantees procedure, with rises being interpreted as an increase in the welfare of the agricultural community. Though microeconomic information on the income developments of particular types and sizes of farm were used to give particularly favourable treatment to individual commodities, such as those produced by small farmers, this was subsidiary to the notion of remunerating farmers "as a whole" (Kirk, 1958) and of guarantees determined in close relationship to supply and demand.

In the USA, as in the UK, the assumption of a strong link between the branch and the individual farm may have been appropriate in the 1920s when the present conceptual framework was set up. Farms then were overwhelmingly family operated and there was less specialisation. Policy was largely concerned with agriculture's share of the national income and comparisons of the evolution of the purchasing power of farmers relative to the urban population (Riemenschneider, 1983). However, in the USA the structure of farming has evolved away from the simple model, not only in the rise of specialisation and the emergence of corporate domination of certain sectors (poultry, pigmeat) but also in the growth of part-time (multi-activity) farming. In the USA not only has the industry changed: so has the policy agenda, with much more attention given to issues of equity, such as the distribution of benefit from government programmes. The perpetuation of indicators pertinent to an earlier scenario is termed conceptual obsolescence (AAEA, 1972); the aggregate measurement of income in agriculture is a prime example.

Agricultural policy has also changed in the EU; it is less concerned with issues of adequacy of the quantity supplied by the domestic agricultural industry and improvements in its productivity. Chapter 2 showed that the CAP and the national policies of Member States have as a fundamental concern the living standards of the agricultural population, an objective which is thrown into relief by the ample fulfilment of other objectives such as food security. There is an increasing preoccupation with "social" and environmental problems, yet fundamental policy reorientation to accommodate them is constrained because of the feared implications for the livelihoods of farmers and their families. These issues cannot be tackled using estimates of the income from agricultural production alone, based on units that are largely fictitious and assumed only to be exclusively involved in generating agricultural commodities. Rather they demand an approach based on real units, which implies agricultural households; such statistics must take into account all the sources of income received by farmers and their families, whether or not this arises from agriculture. Yet the official measurement systems of agricultural incomes in the EU have clung to the production approach; until very recently, in most EU countries, including the UK, no indicator has been available of the total income of agricultural households to set alongside the income-from-production estimates, and no harmonised system of data at the household level exists or is in prospect.

7.3 Evidence on the way that income indicators are used in policy-making

The way that income indicators are used to guide policymaking is rarely spelled out in detail by those involved. Outside observers usually have to be content with general statements on the factors considered when reaching particular decisions, a knowledge of the data which are available, and a few instances where the governmental veil is pulled aside. An example of the last was the investigation in the UK by the National Audit Office into the measurement of farmers' incomes (NAO, 1987) and the examination by the House of Commons' Public Accounts Committee of the Ministry of Agriculture on the basis of the NAO report (House of Commons, 1987). Here we will concentrate on the use of income information in the UK for the shaping of national policy and the stance of the UK in negotiations within the CAP, and in the central decision shaping within the EU. The nature of the explanations in these two examples implies that similar situations are likely to be found elsewhere.

7.3.1 The United Kingdom

First, a reminder of the two main information sources available in the UK. These consist of:

(a) The aggregate Economic Accounts for Agriculture with their associated income indicators, principally the "Total Income From Farming" (TIFF) which has recently gained predominance over the longer-established similarly formulated "Farming Income" (see Chapter 4). This type of estimate has been made for over fifty years. Up to 1998 the coverage was strictly limited to agricultural production activity but embraced all of it taking place in the UK; from 1999 it has broadened marginally to include some secondary activities associated with agriculture that cannot be separated in data sources, but it no longer includes the output of kitchen gardens and other very small units;

(b) Microeconomic information from the Farm Business Survey, with its "Net Farm Income" (now augmented by "Occupiers' Net Income" using different treatment of imputed rents and interest payments). This series goes back to 1936. There are related occasional special studies of individual enterprises and of very small farms. Limited data has been collected since 1998/89 from survey farms on off-farm income, though the representativity of this information is open to some doubt.

The focus at both levels is the income from agricultural production, not the incomes of farmers and their families. At present data from tax returns (Survey of Personal Incomes), which could give indications of the total incomes of farmers and spouses, are not developed to the level at which they are comparable numerically with the more established sources; they have been published as part of the UK's Farm Incomes reports only since 1986. Other data relating to incomes can be found in occasional studies and is collected and used in tests of eligibility as part of the administration of claims for grant aid to investment on farms. But without doubt the main income information sources used to guide official policy are the aggregate EAA figures and those from the Farm Business Survey.

According to the NAO report, the main purposes of monitoring farming incomes are to inform the consideration of policies governing the substantial financial support to UK agriculture (over £1.5 billion in 1986-87, rising to £2.9 billion in 1993-94 and £3.3 billion in 1998-99) from EU and UK public funds, and to provide data as a basis for economic and financial advice to farmers (NAO, 1987). The aggregate income indicators were used by the government departments concerned (Ministry of Agriculture, Fisheries and Food for England (MAFF), the Department of Agriculture Northern Ireland (DANI)), the then Welsh Office Agriculture Department (WOAD) and Scottish Office Agriculture and Fisheries Department (SOAFD)) "to inform themselves and the public of trends in the financial results and well-being of the industry and its contribution to the economy, and to provide a background to policy-making" (NAO, 1987). One important use of this aggregate data has been to set the UK stance in the annual price-fixing round of the Common Agricultural Policy, now diminished in importance as the result of setting a schedule for price reduction for some major commodities (notably cereals, accompanied by compensatory payments on an area basis) as part of the 1992 CAP reforms, but still a regular event for negotiating on major issues. The timing of the calculation of the agriculture branch (now the 'industry') income is such that an estimate for the calendar year can be available in time for the spring meeting of agricultural ministers in the next year. The macroeconomic method of calculation enables this rapid estimate to be made, catching the latest harvest.

The UK's farm-level data from the FBS is used "to inform consideration of individual policy measures, to provide data to the European Commission and its Farm Accountancy Data Network, and as a basis for research and advice to farmers, by the Agricultural Development and Advisory Service (ADAS)." (NAO, 1987) Again, this implies that the data can help set the bargaining stance of UK ministers in the annual EU price fixing, with estimates corresponding to the June-July year ending in the previous calendar year being to hand. This is not as up-to-date as the macroeconomic estimate as it will not cover the latest harvest, though forecasts can be made.

More specifically, the microeconomic income data for the UK is used in the annual review of the support to farming in Less Favoured Areas. European legislation provides for various aids which countries can pay to farmers in these areas, such as annual headage payments (Hill Livestock Compensatory Allowances), which take account of the special natural conditions in these areas and to ensure reasonable incomes for farmers, thereby maintaining the rural population. Information from the farm accounts survey is used in support of the case to the Treasury for increasing these payments. The incongruity of using a farm-business income concept in order to assess well-being of farmers will not be missed by readers, nor was it by the NAO.

The MAFF, while officially subscribing to both the aims of the CAP including its fair standard of living for the agricultural population and the more detailed aims of individual Community support measures, did not seem to regard the lack of personal income data a handicap. In answer to questions of the Select Committee on the necessity of having information on which farmers were most in need of support, the Permanent Secretary of MAFF commented that this would be the case it the government wished to differentiate between one type of farm rather than another on income criteria, but that in general this was not a characteristic of the present support system so the need for information did not arise. MAFF knew that the Commission in Brussels had been thinking for some time of putting forward proposals for some kinds of income aids for farmers unrelated to production, on some basis of (total) income criterion, and if that happened more detail on total incomes would be needed. However, MAFF would not necessarily support such proposals (House of Commons, 1987). In reply to a further question on whether one of the policy objectives which is served by the collection of income information was the maintenance of adequate incomes for farmers, the Permanent Secretary stated that one of the reasons was to know where farm incomes are, but he did not recognise the phrase "adequate farm incomes" as a specific statement.

In similar vein was the reply by the Minister of Agriculture to a House of Lords' Select Committee enquiring into EC rural development policy (House of Lords, 1990). Evidence had been given by the European Commission on its view of the CAP as being primarily a social policy; its representative had commented that its principal motivation was a social one, to protect the poorer categories of society in Europe by means of price and market support (House of Lords, 1990, p166). However, this was clearly not the view of the UK Minister. In response to the question on whether adequate data were available about the nature and scale of economic problems affecting farm households to provide a proper basis for policy-making the Minister replied:

> I think we have the data we need for the proper application of the CAP. We do not have data for some of the things suggested, but they are not the sorts of thing which ought to be solved through the CAP. ..... On what basis do you argue that they should have something special compared with anybody else who would otherwise look to the social security system? I do not think you can do that. The support you are giving to a farmer as a farmer is because he is looking after the land and producing food; that is why the support is there. You cannot say you are giving support for a third reason, which is that he himself has family circumstances of poverty, because once you get into that area you are making judgements which I find very hard to defend in public. To do something for him on grounds which are the same grounds as applying to the unemployed steel worker over here is, I think, a very difficult argument to maintain (House of Lords, 1990 p315).

In sharp contrast, a later discussion of how the CAP should be changed to meet the needs of the future, jointly authored by a former Permanent Secretary, left no doubt as to the importance of the incomes of farmers to the past direction of EU agricultural policy and the need to take them into account when making proposals for change (Ockenden and Franklin, 1995). Nevertheless, these authors manage to misuse results from the production-related income indicators by implying that these show what has been happening to the income of farmers.

The ambivalent attitude of MAFF towards indicators of personal incomes of farmers might reflect a genuine difference of interpretation of the Treaty of Rome's objectives, in line with the views expressed by the Minister above. However, the clarity of the Treaty's reference to fair living standards and the broad nature of that concept makes this unlikely. The more probable explanation lies in a combination of more pragmatic reasons and reflects the way that policy is determined, often in the face of declared aims. The following factors seem relevant:

a) Political demands: Historically, there has been no demand by British Ministers of Agriculture for such an information either for national purposes or for use in negotiations within the CAP (though there is some indication of an awakening interest following the sharp fall in the prosperity of UK farming in the late 1990s and the agreement of the *Agenda 2000* package). The UK has never tried to apply the notion of poverty to its farmers, in the sense of establishing a poverty line and assessing incomes and numbers of cases with respect to it. No strong political pressure has existed for a detailed analysis of the personal income (and wealth) of UK farmers, and isolated attempts to do so (such as Parliamentary Questions notably by Austin Mitchell in the 1980s) have not been enough to stimulate other politicians whose interests lie elsewhere. This lack of concern is perhaps a reflection of the relatively high proportions of MPs, peers and ministers who have been farmers, landowners or have had strong links with the industry (Howarth, 1985). Ministers do not seem to have demanded more, even when negotiating for Britain at times of price fixing within the CAP. What seems to be required in such circumstances is a fairly small number of indicators which can be used to maximum national advantage. The aggregate income information on production rewards, supplemented by farm or enterprise estimates, has proved sufficient.

b) Precedent: Though doubts can be expressed over whether it was ever appropriate to take the aggregate branch income indicator as a proxy for the welfare of farmers, this is the way that is has become interpreted. A similar view has been taken of the Farm Business Survey's income measures, particularly its concept of Net Farm Income, commonly misinterpreted as being personal income. Once the perception has been established and the estimates built into policy, there is a tendency to keep to the system, even to the extent of encountering obvious statistical obsolescence.

c) National interest: If, as seems likely, the personal income position of UK farmers turns out to be very satisfactory on average compared with other UK occupational groups and, more critically, when stood against other farmers in the EU, there could be damage to the national position of the UK in its ability to draw on the EU's budget. This was reflected in the agreement by the then MAFF Permanent Secretary with view of one member of the Select Committee that the UK has to go carefully with the way that it presents its income figures, in the interests of its farmers (House of Commons, 1987).

d) Pro-farmer stance of the agriculture departments: Directly related to the point above, a characteristic noted by many writers on UK agricultural policy is that MAFF has acted predominantly as a ministry *for farmers* rather than *of agriculture,* but not all types of farmer have carried the same weight in its attentions. It has been a ministry that has typically been concerned with production and commodities. This has caused MAFF to concentrate on the large commercial farmers. Small (and by implication low income) farmers have been a minor part of its interest. Therefore any change in the presentation of income information which might result in a shift in its traditional stance, to a more social-support role, would not be in line with its past practice. Moreover, such a change would make the social function of agricultural policy more transparent, perhaps to the extent of raising questions about the need for a Ministry of Agriculture at all. Low incomes in agriculture are just one example of poverty, which might be better handled by general welfare policy and by a ministry responsible for social security.

(e) Administration of support: There are no specific income aids within UK agricultural policy which have ever required the rigorous measurement of the total incomes of farmers. Though these are implied in the aims of certain forms of payment under the Guidance part of the agricultural budget of the CAP (headage payments on stock in LFAs, eligibility tests under Structural Policy measures) the UK has managed to avoid the issue on individual farms or has only collected data on a confidential basis, not even released to other parts of MAFF.

(f) Agencies for providing information: The MAFF and other Agriculture Departments are responsible for estimating the aggregate branch income of the industry and for overseeing the farm-level business surveys. But in Great Britain income data are collected by other agencies. Therefore

MAFF may not be able simply to direct that information on the total income of farmers and/or their households be prepared; negotiations with the agencies will be necessary. For example, the preparation of estimates of the personal income of farmers from tax records is outside the control of MAFF; the Inland Revenue conducts this exercise with the primary purpose of tax studies, not of income monitoring. Though the Inland Revenue may reasonably be expected to respond to MAFF requests for co-operation, in times of strained resources the order of its priorities in ironing out problems will be not to MAFF's advantage. At the farm accounts survey level, in Britain data collection is contracted out to universities and colleges. When the idea of extending the coverage of questions to the non-farm incomes of their co-operator farmers was first proposed, these agents were not enthusiastic. MAFF acquiesced in this; in course of questioning by the UK Public Accounts Committee the Permanent Secretary commented that he felt fairly strongly that if attempts were made to probe for data on their non-farm sources of income farmers might well react adversely in what is a voluntary exercise, and that could jeopardise the rest of the survey (House of Commons, 1987). Such question were, in fact, introduced on a voluntary basis for the year 1988-89 without, it appears, any disastrous impact on the willingness of co-operators to provide the usual information and a response rate to the new questions reputedly of the order of 80 per cent (though lower where individual collecting institutions were unsympathetic).

7.3.2 The European Union

Income information at EU level used in shaping the CAP is almost exclusively confined to the rewards derived from agricultural production. As described in Chapter 4, Eurostat publishes three aggregate indicators of the income from agricultural activity of individual Member States and the EU as a whole using data provided to a harmonised methodology. Rather confusingly, these indicators were formerly referred to as the Sectoral Income Index although they related to a branch of the economy (agriculture) and not a sector (such as farm businesses, which would encompass their non-farming activities, or agricultural households). The convention of expressing these Indicators per labour unit could reinforce the misapprehension that the results refer to personal incomes, which they certainly do not. The misapprehension was perhaps reinforced by the title of the Eurostat publication in which they appeared - *Agricultural Income* – until renamed more realistically in 1999 the *Income from Agricultural Activity*. As also noted in Chapter 4, there has been a change in basic methodology and a revision of the indicators, to be first used in the report published in 2000 (covering 1999 and back to 1995), though in reality there will be a great deal of continuity with the superseded system.

There is a strong and understandable preference for using an index presentation rather than absolute figures; not only does this suit the available data sources and the way that the figures are calculated but also it avoids the pitfalls that could result from attempting to rank incomes of farmers in one country against those in another on the basis of macroeconomic estimates of rewards to factors of production. In particular, disputes over the appropriate currency conversion rates are avoided. Nevertheless, in response to questions about the differences between the absolute incomes from one members state to another and between regions, and despite the problems of comparisons across national boundaries, Eurostat from its 1986 incomes report (Eurostat, 1987) onwards has published absolute figures for the three aggregate indicators.

The timing of the aggregate income calculations is such that indicators are published in the spring of the year after one to which they relate, (that is, the estimates for year *t* have appeared in year *t+1*, in the first month in an incomplete provisional form and a little later - typically March – as a publication containing all three Indicators). Internally the figures for the latest year will be available several months earlier and in time to be taken into account in the preparation of price proposals by the Commission. A forecasting model is also used (SPEL).

The other source of income information open to the Commission is the Farm Accountancy Data Network (FADN/RICA). For historical reasons this is under the control of the Directorate-General for agriculture in the Commission (DG VI) rather than the Eurostat, an arrangement that now looks anomalous and an impediment to improving the EU's information system. Because FADN data is collected from actual farm businesses by national agencies (in the UK it is a subset of the Farm Business Survey) there is an inevitable delay between the end of the accounting year and when the results are published, necessary to cover data checking, transfer and analysis (Lommez, 1984). Latest observed FADN data are normally at least 2 years behind the current year. This has restricted the role of FADN to one of indicating the historical picture and providing the means for the analysis of detail where very recent data was not critical (Bryson, 1985). However there is now a forecasting system in order to help fill the gap by providing updates of the latest available figure using coefficients of price and quantity of a predefined list of products and inputs, which are combined in an econometric model (Brookes, 1987).

When we look at the use of income information in policy-making it is evident that greater emphasis has traditionally been placed on the macroeconomic income measures than on FADN/RICA, largely because of availability at the time needed. Among the three aggregate indicators, most attention has gone on Indicator 1 (Net Value Added per Annual Work Unit), the longest-established and considered the most statistically reliable of the three, even though it is conceptually a long way from income or business profit. Under the revised methodology this entity continues as Indicator A in publications from 2000 onwards.

The importance of the aggregate income indicator as a direct influence on the Community's annual price-fixing exercise lessened with the abandonment by the early 1980s of the "objective method" for setting prices. Starting with the Commission's price proposals for the year 1972/73, the "objective method" purported to establish the price increases that were necessary to cover increases in costs of production and to ensure to farmers on modern, viable farms a development of income (labour income and return to capital) comparable to that of other sectors. In response to escalating surpluses, budgetary problems, unacceptably large price rises that were sometimes suggested, other technical difficulties, and the apparent restriction on the power of the Council to reach political compromises, the Commission ceased to present price proposals based on this principle, though COPA continued to apply the methodology and used the outcome as the basis of its price-increase request (Mortensen, 1984).

Despite the displacement of the mechanistic approach, within the EU institutions the aggregate Income Indices remain the parameter most regarded as indicating movements in the fortune of farming, a view severely criticised by the European Parliament because of the inability of any aggregate figure to reveal what is happening to the distribution of rewards from farming and to individual earnings (European Parliament, 1983).

7.3.3 *Characteristics of the use of income indicators*

There are features of the use of production-based income indicators within the policy environment, shared by the EU and the UK, that cause concern. First is the emphasis on *short-term movements in income* between the latest year and the one before. This happens despite the common knowledge that farming incomes are subject to large variations because of the effect of transient factors, especially of weather. Emphasis in Eurostat's annual Incomes Report falls on comparisons between the latest two years; this is what is supplied first to decision-makers and highlighted in press releases.

Reports from the Farm Accountancy Data Network also feature this short-term change. This implies that it is the changes observable in income which are important to agricultural policy-makers, not so much the absolute level or the distribution by farm size and type. Also, in the UK's annual publications reviewing the aggregate income situation, special attention is given to the latest changes. At the level of the UK Farm Business Survey, again there is emphasis on comparing the results of one year with the previous year, and the data are specially arranged (using the same sample of businesses in each year) to facilitate this. Though MAFF is obviously aware of longer-term income movements, the way that the information is presented is suggestive of a political preoccupation with the immediate past and the short-term.

Second, there is little concern with *distributions of incomes*. This mainly concerns the farm level information. Both in the EU's FADN and the UK's FBS analysis is routinely presented in the form of group averages, by farm type, by size, by level of indebtedness and so on but not, it should be noticed, by level of income. Such tables showing the numbers of farms in various income bands have been published for the FADN as part of a special report on income developments in the 1980s (Hill and Brookes, 1993) and formerly for the Farm Business Survey, but not in recent years. A likely reason for this in the UK is that the FBS is not a random sample of UK farms and cannot be grossed up to give acceptable national estimates of farm numbers by income band. On the other hand, the same basic data is used by the Commission as the basis of weighted results relating to FADN's entire field of observation.

Third, in the 1980s and 1990s the level of incomes seems to be viewed as the *fairly passive outcome of decisions,* taken for other reasons, rather than the driving force of policy. Notwithstanding the central importance of incomes to the CAP, in practice, policy tends to comprise responses to problems when they occur. In conflicts between the important and the urgent in policy-making, the latter dominates. As such, farm incomes (and especially the incomes of farmer's families) are not at the top in the order of priorities. The use and later abandonment of the "objective method" for setting CAP support prices has already been mentioned. In the UK, although in the immediate post-war period there were assurances that increases in costs faced by farmers would be recompensed by higher revenues, protecting income in aggregate, for most of the time the main areas of concern have related to the balance of demand and supply on commodity markets, import substitution and improving the performance of the industry (mostly in terms of generating more output). The NAO reported that MAFF took the view that the urgent need to restrict surpluses and restrict the costs of the CAP meant that less attention could be paid to the objective of maintaining farm incomes than would otherwise be the case (NAO, 1987). Nevertheless concern with incomes has acted as a very effective brake against too speedy a price reform.

Lastly, it should not go unnoticed that the wealth or net worth of farmers has barely been mentioned in the context of assessing the need for agricultural policy and monitoring its performance. In Chapter 6 we found that no official balance sheets are drawn up by Eurostat for the agricultural industry in EU Member States, though these are available for individual farm businesses in FADN. In the UK balance sheets for the industry and individual farm businesses are calculated, but the NAO reported that the UK agriculture departments paid little attention in their policy-making to farm balance sheet information, for example to consider the existence of reserves as a cushion against lean years or how far income had been used for reinvestment (NAO, 1987). Though no doubt changes in the balance sheet have played a part in setting the background of agricultural support, the impression from reading the NAO report and the response which MAFF gave to it is that it had for long remained an undeveloped type of information, both in its collection and analysis. A fuller consideration of changes in the balance sheets would certainly have made the argument for agricultural support more complex, and at times diminish the case. As the then head of economics and statistics once pointed out (Capstick, 1983), increases in land prices have often been seen at times when incomes have been under the severest pressure, and a situation of falling incomes yet rising net worth, increasing the wealth of land-owning farmers, is not a mixture which would bear too close a public examination.

To sum up, the income information available to those responsible for shaping European Commission proposals on agricultural prices and other matters is consists predominantly of aggregate indicators that take the branch agriculture approach. To some extent farm-level data are used to flesh-out the national averages, but lack of timeliness limits their influence.

7.4 The absence of EU estimates of the personal income of farm households

7.4.1 Awareness of the information gap

What has certainly *not* been available to the policy-designers in the Commission's Directorate-General for Agriculture until very recently is a set of Community-wide harmonised data on the personal incomes of farmers and their households. Parts of the Commission seem aware of the difference between the nature of the income measures used and the personal incomes of farmers, more so than many national administrations. For example, in a major document describing the available income data series the Commission in 1985 warned that "agricultural income" was defined in the context of the official monitoring systems as income from farming.

> It should not be forgotten that many of the Community's eight million farmers, with their families, have other incomes: this takes the form of unearned accruals (e.g. social security) or remuneration for other part-time work, which may be regular or may be restricted to certain periods of the year. The disposable income of farmers can also be influenced by other factors (e.g. taxation) the importance of which it is not easy to assess at Community level (Commission, 1985a).

In the Perspectives Green Paper (Commission, 1985b) the Commission stated "In fact, part-time farming combined with a gainful outside gainful activity has taken on such proportions that it would be an error to ignore the phenomenon. The growing importance of part-time farming with outside gainful activity corrects, to some extent, the overall picture of low agricultural incomes..." . In this document various forms of income aid were discussed which could be used to soften the impact of price cuts seen as necessary to achieve better market balance. Included among these was a system of social payments, in which the total income from farm and non-farm sources would be compared with some income standard for all workers in the same region and the gap narrowed by direct payments. This aid was seen very much as a last resort. However, the Commission had made some rough estimates of the numbers of farmers who would be concerned in such a scheme (1 to 1.5 million) and the cost (1,000 million ECU at the beginning); the assumptions lying behind these calculations have never been published.

It is undoubtedly true that the ability of the Commission to propose support systems aimed at the personal incomes of farmers has been limited by the lack of information in this area. One official, widely thought to have been responsible for drafting much of the income-related material in the Perspectives Green Paper, has described the need to provide better income information as urgent (Avery, 1985). It was such prompting that caused Eurostat to embark in 1986 on the creation of its Total Income of Agricultural Households (TIAH) statistics, now called the Income of Agricultural Households (IAHS) statistics, described in Chapter 5. After a long period of preparation, these aggregate statistics are now becoming available (Hill, 1992, 1995,(Eurostat, 1998)). It remains to be seen how policy-makers use them, though the first sets of results are handicapped by the coverage being less than complete and up-to-date. However, already it is clear that they are forming part of the background against which decisions are made rather than as critical elements in the decisions themselves. The development of equivalent microeconomic data, which might be used for example to identify farm households where total incomes were unsatisfactorily low, is proving much more difficult.

7.4.2 An explanation for the information gap

An explanation must be sought for the contrast between, on the one hand, the awareness of the Commission of the difference between factor rewards and personal incomes of farmers, and on the other hand the continued predominance of indicators of branch activity in policy determination and the lack of urgency felt among much of the Commission for better information on the personal income of farmers and their households. The likely reasons include the following:

(a) The income indicators for the agricultural branch of the economy were established long ago, under historical circumstances that largely dictated the form they took. Consequently they are now are solidly established and use a well harmonised methodology. Statisticians are confident in their underlying principles and in the quality of the basic data on which they draw; there is much professional investment in them. Policymakers have come to regard them as reliable and consistent and are thus not willing to easily abandon them. This means that other approaches to income measurement will find it hard to become accepted. Eurostat's IAHS statistics are too new to have made much impact and will only be given great attention once they can be made more timely and greater harmonisation between countries is assured.

(b) Policy in the EU is settled primarily commodity by commodity. Although the income implications may be taken into account in a general way when considering price reductions or other changes, incomes are secondary. Frequently it is difficult to predict the impact at the farm level because of possible substitution of products and input saving. Consequently, it is not a matter of setting income objectives first and then using commodity-linked and other measures to arrive at the desired income goals, but the other way round.

(c) Though there is an awareness within the Commission of the importance of other sources of income to agricultural households, the Directorate-General for agriculture has no single and consistent view of the beneficiaries of the CAP or of the way in which incomes should be assessed for policy purposes. Even within the Perspectives Green Paper of 1985 there was a rather obvious split between the market-balance view and the more radical income support/social instrument approach. Within the Commission there are many staff, primarily concerned with commodity markets, who remain to be convinced of the relevance of farmer household incomes.

(d) The development of statistics is a task shared between Eurostat and the statistical authorities in Member States. Much of the statistical system operates on a set of "gentleman's agreement" rather than having a legal basis by which Member States would be required to provide data. Consequently, progress in new areas can be only made by mutual goodwill. Though the aggregate Economic Accounts for Agriculture and their related income indicators lack a legal base, there is strong impetus behind them because they are well-established, in demand by agricultural policymakers, and Member States use the same basic data to estimate agriculture's contribution to national accounts (which have a very high priority). However, they feel no such urgency for the development of household sector statistics, particularly where Member States face a lack of suitable basic data and at a time when there is a requirement to devote scarce resource to revising the methodologies of more established statistics; there is no legal requirement to supply the household-based data, as yet the demand expressed by officials is weak (though strong from many other policy commentators) and there is no pressure from the system of national accounts for the information about agricultural households (though a subdivision of the whole household account into socio-professional groups is a planned action of the European System of Accounts in its 1995 manifestation, no timetable has yet been set). The provision of a legal base would not necessarily improve matters. Though the provision of FADN/RICA farm business data is a legal obligation, attempts to add compulsory question on non-farm income requires change in the legislation, to which some Member States are hostile (Robson, 1996). In particular, in France objections have come mainly from farmers' unions and in Luxembourg a repeat of questions on non-farm income posed in 1989 has been ruled out as politically too sensitive.

7.5 The organisational process, pressure groups and bureaucratic politics

While the lack of development of statistics in the EU on the income situation of agricultural households might be explained, in large part, by historical factors, there is another phenomenon that suggests other factors are involved. Even where statistics exist on the income situation of agricultural households, this does not necessarily mean that they are used to formulate and monitor agricultural policy, though their relevance to the fundamental problem that policy attempts to address is undeniable. In countries with good quality information on farm household incomes, such as USA, Canada, Germany, Denmark, it seems to be ignored or marginalised. In the latter two cases this might be explained in terms of having to operate a common agricultural policy within a EU largely devoid of such data. Such constraints do not apply in north America, but still the situation persists. In the USA, where there is regular data collection on the total income situation of its farm occupiers and official poverty lines for farm families, the impression given by staff involved in supporting the political decision-makers is that such information is not treated as a significant input. Similarly in Canada, probably the country best equipped with microeconomic data on farmers' total incomes, there is no indication that they are used in ways which are directly coupled to policy; once again it is the industry branch income and the results of surveys of farmers which are the officially-recognised income indicators.

The explanation of this lack of interest in the development and/or use of information on farm household incomes can usefully consider theories of public decision making and, particularly, the range of economic and political factors - both long and short-term - which impinge on those responsible for designing and operating policies. The importance of this area of economics is becoming increasingly recognised (reviewed in de Gorter and Swinnen, 1994 and in (van der Zee, 1997)). From this approach it seems likely that farm household incomes have been ignored because it has not been in the interest of any effective group to make them an issue; as such, they have been treated as marginal.

Agricultural policy has been described as being determined in the short run by conflicts of interest regulated through political institution, whereas in the long run general economic forces play a critical role (Petit, 1985 and

Petit *et al.,* 1987). According to this approach, while economic phenomena play an important part in the shaping of policy, their influence is exerted through the mediation of the political process. The result is that decisions are not the result of economic rationality but are heavily influenced by groups representing interested parties; these will include pressure groups acting for particular types of individuals (for example, farmers' unions) and the governmental institutions involved with policy. Consequently, the explanation of the outcome of a policy decision will need to take into account from which directions attempts are made to bring influence to bear and the stages at which pressures are applied.

In a piece of allegorical writing almost as effective as Pen's famous parade of dwarfs and giants describing the distribution of incomes in society (Pen, 1971), and building on ideas put forward by Allison (1971) in the context of international relations, Petit describes the agricultural policy process as a play in which the actors are representatives of interest groups and government organisations. As in a play, these actors in the policy process have their entrances and exits, and some are more important than others. At times one will take the centre stage, later to move to the wings. While the role of each actor is determined within the play, this is not totally set out and there is room for interpretation and possibilities for improvisation. Some of the interactions will be played out behind the scenes, out of the view of the public. And as in an ancient Greek drama, there may be a chorus who comment on the action but take no part in it, a function perhaps of the modern professional critic. Within the agricultural policy process of both the EU, UK and many other countries there is no shortage of actors to fill the roles of the Petit play.

Two other important points made by Petit are that, first, policy is a process in time, so that a particular decision can only be satisfactorily viewed in the context of earlier decisions and will, in turn, influence later decisions. Second, as policy debates take place in an atmosphere of uncertainty this will be reflected in the behaviour of participants in the process who will display a range of characteristics to cope with uncertainty (hedging, waiting to see, seeking more information and so on). As time passes, controversial issues may fade away as more information reduces the extent of uncertainty and arguments against newly-emerged data are shown to be invalid and likely to undermine the credibility of their advocates.

The dynamic nature of the policy process has been further elaborated by Moyer and Josling (1990) who see, in addition to the longer-term economic forces which shape policy, a parallel set of political forces, such as the declining voting power of the agricultural population and the changing perception of the farmer within society. In the medium term there will be interest groups which create the economic and political background against which decisions are made, but also there will be short-term problems to be faced which may force decisions to be taken which may run against the pressures of these groups. For example, the imposition of milk quotas within the EC was forced on the Council of Ministers by impending budgetary disaster. Moyer and Josling point to the structure of the decision-making process itself as being very important, including the numbers of individuals, groups and stages involved. The various actors in the process are likely to have different goals, based on their own individual and organisational interests as well as the general aim to which agricultural policy is directed. They will tend to see the aims differently and to vary in their responsiveness to external influences. Typically, agricultural policy is fragmented, so that different organisational groups deal with different parts of agricultural policy, tending to an uncoordinated policy in which the fundamental aims are likely to be under-represented. As a general hypothesis, Moyer and Josling suggest that the greater the number of actors in the policy process and the greater the number of steps in decision making, the stronger the bias toward maintaining the status-quo, because the bargaining costs of achieving change increase with the complexity of the process. Organisations, being risk averse, will prefer to maintain their present ways of doing things, only making incremental changes where required to do so. Furthermore, the earlier that influence can be brought to bear within the policy process, the more likely that this will continue right through to the outcome, as it becomes increasingly difficult to overturn something that forms an integral part of a proposal.

In the context of the EU the way that the income objective is handled within agricultural policy and, consequently, the way in which incomes are monitored seem to be explained quite well in terms of the above decision models. Firstly, there are the longer-term influences on policy. The economic explanation why there is a persistent downward pressure on aggregate farming income and why the farm-size threshold of commercial viability is rising inexorably was given in Chapter 2. Pressure for government intervention is filtered through the political process and interpreted by civil servants. Until recently this provided an environment which was favourable to support for the incomes of farmers. In the USA the protection of the family farm seems to hold a prominent place in political priorities, and this is felt too in some EU Member States, particularly France; it is often expressed most strongly by those who are separated from farming by one or more generations. In contrast, UK support for farm incomes, though a declared aim of policy, seems to have ridden on the back of political goals of securing a reliable food supply or increasing self-sufficiency, rather than being an issue in its own right. This is the way that agricultural civil servants seem to have interpreted their political masters' wishes.

It is interesting that, in the later 1980s and 1990s, the changing political environment has shifted as more voters become concerned with environmental questions and the imperfections of the CAP become matters for common conversation. This represents a change in one of the longer-term political influences on policy. Reflecting this, agricultural ministers have changed noticeably in their receptiveness to ideas of supporting the incomes of farmers through forms of direct income payment rather than by product price enhancement; the introduction of arable area payments and livestock headage payments made direct to farmers as part of the 1992 CAP reforms were accepted with little difficulty by the Council of Ministers. Probably significant to this acceptance was the description of such payments as compensation for the cuts in support prices that were anticipated would lead to falls in market prices received by farmers; in practice market prices for cereals did not fall in the first years, thus leading to a sharp rise in incomes of cereal producers (Cook, 1999). The extension of direct payments by the 1999 *Agenda 2000* package was not seriously challenged, the only matters of substantial dispute being whether these payments should be "degressive" (having a planned reduction over time as the justification for compensation diminishes) and "modulated" (so that they do not rise *pro rata* with the size of farm). The fact that some of the direct payments to farmers are linked to the provision of environmental services, and are thus legitimised, has probably assisted the political acceptance of those that are not so linked.

Secondly, present policy decisions are to be viewed in the context of past policy. Perhaps nowhere is this more apparent than with incomes, where the practice of monitoring their development over time has maintained an approach that is now patently inadequate. Changes in income of the industry and of businesses from one year to the next have become regarded as an acceptable indicator of well-being of farmers in the face of ample evidence that this sort of data is largely unsatisfactory for indicating living standards. The system of support mainly through raising the prices received by farmers for their products, set up at a time when higher output was welcomed and was consonant with income objectives, has proved to be a constraint on using instruments which are directly aimed at incomes. It has also hindered the more general reform of policy to meet budgetary constraints and the conditions for achieving a successful GATT outcome in 1993. On the other hand, the steps taken in the 1990s to dismantle price support seem to offer the possibility to tackle income problems in a more direct way.

Third, the institutional structure has been important in preserving the use of the aggregate agricultural production income indicators and, at micro level, farm business incomes. Among interest groups there are no significant ones pressing for a farmer-household income measure. Farmer organisations will naturally not wish to bring attention to the existence of other sources of income which might lesson their case for support of farm prices. In early discussions on the possibility of using direct forms of income aid (which would imply a fuller knowledge of farmers' total incomes), COPA adopted a negative attitude, and in 1980 the German farmers' union rejected direct income aids as "reducing farmers to the status of recipients of social assistance from the state" (quoted in Neville-Rolfe, 1984). It is evident that the leaders of such organisations, whether at international, national or local level, tend to be among those large-scale operators who might expect to suffer personally by any reorientation of policy towards a more direct assault on the problems of farm families with low incomes.

Within the EU's Council (of agriculture ministers) there has been little inclination to adopt a more rigorous attitude to farmer incomes. Partly this comes from a shared common pro-farmer stance, but is also a reflection of the absence of any strong national interest in turning income support systems into a high-profile issue. In Germany, which could reasonably be expected to save most from a better control of agricultural support spending, there are substantial political pressures to maintain the status quo, and in the UK a full-income assessment for farmers could well act against the national (budgetary) interest. Mediterranean countries, though perhaps benefiting from a changed system, and with more funds going to the EU's Regional and Social Funds, face the problem of lack of information and internal political problems if this sort of data were to be collected from farmers.

Groups that might be expected to express concern with the current way that policy towards incomes of farmers are supported and assessed would include consumers' and taxpayers' organisations, non-agricultural national government departments and Community institutions and politicians representing non-agricultural interests. For EU consumer groups the incomes of farmers appear not to be a high profile issue, perhaps because of what seem to be daunting technical complexities and a weak link with food prices. Within the European Commission agricultural matters are mainly left in the hands of the specialists – the Directorate-General for Agriculture and in the UK government service to the agriculture departments. Only occasionally have other parts of the administration or institutions shown much interest. Agriculture administrations seem to exhibit to a marked degree a preference for the status quo, an incrementalist attitude towards change and a keen awareness of self-interest. One exception to the disinclination of other governmental (or quasi-governmental) institutions to extend activities into agriculture matters has been the UK's National Audit Office (for example, NAO 1985, 1987) but the agriculture departments have proved adept at acting swiftly to counter criticism and to suggest that national interest might be harmed (within the EU) if too full an income position of UK farmers was presented. In contrast, parts of the European Parliament have been vocal critics of the present system of income measurement (European Parliament, 1983) though in practice this has not influenced the general approach of the CAP to income issues; recently a report for the Parliament on evaluating the CAP concluded that information on living standards was needed, both average and distributional information and that the present production-centred measures contained well-known deficiencies (Tangerman, 1999).

Earlier in this Chapter it was noted that in the UK MAFF in the 1980s did not see the necessity of collecting and publishing data on the disposable household income of farmers. This view is still shared by some, but not all, parts of the European Commission. The breakdown of the organisations implementing policy into parts dealing with specific groups of commodities seems largely to blame; this accords with the institutional view of decision-making which suggests that, as the result of policy fragmentation, it is difficult to keep the overall problem in perspective and to judge whether the combined partial solutions will deal effectively with the total problem. Hence, questions of how policy relates to the income of farmers tend to be relegated to the periphery of decision-making instead of forming its central pivot. If personal incomes were to be given a more central role there would be demands that farmers should be measured by yardsticks applicable generally across society, removing the uniqueness of the farm income issue. This might pose a threat to the existence of the agricultural departments themselves and could therefore be expected to be resisted.

Within the EU policy process there seems to be little pressure for the full income position of farmers to be taken into account since there are no influential parties in whose interest it would be desirable to promote this approach. Existing players are well served by the present arrangements and, except in the presence of some CAP crisis that might force a reappraisal of the way incomes are viewed, there is an inertia opposing change. This also provides an explanation for the ignoring of information on farm operator total incomes in the USA.

One might reasonably expect that the academic fraternity would question the role of income support and measurement. While there have been several analyses by academics of the impact of policy on incomes in the UK (see for example Josling and Hamway, 1976; Traill, 1982; Harvey and Thomson, 1985) these have confined themselves to the rewards from agricultural production, not the personal incomes of farmers and their households. The study of the personal incomes of farmers is not strong in British university departments of agricultural economics (with the exception of Britton 1981, Hill 1982 to 1999; Howarth, 1984, 1990). There has been a marked reluctance on the part of their staffs to explore the interface between the business and personal affairs of farmers and to collect data for this purpose, or encourage the official income measurement systems to do so. Even in its most developed aspect (the study of part-time farming) quantitative exploration of the interaction between incomes from the farm and non-farm sources is weak in the university departments of agricultural economics in UK (though stronger in Germany, see Schmitt 1988 to 1994). UK studies involving pluriactivity tend to have been primarily qualitative, presumably because of lack of suitably detailed income information (see for example, Gasson, 1988; Gasson *et al.,* 1988; Gasson and Errington, 1993; Shucksmith *et al.,* 1989; Shucksmith and Smith, 1991; Shucksmith, 1993).

The lack of income data, and of interest in the subject, may reflect what appears to be a general characteristic of today's agricultural economists. Bonnen (1988, 1990) suggests that, in the US, an imbalance has developed between the three elements of empirical agricultural economics research that consist of (a) theory (including disciplines other than economics), (b) statistical and other quantitative measurement techniques, and (c) data, which must be defined in the same terms as the theory being supported or negated. The specification of data requires the same underlying causal logic and rigour demanded of economic theory and statistical methods (Churchman, 1971). Bonnen criticises the American agricultural economics profession for increasingly ignoring the data element of research and rewarding theory and statistical methods. Consequently, in his view, the capacity of agricultural economics as a science was being undermined. A case could be made that the situation found in the EU and UK parallels that of the US.

Additionally, in the UK perhaps this reluctance to probe the relationship between the farm and other activities and to collect data with this in mind has something to do with the financial interest which university departments of agricultural economics have in maintaining contracts to carry out the annual Farm Business Survey on behalf of MAFF and the respective government agriculture departments in Wales (WOAD /NAWAD) and Scotland (DAFS/SOAFD/SERAD); the relationship is more likely to be continued if the universities are seen to adopt the attitude exhibited by the sponsor. In part it is a matter of convenience, since it has been felt that overtures into the non-farming activities of farmers might cause difficulties for the Farm Business Survey, which relies on voluntary co-operation. Partly it is because of a feeling that the non-farming incomes should be of no concern to institutions designated as agricultural. This reflects the roots of the UK profession in farm management monitoring and advice (Whetham, 1981; Colman, 1987). Also there has been a tendency for such university departments to regard themselves as acting *for* the benefit of the agricultural industry rather than with its objective study.

It is an indication of the way that professional agricultural economists are seen by others that, when two academic economists wrote a book critical of British agricultural policy, they felt it necessary to point out that they were not connected with the agricultural economics departments of their respective universities (Bowers and Cheshire, 1983). In that a substantial proportion of the money flowing to universities for agricultural economic research comes either directly from MAFF, or MAFF's advice is sought by other sponsors, it follows that the ability to undertake studies in this area is dependent on MAFF's support. In a situation in which this support is not forthcoming, it is not surprising that the body of research concerning the personal income position of UK farmers is weak.

7.6 Pressures for change, and the direction of development

There are signs that the way in which the income support functions of the CAP are viewed is changing. To return to Petit's theatre analogy, there is a time when the management realises that the existing play has reached the end of its run. It no longer appeals and changes have to be made. In the short term it may be possible to rewrite parts, add new scenes or change the personnel to freshen up the action on stage, but eventually this will not be enough. The biggest shake up at the theatre occurs when some crisis, such as a threatened financial collapse, forces a whole new play to be put on in which the interactions between the players take on an entirely different context. As with any company, there may be new roles for existing actors and, though the parts they play are substantially different, there may be obvious hangovers and typecasting. And the mounting of any new play will require preparation of the production while the old drama is still being staged.

Four aspects of change are, firstly, the perception of need for change and, secondly, the growth of pressure for that change. Thirdly, there must be preparation of the means by which change can be brought about and, fourthly, actions must be taken to effect the change. There is no shortage of reports on the need to reform the CAP, from the early (1968) Mansholt "plan" to restructure agriculture, through to the "Larsen Report" (Commission, 1994) and Ockenden and Franklin (1995). Milestones are the Commission's own Perspectives Green Paper of 1985, the "MacSharry" reform proposals of 1991 (agreed in modified form in 1992) and the *Agenda 2000* analysis and proposals, first publiched in 1997 (Commission of the European Communities, 1997)and agreed (again in a somewhat watered-down form) in March 1999. A common feature is that they all propose allowing the market a greater role in setting the prices that farmers receive for agricultural commodities and of achieving policy objectives in more direct ways.

The impetus for change in the past has come largely from the need to contain the costs of the CAP, to which more recently have to be added the political will to curb the damage to the environment caused by some forms of modern farming which have been encouraged by the system of poorly-targeted support and to harness the environmental enhancements that other forms can bring, the requirement to reduce the level of market distortion to comply with the GATT agreement of 1993, and the impending enlargement of the EU to include countries of eastern Europe. These are proving to be the factors at the level of the European Commission that galvanise action on reassessing the agricultural income problem and policies directed at its alleviation. If the income problem is shown to be smaller, less pervasive or more easily remedied than is commonly assumed, then actions to solve the other problems faced by the CAP become easier and less painful.

But the ground has also been prepared by a greater awareness of the pluriactive nature of many agricultural households, the complexity of their income composition, their relative income position compared with other groups in society, and their wealth. The EU regularly publishes the results of the Farm Structure Survey, which includes data on the percentages of farms where the occupier (and members of his family) have other gainful activities. Of more significance in the long term is information on the personal income position of farmers throughout the Community that is becoming available in the 1990s through Eurostat's statistics for the agricultural households sector; the main results were described in Chapter 5. These call into question some of the fundamental assumptions of agricultural support policy (such as that farmers are a relatively poor group in society) and are likely to carry repercussions for its design in the future, dealt with below.

The development of IAHS statistics also forms part of the means by which a change in the way that incomes in agriculture are monitored can be brought about. All EU statistics, if they are to be taken seriously, much be harmonised across Member States, be accurate, reliable, pertinent and timely. The methodology behind IAHS statistics has made important steps in this direction, though these currently only apply at the level of the entire agricultural household sector. Official EU microeconomic information can be expected to follow once a harmonised methodology has been agreed, though for institutional reasons progress at this level is likely to be slow and coverage of Member States initially incomplete.

Implementation of the change of orientation towards measuring the incomes of people in agriculture, in addition to that of arising from agricultural production, will pose problems for statisticians, particularly in selecting the basic unit over which income is measured. While for administrative purposes it is often convenient to assume that each holding has one household and one farmer-manager, when looking at the income of agricultural households the acceptance of this "myth" (Schertz, 1982, 1987) is no longer tenable. Statisticians working with agriculture will need access to data sources and approaches that will be unfamiliar. They will also have to face the difficult problem of devising an appropriate treatment for those households found on large-scale co-operative farms in countries in Central and Eastern Europe whose accession to the EU is expected within the first decade of the twenty-first century. They do not fit the 'western' model of family farmers that lies behind much of the agricultural statistics of EU and other OECD countries. Though a solution is also needed to accommodate those large units that the unification of Germany brought in, this has not yet been worked out.

Implementation will be difficult unless users of statistics demonstrate the need for and the utility of such statistics. Here there may be problems, because the preliminary information from the IAHS and the glimpses provided by microeconomic data sources (reviewed in Chapter 5) suggest that there are some unsettling lessons to be learned about the income situation of farmers and their households.

7.7 Implications for policy-making

The information presented in this book on the income situation of farmer households has some important policy implications.

First, there is considerable evidence that in the EU (excepting Portugal), and among other OECD countries cited, there is no income problem for many farm families, in the sense that their overall incomes are not low but compare favourably with households in general. Among families on small farms this is achieved in large part through the diversification of income sources. However, the occupiers of large farms, which are capable of generating incomes from agriculture that would put their operators' households at least on a par with national averages, also have significant quantities of non-farm income. There is plenty of evidence to show that, when assessing the income situation of a household, a low income from agriculture is no reliable guide to the total income received. Where income problems exist, they are likely to be linked with the combination of a number of socio-economic factors, such as size and type of farm, location, ages and educational background of the operators.

Second, many farm families depend only to a small extent on the farm for their livelihoods; on something like half the holdings in the EU farming is not the main income source of the head of household, and these families receive only a very small proportion of their total incomes from agriculture (typically less than 10 per cent). This underlines the heterogeneity of the households that are associated with agriculture. A more detailed consideration is required of what is meant by an "agricultural" household and which households should be the target of agricultural support. If assistance for income support is to be directed at those that derive most of their income from farming, it means that many households who operate holdings will be deemed to fall outside the sphere of interest of agricultural policy. This will mainly involve the smallest holdings. However, the application of a main-income criterion could exclude some large agricultural producers from support schemes if they have large non-farming incomes, as many do. National agricultural ministers are unlikely to accept easily that some of their farmers who currently receive some of the benefits from product price support are not "real" farmers and should be excluded. The greater the proportions of pluriactive farmers the greater the political cost of leaving them out. Of course, for policies that are primarily environmental in nature the target group will be different and might include all the occupiers of land; personal incomes will be then irrelevant.

Third, the general low income dependency of small farms on farming, coupled with their relatively small volumes of output, imply that the present system of income support is highly inefficient in terms of welfare transfer to them. Under current commodity support regimes a very high proportion of transfers accrue to a relatively small proportion of farmers - those who are the largest producers. This distribution of benefit is becoming increasingly apparent and attracting unfavourable comment as, under the reforms to the CAP cereals regime, direct payments are made to farmers as compensation for lower support prices. The importance of the household income information is that it makes clear that increasing the prices paid to low output farmers on small farms would not greatly enhance their personal incomes. On average, their overall incomes are much more likely to be affected by the health of the broader economy in which they operate and the opportunities it provides, factors which will determine their earnings from other, mainly off-farm activities, and by the welfare transfers that can be offered to them by the rest of society.

Fourth, adopting an overall view of the income of agricultural households reduces the uniqueness of farm incomes and the agricultural income problem. At present the monitoring of incomes in agriculture is a special process used in helping shape policy for this industry, albeit only indirectly. However, taking a household income approach puts the incomes of agricultural households on the same basis as those of any other groups of households. Low incomes among farmers are then presented as primarily an income distribution problem, not one peculiar to agriculture. While there may still be a case for supporting incomes of farmers using agricultural means, its strength is reduced. The ministers and staffs in the institutions bound up with agricultural policy could be expected to see their positions under attack if this approach to income meausrement became prevalent, and interest groups within the bureaucracy are likely to attempt to slow or prevent change.

Fifth, when income results are available both on the rewards from agricultural production (the traditional approach) and on the household incomes of farmers (such as Eurostat's new IAHS statistics) a far more complex income picture will be presented to politicians responsible for determining agricultural policy. As has been pointed out earlier, income movements for the agricultural branch of the economy may show trends at variance with those of the personal incomes of farmers' households. When agricultural incomes are under pressure, household incomes are likely to show a less gloomy picture. The direction of required action on the part of policy makers is then less clear, and the non-agricultural options are underlined. This further reduces the uniqueness of agricultural solutions as answers to income problems among farmers and threatens the position of the agricultural bureaucracy.

When these strands are brought together it is clear that the present form of the CAP is very inefficient at tackling the basic income problem in agriculture. The elaborate price support mechanisms still account for more than 70 per cent of the total assistance to agricultural producers generated by agricultural policies in the OECD countries yet are "entirely inappropriate for many categories of farm households" (Cahill, Fulponi and Morenddu, 1993). The agricultural Commissioner (MacSharry) asserted in 1991 that 80 per cent of support was then being received by only 20 per cent of farmers, the implication being that these were the largest ones. One commentator claimed that only about 10 per cent of support reached the small low-income farmer (Gardner, 1996). A better approach would seem to be the greater use of more targeted instruments aimed at alleviating specific impediments to adjustment at the farm household level, and of stimulating the local rural economy so that the opportunities of income diversification are available. This attempts to tackle the income problem in agriculture at its root. In addition, direct payments may be made to farm operators in return for the provision of some service valued by society but which the market fails to supply, such as conservation of the environment or access for recreation. It often happens that farms under income pressure on their "private good" markets, such as those facing difficult production conditions in hill areas, are well endowed with resources that generate "public goods" such as an attractive landscape. A danger with rewards that compensate for market failure is that they may be used as a justification for the continuation of existing support without an adequate scrutiny of the services offered in return. A common recommendation is that such direct payments should be "decoupled", in the sense that they should be designed so that changes in their levels should not impinge on farmers' production decisions (unless, of course, a change in production is integral to achieving a particular environmental target); in practice, complete decoupling is difficult if not impossible to achieve. Separating the various strands of policy and using appropriate mechanisms to achieve the aims of each is in line with the general ('Tinbergen') principle that any set of policies should have at least the same number of instruments as targets.

Where there are remaining poverty problems after the possibilities of payment for non-market services, diversification and rural development have been exhausted, these constitute essentially a social problem rather than an agricultural one. In some countries this residual income problem could be left to the general welfare net, whereas for others some more active stance for farmers might be required as such nets may not be capable of catering adequately for self-employed cases, especially in countries where farmers do not commonly keep accounting records. The "Larsen" report (Commission, 1994) suggested that this poverty problem was essentially an issue of income distribution that was best treated as a matter for national governments. But in practice, achieving subsidiarity in this key EU policy would require major adjustments from the present in both the way that the CAP is run and in how the EU is financed. As has been demonstrated, present systems and institutional interests may severely restrict the possibilities for change.

7.8 Summary and conclusions

At the outset of the argument contained in this book it was shown that the income objectives of agricultural policy, particularly the CAP, are primarily concerned with the living standards of the agricultural population. These objectives have not been articulated precisely in official documents, though the general intentions are clear. Incomes of farmers and their households are still at the centre of policy either directly, such as how they might be affected by alternative policy scenarios, or indirectly, such as through the assumed link between the prosperity of farmers and the maintenance of rural populations and the appearance of the countryside. However, the EU's system of income monitoring for the agricultural community and the ways that incomes are taken into account in policy formation are inappropriate for meeting this purpose. The present practice has helped perpetuate a policy that, through failing to attack the problems of low incomes where they occur in a straightforward way, has helped create large and costly imbalances in supply and demand for farm products.

The failure of the income monitoring system to provide the necessary income information does not seem to be the result of any conspiracy to maintain the status quo. Rather, the present systems and organisations are the legacy of previous phases of agricultural policy. When it was desirable to expand the level of farm output and when farmers were thought of as not having other sources of incomes, a monitoring system which used the income of the agricultural branch of the economy as a proxy for the well-being of farmers was a statistical convenience. Similarly, at the farm level, the incomes of the farm business could be assumed to represent that of the farm household. Such assumptions are no longer acceptable. Farming is seen to be a much more heterogeneous activity and the emphasis of policy has shifted away from the encouragement of production. The information systems have not adjusted to the current requirements of policy; they are an example of statistical obsolescence.

Why this obsolescence has happened can be explained largely in terms of individuals and groups pursuing their self interest. These include not only farmers and their representatives but also those involved in the policy-making process itself - politicians and administrators. Put simply, it has not been to the advantage of anyone with influence to change fundamentally the system by which incomes are supported and, as a consequence, the ways in which information on incomes is collected and used. Though there are groups who might have benefited from a change these have not proved sufficiently powerful to effect the change. Among these potential beneficiaries would be small farmers without alternative income sources for their families, consumers, taxpayers, and groups who could receive greater benefits from a diversion of funds from agriculture to social and regional spending. Perhaps the most influential are the environmental lobby who could see a more direct form of support for small, low-income farmers being in harmony with their desired pattern of land use.

Against these, there are the substantial forces with an interest in maintaining the status quo, primarily the groups representing farmers (with a bias towards the interests of the medium and larger producers) and the bureaucracy. Only when there is a threat to the entire system, such as the budgetary crisis in the EU, do these groups advocate reform. The need to consider seriously the objectives and mechanisms in the face of inadequate resources introduces a fluidity that is sorely needed.

It is increasingly accepted that the sort of CAP support policy that the EU operated up to the early 1990s was unsustainable. To try to continue along those lines was counter to the history of agriculture's role in economic development in industrialised countries and increasingly disrupted the pattern of world trade. There was a fundamental incompatibility between rising levels of supply at supported prices and static effective domestic demand. Reform of the CAP, as yet far from complete, has taken the form of restoring the market as the main determinant of farmer's production decisions and, at the same time, expanding the use of instruments aimed at environmental, social and rural development objectives. In the late-1990s the policy agenda has been dominated by the transition problems of moving from the former system of support, with meeting the agricultural requirements of the 1993 GATT agreement, with preparing for the impact of the entry to the EU of countries to the east and with coping with unanticipated crisis (the problem of BSE among cattle, consumer worries about hormones in beef production, food and environmental concerns about genetically-modified plants etc.).

In all this it is necessary to remind ourselves that longer-term changes are taking place in EU agriculture, with local variations. At the farm level the average income from agriculture will continue to trend downwards. The wide diversity of farm sizes and structures will continue within a declining number of independent units. The minimum size of business capable of generating an acceptable income for its occupier and his family as a full-time farm will continue to rise. The number of farms run by households where the main source of income comes from outside agriculture will increase and an increasing proportion of part-time farmers will treat their holdings primarily as domestic assets. The proportion of total income of households living on farms coming from non-farm sources will also rise.

These are well-established trends, the rate of which can be altered for a time by agricultural policy, but the underlying forces of which cannot be overcome. They give rise to political implications. The numbers of households that can be classed as agricultural, in that farming is the main source of their incomes, will continue to shrink, and less attention will be given by politicians to these and more to the voters in households who operate farms in some part-time capacity and to those with broader concerns with the environment and the countryside. Greater public awareness of the size and composition of the total personal income of farmers will encourage a more direct approach to those whose incomes are unsatisfactorily low; they are more likely to be treated as constituting a social problem rather than an agricultural problem and subject to the general welfare net than at present, though special agricultural income support programmes will be needed in those Member States where the social security administration is not effective at tackling income problems among the self-employed. Consequently, support for other types of farm operators - those with substantial incomes either because their farm businesses are of adequate size or because of other incomes - will be reduced unless this is in return for providing environmental or other services.

However, the rapidity with which these movements are translated into agricultural policy is heavily dependent on the bureaucracy. As pointed out above, it is in the interest of many involved in the process to prevent or impede change. This applies both to the implementation of policy and to the statistics that that policy depends on. However the steps taken by Eurostat to create an aggregate indicator of the total disposable income of agricultural households, coupled with the demands for such an indicator from some parts of the Commission, marks an expansion in the public knowledge of the income situation of farmers that is not reversible. Its creation is probably adequate, within the framework of Community institutions, to ensure that its findings cannot be ignored. There are groups within the policy-shaping bureaucracy (notably those concerned with structure policy and with non-agricultural aspects of EU activities which find themselves starved of funds by agriculture) who have an interest in using this new information.

However, aggregate information on the overall income situation of farmers is not by itself adequate for servicing the statistical needs of the CAP. Progress at microeconomic level is needed to throw light on to many of the pressing policy questions concerning incomes. For example, what is the appropriate basic household unit over which incomes are to be measured and how does the picture change with alternative definitions of the household? To what extent should a run of years be considered when assessing income of the basic household unit? How are the households on large-scale co-operative farms in Germany and (looking forward) in candidate countries to be treated? Assuming such methodological problems can be resolved, where and with what frequency are farm families with low total incomes to be found? On what types and sizes of farm, in which regions, and what are the personal characteristics of their occupiers? Though there is some fragmentary information for the EU, a much more secure statistical base is needed from which to identify the extent of problems and to design and monitor policy. This implies the development of robust data sources. Though information from tax records and household budget surveys may play a role here, the main expectation must be attached to the Farm Accountancy Data Network (FADN), the EU's official survey of farm businesses. Political obstruction from a few Member States has so far prevented this survey from collecting data that would enable a full picture of the incomes of farms and farm households to be presented. The physical separation of the parts of the Commission responsible for the aggregate income estimates and for microeconomic data in both institutional and geographical senses (Eurostat in Luxembourg and the Directorate-General for Agriculture in Brussels) has hardly made communication easy on matters such as co-ordinating methodological developments and the comparison of results. A joint work-programme involving co-operation between Eurostat and FADN is a fundamental requirement for progress towards facilitating a more rational CAP and for the continued monitoring of objectives leading to modifications in the policy instruments and, if necessary a reweighting of the various policy elements. Thus the apparent disharmony between the aims of policy in regard to incomes in agriculture and the information by which intentions are approached and achievements monitored may be better resolved.

Bibliography

AAEA (American Statistical Association - American Agricultural Economics Association Joint Committee on Agricultural Statistics) (1972), 'Our obsolete data systems: new directions and opportunities', *Amer. J. agric. Econ.*, 54, 867-80.

Abrams, M. (1973), 'Subjective social indicators', *Social Trends*, 4.

Ahearn, M (1986), *Finanacial Well-being of Farm Opertors and Their Households*, Economic Research Service, US Department of Agriculture, Report No. 563.

Ahearn, M. (1990), 'The Role of the Farm Household in the Agricultural Economy', *Agricultural Income and Finance: Situation and Outlook Report*, USDA, ERS. AFO-37.

Ahearn, M. (1996), 'Methodological issues in the measurement of the income of farm households in the USA', in Hill, B.(ed), *Income Statistics for the Agricultural Household Sector*, Eurostat, Luxembourg.

Ahearn, M. and Lee, J. E. (1991), 'Multiple Job-holding among Farm Operator Households in the United States', in Hallberg, Findeis and Lass (1991) *op. cit.*

Ahearn, M. C., Perry, J. and El-Osta, H. S. (1993), *The Economic Well-Being of Farm Operator Households, 1988-90*, Agricultural Economic Report, No. 666, USDA ERS, Washington.

Ahearn, M., Johnson, J. and Strickland, R. (1985), 'The Distribution of Income and Wealth of Farm Operator Households', *Amer. J. agric. Econ.*, 67(5), 1087-94.

Allanson, P. and Hubbard, L. (1999). 'On the comparative evaluation of agricultural income distributions in the European Union', *European Review of Agricultural Economics*, 1-17.

Allison, G. T. (1971), *The Essence of Decision - Explaining the Cuban Missile Crisis*, Little Brown, Boston.

Andersson, B. and Bengtsson, B. -A. (1984), *Capital gains and losses in the income statement of the agricultural firm. A simulation study of some alternative methods*, Report 235, Swedish University of Agricultural Sciences, Department of Economics and Statistics, Uppsala. Cited in Puurunen (1990), *op cit.*

Atkinson, A. B. (1975), *The Economics of Inequality*, Oxford University Press, Oxford.

Atkinson, A. B. (ed)(1980), *Wealth, Income and Inequality*, Oxford University Press, Oxford.

Avery, G. (1985), *Guarantee Thresholds and the Common Agricultural Policy*, Paper given to the 1985 Agricultural Economics Society Conference, Edinburgh.

Banks, V, Butler, M. and Kalbacher, J. (1989), *Alternative Definitions of Farm People*, Staff Report No 89-9, USDA ERS, Washington.

Banks, V. J. and Kalbacher, J. Z. (1981), *Farm Income Recipients and their Families: A Socioeconomic Profile*, Rural Development Research Report No. 30, USDA ERS, Washington.

Bannock, G., Baxter, R. E. and Rees, R. (1978*)*, *The Penguin Dictionary of Economics*, Penguin Books, Harmondsworth.

Barlett, P. F. (1993), *American Dreams, Rural Realities. Family Farms in Crisis.* University of North Carolina Press. Chapel Hill.

Barnett, A. (1987), 'Review of MAFF Statistics', In *Agriculture and Food Statistics. Papers of the Statistics Users Annual Conference*, Nov. 1986.

Baum, K. and Johnson, J. (1986) 'Microeconomic Indicators of the Farm Sector and Policy Implications,' *Amer. J. agric. Econ.*, 68(5),1121-29.

Becker, G. S. (1976), *The Economic Approach to Human Behaviour*, University of Chicago Press.

Bellerby, J. R. (1953), 'Distribution of Farm Income in the United Kingdom, 1867-1938,' *Journal of the Proceedings of the Agricultural Economics Society.*

Bellerby, J. R. (1954), 'Gross and Net Farm Rent in the United Kingdom, 1867-1938,' *Journal of the Proceedings of the Agricultural Economics Society.*

Bellerby, J. R. (1955), 'Agricultural Income,' *Journal of the Royal Statistical Society*, 118:3.

Bellerby, J. R. (1956), *Agriculture and Industry Relative Income*, Macmillan, London.

Bhatia, K. B. (1970), 'Accrued Capital Gains, Personal Income and Saving in the United States 1948-64,' *Rev. Income and Wealth*, 16(4), 363-78.

Bhatia, K. B. (1971), 'On Estimating Capital Gains in U.S. Agriculture,' *Amer. J. agric. Econ.*, 53, 502-6.

Bhatia, K. B. (1972), 'Capital Gains and the Aggregate Consumption Function,' *American Economic Review*, 62, 866-79.

Bjornsen, H., -M. (1999). 'Off-farm labour decisions of Norwegian farm households'. Paper to the research seminar "Living conditions and income". NILF/Statistics Norway, Oslo, Norway.

Bollman, R. D. (1980), 'A Comparison of the Money Incomes of Farmers and Non-farmers,' *Can. J. agric. Econ., Proceedings of Annual Meeting*, 1980.

Bollman, R. D. and Smith, P. (1987), 'The Changing Role of Off-farm Income in Canada', *Proceedings: Canadian Agricultural Outlook Conference*, December 1987.

Bonnen, J. T. (1975), 'Improving Information on Agriculture and Rural Life' *Amer. J. agric. Econ.*, 57, 753-63.

Bonnen, J. T. (1977), 'Assessment of the Current Agricultural Data Base: an Information System Approach.' in Martin, L. R. (1977), vol 2, *op cit.*.

Bonnen, J. T. (1988), 'Improving the Socioeconomic Data Base', in Hildreth, J., Lipton, K., Clayton, K. and O'Conner, C. (eds), *Agriculture and Rural Areas Approaching the 21st Century: Challenges for Agricultural Economics.* Iowa State University Press, 452-83

Bonnen, J. T. (1990) 'On the Role of Data and Measurement in Agricultural Economic Research', *Journal of Agricultural Economics Research*, 41 (4), 2-5.

Bonnen, J. T. and Schweikhardt, D. B. (1998), 'The Future of U.S. Agricultural Policy: Reflections on the Disappearance of the "Farm Problem"', *Review of Agricultural Economics,* 20(1), 2-36.

Booth, C. (1902), *Life and Labour of the People of London,* Kelly.London.

Bowers, D. E. (1997). *Rural Conditions and Trends, Vol. 8 No. 2,* US Department of Agriculture, Washington,

Bowers, J.K. and Cheshire, P. (1983*), Agriculture, the Countryside and Land Use,* Methuen, London.

Roxley, R. F. (1989), 'Agricultural and Rural Data Paradigms', *Journal of Agricultural Economics Research*, 41(1), 21-6.

Bradley, T. (1986), 'Poverty and Dependency in Village England.', in Lowe, Bradley and Wright *op cit.,*

Bradley, T., Lowe, P. and Wright, S. (1986), 'Rural Deprivation and the Welfare Transition.' in Lowe, Bradley and Wright *op cit.*

Brandow, G. E. (1977), 'Policy for Commercial Agriculture', in Martin (1977) Vol. 1 *op. cit..*

Brangeon, J. L., and Jégouzo, G. (1992). 'L'estimation du revenu des ménages agricoles: approches microéconomiques'. *Cahiers d'économie et sociologie rurales* 23.

Brangeon, J.-L., Jégouzo, and Roze, B. (1991), *Une contribution a la connaissance des revenus totaux des familles d'agriculteurs; resultats d'un depoullement particulier d'une enquete CERC sur les revenus de l'anne 1978,* INRA, Station d'Economie et Sociologie Rurales, Rennes.

Brinkman, G. L. (1980), 'Reflections on Farm Incomes in the 1970s,' *Can. J.agric. Econ., Proceedings of Annual Meeting, 1980.*

Brinkman. G. L. (1983), 'Agricultural Policy Formation and Farm Income Data Needs', in Loyns et al. *op cit..*

Britton, D. K. (1980), 'Some Aspects of Income Distribution Within the Farm Sector', Paper given to the Agricultural Economics Society one-day conference on Investment, Income and Taxation in Agriculture, Nov. 1981.

Britton, D.K. (1981), *Agricultural Policies and Agricultural Incomes, Inaugural Winegarten Memorial Lecture,* National Farmers' Union, London.

Brookes, B. (1987) 'Farmers' incomes in the European Community', in *Agriculture and Food Statistics. Proceedings of the Conference of the Statistics Users Council,* November 1986.

Bryant, W. K., Bawden, D. L. and Saupe, W. E. (1981), 'The Economics of Rural Poverty - a Review of the Post-World War II United States and Canadian Literature', in Martin (ed.) *op cit..*

Bryden, J., Hawkins, E., Gilliatt, J., MacKinnon, N., and Bell, C. (1992). *Farm Household Adjustment in Western Europe 1987-1991, Final Report on the Research Programme on Farm Structure and Pluriactivity, Vol. 1*, Arkleton Trust, Nethy Bridge.

Bryson, J. E. (1985), *The Validity and Usefulness of the EC Farm Income Comparisons*, unpublished PhD thesis, Wye College, University of London.

Buhmann, B., Rainwater, L., Schmaus, G. and Smeeding, T. M. (1987), 'Equivalence Scales, Well-being, Inequality, and Poverty Sensitivity Estimates Across Ten Countries Using the Luxembourg, Income Study (LIS) Database,' *Review of Income and Wealth*, 33, 115-42.

Burrell, A., Hill, B. and Medland, J. (1987), *Statistical Handbook of UK Agriculture*, Wye College, University of London, Ashford.

Cahill, C., Fulponi, L. and Moreddu, C. (1993) 'The total income situation of farm households in the OECD: linkages to the rural economy'. Paper presented to the Agricultural Economics Society meeting on Rural Sustainability, London, Dec. 13th, 1993.

Caillavet, F., Guyomard, H. And Lifran, R. (eds)(1994), *Agricultural Household Modelling and Family Economics*, Developments in Agricultural Economics 10, Elsevier, Amsterdam.

Capstick, C. W. (1983), 'Agricultural Policy Issues and Economic Analysis', *J. agric. Econ.*, 34(3), 263-78.

Carlin, T.A. and Reinsel, E.I. (1973), 'Combining Income and Wealth: An Analysis of Farm Family Well-being', *Amer. J. agric. Econ.*, 55, 38-44.

CAS (1978), *Capital for Agriculture*, Report No. 3, Centre for Agricultural Strategy, University of Reading, Reading.

Cecora, J. (1986), 'Agriculture - Its Effects on the Level-of-Living and Subsistence Technology of Farming Households', in EAAE (1986) *op cit.*.

Chase, L. (1980), 'Inflation, Capital Gains and Farmers' Economic Well-being', *Can. J. agric. Econ.*, *Proceedings of Annual Meeting, 1980*.

Chase, L. and Lerohl, M.L. (1981), 'On Measuring Farmers' Well-being', *Can. J. agric. Econ.*, 29.

Churchman, W. (1971), *The Design of Inquiring Systems*, Basic Books, New York.

Cochrane, W. W. (1985), 'The Need to Rethink Agricultural Policy in General and to Perform Some Radical Surgery on Commodity Programs in Particular', *Amer. J. agric. Econ.*, 67, 1002-9.

Cochrane, W. W. and Ryan, M. E. (1976), *American Farm Policy, 1948-1973*, University of Minnesota Press, Minneapolis.

Colman, D. (1987) 'The Development, Organisation and Orientation of Agricultural Economics in the UK'. Paper to the Inaugural Conference of the Franco-British Assiciation for Rural Studies, Oxford, March 26-28, 1987.

Commission of the European Communities (1981*)*, *Factors Influencing Ownership, Tenancy, Mobility and Use of Farmland in the United Kingdom*, Information on Agriculture No. 74, The Commission, Luxembourg.

Commission of the European Communities (1982*)*, *Indicators of Farm Income*, Working document of the Services of the Commission, VI/308/82-EN (0082d).

Commission of the European Communities (1983*), Examination of the different concepts regarding farm incomes,* Community Committee on the Farm Accountancy Data Network, VI/A-3, RI/CC 828.

Commission of the European Communities (1984a), *The Outlook for Europe's Agricultural Policy,* Green Europe Newsletter 25. The Commission, Brussels.

Commission of the European Communities (1984b), *Agricultural Incomes in the Community in 1983,* Green Europe Newsflash 26, The Commission, Brussels.

Commission of the European Communities (1985a*), Agricultural incomes in the Community.* Green Europe Newsflash 29, The Commission, Brussels.

Commission of the European Communities (1985b), *Perspectives for the Common Agricultural Policy,* COM(85) 333 Final, The Commission, Brussels (also published as Newsflash 33).

Commission of the European Communities (1985c), *A Future for Community Agriculture. Commission Guidelines,* Newsflash 34, Green Europe, The Commission, Brussels.

Commission of the European Communities (1985d), *Income Disparities in Agriculture in the Community,* Green Europe 208, The Commission, Brussels.

Commission of the European Communities (1986), *Study of Outside Gainful Activities of Farmers and their Spouses in the E.E.C.,* Document series, The Commission, Luxembourg.

Commission of the European Communities (1988a), *The Agricultural Situation in the Community: 1987 Report,* The Commission, Luxembourg.

Commission of the European Communities (1988b*), The Future of Rural Society,* COM(88)501, Final/2, The Commission, Luxembourg.

Commission of the European Communities (1989), *The European Rarm Accountancy Data Network: an A-Z of Methodology,* Directorate General for Agriculture, Unit A-3, Analysis of the situation of Farm Holdings, The Commission, Brussels.

Commission of the European Communities (1991a), *The Development and Future of the CAP: Reflection Paper of the Commission. Communication of the Commission to the Council,* COM (91) 100 final, The Commission. Brussels.

Commission of the European Communities (1991b), *The Development and future of the Common Agricultural Policy: Proposals of the Commission,* Green Europe 2/91, The Commission, Brussels.

Commission of the European Communities (1992). "Farm Take-over and Farm Entrance within the EEC", Document series, Commission of the EC, Brussels, ISBN 92-826-3667-4.

Commission of the European Communities (1993), *Farm Incomes in the European Community 1990/91 including selected results for 1986/87 to 1989/90.* Document series. The Commission, Luxembourg.

Commission of the European Communities (1994a), *EC Agricultural Policy for the 21st Century* (the Larsen report), European Economy, Reports and Studies No. 4, The Commission, Brussels.

Commission of the European Communities (1994b), *The Economics of the Common Agricultural Policy*, European Economy, Reports and Studies No. 5, The Commission, Brussels.

Commission of the European Communities (1997), *Agenda 2000 - Volume 1 - Communication: For a Stronger and Wider Union*, DOC/97/6, The Commission, Brussels.

Cook, E., and Hill, B. (1999), *Economic aspects of cereal production in the EU, 1999 edition*, Theme 5, Eurostat, Luxembourg.

Cornet, P. P., Blanc, M., Cavailhes, J., Dauce, P. And Le Hy, A. (1991), *Farm Take-Over and Farm Entrance within the E.E.C.*, Document series, The Commission of the EC. Brussels.

CSO (1998), *Demographic, Social and Economic Situation of the Farming Community in 1991: Censuses of Agriculture and Population*, Central Statistics Office of Ireland, Cork, Ireland.

CSO (Central Statistical Office)(1985*)*, *United Kingdom National Accounts: Sources and Methods*, HMSO, London.

Culver, D., O'Connor, K. And Yap, S. (1992) Comparison of the Incomes of Self Employed Farm Operators with Other Self Employed Occupations. Farm Analysis Bulletin No 43, Agriculture Canada, Ottawa.

Dancy, R. J. (1983), 'Farm Management Advisory Work; the Present and the Future,' J. agric. Econ., 34(3), 329-36.

Davey, B. (1996), 'Income Statistics in Countries Outside the EU and their Relevance to Agricultural and Rural Development Policies in the 1990s: Lessons from Canada'. In Hill, B. (ed.), *Income Statistics for the Agricultural Households Sector,* Eurostat, Luxembourg, 23-33.

Davy, B., Josling, T. E. and McFarquar, A. (1976), *Agriculture and the State: British Policy in a World Context,* Macmillan, London.

de Gorter, H. and Swinnen, J. (1994), 'The Economic Polity of Farm Policy', *J. agric. Econ.*, 45(3), 312-326.

de Paula, F. C. (1973), *Land Prices and New Capital for Agriculture*, Agricultural Mortgage Corporation, London.

Dinwiddy, R. (1980), *The Concept of Personal Income in the Analysis of Income Distribution,* Government Economic Service Working Paper No. 30, Departments of Environment and Transport, London.

Drynan, R. G. and Hodge, I. D. (1981) 'The Value of Unrealised Farm Land Capital Gain: Comment', *Amer. J. agric. Econ.*, 63, 281-2.

Dubgaard, A., Grassmugg, B. and Munk, K. J. (eds)(1984), *Agricultural Data and Economic Analysis,* European Institute of Public Administration, Maastricht, and Jordbrugsokonomiske Institut, Copenhagen.

Dunford, R. W. (1980), 'The Value of Unrealised Land Capital Gains: Comment,' *Amer. J. agric. Econ.*, 62, 260-2.

EAAE (European Association of Agricultural Economists)(1986), *Income Disparities Among Farm Households and Agricultural Policy,* Papers presented to the 14th European Seminar, INRA, Rennes, France.

Eboli, M. G. (1996), 'Farm Household Income, Work and Pluriactivity' In Hill, B. (ed) *Income Statistics for the Agricultural Household Sector*, Eurostat, Luxembourg.

Eboli, M. G. and Turri, E. (1988), 'Toward a Behavioural Model of Mutiple Job-Holding Farm Families', *Agricultural Economics, 2, 247-58*.

EDC for Agriculture (1977a), *Agriculture into the 1980s: Finance*, HMSO. London.

EDC for Agriculture (1977b), *Agriculture into the 1980s: Taxation,*.HMSO, London.

Efstratoglou, S. (1994), *Pilot Survey of Incomes of Farm Households in Greece: Report on Methodology and Results,* (Vakakis International), Commission of the European Communities DG VI/A-3, Brussels.

European Parliament (1983), *Interim Report drawn up on behalf of the Committee on Agriculture on the Level of Agricultural Income,* Working documents 1982-83, 1-1327/82, Rapporteur Maher, T. J.

Eurostat (1978), *Harmonisation of National Family Budget Surveys,* Doc. No 3238/77 Rev. 1., Eurostat, Luxembourg.

Eurostat (1979), *European System of Integrated Economic Accounts. Second Edition,* Statistical Office of the European Communities, Luxembourg.

Eurostat (1980), *Methodology of Surveys on Family Budget,* Eurostat, Luxembourg.

Eurostat (1981), *The 1979 Harmonised Family Budget Surveys: Review of the Methodological Aspects of the Questionnaires in the ten Member States,* Eurostat, Luxembourg.

Eurostat (1985), *Family Budgets: Comparative Tables - Federal Republic of Germany, France, Italy, United Kingdom,* Eurostat, Luxembourg.

Eurostat (1986), *Farm Structure: Methodology of Community Surveys*, Theme 5 Series E, Eurostat, Luxembourg, ISBN 92-825-5919-X.

Eurostat (1986a), *Familiy Budgets: Comparative tables: Netherlands, Belgium, Ireland, Denmark, Greece, Spain,* Eurostat, Luxembourg.

Eurostat (1986b), *Family Budgets: Comparative tables (twelve countries),*Eurostat, Luxembourg.

Eurostat (1986c), *Farm Structure - 1983 survey: main results,* Theme 5, Series C, Eurostat, Luxembourg.

Eurostat (1987), *Manual on Economic Accounts for Agriculture and Forestry,* Theme 5 Series E. Eurostat, Luxembourg.

Eurostat (1988), *Agricultural Income: Sectoral income index analysis 1987,* Theme 5, Series D, Eurostat, Luxembourg.

Eurostat (1990a), *Family Budgets: Comparative tables: FR of Germany, Spain, France, Ireland, Italy, Netherlands,* Theme 3 Series C, Eurostat, Luxembourg.

Eurostat (1990b), *Manual on the Total Income of Agricultural Households,* Theme 5 Series E, Eurostat, Luxembourg.

Eurostat (1990c), *Family Budgets: Methodological handbook*, Theme 3 Series C, Eurostat, Luxembourg.

Eurostat (1991), *Farm Structure: 1987 survey - main results,* Theme 5 Series C, Statistical Office of the European Communities, Luxembourg.

Eurostat (1993), *Family Budget Surveys in the EC: Methodology and Recommendations for Harmonisation,* Theme 3 Series E, Eurostat, Luxembourg (see also under Verma and Gabilondo, 1993).

Eurostat (1995a), *Agricultural Income 1994,* Theme 5 Series A, Eurostat, Luxembourg.

Eurostat (1995b), *European System of Accounts: ESA 1995.* Eurostat, Luxembourg.

Eurostat (1995c), *Manual of the Total Income of Agricultural Households (Rev.1),* Theme 5 Series E, Eurostat, Luxembourg.

Eurostat (1996a), *European System of Accounts: ESA 1995,* Eurostat, Luxembourg,

Eurostat (1996b), *Manual of the Total Income of Agricultural Households* (Rev.1) Theme 5 Series E, Theme 5 Series E, Eurostat, Luxembourg, ISBN 92-827-5227-5.

Eurostat (1997a), *Agricultural Labour Input in the EU,* Theme 5 Series c, Eurostat, Luxembourg, 92-827-9311-7.

Eurostat (1997b), *Manual on the Economic Accounts for Agriculture and Forestry (Rev.1),* Eurostat, Luxembourg,

Eurostat (1997c), *Total Income of Agricultural Households: 1996 Report,* Theme 5 Series .C, Eurostat, Luxembourg, 92-827-9614-0.

Eurostat (1998), *Income of the Agricultural Households Sector 1997 Report,* Theme 5 Series C, Eurostat, Luxembourg, 92-828-3638-X.

Eurostat (1999), *Income from agricultural activity 1998,* Theme 5, Eurostat, Luxembourg, ISBN 92-828-6029.

FAO (1996), *" A System of Economic Accounts for Food and Agriculture,* FAO Statistical Development Series 8," Food and Agriculture Organisation of the United Nations, Rome,

Farmer, L. and Strickland, R. (1986), 'Financial indicators of the U.S Department of Agriculture', in Loyns et al. (1986), 70-90, *op cit..*

Fennell, R. (1985), 'A Reconsideration of the Objectives of the Common Agricultural Policy', *J. Common Market Studies,* 23:3, 257-76.

Fennell, R. (1987), *The Common Agricultural Policy of the European Communities,* BSP Professional Books.

Fennell, R. (1997), *The Common Agricultural Policy: Continuity and Change,* Clarendon Press, Oxford, ISBN0-19-828857-3.

Fitzpatrick, J. M. and Parker, C. V. (1965), 'Distribution of income and Canadian agriculture', *Can. J. agric. Econ.,* 13(2), 47-64.

Floystrup-Jensen, J. and Dyreborg-Carlson, B. (1981), *Factors Influencing Ownership, Tenancy, Mobility and Use of Farmland in Denmark.* Commission of the European Communities, Luxembourg.

Forse, T. (1979), 'Beneficial Land Ownership'. in Commission (1981) *op cit..*

Fox, K. A. (1986), 'The Present Status of Objective Social Indicators: A Review of Thoery and Measurement', *Amer. J. agric. Econ.,* 68(5),1113-20.

Friedman, M. (1957), *A Theory of the Consumption Function*, Princeton University Press, Princeton, New Jersey.

Fuller, A. M. (1991), 'Multiple Job-holding among Farm Families in Canada', in Hallberg, Findeis and Lass *op cit.*

Furness, G. W. (1982), 'Some Features of Farm Income and Structure Variations in Regions of the United Kingdom', *J. agric. Econ.*, 33, 289-309.

Furness, G. W. (1983), 'The importance, distribution and net incomes of small farm businesses in the UK'. In Tranter (1983) *op cit.*.

Gardner, B. (1996), *European Agriculture: Policies, production and trade*, Routledge, London, ISBN0-415-08532-2.

Gardner, B. L. (1972), *Measuring the Income of Rural Families: Results of a Survey of Sampson County, North Carolina*, Economics Research Report No. 20, Dept. of Economics, North Carolina State University, Rayleigh.

Gardner, B. L. (1975), A *Full Income Approach to the Measurement of Rural Poverty*, Economics Research Report No. 34, , Department of Economics and Business, North Carolina State University, Raleigh.

Gardner, B. L. (1992), 'Changing Economic Perspectives on the Farm Problem', *Journal of Economic Literature*, 30 (March 1992), pp.62-101.

Garfinkel, I. and Haveman, R. (1977), 'Earnings capacity, economic status, and poverty,' *J. Human Relations*, 12(1), 49-70.

Gasson, R. (1973), 'Goals and values of farmers', *J. agric. Econ.*, 18(3), 521-42.

Gasson, R. (1983), *Gainful occupations of farm families*, Wye College, University of London, Ashford.

Gasson, R. (1986), *Farm families with other gainful activities*, Wye College, University of London, Ashford.

Gasson, R. (1988), *The Economics of Part-time Farming*, Longmans.

Gasson, R. and Errington (1993), *The Farm Family Business*, CAB International, Wallingford.

Gasson, R., Crow, G., Errington, A., Hutson, J., Marsden, T. and Winter, M. (1988), 'The Farm as a Family Business: a Review', *J. agric. Econ.*, 39(1), 1-42.

Gebauer, R. H. (1982*), Die Problematik intersektoraler Einkommenstver-gleiche*. Gottinger Schriften zur Agrarokonomie, Gottingen.

Gebauer, R. H. (1986), 'Socio-economic Classification of Farm Households', in EAAE (1986) *op cit.*.

Ghelfi, L. M. (1988), 'About that Lower Cost of Living in Nonmetro Areas', *Rural Development Perspectives*, 5(4), pp30-34.

Grootaert, C. (1983), 'The Conceptual Basis of Measures of Household Welfare and their Implied Survey Data Requirements', *Rev. of Income and Wealth*, 29(1), 1-21.

Gulbransen, O. and Lindbeck, A. (1973*), The Economics of the Agricultural Sector*. The Industrial Institute for Economic and Social Research, Almqvist and Wiksell, Stockholm.

Hagenaars, A. J. M. and Van Praag, B. M. S. (1985), 'A Synthesis of Poverty Line Definitions', *Rev. of Income and Wealth*, 31(2), 139-54.

Hagenaars, A. J. M., de Vos, K. and Zaidi, M. A. (1994), *Poverty Statistics in the Late 1980s: Research based on micro-data,* Theme 3 Series C, Eurostat, Luxembourg.

Hall, J. (1976), 'Subjective measures of the quality of life in Britain,' *Social Trends,* 7.

Hallam, A. (ed.)(1993), *Size, Structure and the Changing Face of American Agriculture,* Westview Press, Boulder, CO.

Hallberg, M. C., Findeis, J. L. and Lass, D. A. (eds.)(1991), *Multiple Job-holding among Farm Families,* Iowa State University Press, Ames.

Halsey, A. H. (1987), 'Social trends since World War II', *Social Trends,* 17.

Hamilton, E. F. (1986), 'Measuring the Economic Welfare of Farmers: a Theoretical Approach'. in Loyns et al (1986), 105-22, *op cit.*.

Harbury, C. D. and McMahon, P. C. (1973), 'Inheritance and the Characteristics of Top Wealth Leavers in Britain', *Economic Journal,* 1973, pp 810-33, cited in Atkinson (1980).

Harrison, A. (1975), *Farmers and Farm Businesses in England.* Miscellaneous Studies 62, Department of Agricultural Economics and Management, University of Reading.

Harrison, A. and Tranter, R. B. (1989), *The Changing Financial Structure of Farming.* CAS Report 13, Centre for Agricultural Strategy, University of Reading.

Harrison, Anne (1999), 'Linking micro and macro income distribution', paper to the *Eurostat Seminar on Income Methodology for Statistics on Households,* Luxembourg 13014 December 1999, Organisation for Economic Co-operation and Development, Paris.

Harvey, D. R. and Thomson, K. J. (1985), 'Costs, Benefits and the Future of the Common Agricultural Policy', *J. Common Market Studies,* 24(1), 1-20.

Hastings, M. R. (1983), 'Transferring Management Control', *Farm Management,* 5, 397-405.

Hastings, M. R. (1984), 'Succession on Farms', *Agricultural Manpower,* 8, 4-8.

Hathaway, D. E. (1963), *Government and Agriculture,* Macmillan, New York.

Hearn, S. (1977), *Farm Incomes and Capital Gains: Implications for Structural Change,* PhD thesis (unpublished), Wye College, University of London.

Hegrenes, A. (1999), 'Total income of agricultural households in Norway, some evidence an suggestions for an accounting system',.Seminar on standard of living and income, May 1999, NILF/Statistics Norway, Oslo.

Hegrenes, A., Hill, B. and Lien, G. (2000), *Income instability among agricultural households – evidence from Norway,* Discussion Paper, Department of Agricultural Economics and Business Management, Wye College, University of London, Ashford, UK.

Hendriks, G. (1994), 'German Agricultural Policy Objectives', in Kjeldahl, R. and Tracy, M. (eds) *Renationalisation of the Common Agricultural Policy?* Institute of Agricultural Economics, Copenhagen, and APS, La Hutte (Genappe), Belgium.

Herrmann, R., Jensen, U., Schafer, A. and Terwitte, H. (1985), *Views, Concensus and Dissention Among Agricultural Economists: Results of a Statistical Survey*, Erschienene Diskussionsbeitrage des Instituts fur Agrarpolitik und Marktlehre der Universitat Kiel, Nr. 46. Kiel University.

Herzberg, F. W. *et al.* (1957), *The Motivation to Work*, Wiley, New York

Hicks, J. R. (1946), *Value and Capital: and Inquiry into Some Fundamental Principles of Economic Theory.*, 2nd. ed., Clarendon Press, Oxford.

Higgins, J. (1979), 'Price Determination and Price Control in the Agricultural Land Market,' *Irish J. agric. Econ. rur. Sociol.*, 7(2), 127-48.

Higgins, J. (1986), 'The Distribution of Income on Irish Farms', in EAAE (1986) *op cit.*.

Hill, B. (1982), 'Concepts and Measurement of the Incomes, Wealth and Economic Well-being of Farmers', *J. agric. Econ.*, 33(3).

Hill, B. (1984), 'Information on Farmers' Incomes: Data from Inland Revenue Sources', *J. agric. Econ.*, 35(1), 39-50.

Hill, B. (1987), 'Multiple Sources of Income: Implications for Farm Incomes and Farm Income Support', *J. agric. Econ.*, 38(2), 182-9.

Hill, B. (1988), *Total Incomes of Agricultural Households*, Theme 5 Series D, Eurostat, Luxembourg.

Hill, B. (1990a), *An Introduction to Economics for Students of Agriculture*, second edition, Pergamon, Oxford.

Hill, B. (1990b), 'In search of the Common Agricultural Policy's "agricultural community"', *J. agric. Econ.*, 41(3), 316-26.

Hill, B. (1991), *Calculation of Economic Indicators: Making use of RICA (FADN) accountancy data*, Document series, Commission of the EC., Brussels:, ISBN 92-826-3037-4.

Hill, B. (1992), *Total Income of Agricultural Households: 1992 Report*, Theme 5 Series C, Eurostat, Luxembourg.

Hill, B. (1993), 'The 'Myth' of the Family Farm: Defining the Family Farm and Assessing its Importance in the European Community', *Journal of Rural Studies*, 9, 359-370.

Hill, B. (1994), *Total Income of Agricultural Households: Progress in 1993*, Theme 5 Series D, Eurostat, Luxembourg.

Hill, B. (1995), *Total Income of Agricultural Households: 1995 Report.* Theme 5 Series D, Eurostat, Luxembourg.

Hill, B. (1996), 'Monitoring incomes of agricultural households within the EU's information system - new needs and new methods', *European Review of Agricultural Economics*, 23, 27-48.

Hill, B. (ed.) (1998a), *Agricultural Statistics for Central European Countries: Proceedings of the Fifth IWG-AGRI Seminar, Budapest, 12-14 November 1997., "*. Eurostat, Luxembourg, ISBN 92-828-3485-9.

Hill, B. (1998b), 'The Implications for Agricultural Statistics of Changes in the System of National Accounts'. *J. agric. Econ.*, 49, 359-77.

Hill, B. and Brookes, B. (1993), *Farm Incomes in the European Community in the 1980s*, Document Series, The Commission of the EC, Brussels.

Hill, B. and Ray, D. (1987*), Economics for Agriculture: Food, Farming and Rural Economics,* Macmillan, London.

Hill, G. P. (1984), 'Measuring Farming Income under Conditions of Inflation - the Gains from Borrowing', *J. agric. Econ.,* 35, 51-60.

HMSO (1975), *Food From Our Own Resources,* Cmnd. 6020, HMSO, London.

HMSO (1979), *Agriculture and The Nation,* Cmnd. 7458, HMSO, London.

HMSO (annual), *Annual Review of Agriculture,* HMSO, London.

Hoover, D. M. (1962), 'The Measurment and Importance of Real Capital Gains in United States Agriculture', *J. Farm Econ.,* 44, 929-40.

House of Commons (1987), *The Measurement of Farming Incomes, Ministry of Agriculture, Fisheries and Food,.* Proceedings of the Committee of Public Accounts, Session 1987-88, HMSO, London.

House of Lords (1990), *The Future of Rural Society,* Report of the Select Committee on the European Communities, Session 1989-90, HMSO, London.

Howarth, R.W. (1985), *Farming for Farmers?* Hobart Paperback 20, Institute of Economic Affairs, London.

Howarth, R.W. (1990), *Farming for Farmers? A Critique of Agricultural Support Policy.* Second edition, Institute of Economic Affairs, London

Huff, H. B. and MacAulay, T. G. (1973), 'Summing Components of Real Capital Gains', *Amer. J. agric. Econ.,* 55, 69-72.

Huigen, R., Van De Stadt, H. And Zeelenberg, K. (1989), 'Socio-Economic Accounts for the Netherlands', *Review of Income and Wealth,* 35(3), 317-334

Jégouzo, G., Brangeon, J-L., Roze, B. (1998), *Richesse et pauvrete en agriculture,* Collection economie agricole et agro-alimentaire, INRA, Paris, ISBN-INRA 2-7380-0832-1.

Johnson, C. (1987), 'The balance sheet of British agriculture', in Statistics Users Council (1987) *op cit..*

Johnson, C. D. (1990), *A Historical Look at Farm Income,* Statistical Bulletin Number 807, US Department of Agriculture, Economic Research Service, Washington.

Jones, R. B. (1969), 'Stability in Farm Incomes', *Journal of Agricultural Economics,* 20(1), 111-124.

Josling, T. E. (1974), 'Agricultural Policies in Developed Countries: A Review', *J. agric. Econ.,* 25(3).

Josling, T. E. and Hamway, D. (1976), 'Income transfer effects of the Common Agricultural Policy', in Davy, Josling and McFarquar (1976) *op cit..*

Kada, R. (1980), *Part-time Family Farming,* Center for Academic Publications, Tokyo.

Kirk, J.H. (1958), 'Some Objectives of Agricultural Support Policy', *J. agric. Econ.,* 13.

Kirk, J. H. (1964), 'The Economic Activities of the Ministry of Agriculture, Fisheries and Food', *J. agric. Econ.,* 16(2).

Kjeldahl, R. (1994), *Direct Income Payments to Farmers: Uses, implications and an empirical investigation of labour supply response in a sample of Danish farm households,* PhD thesis, Wye College, University of London.

Knudsen, O., Nash, J., Bovard, J., Gardner, B. and Winters, L. A. (1990), *Redefining the Role of Government in Agriculture for the 1990s,* World Bank Discussion Papers, No. 105, The World Bank, Washington.

Kuipers, A. D. (1994), 'Agricultural Households and ther Incomes in the Netherlands', in Hill (1994) *op. cit.*

Kulshreshtha, S. N. (1966), 'An Approach to Develop Comparisons of Farm and Non-farm Incomes in Canada', *Can. J. agric. Econ.*, 14(2), 61-76.

Kulshreshtha, S. N. (1967), 'Measuring the Relative Income of Farm Labour 1941-61', *Can. J. agric. Econ.*, 15(1), 23-43.

Larson, D. K. (1975), 'Economic Class as a Measure of Farmers' Welfare', *Amer. J. agric. Econ.*, 57(4), 658-64.

Lee, W. F. and Rask, N. (1976), 'Inflation and Crop Profitability: How Much Can Farmers Pay for Land?', *Amer. J. agric. Econ.*, 58, 984-89.

Little, I, M. D. (1957), *A Critique of Welfare Economics,* 2nd ed, Oxford University Press.

Lommez, J. (1984), 'The Farm Accountancy Data Network: A Tool for Observing and Analysing the Agricultural Situation in the European Community', in Dubgaard, Grassmugg and Munk (eds), *op.cit.*.

Lowe, P., Bradley, T. and Wright, S. (1987*)*, *Deprivation and Welfare in Rural Areas*, Geobooks, Norwich.

Loyns, R. M. A., Freshwater, D. and Hamilton, E. F. (eds) (1986), *Proceedings of the seminar on the theory and practice of agricultural wealth accounts*, Occasional Series No. 16, Department of Agricultural Economics and Farm Management, Faculty of Agriculture, University of Manitoba, Winnipeg.

Loyns, R. M. A., Freshwater, D., and Beelan, G. (eds) (1983), *Proceedings of the Seminar on Farm Income Statistics,* Research Bulletin No. 83-2, Department of Agricultural Economics and Farm Management, Faculty of Agriculture, University of Manitoba, Winnipeg.

Lund, P.J. and Watson, J.M. (1981), 'Agricultural incomes: a review of the data and recent trends', *Economic Trends*, 338, 103-21.

Madden, J.P. (1975), 'Poverty measures as indicators of social welfare', in Wilber, G.L (ed) *Poverty: new perspectives.*, University of Kentucky Press, Lexington.

MAFF (1977), *The changing structure of agriculture,*.HMSO, London.

MAFF (1984), *Departmental Net Income Calculation: Sources and Methods,* MAFF Statistics Division 1, London.

MAFF (1987), *Farm Incomes in the United Kingdom: 1987 Edition*, HMSO, London.

MAFF (1989a), *Agriculture in the United Kingdom: 1988,* HMSO, London.

MAFF (1989b), *Farm Incomes in the United Kingdom: 1989 Edition.* HMSO, London.

MAFF (1994), *Farm Incomes in the United Kingdom 1992/93,* HMSO, London.

MAFF (1995), *European Agriculture: The Case for Radical Reform.* Working Papers, Ministry of Agriculture, Fisheries and Food, London.

Males, W. and Poulter, D. (1987), 'Off-farm income and rural adjustment', *Quarterly Review of the Rural Economy*, 9(2),160-9.

Martin, J., Cheesbrough, S., Dodd, T., Farrant, G. and McKernan, A. (1996), 'Asking the Self-employed about their Income', *Survey Methodology Bulletin* 39, (July 1996), 11-15.

Martin, L. (1981), *A Survey of Agricultural Economics Literature - Volume 3. Economics of Welfare, Rural Development, and Natural Resources in Agriculture, 1940s to 1970s,* University of Minnesota Press, Minneapolis.

Martin, L. R. (1977), *A Survey of Agricultural Economics Literature. - Volume 1. Traditional Fields of Agricultural Economics 1940s to 1970s. - Vol. 2. Quantitative Methods in Agricultural Economics, 1940s to 1970s,* University of Minnesota Press, Minneapolis.

Maslow, A. H. (1954), *Motivation and Personality,* Harper and Rowe, New York

Massey, D. and Catalano, A. (1978), *Capital and Land: Landownership by Capital in Great Britain,* Edward Arnold, London.

Melichar, E. (1979), 'Capital gains versus current income in the farming sector', *Amer. J. agric. Econ.,* 61.

Mortensen, J. (1984), 'COPA's Use of Data on Agricultural Incomes in the Context of the Annual Price Review for Agriculture in the EC', in Dubgaard, Grassmugg and Munk, *op.cit.*

Moyer, W. snd Josling, T. E.(1988*), Agricultural Policy Reform: Politics and Process in the EC and USA,* Iowa State University Press.

Mullen, J. D., Powell, R. A. and Reece, B. F. (1980), 'The Income and Consumption Experiences of a Sample of Farm Families', *Austr. J. agric. Econ.,* 268-82.

Murphy, M. (1984), *Report on Farming in the Eastern Counties of England, 1982/83,* Agricultural Economics Unit, Department of Land Economy, University of Cambridge.

Nakajima, C. (1986), *Subjective Equilibrium of the Farm Household,* Elsevier. Amsterdam.

National Audit Office (1985), *Achievements and Costs of the Common Agricultural Policy in the United Kingdom,* Report by the Comptroller and Auditor General, No. 578, HMSO, London.

National Audit Office (1987), *The Measurement of Farming Incomes,* Report by the Comptrollor and Auditor General No 189, HMSO, London.

National Economic and Social Council (1982), *Farm Incomes: Analysis and Policy,* NESC, Dublin.

Nersten, N. K. (ed) (1998), *Norwegian Agriculture: Status and Trends 1998,* Norwegian Agricultural Economics Research Institute, Oslo, ISBN 82-7077-291-7.

Neville-Rolfe, E. (1984*), The Politics of Agriculture in the European Community,* European Centre for Policy Studies, Policy Studies Institute. London.

Newby, H., Bell, C., Rose and Saunders, P. (1978*), Property, Paternalism and Power,* Hutchinson. London.

Niessler, R. (1986), 'Income Distribution in Austrian Agriculture'. in EAAE (1986) *op cit.*.

Northfield (1979), *Report of the Committee of Inquiry into the Acquisition and Occupancy of Agricultural Land*, Cmnd. 7599, HMSO, London.

Ockenden, J. And Franklin, M. (1995*), European Agriculture: Making the CAP Fit the Future*, Chatham House Papers, The Royal Institute of International Affairs. London.

OECD (1964), *Low incomes in agriculture: problems and policies*, Organisation for Economic Co-operation and Development, Paris.

OECD (1974*), Agricultural Policy in the United State*, Organisation for Economic Co-operation and Development, Paris

OECD (1978*), Part-time Farming in OECD Countries*, Organisation for Economic Co-operation and Development, Paris.

OECD (1979), *The Taxation of Net Wealth, Capital Transfers and Capital Gains of Individuals*, Organisation for Economic Co-operation and Development OECD, Paris.

OECD (1982*), The OECD List of Social Indicators*, Organisation for Economic Co-operation and Development, Paris.

OECD (1983a*), Review of Agricultural Policies in OECD Member Countries 1980-1982*, Organisation for Economic Co-operation and Development, Paris.

OECD (1983b*), The Implications of Different Means of Agricultural Income Support*, Organisation for Economic Co-operation and Development, Paris.

OECD (1987), *National Policies and Agricultural Trade*, Organisation for Economic Co-operation and Development, Paris.

OECD (1992), *Economic Accounts for Agriculture 1977-1990*, Organisation for Economic Co-operation and Development, Paris, ISBN 92-64-03701-2.

OECD (1994), *Agricultural Policies, Markets and Trade*, Organisation for Economic Co-operation and Development, Paris.

OECD (1995), *A Review of Household Income in OECD Countries: Notes by Country*, (OECD/GD/(95)97), Background paper to *Adjustment in OECD Agriculture: Issues and Policy Responses*, Organisation for Economic Co-operation and Development, Paris.

OECD (1996), *Factors conditioning the transfer efficiency of agricultural support*, Directorate for Food, Agriculture and Fisheries, Organisation for Economic Co-operation and Development, Paris.

OECD (1997), *Future Developments of Economic Accounts Statistics: Issues and Directions*, OCDE/GD(97)108., Organisation for Economic Co-operation and Development, Paris.

OECD (1998), *Adjustment in OECD Agriculture: Reforming Farmland Policies: Part 1, Policies affecting farmland mobility*, Organisation for Economic Co-operation and Development, Paris, ISBN 9-789264-260279.

OECD (1999), *Distributional Effects of Agricultural Support in Selected OECD Countries*, AGR/CA(99)8/FINAL, Organisation for Economic Co-operation and Development, Paris.

Outlaw, J.E. and Croft, G. (1981), 'Recent Developments in Economic Accounts for Agriculture', *Economic Trends*, 335, 95-103.

Pen, J. (1971), *Income Distribution*, Penguin, Harmondsworth.

Perry, G. M., Rister, E., Richardson, J. W. and Leatham, D. J. (1986), 'The Effects of Equity Position, Credit Policy, and Capital Gains on Farm Survival', *Agricultural Economics Research*.

Peters, G. H. (1987) 'Factor Returns', in Statistics Users Council (1987), *op cit.*.

Peters, G.H. (1980), 'Some thoughts on capital taxation,' *J. agric. Econ.*, 31.

Peterson, G. M. (1933), 'Wealth, Income and Living', *Journal of Farm Economics*, 15(3), 421-51.

Petit, M. (1985), *Determinants of Agricultural Policies in the United Dtates and the European Community*, Research Report 51, International Food Policy Research Institute, Washington.

Petit, M., de Benedictis, M., Britton, D, deGroot, M., Henrichsmeyer, W. And Lechi, F. (1987), *Agricultural Policy Formation in the European Community: The Birth of Milk Quotas and CAP Reform*, Developments in Agricultural Economics 4, Elsevier, Amsterdam.

Phimister, E. (1993), *Savings and Investment in Farm Households: Analysis using life cycle*. Avebury, Aldershot.

Plaxico, J. S. and Kletbe, D. D. (1979), 'The Value of Unrealised Farm Land Capital Gains', *Amer. J. agric. Econ.*, 61, 327-30.

Plaxico, J. S. and Kletbe, D. D. (1981), 'The Value of Unrealised Farm Land Capital Gains', *Amer. J. agric. Econ.*, 62, 283-4.

Pollack, R. A. (1985), 'A transactionist approach to families and households', *Journal of Economic Literature*, 23, 581-668.

Poppe, K. amd Zachriasse, L. C. (1986), 'Income Disparities Among Farm Households and Agricultural Policy. Case: the Netherlands', in EAAE (1986), *op cit.*

Pratschke, J. L. (1982) 'Aspects of Agricultural Incomes in Ireland', *Irish J. agric. Econ. rur. Sociol.*, 9, 1-16.

Pratschke, J. L. (1984), 'Aspects of the Redistribution of Income in Rural Ireland 1973-1980', *Irish J. agric. Econ. rur. Sociol.*, 10(1), 13-28.

Puurunen, M. (1990), *A Comparative Study on Farmers' Income*, Research Publications 62-1990, Agricultural Economics Research Institute, Helsinki.

Riemenschneider, C. H. (1983), 'Conceptual obsolescence and farm income data', in Loyns et al (1983), 3-22, *op cit.*.

Robson, N. (1996), 'Practical and legal challenges of developing pluriactivity and non-farm incomes data using the EU's Farm Accountancy Data Network', in *Income Statistics for the Agricultural Households Sector*, (B. Hill, ed.), pp. 69-77. Eurostat, Luxembourg.

Rowntree, B. S. (1901), *Poverty - a Study of Town Life*, Macmillan, London.

Royal Commission on the Taxation of Profits and Income (1955), *Final Report*, HMSO, London.

Ruggles, R. And Ruggles, N. D. (1986), 'The integration of macro and micro data for the household sector', *Review of Income and Wealth*, 32, 245-76.

Runciman, W. G. (1974) 'Occupation class and the assessment of economic inequality in Britain', in Wedderburn, D. (ed)(1974*)*, *Poverty, inequality and class structure*, Cambridge Univerity Press.

Sand, R. (1999), *The marginal propensities to consume and implications for saving: An application to Norwegian farm households,* Notat 1999:12, Norwegian Agricultural Economics Research Institute, Oslo.

Sarris, H. a. Z., S. (1996), 'Agricultural income statistics and policy: a view from southern Europe', in *Income Statistics for the Agricultural Household Sector,* (B. Hill, ed.). Eurostat, Luxembourg.

Schertz, L. P. (1982), 'Households and Farm Establishments in the 1980s: Implications for Data', *Amer. J. agric. Econ.,* 64, pp115-8.

Schertz, L. P. (1987), 'Toward Consensus in Adopting Improved Data Concepts', in proceedings of symposium on *Relevance of Agricultural Economics: Obsolete Data Concepts Revisited,* American Agricultural Economics Association annual meeting, East Lancing.

Scheuch, E. K. (1994), 'The Puzzle of "Quality of Life"', in D'Antonio, W. V., Sasaki, M. And Yonebayashi, Y. (eds)(1994), *Econogy, Society and the Quality of Social Life,* Transaction Publishers, New Brunswick and London.

Schmitt, G. (1988), 'What do Agricultural Income and Productivity Measurements Really Mean?' *Agricultural Economics,* 2, 139-57.

Schmitt, G. (1989), 'Farms, farm households, and productivity of resource use in agriculture'. *European Review of Agricultural Economics,* 2, 257-84.

Schmitt, G. (1991), 'Why is the agriculture of advanced Western economies still organised by family farms?' *European Review of Agricultural Economics,* 18, 443-58.

Schmitt, G. (1993), 'Über die Zusammenhänge zwischen Haushalts- und Betriebsgröße, Einkommensniveau und -struktur im Anpassungsprozeß der Landwirtschaft: Eine empirische Untersuchung füdie Bundesrepublik Deutschland 1975 bis 1990', *Berichte über Landwirtschaft,* 71, 189-213.

Schmitt, G. (1994), 'Wenig dazugelernt: Zur Darstellung der Agarstruktur und der "sozialen Lage" im Agrarbericht 1994', *Agrarwirtschaft,* 43, (8/9), 308-18.

Schmitt, G. und Burose, C. (1994*), Abwanderungsdruck oder Abwanderungs-sog? Zu den Triebkräften des agrarstrukturellen Anpassungsprozesses un der Bundesrepublik Deutschland.* Diskussionsbeitrag 9403, Institut für Agrarökonomie der Universität Göttingen.

Schultz, T. W. (1945), *Agriculture in an unstable economy,* McGraw-Hill, New York.

Sexton, R. N. and Duffus, G. W. (1977), 'On Economic Welfare and Farmer Annuity Schemes', *Quarterly Rev. agric. Econ.,* 30(2),117-32.

Shaw, R.P. (1979), 'Canadian Farm and Non-farm Family Incomes', *Amer. J.agric. Econ.,* 61(4), 676-82.

Shoard, M. (1980), *The Theft of the Countryside,* Temple Smith, London.

Shucksmith, M. (1993), 'Farm Household Behaviour and the Transition to Post-Productivism', *J.agric.Econ.,* 44(3), 466-478.

Shucksmith, M. and Smith, R. J. (1991), 'Farm Household Strategies and Pluriactivity in Upland Scotland', *J. agric. Econ.,* 42(3), 340-353.

Shucksmith, M., Bryden, J., Rosenthall, P., Short, C. and Winter, M. (1989) 'Rural Change, Farm Structures and Pluriactivity', *J. agric.Econ.,* 40, 340-352.

Simons, H. (1938), *Personal Income Taxation,*.University of Chicago Press.

Slattery, M. (1966), 'Relative Income of Farmers: Some International Comparisons,' *Quarterly Rev. agric. Econ.*, 115-127.

Sommer, J. E., Hoppe, R. A., Greene, R. C., Korb, P. J. (1998), *Structural and Financial Characteristics of U.S. Farms, 1995: 20th Annual Family Farm Report to the Congress*, Economic Research Service, US Department of Agriculture, Washington.

Statistics Canada (1993), *Whole Farm Data Base Reference Manual,* Statistics Canada, Ottawa.

Stoeckel, A. B., Cuthbertson, A. G. and Curran, W. R. (1974), *Income and Net Worth: Implications for Economic Welfare,* Paper to the 18th Annual Conference of the Australian Agricultural Economics Society.

Stovall, J. G. And Hathaway, D. E. (1995), 'The 1995 Farm Bill: Issues and Options', *Choices*, second quarter, 8-12.

Sturgess, I. (1984), *Collection and Analysis of Economic Data Through Farm Surveys By British Universities,* Occasional Paper No.35, Agricultural Economics Unit, Department of Land Economy, University of Cambridge.

Tangerman, S. and. Buckwell, A. (1999), *The Purpose and Methodology of Evaluation in regard to EU Agricultural Expenditure*, Budgetary Series, BUDG-102 EN, European Parliament, Luxembourg.

Terluin, I. J. (1991), *Production, Prices and Incomes in Agriculture: An analysis of the Economic Accounts for Agriculture 1973-1988,* Eurostat, Luxembourg.

Thorner, D., Kerblay, B. and Smith, R.E.F. (eds)(1966), *A.V. Chayanov on the Theory of Peasant Economy,* The American Economic Association, Illinois.

Toland, S. (1980), 'Social Commentary: Changes in Living Standards Since the 1950s', *Social Trends*, 10.

Traill, B. (1982), 'The Effect of Price Support Policies on Agricultural Investment, Employment, Farm Incomes and Land Values in the United Kingdom,' *J. agric. Econ.*, 33(3), 369-86.

Tranter, R. (ed)(1983), *Strategies for family-worked farms in the UK,*.CAS Paper 15, Centre for Agricultural Stratergy, University of Reading.

Tubman, W. (1977) 'A Note on Off-Farm Income of Farm Families in Australia', *Australian J. agric. Econ.*, 21(3), 209-14.

Tweeton, L. (1971), *Foundations of Farm Policy,* Westview Press, Boulder, CO.

Tweeon, L. and Zulauf, C. (1997) 'Public Policy for Agriculture after Commodity Progams', *Review of Agricultural Economics,* 19(2), 280-89.

UN (1968), *System of National Accounts 1968,*.United Nations, New York.

UN (1977), *Provisional Guidelines on Statistics of the Distribution of Income, Consumption and Accumulation of Households,* Studies in methods M61, United Nations, New York.

UN (1993), *System of National Accounts 1993*, Commission of the European Communities - Eurostat, International Monetary Fund, Organisation for Economic Co-operation and Development, United Nations, World Bank, Brussels/Luxembourg, New York, Paris, Washington, D.C., ISBN 92-1-16352-3.

USDA (1969), *Major Statistical Series of the USDA. Vol. 3. How they are constructed and used: Gross and Net Farm Incomes*, USDA, Washington.

USDA (1981), *Farm Income Recipients and Their Families: A Socioeconomic Profile*, USDA, Washington.

USDA (1984), *Farm Income Data: A Historical Perspective*, USDA, Washington

USDA (1986), 'Implications of the 1985 Farm Bill', *Agricultural Outlook*, March.

USDA (1988), *Major Statistical Series of the US Department of Agriculture: How they are constructed and used. Vol No 3 Farm Income*, Economic Research Service, USDA, Washington.

USDA (1997), 'Farm Household Income and Wealth'. In *Rural Conditions and Trends* 8, 79-85.

van der Laan, P. (1999), 'The Problematic Measurement of Income from Self-Employment', paper to the *Eurostat Seminar on Income Methodology for Statistics on Households*, Luxembourg 13014 December 1999, Statistics Netherlands, Voorburg, The Netherlands.

van der Zee, F. (1997), *Political economy models and agricultural policy formation: empirical applicability and relevance for the CAP*, Mansholt studies, Mansholt Institute, Wageningen, The Netherlands, ISBN 90-6754-484-1.

Van Slootan R., and Coverdale, A. G. (1977), 'The Characteristics of Low Income Households', *Economic Trends*, 8, 26-39.

Verma, V. and Gabilondo, L. G. (1993), *Family Budget Surveys in the EC: Methodology and Recommendations for Harmonisation*, Series 3E, Eurostat, Luxembourg.

Verma, V., and Gabilondo, L. G. (1993). "Family Budget Surveys in the EC: Methodology and ecommendations for Harmonisation. Theme 3 Series E," Eurostat, Luxembourg,

Vertrees, J. and Morton, A. (1984), *Crop Price Support Programs: Policy Options for Contemporary Agriculture*, Congressional Budget Office. Washington.

Vickrey. W. (1947), *Agenda for Progressive Taxation*, Ronald Press, New York.

Vincent, D.P. (1976), 'Economic Aspects of Farm Poverty', *Australian J.agric. Econ.*, 20(2), 103-118.

Vincent, D. P., Watson, A. S. and Barton, L. M. (1975), 'Poverty Among Farmers in Three Districts of Victoria. Commission of Inquiry into Poverty', in *Financial Aspects of Rural Poverty*, Government Publishing Service, Canberra.

Weisbrod, S.A. and Hansen, W.L. (1968), 'An income-net worth approach to measuring economic welfare', *Am. Econ. Rev.*, 53, 1315-29.

Weldon, R. N., Moss C. B. and Erickson, K. (1993), 'The Distribution of Farm Wealth in the United States', *Agricultural Finance Review*, 53, pp100-9

Whetham, E. H. (1981), *Agricultural Economics in Britain 1900-1940*, Monograph of the Institute of Agricultural Economics, University of Oxford.

Wilson, G. K. (1977), *Special Interests and Policymaking: Agricultural Policies and Politics in Britain and the United States of America, 1956-70*. Wiley, London.

Winters, L. A. (1990), *The so-called non-economic objectives of agricultural policies,* OECD Economic Studies, No 13, Winter 1989-90, Paris. Also published as Winters (1988), OECD Department of Economics and Statistics Working Paper No. 52, OECD, Paris.

Wolleb, G. (ed.)(1989), *Trends and Distribution of Income: An Overview,* Programme for Research and Actions on the Development of the Labour Market, European Federation for Economic Research, Commission of the European Communities, Brussels.

Yap, S.-S., Culver, D. And St. Jean, J. (1993), *Regional Comparison of Incomes of Self-Employed Farm Operators with Other Self Employed Occupations, Canada, 1990,* Farm Analysis Bulletin No. 54, Agriculture Canada, Ottawa.

Yap, S.-S., O'Connor, K., St. Jean, J. and Culver, D. (1995), *An Economic Overview of Farm Incomes, by Farm Type, Canada 1992,* Agriculture Canada, Policy Branch, Ottawa.

Index

Note: references to EU Member States only include those to particular features of these countries. Where possible, all are included in each of the Tables, Figures and discussions relating to the EU in the main text.

373